Shojo Beat

kimi ni todoke
From Me to You

Vol. 1
Story & Art by
Karuho Shiina

Volume 1

Contents

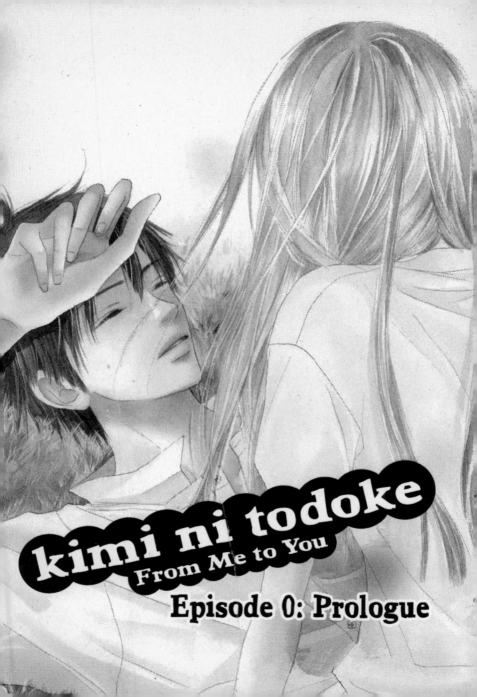

kimi ni todoke
From Me to You

Episode 0: Prologue

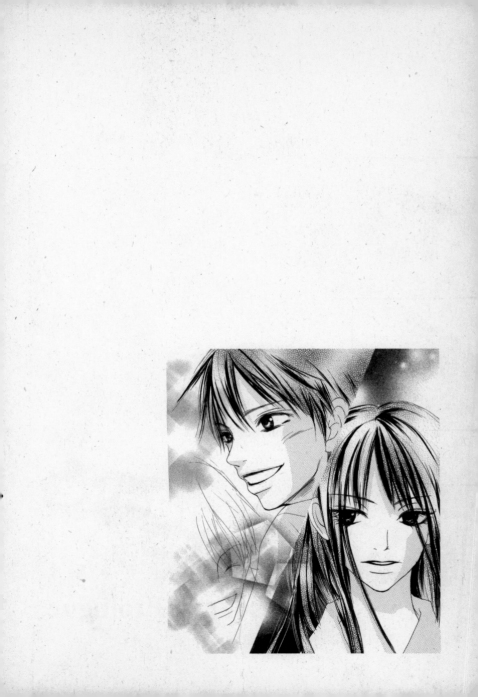

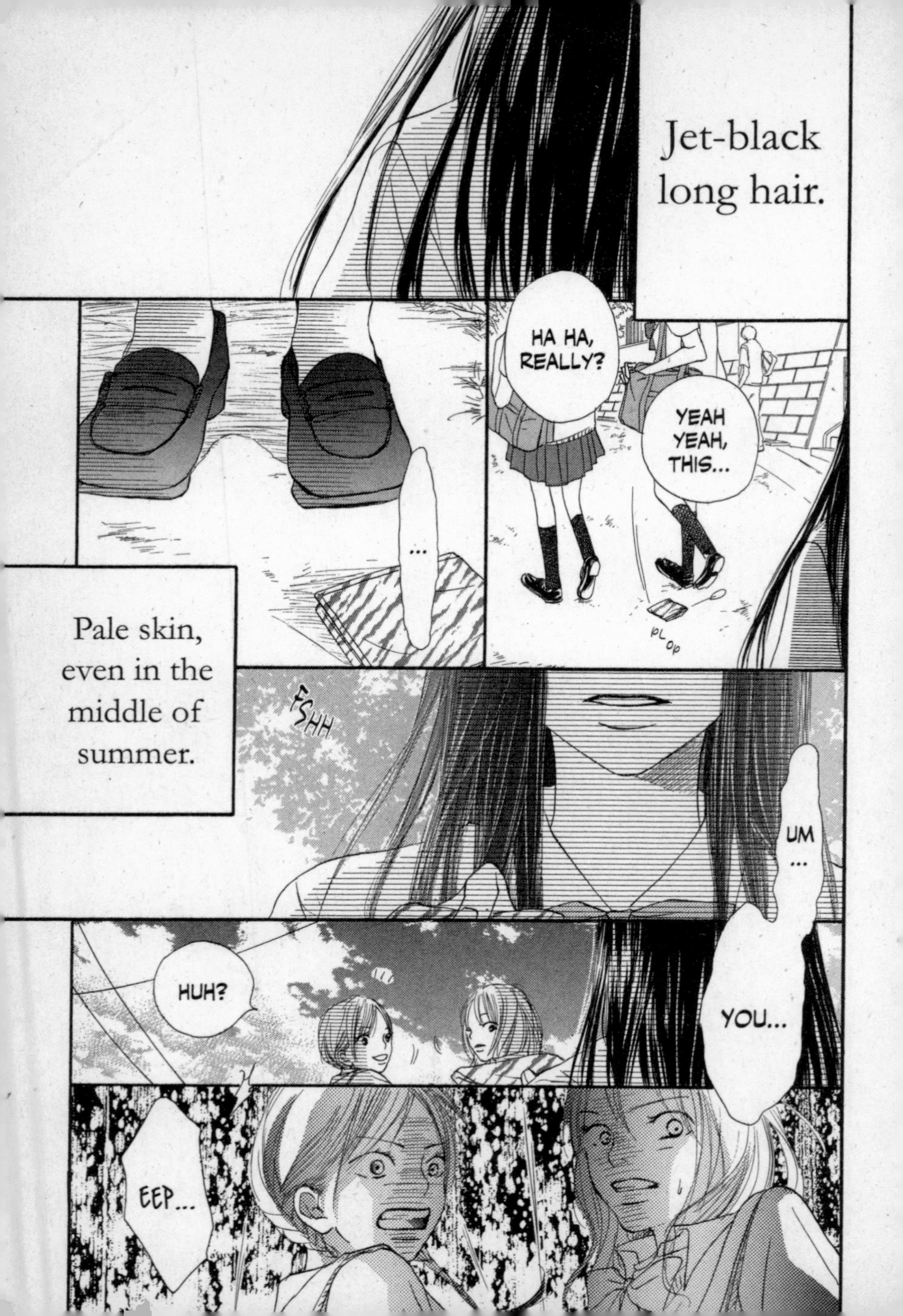
Jet-black long hair.
HA HA, REALLY?
YEAH YEAH, THIS...
PLOP
...
Pale skin, even in the middle of summer.
FSHH
UM ...
YOU...
HUH?
EEP...

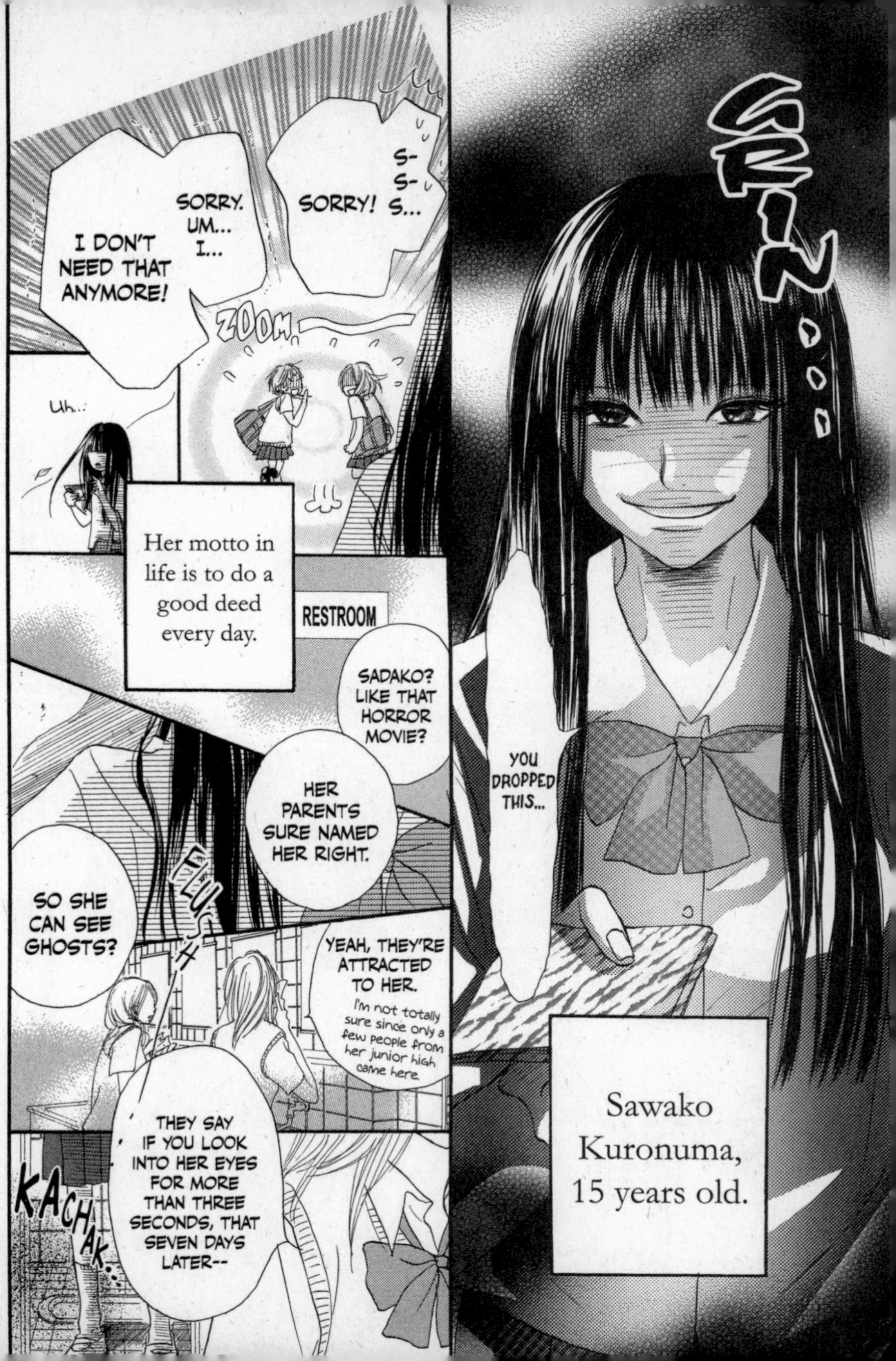
GRIN...
YOU DROPPED THIS...
Sawako Kuronuma, 15 years old.
S-S-S...
SORRY!
SORRY. UM... I...
I DON'T NEED THAT ANYMORE!
ZOOM
Uh...
Her motto in life is to do a good deed every day.
RESTROOM
SADAKO? LIKE THAT HORROR MOVIE?
HER PARENTS SURE NAMED HER RIGHT.
YEAH, THEY'RE ATTRACTED TO HER.
I'm not totally sure since only a few people from her junior high came here.
FLUSH
SO SHE CAN SEE GHOSTS?
THEY SAY IF YOU LOOK INTO HER EYES FOR MORE THAN THREE SECONDS, THAT SEVEN DAYS LATER--
KACHAK...

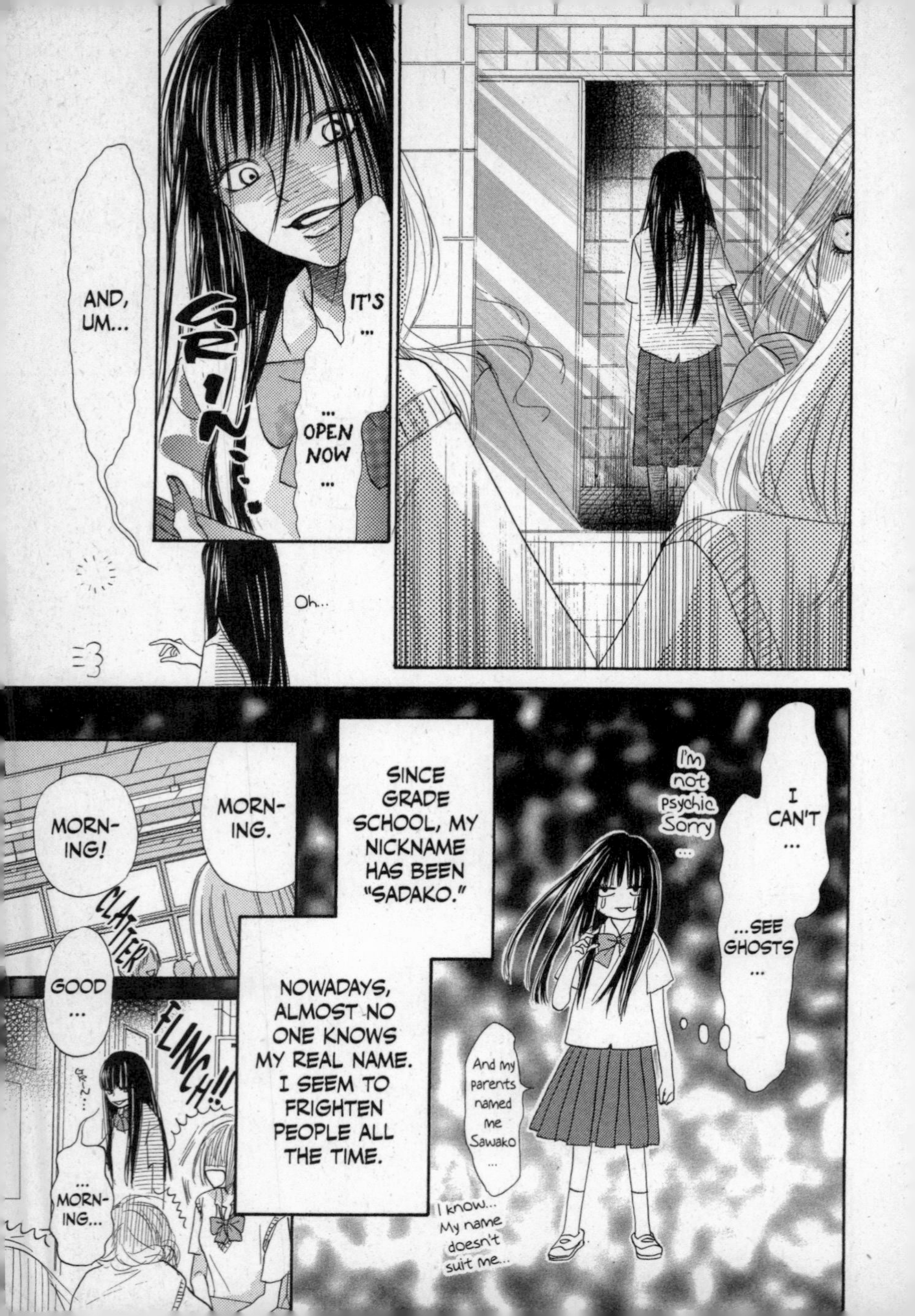

IT'S ... ... OPEN NOW ...
GRIN...
AND, UM...
Oh...
I CAN'T ... ...SEE GHOSTS ...
I'm not psychic. Sorry ...
SINCE GRADE SCHOOL, MY NICKNAME HAS BEEN "SADAKO."
NOWADAYS, ALMOST NO ONE KNOWS MY REAL NAME. I SEEM TO FRIGHTEN PEOPLE ALL THE TIME.
And my parents named me Sawako ...
I know... My name doesn't suit me...
MORN-ING.
MORN-ING!
CLATTER
GOOD ...
FLINCH!!
GRIN...
... MORN-ING...

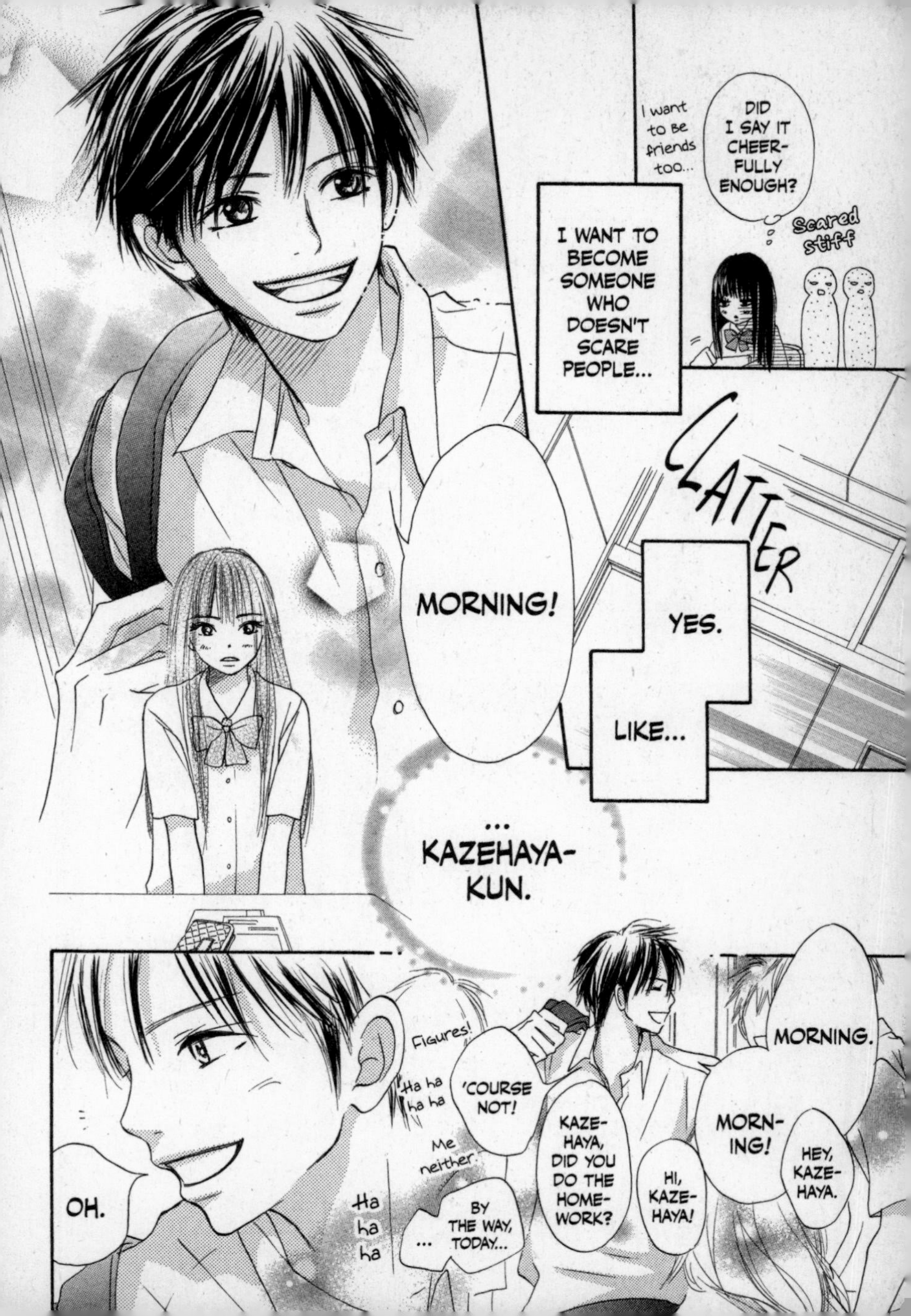
I WANT TO BECOME SOMEONE WHO DOESN'T SCARE PEOPLE...
DID I SAY IT CHEERFULLY ENOUGH?
I want to be friends too...
Scared stiff
CLATTER
YES.
LIKE...
MORNING!
... KAZEHAYA-KUN.
MORNING.
HEY, KAZE-HAYA.
MORN-ING!
HI, KAZE-HAYA!
KAZE-HAYA, DID YOU DO THE HOME-WORK?
'COURSE NOT!
Figures!
Ha ha ha ha
Me neither.
BY THE WAY, TODAY...
...
Ha ha ha
OH.

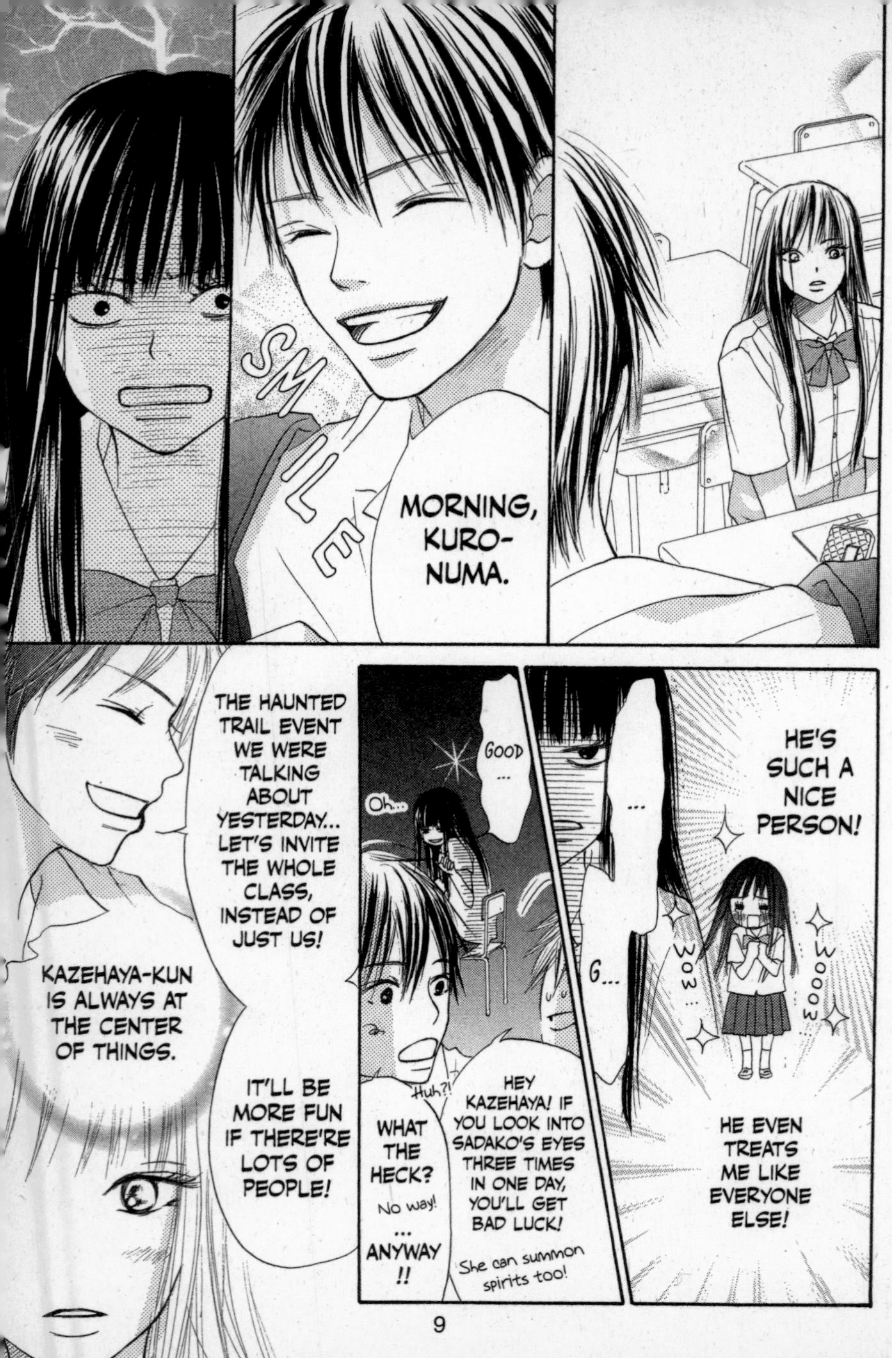
SMILE
MORNING, KURO-NUMA.
HE'S SUCH A NICE PERSON!
...
G...
WOW...
WOOOW...
HE EVEN TREATS ME LIKE EVERYONE ELSE!
GOOD ...
Oh...
HEY KAZEHAYA! IF YOU LOOK INTO SADAKO'S EYES THREE TIMES IN ONE DAY, YOU'LL GET BAD LUCK!
She can summon spirits too!
Huh?!
WHAT THE HECK?
No way!
... ANYWAY !!
THE HAUNTED TRAIL EVENT WE WERE TALKING ABOUT YESTERDAY... LET'S INVITE THE WHOLE CLASS, INSTEAD OF JUST US!
KAZEHAYA-KUN IS ALWAYS AT THE CENTER OF THINGS.
IT'LL BE MORE FUN IF THERE'RE LOTS OF PEOPLE!

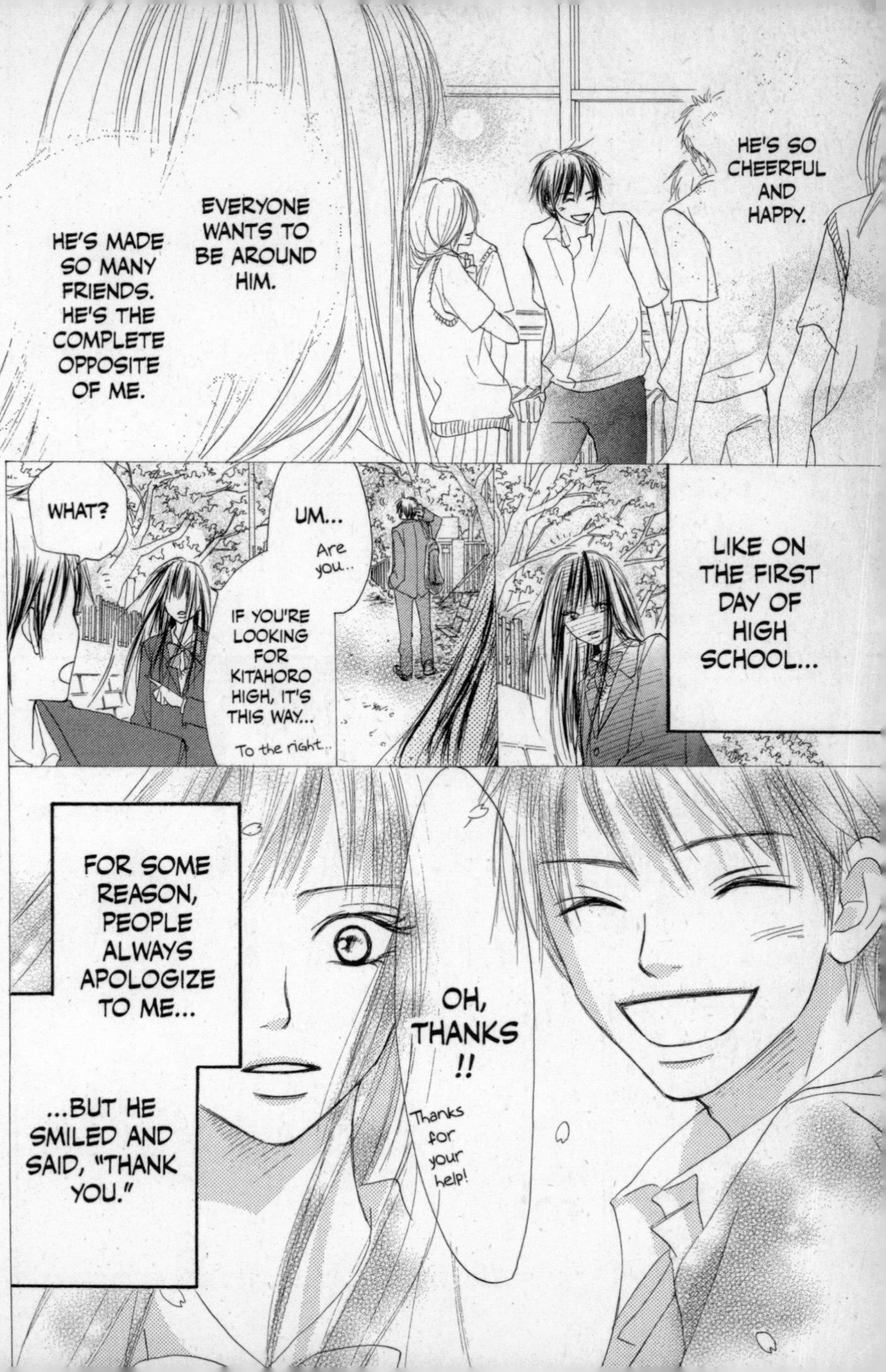
HE'S SO CHEERFUL AND HAPPY.
EVERYONE WANTS TO BE AROUND HIM.
HE'S MADE SO MANY FRIENDS. HE'S THE COMPLETE OPPOSITE OF ME.
LIKE ON THE FIRST DAY OF HIGH SCHOOL...
UM...
Are you...
WHAT?
IF YOU'RE LOOKING FOR KITAHORO HIGH, IT'S THIS WAY...
To the right...
OH, THANKS !!
Thanks for your help!
FOR SOME REASON, PEOPLE ALWAYS APOLOGIZE TO ME...
...BUT HE SMILED AND SAID, "THANK YOU."

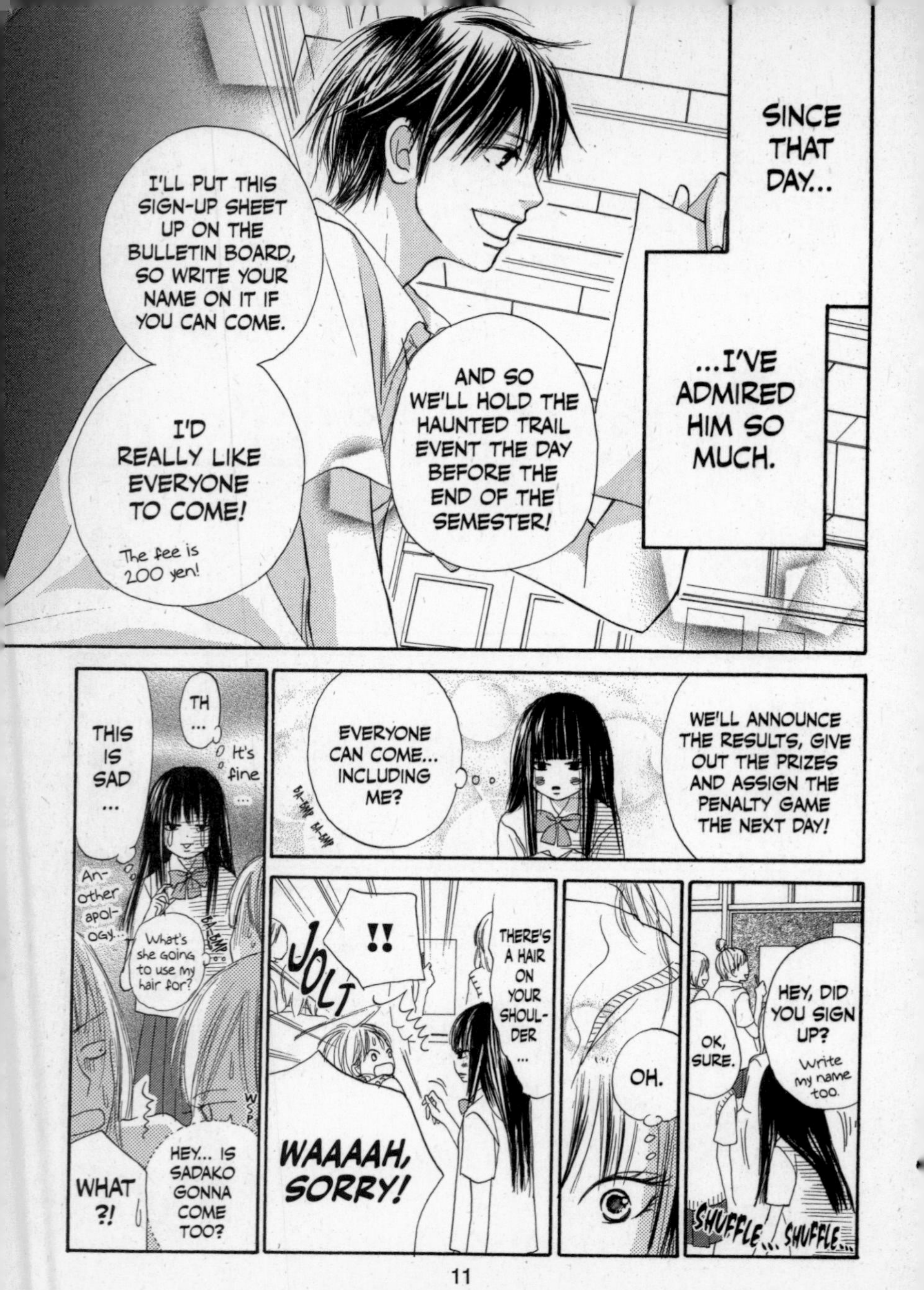
SINCE THAT DAY...
...I'VE ADMIRED HIM SO MUCH.
AND SO WE'LL HOLD THE HAUNTED TRAIL EVENT THE DAY BEFORE THE END OF THE SEMESTER!
I'LL PUT THIS SIGN-UP SHEET UP ON THE BULLETIN BOARD, SO WRITE YOUR NAME ON IT IF YOU CAN COME.
I'D REALLY LIKE EVERYONE TO COME!
The fee is 200 yen!
WE'LL ANNOUNCE THE RESULTS, GIVE OUT THE PRIZES AND ASSIGN THE PENALTY GAME THE NEXT DAY!
EVERYONE CAN COME... INCLUDING ME?
BA-BMP BA-BMP
HEY, DID YOU SIGN UP?
Write my name too.
OK, SURE.
SHUFFLE... SHUFFLE...
OH.
THERE'S A HAIR ON YOUR SHOULDER ...
!!
JOLT
WAAAAH, SORRY!
TH ...
It's fine ...
THIS IS SAD ...
Another apology...
What's she going to use my hair for?
BA-BMP
WSP
HEY... IS SADAKO GONNA COME TOO?
WHAT?!

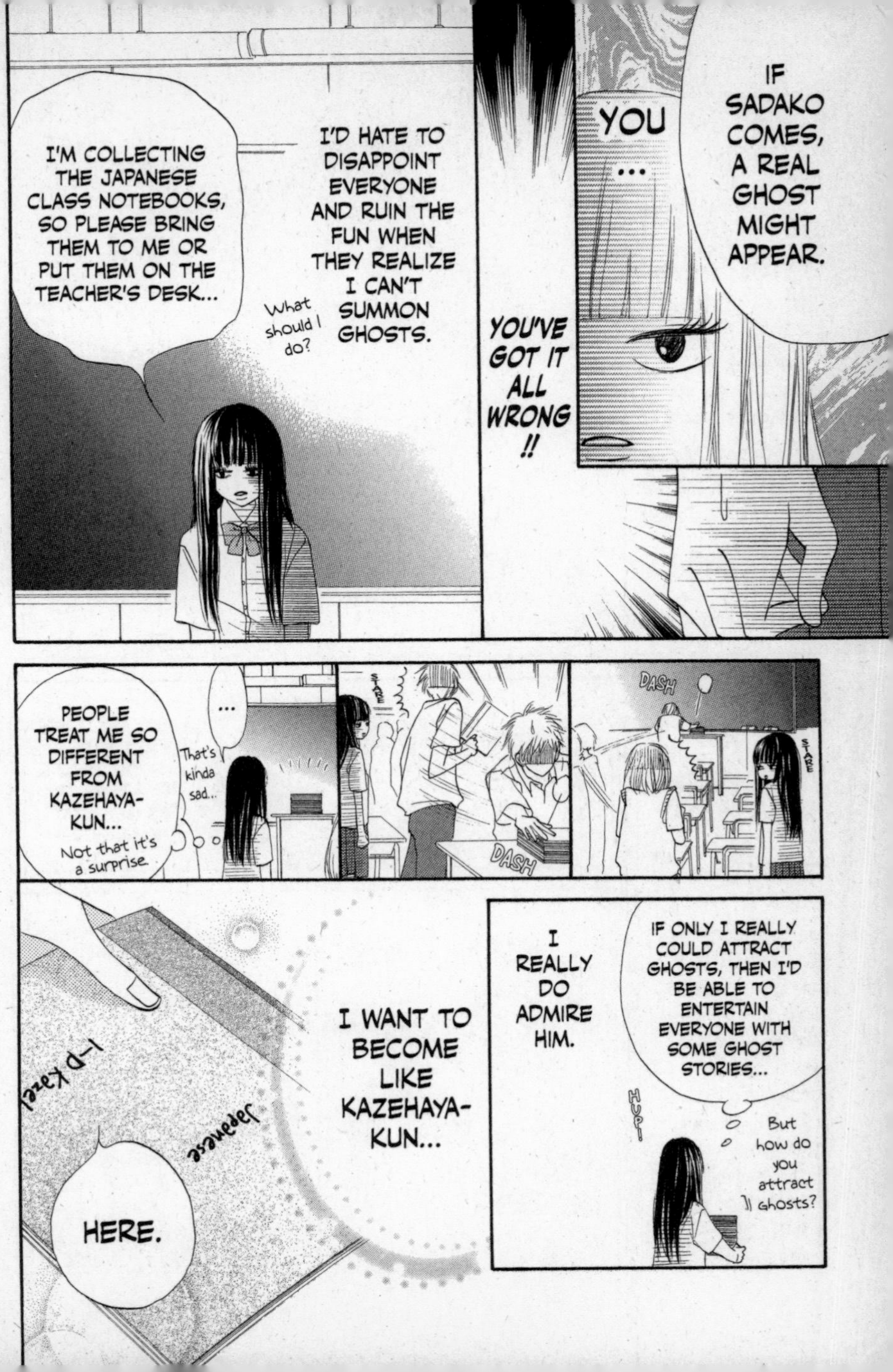
IF SADAKO COMES, A REAL GHOST MIGHT APPEAR.
YOU ...
YOU'VE GOT IT ALL WRONG !!
I'D HATE TO DISAPPOINT EVERYONE AND RUIN THE FUN WHEN THEY REALIZE I CAN'T SUMMON GHOSTS.
What should I do?
I'M COLLECTING THE JAPANESE CLASS NOTEBOOKS, SO PLEASE BRING THEM TO ME OR PUT THEM ON THE TEACHER'S DESK...
DASH
STARE
STARE
DASH
...
That's kinda sad...
PEOPLE TREAT ME SO DIFFERENT FROM KAZEHAYA-KUN...
Not that it's a surprise.
IF ONLY I REALLY COULD ATTRACT GHOSTS, THEN I'D BE ABLE TO ENTERTAIN EVERYONE WITH SOME GHOST STORIES...
But how do you attract ghosts?
HUP!
I REALLY DO ADMIRE HIM.
I WANT TO BECOME LIKE KAZEHAYA-KUN...
1-D Kaze
Japanese
HERE.

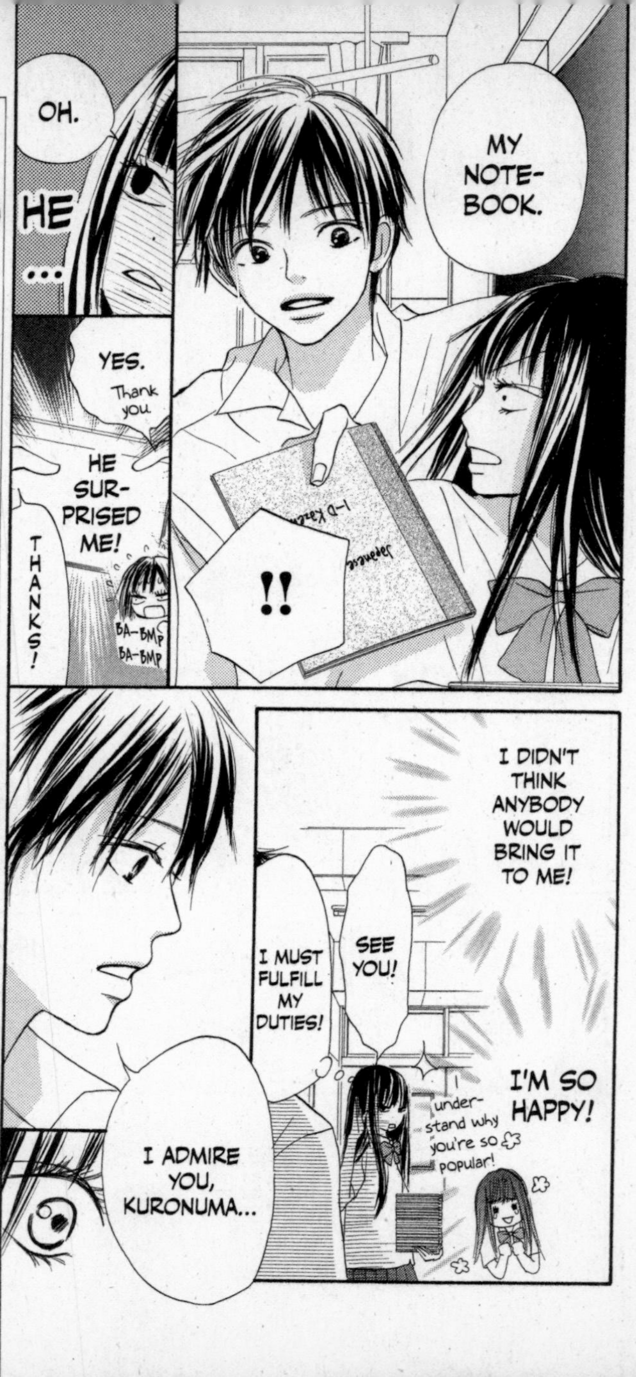
MY NOTE-BOOK.
!!
OH.
HE...
YES.
Thank you.
HE SURPRISED ME!
THANKS!
BA-BMP BA-BMP
I DIDN'T THINK ANYBODY WOULD BRING IT TO ME!
SEE YOU!
I MUST FULFILL MY DUTIES!
I'M SO HAPPY!
I understand why you're so popular!
I ADMIRE YOU, KURONUMA...

KARUPIN on JAPAN 1

Hello! How're you doing?

I'm the author, Shiina Karuho.

It would be so funny if a middle-aged guy who was randomly passing by wrote these sidebars instead of me! But that's not happening, so I have to...

So please stick with me!

It's the beginning of April as I'm writing this, but it's not quite spring yet in Hokkaido. It still snows around this time.

I don't want any more snow.

I hope spring comes soon...

Ao Mimori of Tokyo sent me a photo of some cherry blossoms that were in full bloom from her cell phone. Meanwhile, it was snowing here. Japan is interesting. This book will be on sale at the end of May (2006), so it'll probably be warm by then.

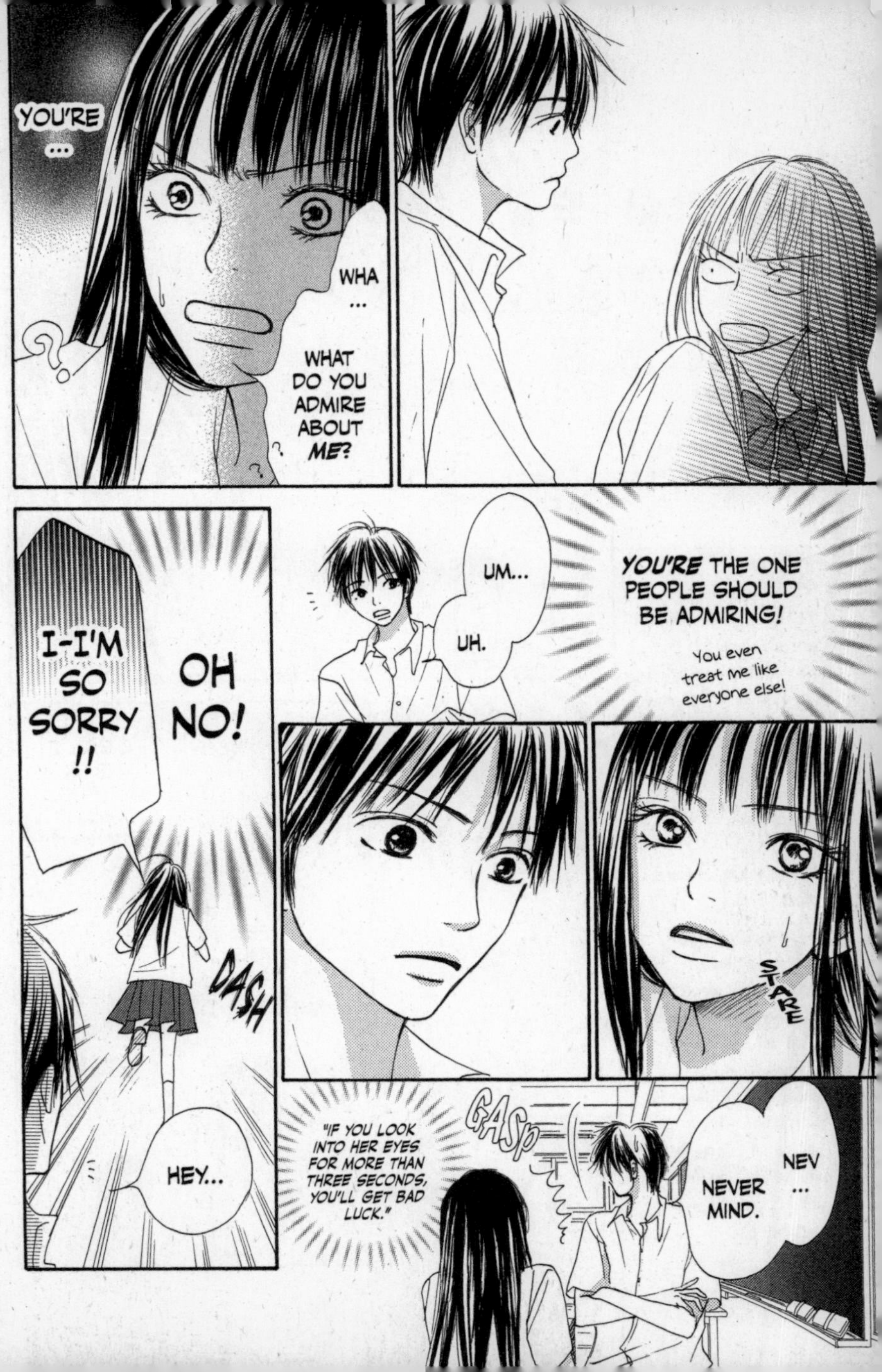
YOU'RE ...
WHA ...
WHAT DO YOU ADMIRE ABOUT ME?
YOU'RE THE ONE PEOPLE SHOULD BE ADMIRING!
You even treat me like everyone else!
UM...
UH.
STARE
NEV ...
NEVER MIND.
GASp
"IF YOU LOOK INTO HER EYES FOR MORE THAN THREE SECONDS, YOU'LL GET BAD LUCK."
OH NO!
I-I'M SO SORRY !!
DASH
HEY...

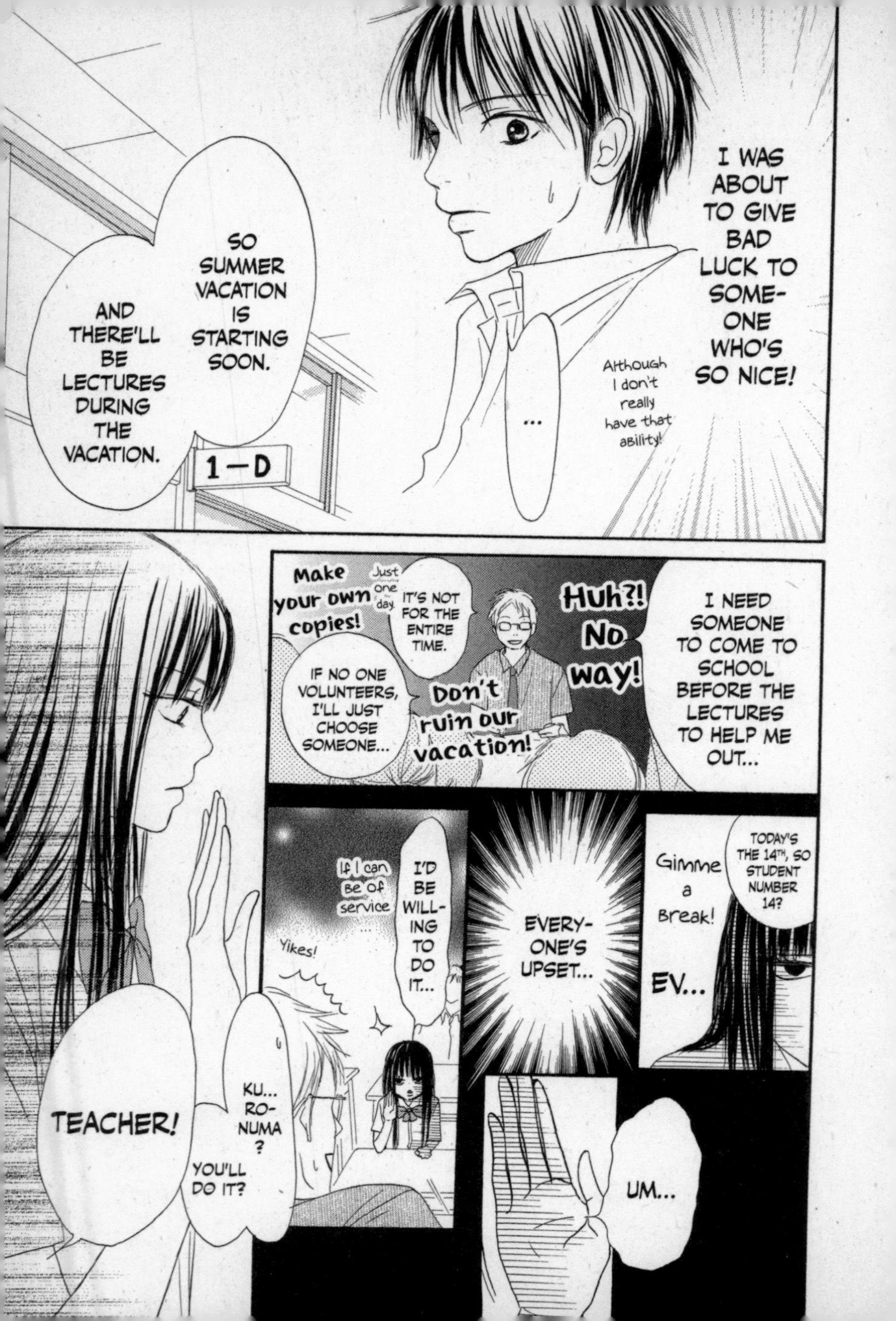
I WAS ABOUT TO GIVE BAD LUCK TO SOME-ONE WHO'S SO NICE!
Although I don't really have that ability!
...
SO SUMMER VACATION IS STARTING SOON.
AND THERE'LL BE LECTURES DURING THE VACATION.
1—D
I NEED SOMEONE TO COME TO SCHOOL BEFORE THE LECTURES TO HELP ME OUT...
Huh?! No way!
Don't ruin our vacation!
IT'S NOT FOR THE ENTIRE TIME.
Just one day.
Make your own copies!
IF NO ONE VOLUNTEERS, I'LL JUST CHOOSE SOMEONE...
TODAY'S THE 14TH, SO STUDENT NUMBER 14?
Gimme a Break!
EV...
EVERY-ONE'S UPSET...
UM...
TEACHER!
I'D BE WILL-ING TO DO IT...
If I can be of service...
Yikes!
KU... RO-NUMA?
YOU'LL DO IT?

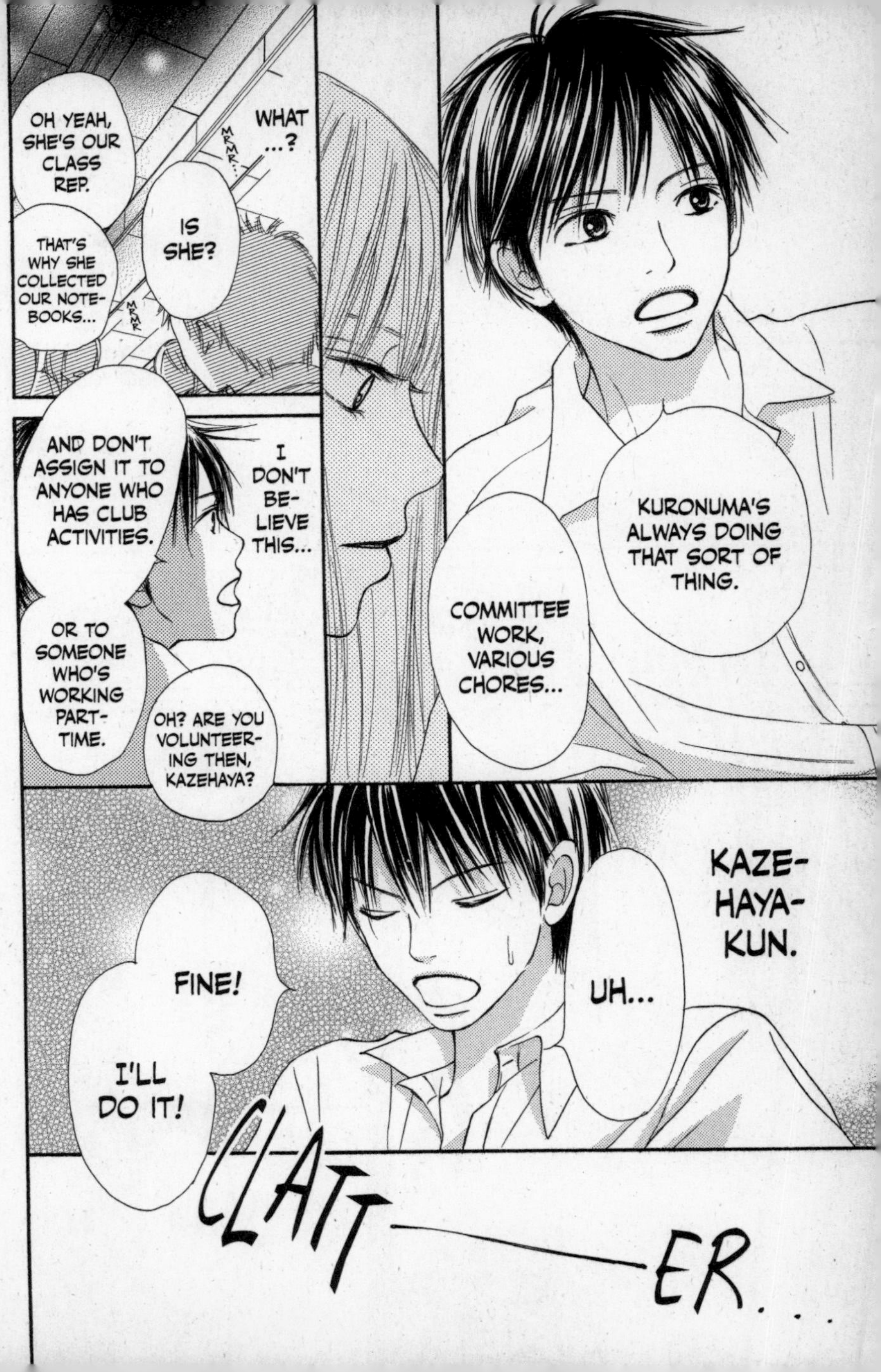
KURONUMA'S ALWAYS DOING THAT SORT OF THING.
COMMITTEE WORK, VARIOUS CHORES...
WHAT ...?
I DON'T BE-LIEVE THIS...
OH YEAH, SHE'S OUR CLASS REP.
MRMR...
IS SHE?
THAT'S WHY SHE COLLECTED OUR NOTE-BOOKS...
MRMR
AND DON'T ASSIGN IT TO ANYONE WHO HAS CLUB ACTIVITIES.
OR TO SOMEONE WHO'S WORKING PART-TIME.
OH? ARE YOU VOLUNTEER-ING THEN, KAZEHAYA?
KAZE-HAYA-KUN.
UH...
FINE!
I'LL DO IT!
CLATT——ER...

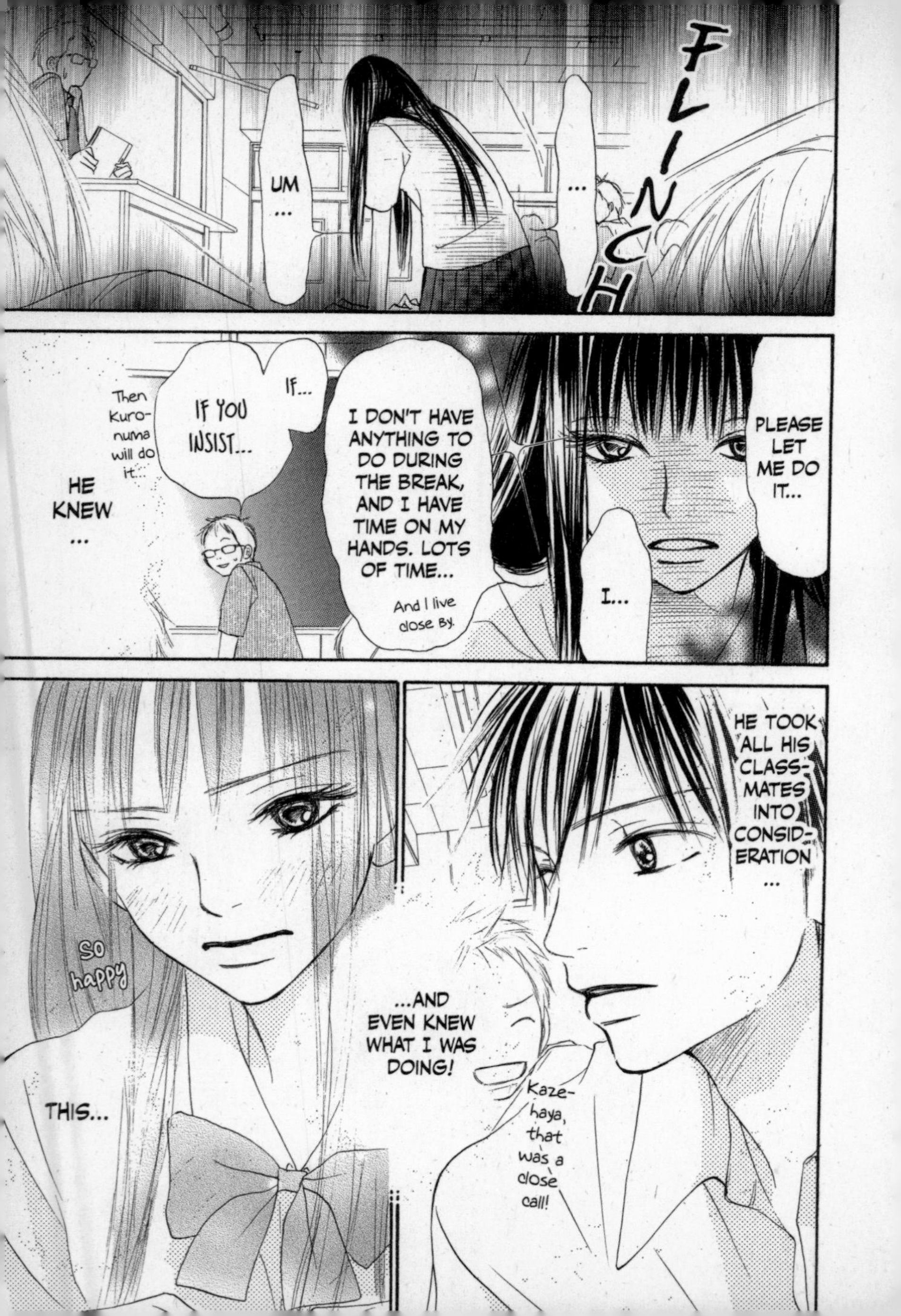
FLINCH
...
UM ...
PLEASE LET ME DO IT...
I...
I DON'T HAVE ANYTHING TO DO DURING THE BREAK, AND I HAVE TIME ON MY HANDS. LOTS OF TIME...
And I live close by.
IF...
IF YOU INSIST...
Then Kuronuma will do it...
HE KNEW ...
HE TOOK ALL HIS CLASSMATES INTO CONSIDERATION ...
...AND EVEN KNEW WHAT I WAS DOING!
Kazehaya, that was a close call!
So happy
THIS...

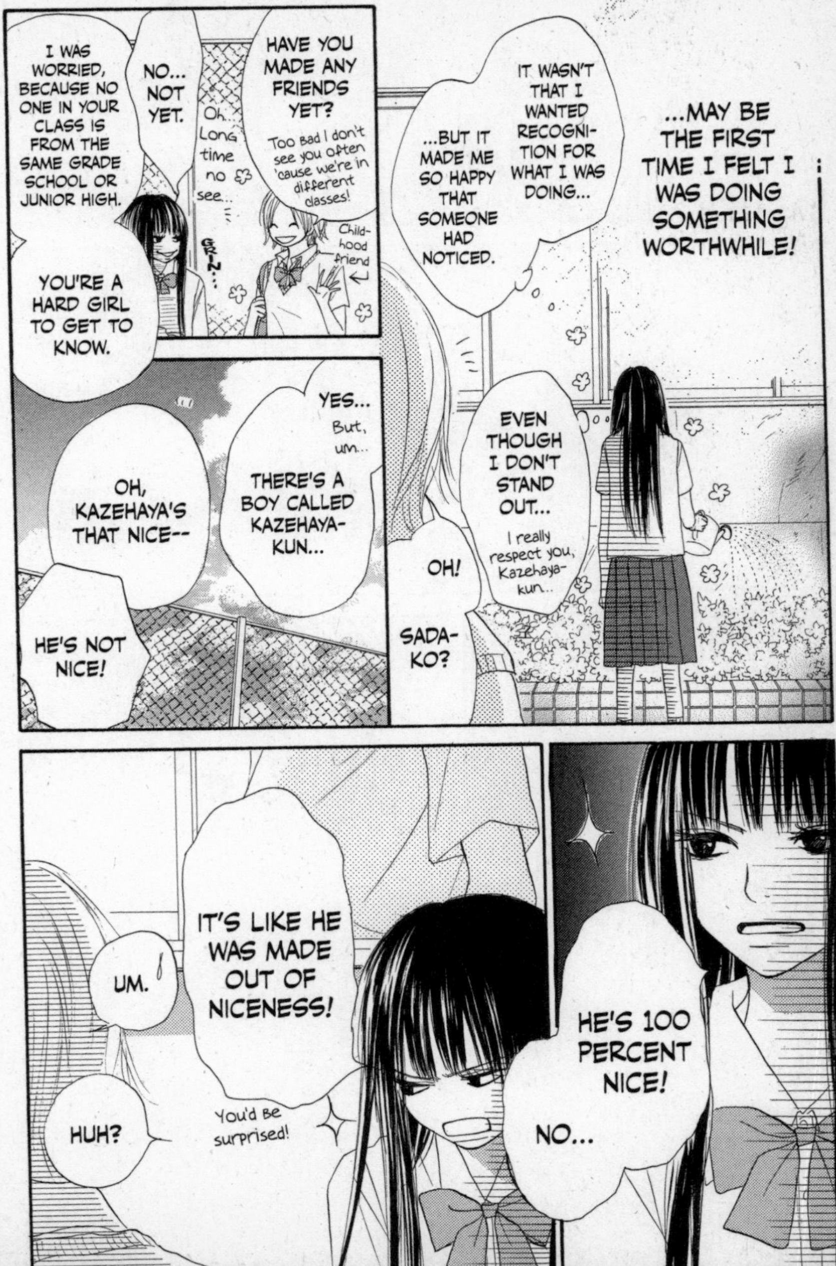
...MAY BE THE FIRST TIME I FELT I WAS DOING SOMETHING WORTHWHILE!
IT WASN'T THAT I WANTED RECOGNITION FOR WHAT I WAS DOING...
...BUT IT MADE ME SO HAPPY THAT SOMEONE HAD NOTICED.
EVEN THOUGH I DON'T STAND OUT...
I really respect you, Kazehaya-kun...
OH!
SADA-KO?
HAVE YOU MADE ANY FRIENDS YET?
Too bad I don't see you often 'cause we're in different classes!
Childhood friend
Oh... Long time no see...
GRIN...
NO... NOT YET.
I WAS WORRIED, BECAUSE NO ONE IN YOUR CLASS IS FROM THE SAME GRADE SCHOOL OR JUNIOR HIGH.
YOU'RE A HARD GIRL TO GET TO KNOW.
YES...
But, um...
THERE'S A BOY CALLED KAZEHAYA-KUN...
OH, KAZEHAYA'S THAT NICE--
HE'S NOT NICE!
HE'S 100 PERCENT NICE!
NO...
IT'S LIKE HE WAS MADE OUT OF NICENESS!
You'd be surprised!
UM.
HUH?

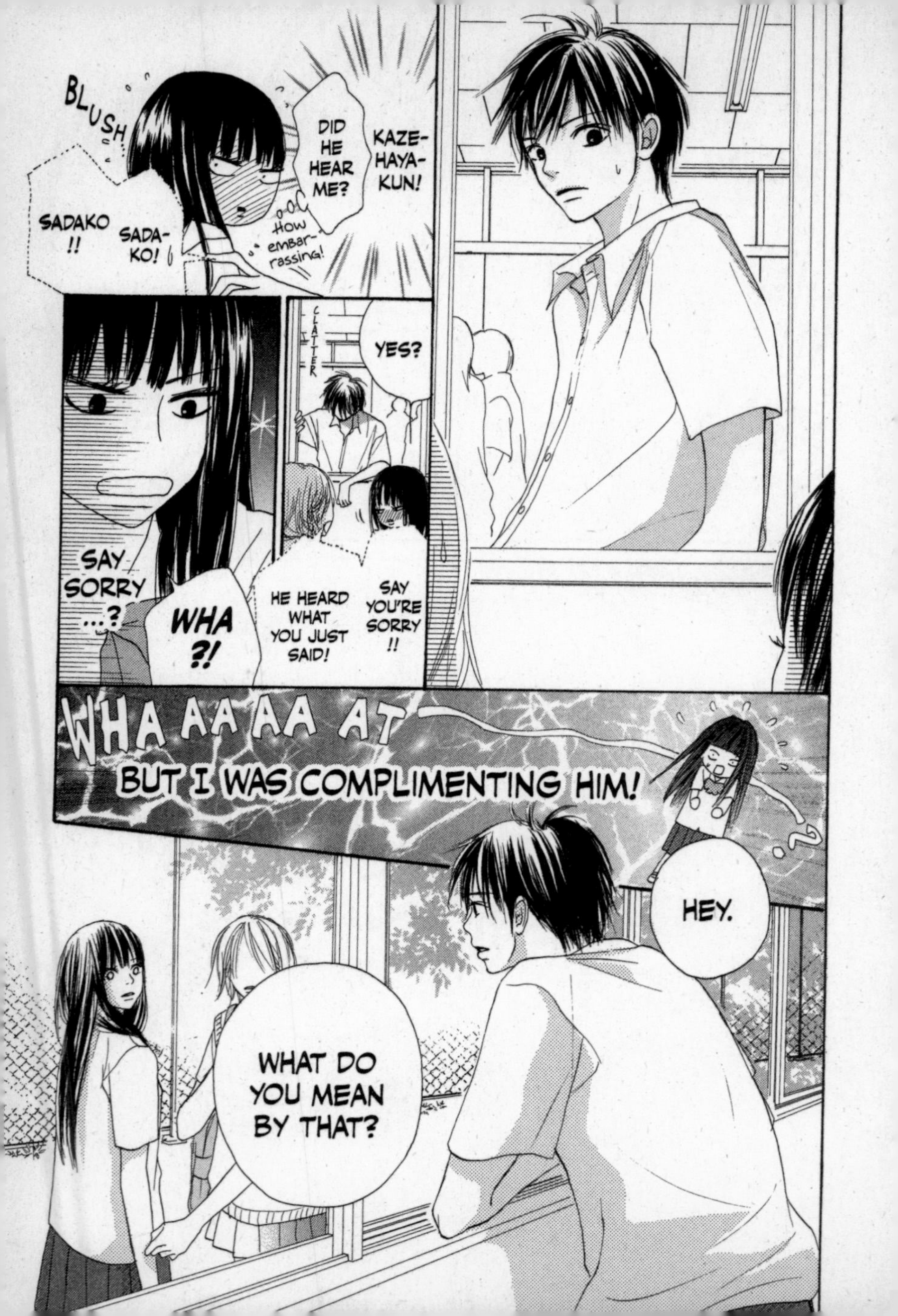

KAZE-HAYA-KUN!
DID HE HEAR ME?
BLUSH
How embarrassing!
SADA-KO!
SADAKO !!
CLATTER
YES?
SAY YOU'RE SORRY !!
HE HEARD WHAT YOU JUST SAID!
WHA ?!
SAY SORRY ...?
WHAAAAAAAT
BUT I WAS COMPLIMENTING HIM!
HEY.
WHAT DO YOU MEAN BY THAT?

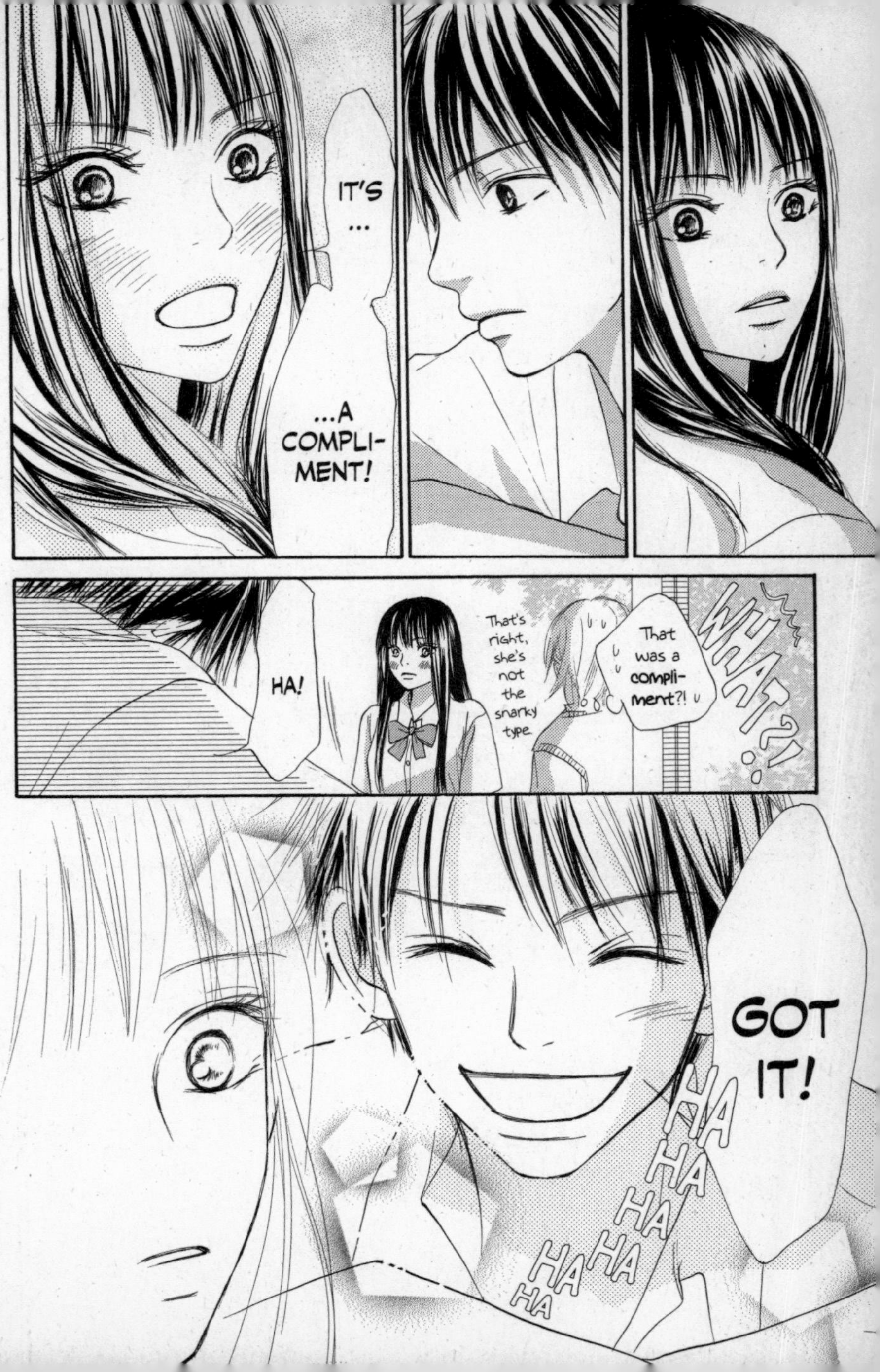
IT'S ...
...A COMPLIMENT!
WHAT?!
That was a compliment?!
That's right, she's not the snarky type.
HA!
GOT IT!
HA HA HA HA HA HA HA HA

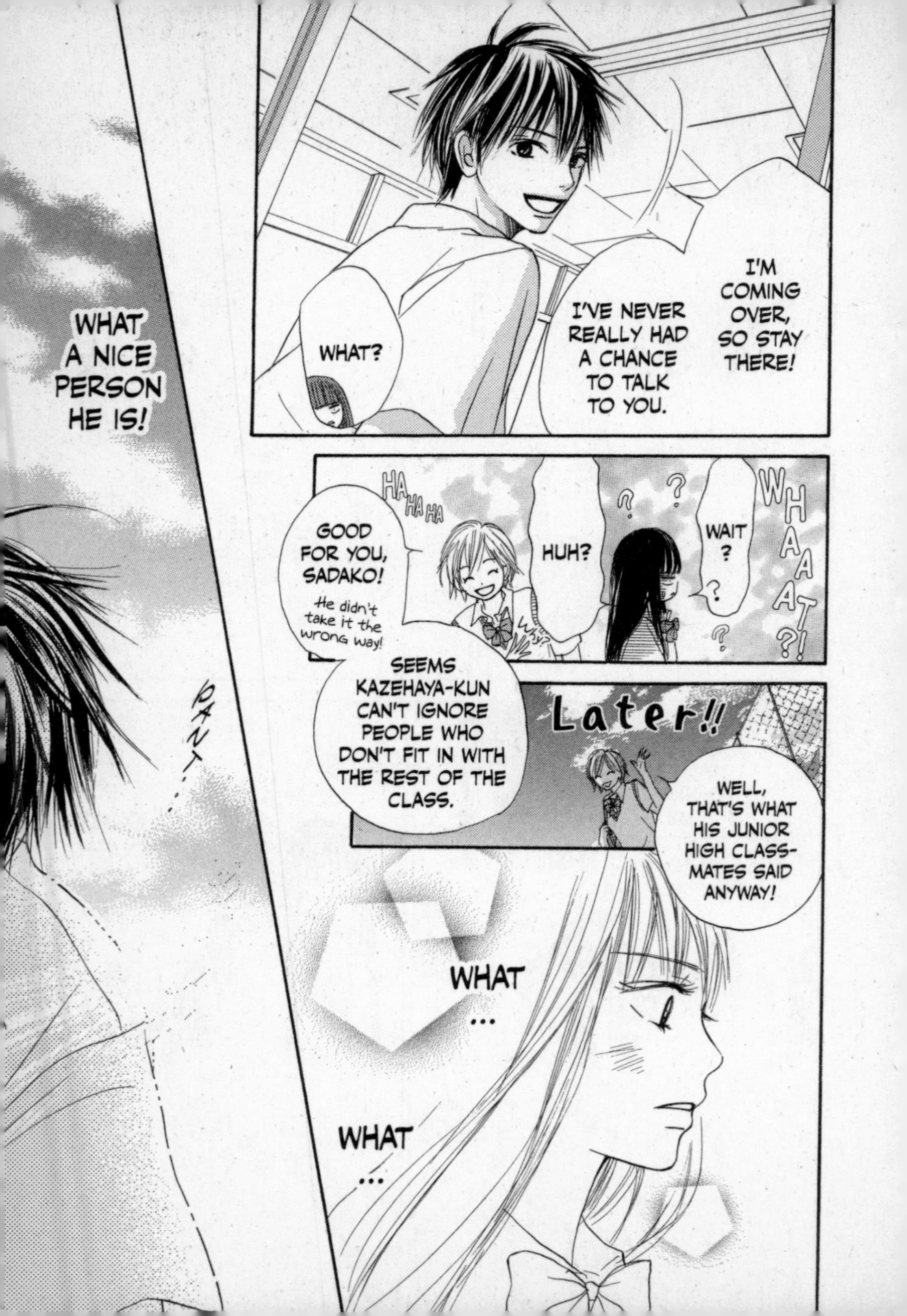
I'M COMING OVER, SO STAY THERE!
I'VE NEVER REALLY HAD A CHANCE TO TALK TO YOU.
WHAT?
WHAAAT?!
WAIT? ? ?
HUH?
Why?
GOOD FOR YOU, SADAKO!
He didn't take it the wrong way!
HA HA HA
Later!!
SEEMS KAZEHAYA-KUN CAN'T IGNORE PEOPLE WHO DON'T FIT IN WITH THE REST OF THE CLASS.
WELL, THAT'S WHAT HIS JUNIOR HIGH CLASS-MATES SAID ANYWAY!
WHAT ...
WHAT ...
WHAT A NICE PERSON HE IS!
PANT...

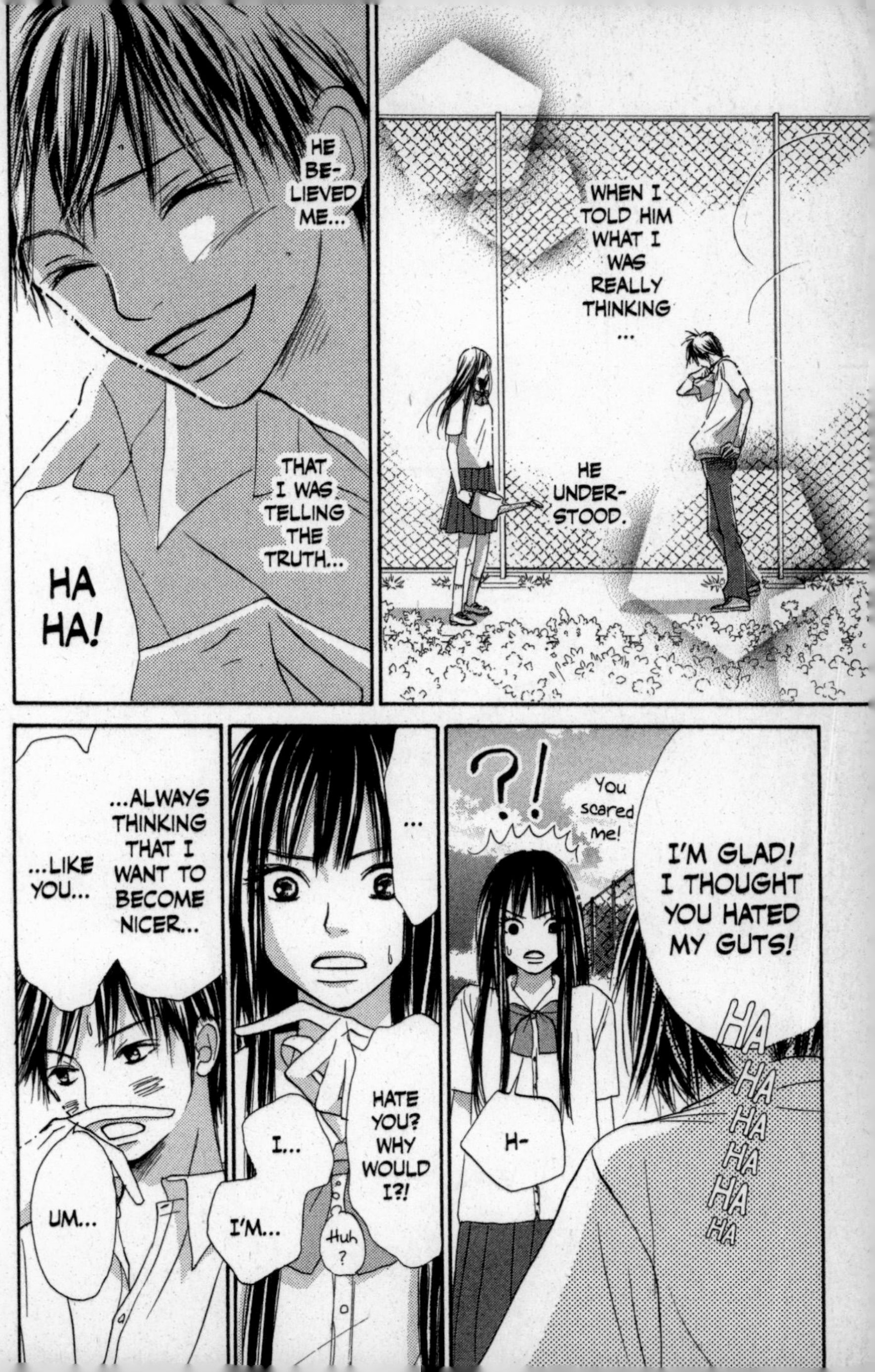
WHEN I TOLD HIM WHAT I WAS REALLY THINKING...
HE UNDERSTOOD.
HE BE-LIEVED ME...
THAT I WAS TELLING THE TRUTH...
HA HA!
I'M GLAD! I THOUGHT YOU HATED MY GUTS!
?!
You scared me!
HA HA HA HA HA HA HA
H-
...
HATE YOU? WHY WOULD I?!
I...
Huh?
I'M...
...ALWAYS THINKING THAT I WANT TO BECOME NICER...
...LIKE YOU...
UM...

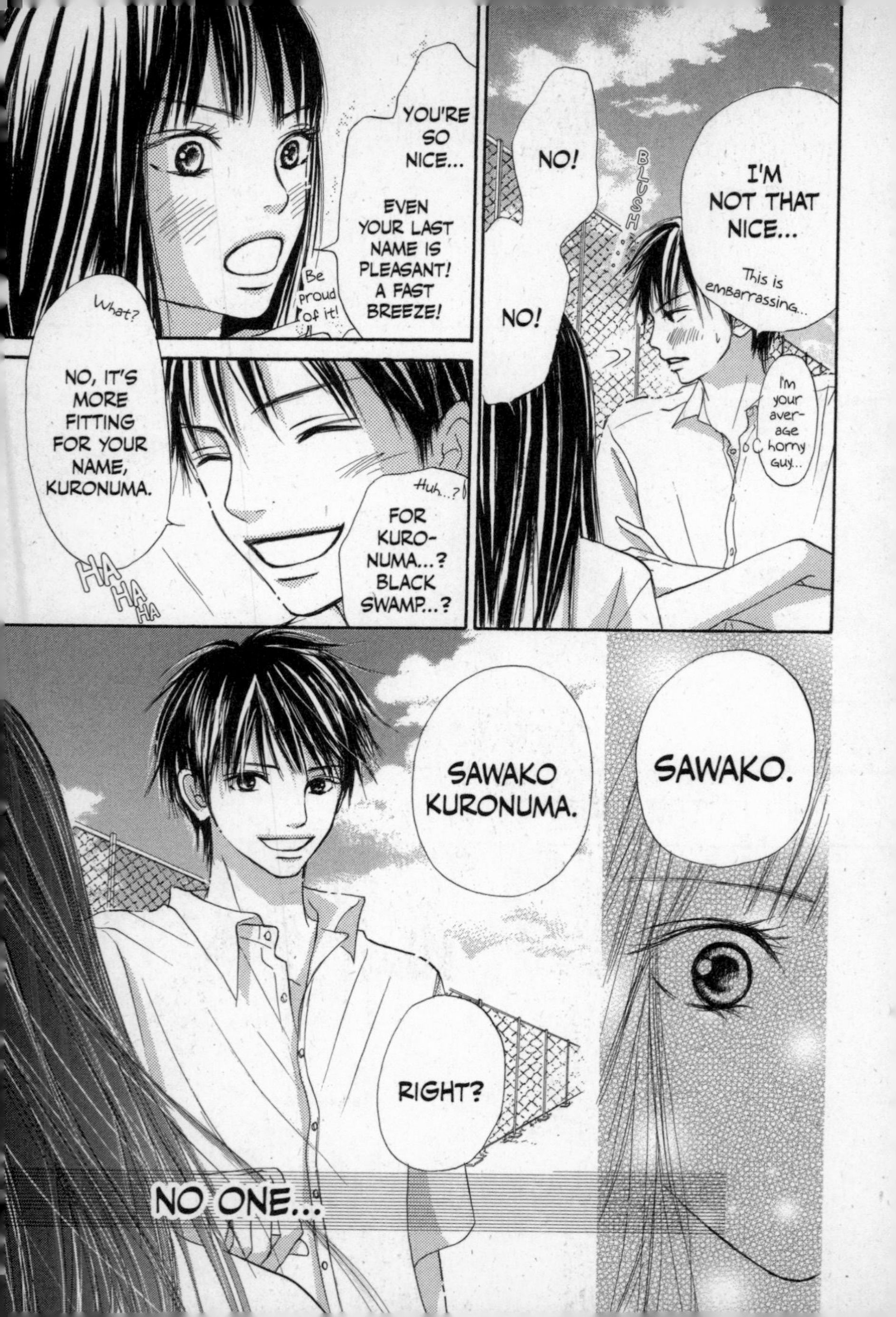
I'M NOT THAT NICE...
This is embarrassing...
BLUSH
NO!
NO!
I'm your average horny guy...
YOU'RE SO NICE...
EVEN YOUR LAST NAME IS PLEASANT! A FAST BREEZE!
Be proud of it!
What?
Huh...?
FOR KURONUMA...? BLACK SWAMP...?
NO, IT'S MORE FITTING FOR YOUR NAME, KURONUMA.
HA HA HA
SAWAKO.
SAWAKO KURONUMA.
RIGHT?
NO ONE...

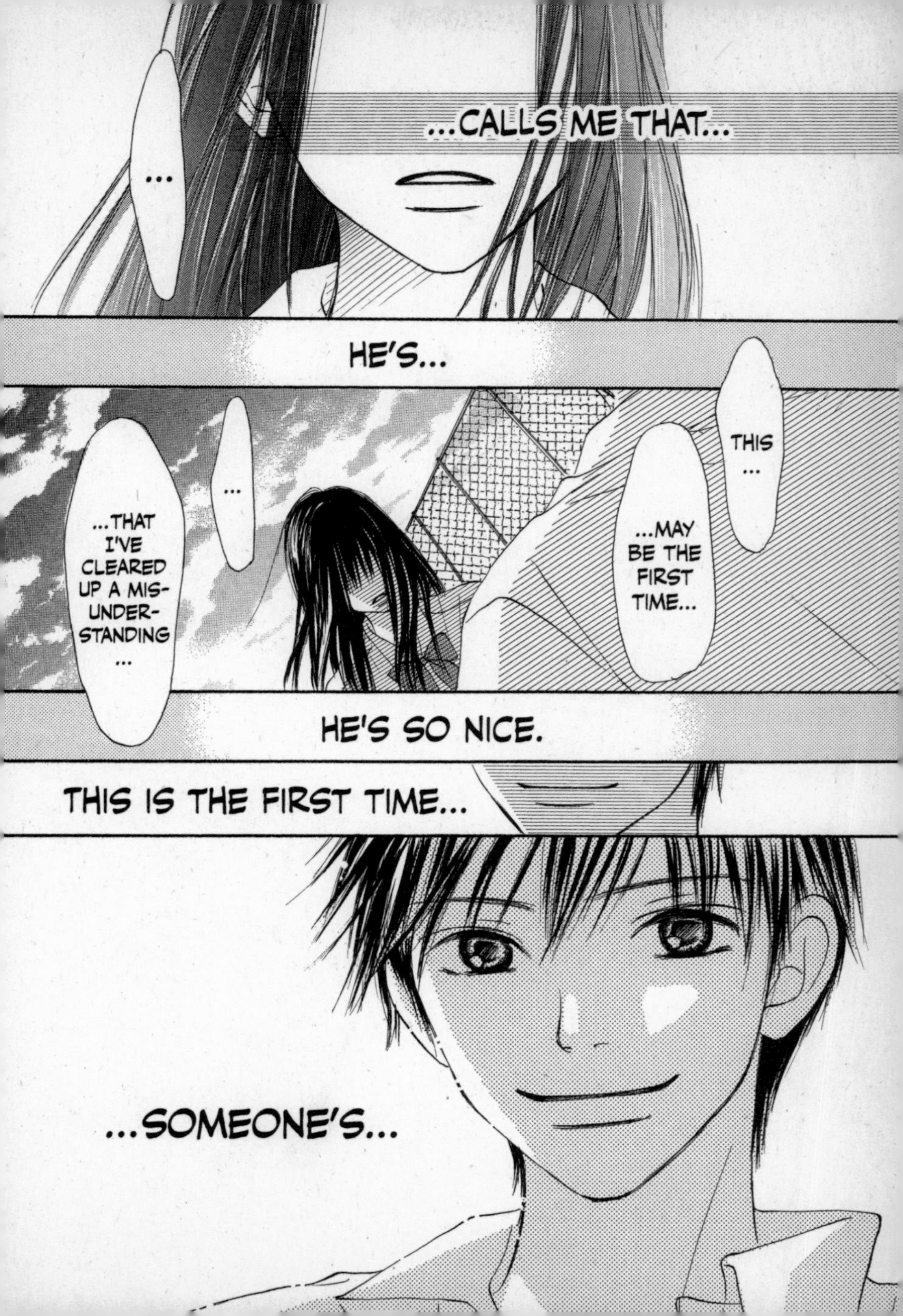
...CALLS ME THAT...
...
HE'S...
THIS ...
...MAY BE THE FIRST TIME...
...
...THAT I'VE CLEARED UP A MIS-UNDERSTANDING ...
HE'S SO NICE.
THIS IS THE FIRST TIME...
...SOMEONE'S...

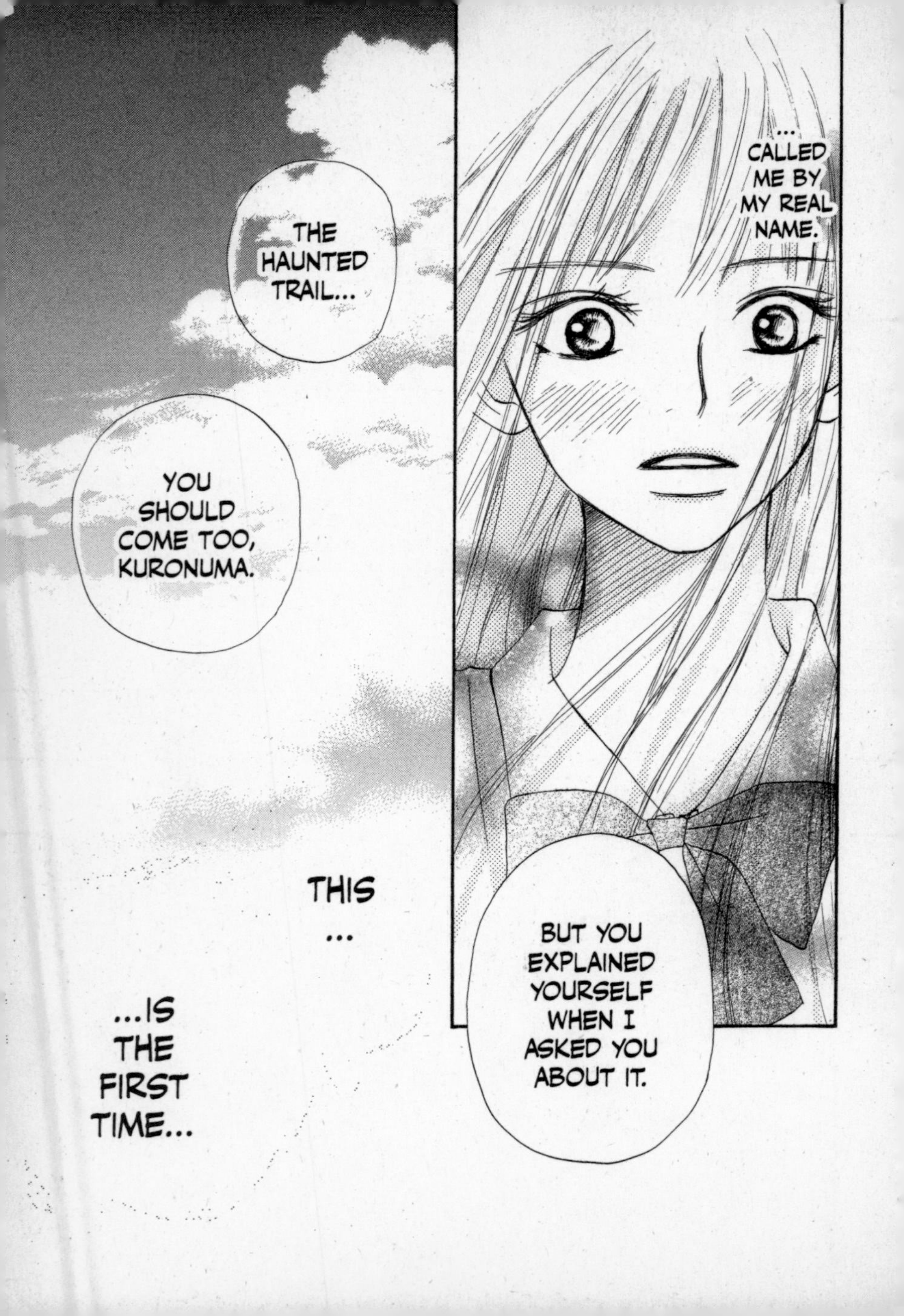
...CALLED ME BY MY REAL NAME.
THE HAUNTED TRAIL...
YOU SHOULD COME TOO, KURONUMA.
BUT YOU EXPLAINED YOURSELF WHEN I ASKED YOU ABOUT IT.
THIS...
...IS THE FIRST TIME...

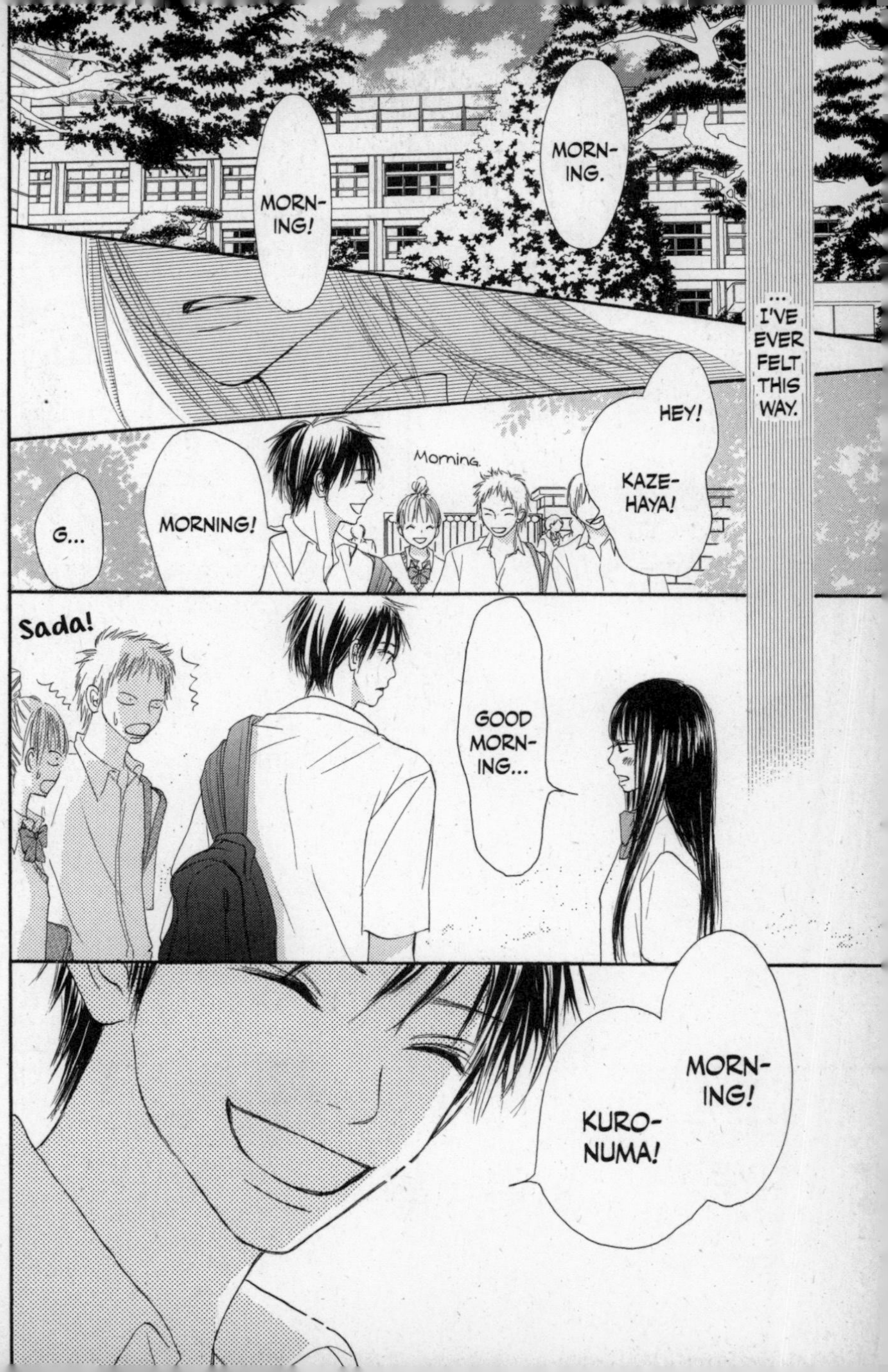

... I'VE EVER FELT THIS WAY.
MORN-ING.
MORN-ING!
HEY! KAZE-HAYA!
Morning.
MORNING!
G...
GOOD MORN-ING...
Sada!
MORN-ING! KURO-NUMA!

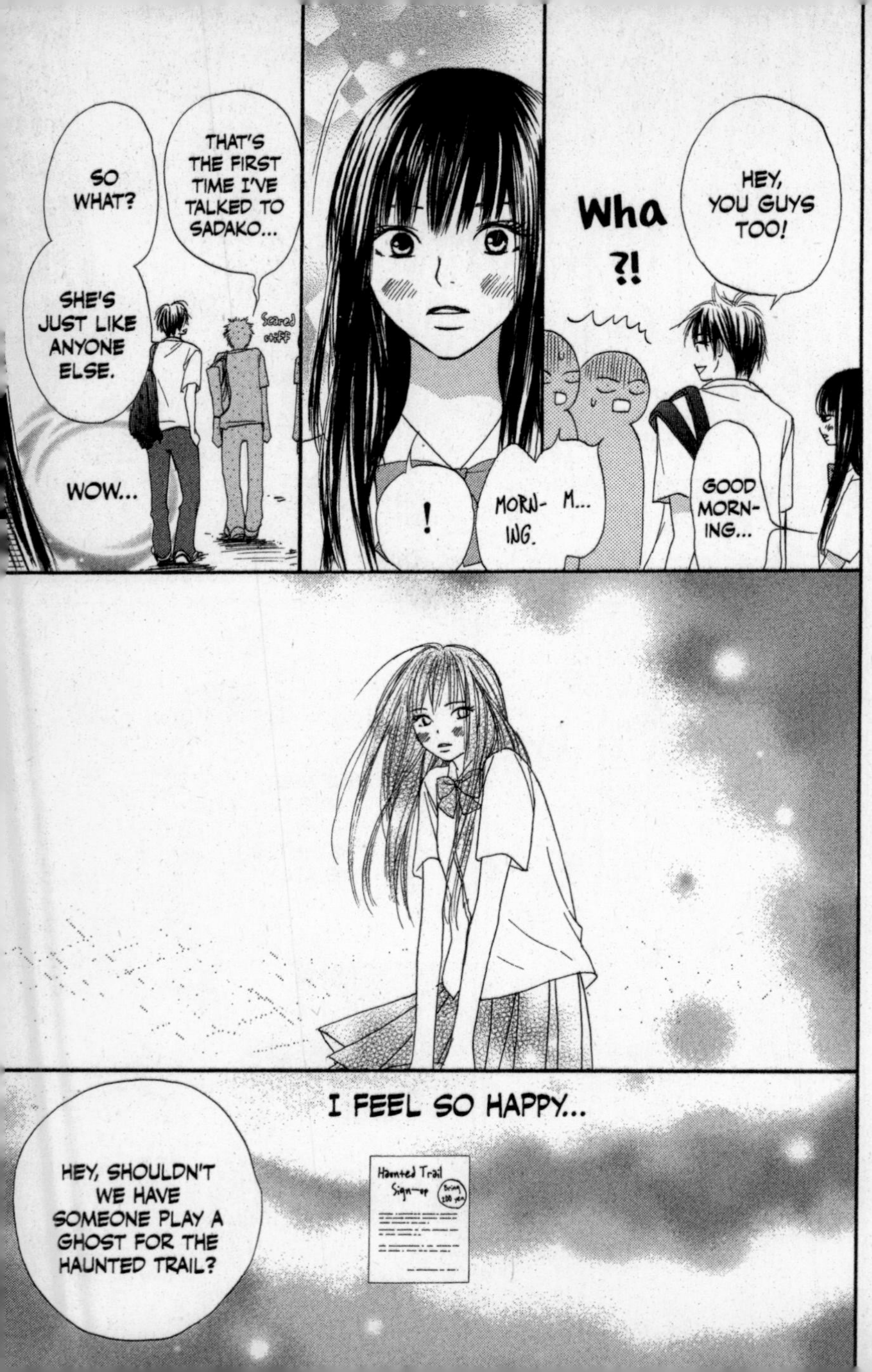
HEY, YOU GUYS TOO!
Wha ?!
GOOD MORNING...
M...
MORN-ING.
!
THAT'S THE FIRST TIME I'VE TALKED TO SADAKO...
Scared stiff
SO WHAT?
SHE'S JUST LIKE ANYONE ELSE.
WOW...
I FEEL SO HAPPY...
Haunted Trail Sign-up
Bring 100 yen
HEY, SHOULDN'T WE HAVE SOMEONE PLAY A GHOST FOR THE HAUNTED TRAIL?

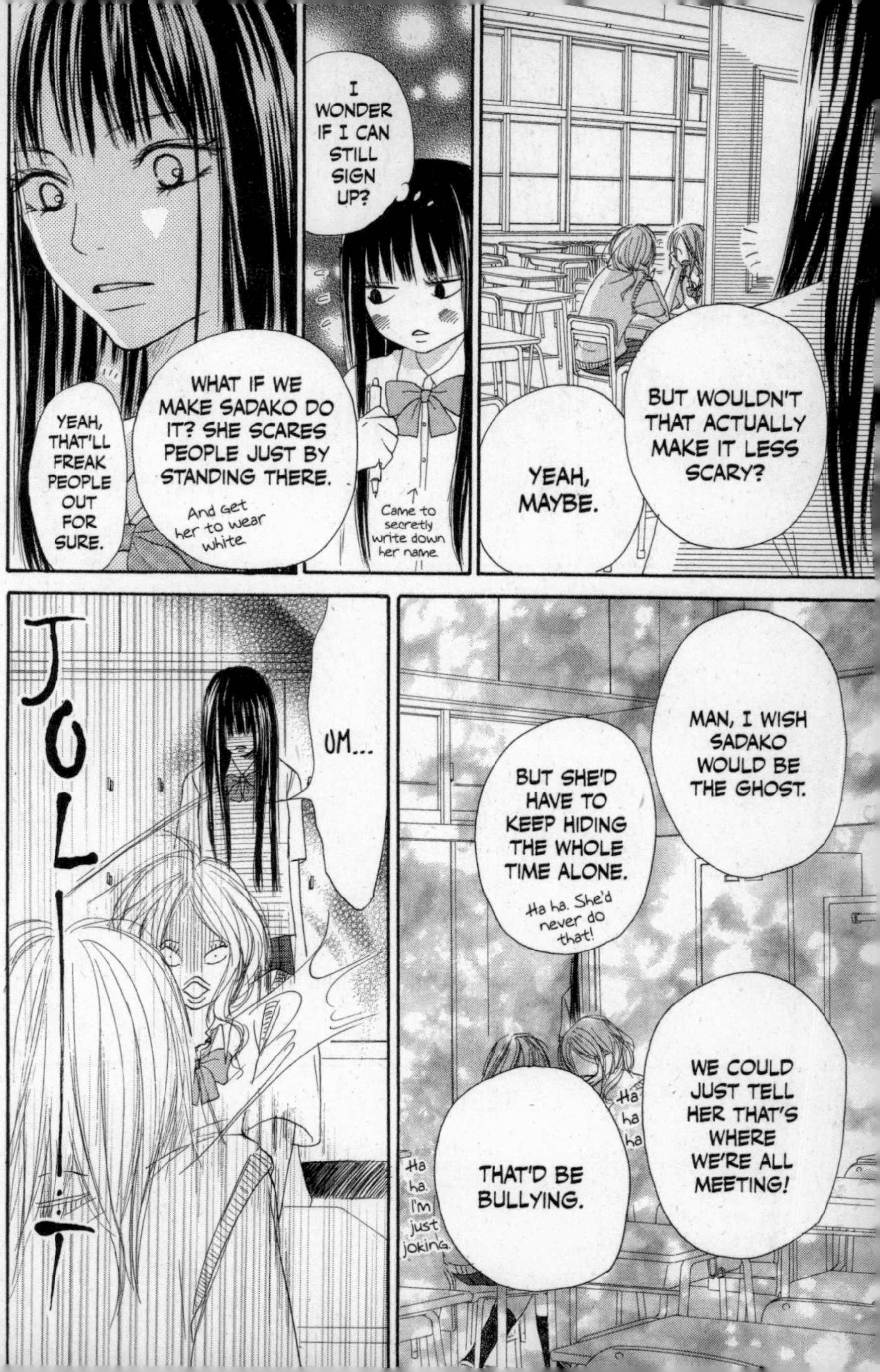
BUT WOULDN'T THAT ACTUALLY MAKE IT LESS SCARY?
YEAH, MAYBE.
I WONDER IF I CAN STILL SIGN UP?
WHAT IF WE MAKE SADAKO DO IT? SHE SCARES PEOPLE JUST BY STANDING THERE.
Came to secretly write down her name.
And get her to wear white.
YEAH, THAT'LL FREAK PEOPLE OUT FOR SURE.
MAN, I WISH SADAKO WOULD BE THE GHOST.
BUT SHE'D HAVE TO KEEP HIDING THE WHOLE TIME ALONE.
Ha ha. She'd never do that!
WE COULD JUST TELL HER THAT'S WHERE WE'RE ALL MEETING!
Ha ha ha
THAT'D BE BULLYING.
Ha ha. I'm just joking.
UM...
JOLT...!

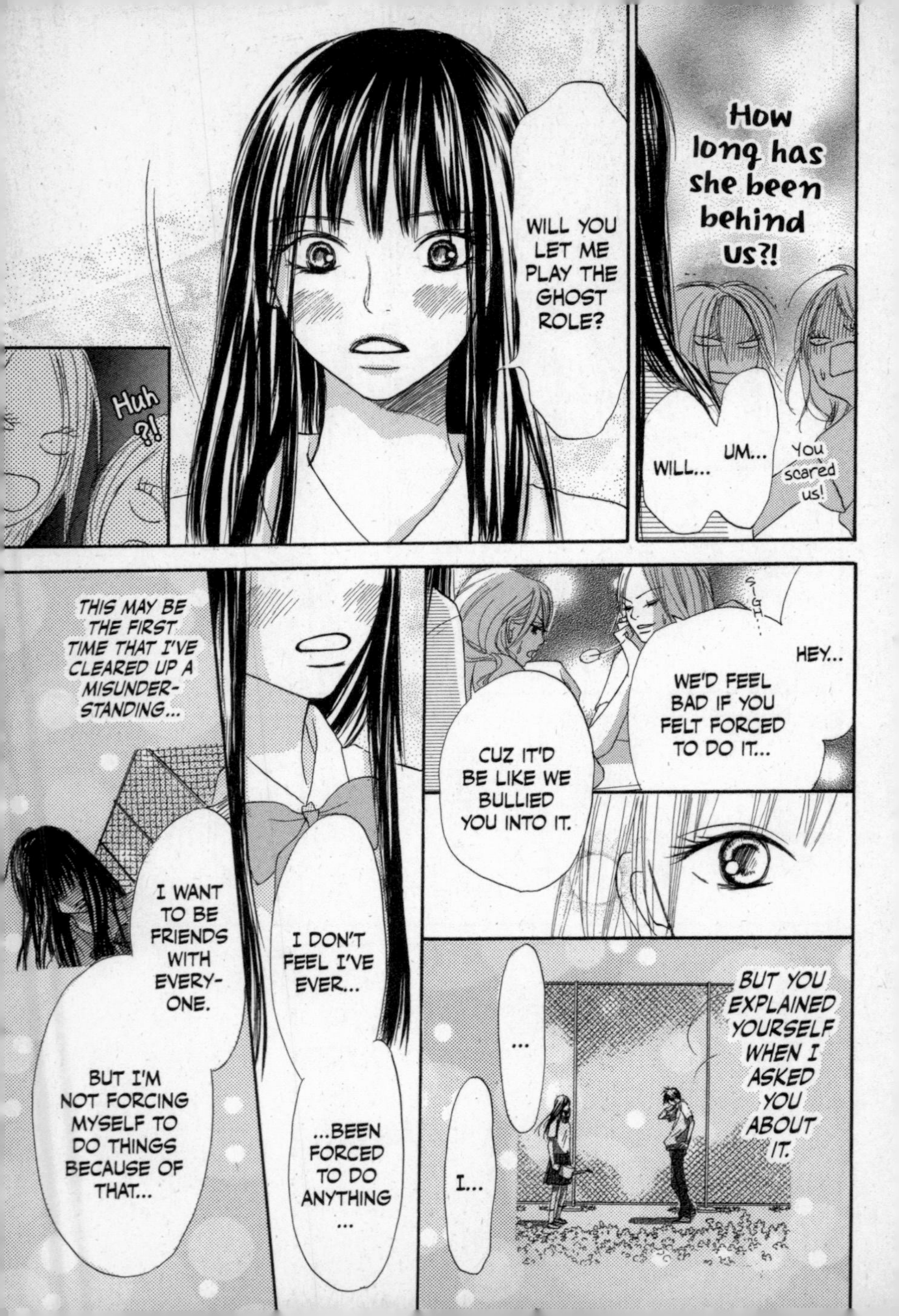

How long has she been behind us?!
You scared us!
UM...
WILL...
WILL YOU LET ME PLAY THE GHOST ROLE?
Huh ?!
SIGH...
HEY...
WE'D FEEL BAD IF YOU FELT FORCED TO DO IT...
CUZ IT'D BE LIKE WE BULLIED YOU INTO IT.
BUT YOU EXPLAINED YOURSELF WHEN I ASKED YOU ABOUT IT.
...
I...
THIS MAY BE THE FIRST TIME THAT I'VE CLEARED UP A MISUNDER-STANDING...
I DON'T FEEL I'VE EVER...
...BEEN FORCED TO DO ANYTHING ...
I WANT TO BE FRIENDS WITH EVERY-ONE.
BUT I'M NOT FORCING MYSELF TO DO THINGS BECAUSE OF THAT...

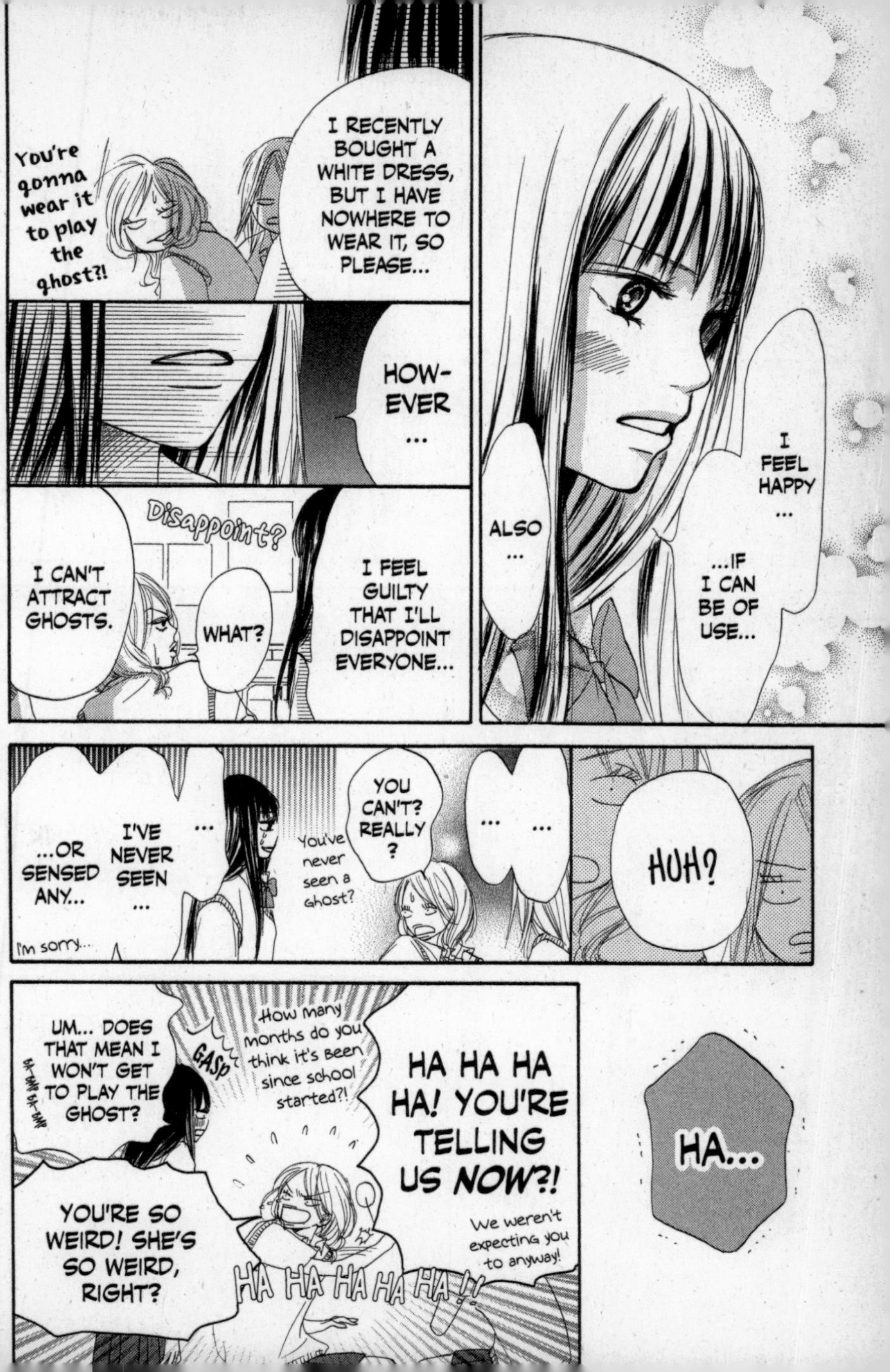
I FEEL HAPPY...
...IF I CAN BE OF USE...
ALSO...
I RECENTLY BOUGHT A WHITE DRESS, BUT I HAVE NOWHERE TO WEAR IT, SO PLEASE...
You're gonna wear it to play the ghost?!
HOW-EVER...
I FEEL GUILTY THAT I'LL DISAPPOINT EVERYONE...
Disappoint?
WHAT?
I CAN'T ATTRACT GHOSTS.
HUH?
... ...
YOU CAN'T? REALLY?
You've never seen a ghost?
...
I'VE NEVER SEEN...
...OR SENSED ANY...
I'm sorry...
HA...
HA HA HA HA! YOU'RE TELLING US NOW?!
How many months do you think it's been since school started?!
GASP
UM... DOES THAT MEAN I WON'T GET TO PLAY THE GHOST?
BA-DMP BA-DMP
We weren't expecting you to anyway!
YOU'RE SO WEIRD! SHE'S SO WEIRD, RIGHT?
HA HA HA HA HA HA!!

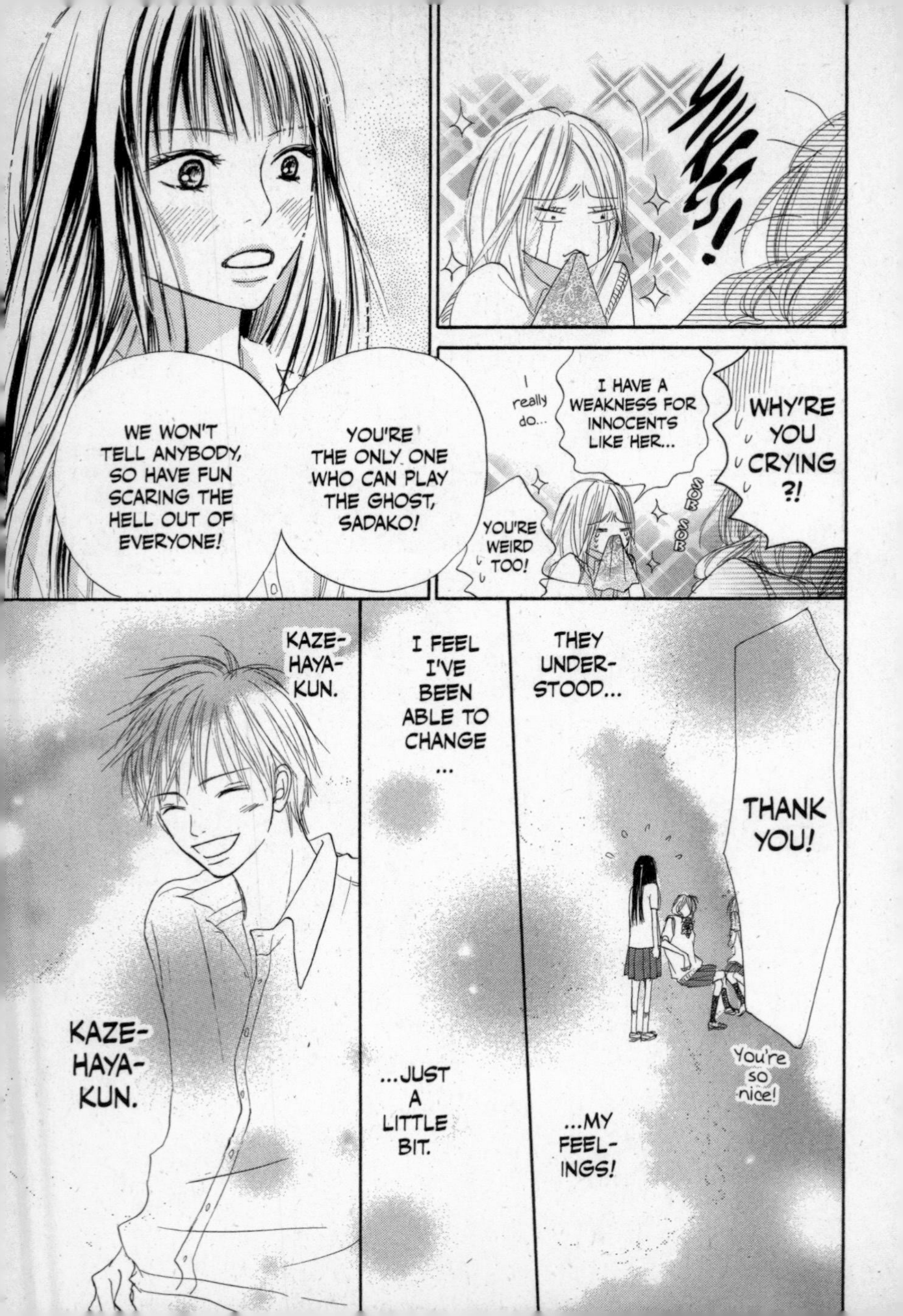
YIKES!
WHY'RE YOU CRYING?!
I HAVE A WEAKNESS FOR INNOCENTS LIKE HER...
I really do...
SOB SOB
YOU'RE WEIRD TOO!
YOU'RE THE ONLY ONE WHO CAN PLAY THE GHOST, SADAKO!
WE WON'T TELL ANYBODY, SO HAVE FUN SCARING THE HELL OUT OF EVERYONE!
THANK YOU!
THEY UNDER-STOOD...
...MY FEEL-INGS!
You're so nice!
I FEEL I'VE BEEN ABLE TO CHANGE ...
...JUST A LITTLE BIT.
KAZE-HAYA-KUN.
KAZE-HAYA-KUN.

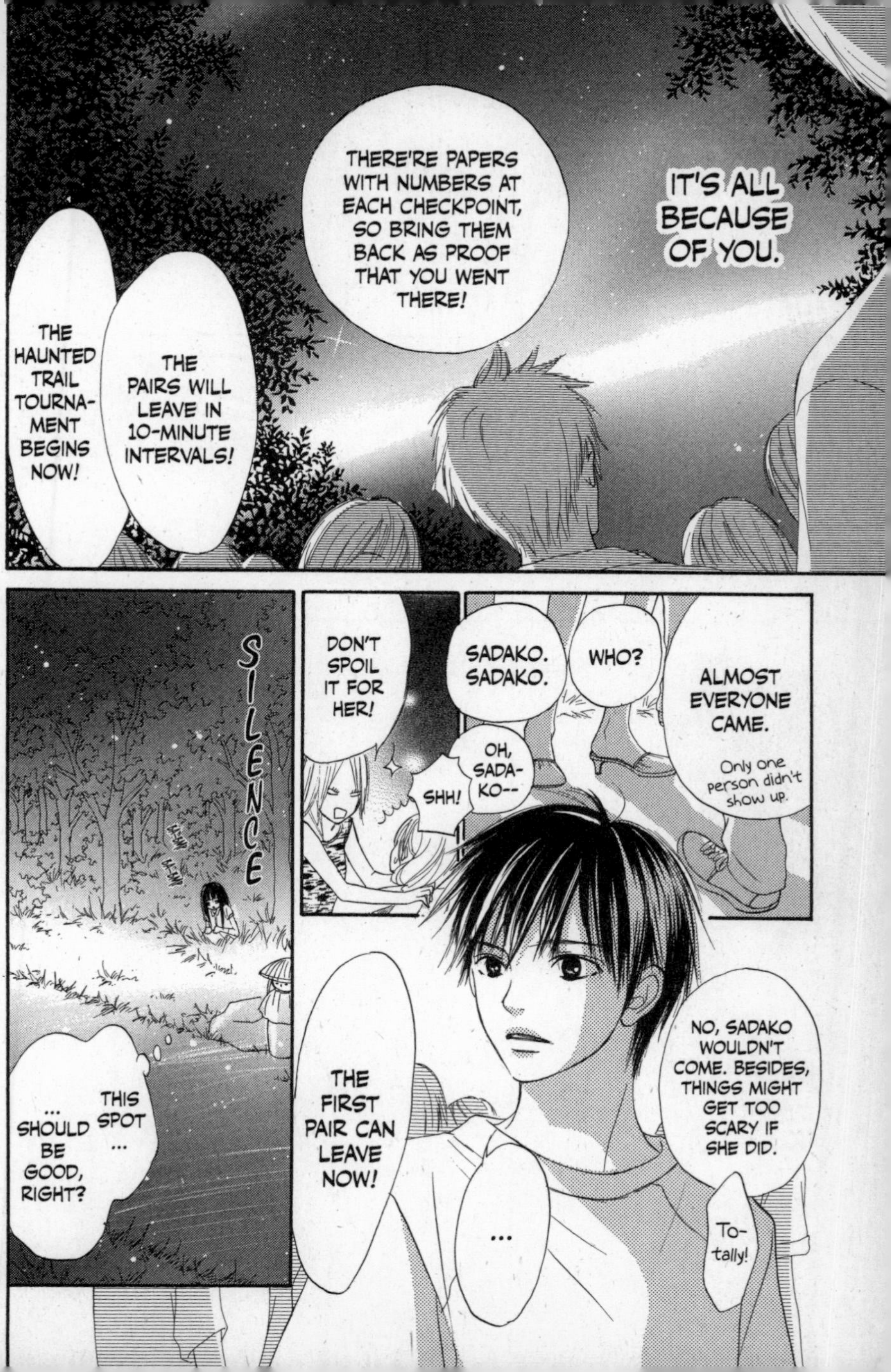
IT'S ALL BECAUSE OF YOU.
THERE'RE PAPERS WITH NUMBERS AT EACH CHECKPOINT, SO BRING THEM BACK AS PROOF THAT YOU WENT THERE!
THE PAIRS WILL LEAVE IN 10-MINUTE INTERVALS!
THE HAUNTED TRAIL TOURNAMENT BEGINS NOW!
ALMOST EVERYONE CAME.
Only one person didn't show up.
WHO?
SADAKO. SADAKO.
OH, SADAKO--
SHH!
DON'T SPOIL IT FOR HER!
NO, SADAKO WOULDN'T COME. BESIDES, THINGS MIGHT GET TOO SCARY IF SHE DID.
To-tally!
THE FIRST PAIR CAN LEAVE NOW!
...
SILENCE
THIS SPOT ...
... SHOULD BE GOOD, RIGHT?

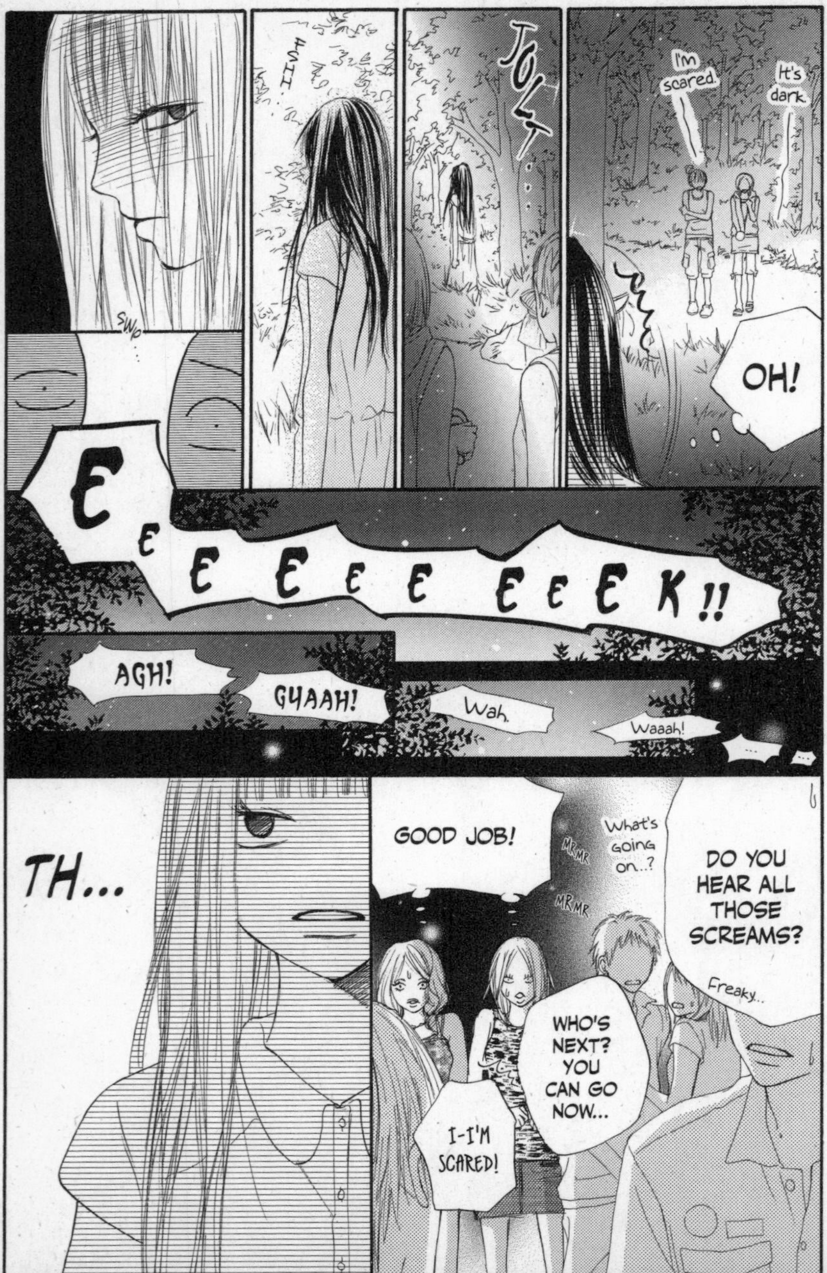
It's dark.
I'm scared.
OH!
JOLT...
FSHH...
SWP...
EEEEEEEEEEEK!!
...
...
Waaah!
Wah.
GYAAH!
AGH!
DO YOU HEAR ALL THOSE SCREAMS?
Freaky...
What's going on...?
MRMR
MRMR
GOOD JOB!
WHO'S NEXT? YOU CAN GO NOW...
I-I'M SCARED!
TH...

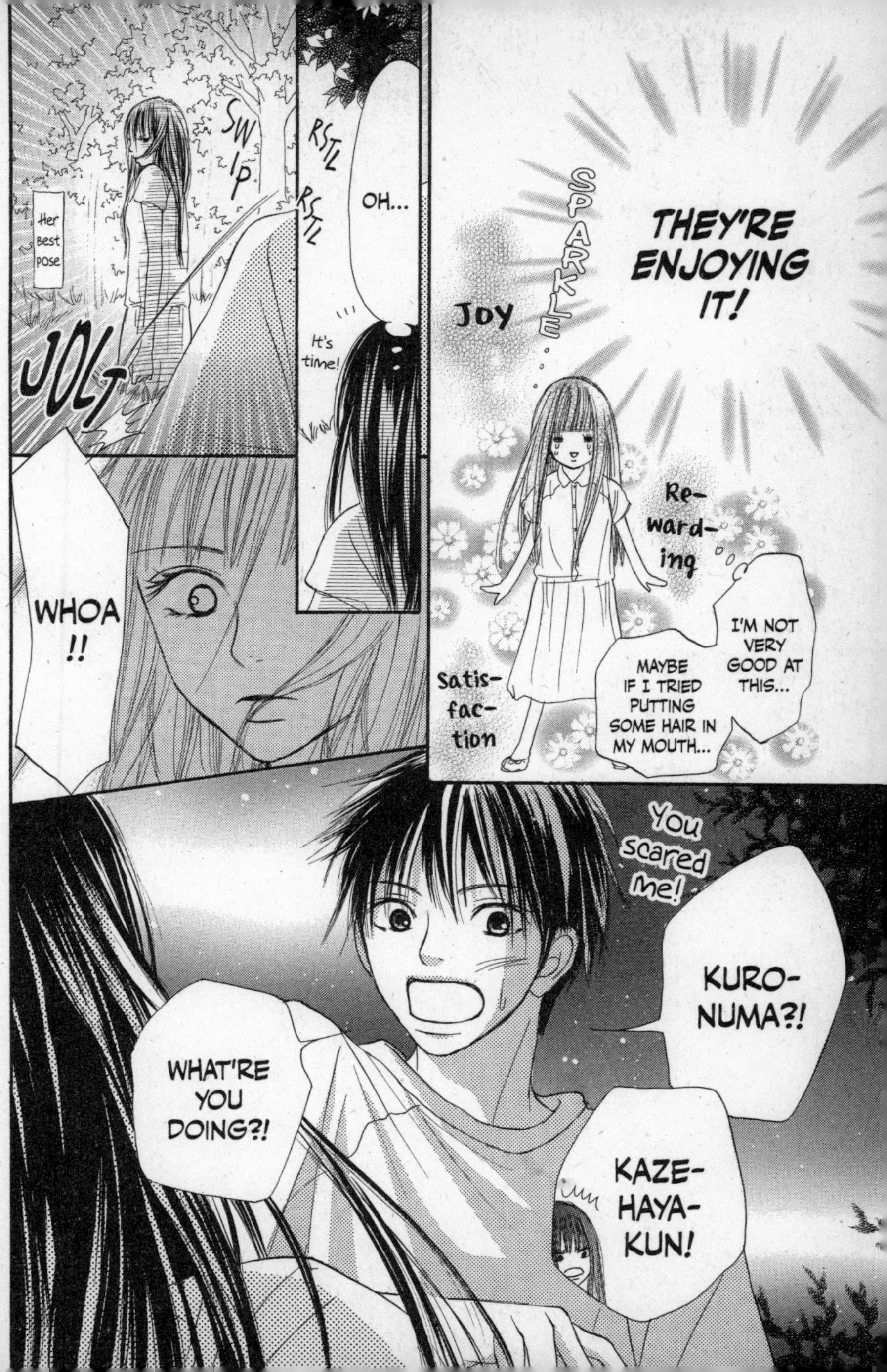
THEY'RE ENJOYING IT!
SPARKLE
JOY
Re-warding
Satis-faction
I'M NOT VERY GOOD AT THIS...
MAYBE IF I TRIED PUTTING SOME HAIR IN MY MOUTH...
RSTL RSTL
OH...
It's time!
SWIP
Her best pose
JOLT
WHOA !!
You scared me!
KURO-NUMA?!
WHAT'RE YOU DOING?!
KAZE-HAYA-KUN!

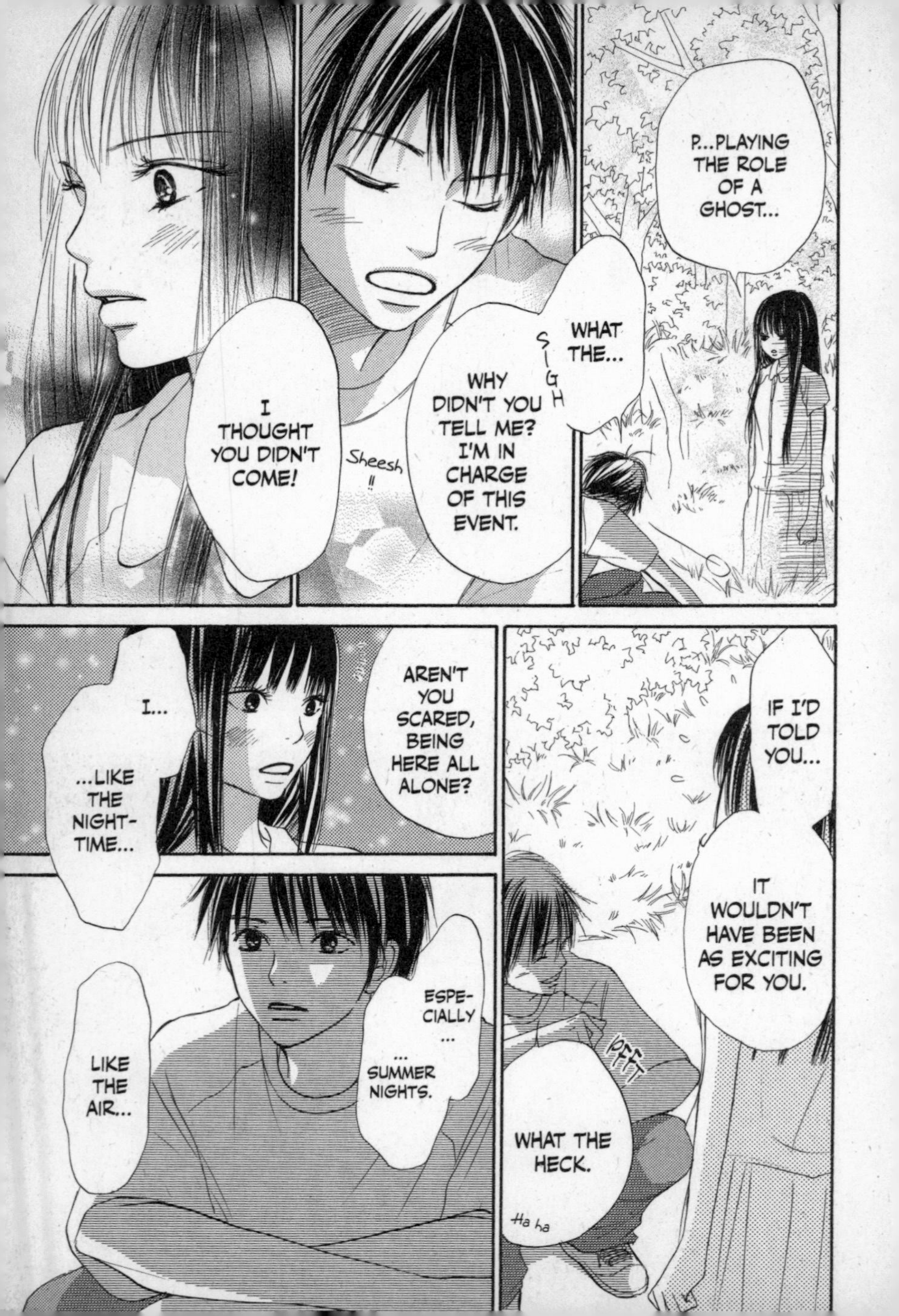
P...PLAYING THE ROLE OF A GHOST...
WHAT THE...
SIGH
WHY DIDN'T YOU TELL ME? I'M IN CHARGE OF THIS EVENT.
Sheesh !!
I THOUGHT YOU DIDN'T COME!
IF I'D TOLD YOU...
IT WOULDN'T HAVE BEEN AS EXCITING FOR YOU.
PFFT
WHAT THE HECK.
Ha ha
AREN'T YOU SCARED, BEING HERE ALL ALONE?
I...
...LIKE THE NIGHT-TIME...
ESPE-CIALLY ...
... SUMMER NIGHTS.
LIKE THE AIR...

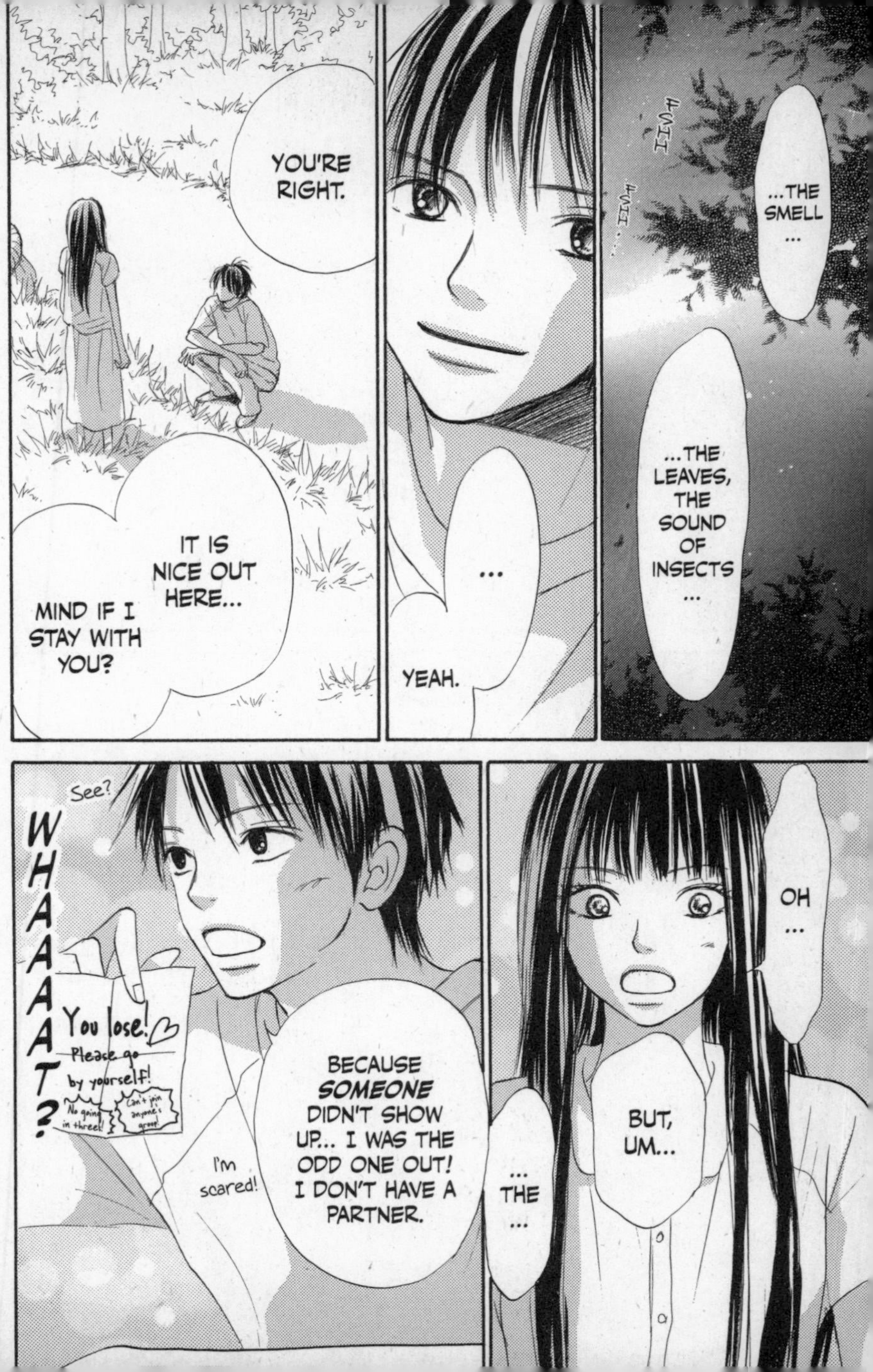
FSHH
FSHH...
...THE SMELL...
...THE LEAVES, THE SOUND OF INSECTS...
...
YEAH.
YOU'RE RIGHT.
IT IS NICE OUT HERE...
MIND IF I STAY WITH YOU?
OH...
BUT, UM...
...THE...
BECAUSE SOMEONE DIDN'T SHOW UP... I WAS THE ODD ONE OUT! I DON'T HAVE A PARTNER.
I'm scared!
See?
WHAAAAAT?
You lose!
Please go by yourself!
No going in threes!
Can't join anyone's group!

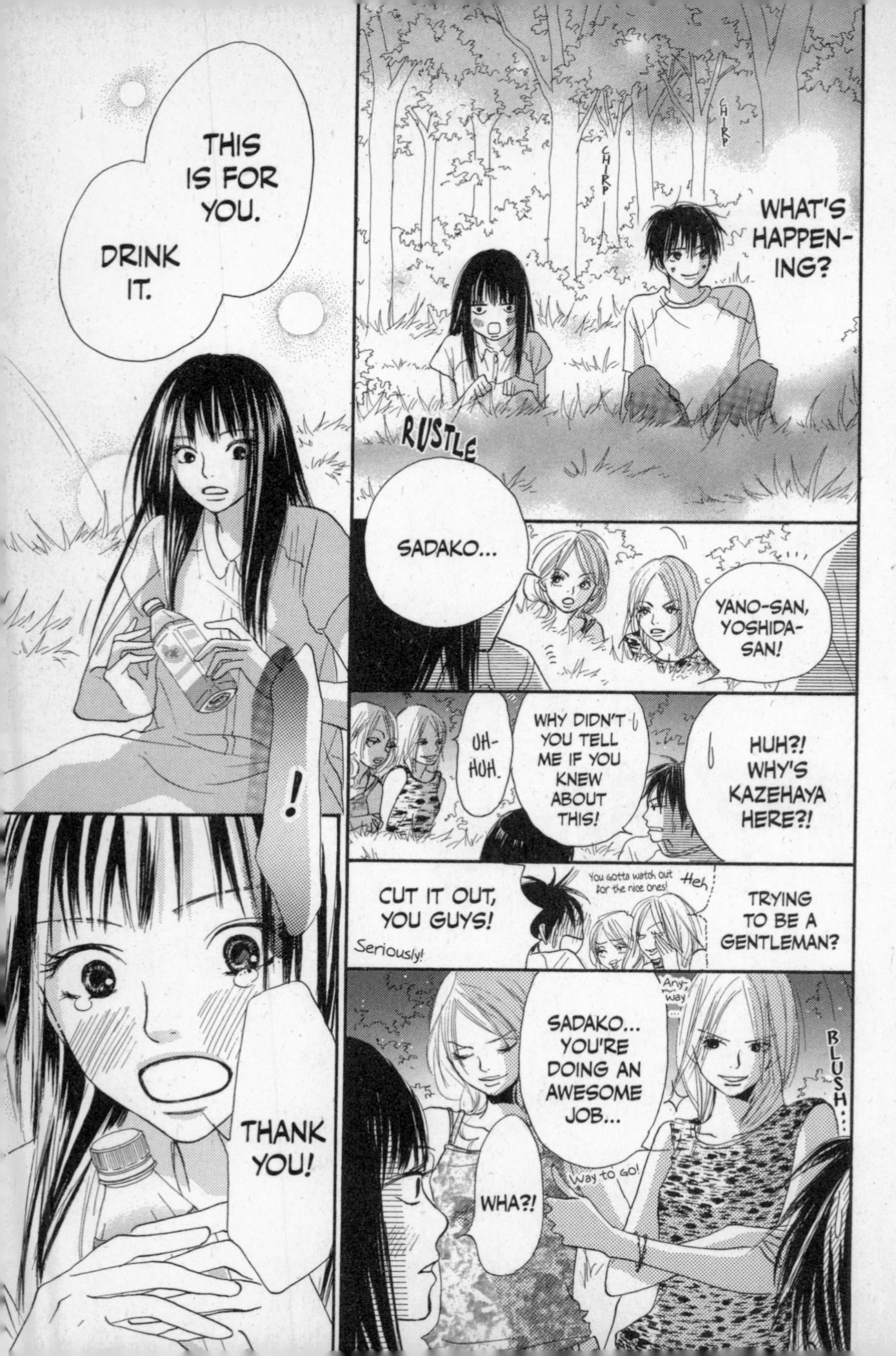
CHIRP
CHIRP
WHAT'S HAPPENING?
RUSTLE
YANO-SAN, YOSHIDA-SAN!
SADAKO...
HUH?! WHY'S KAZEHAYA HERE?!
WHY DIDN'T YOU TELL ME IF YOU KNEW ABOUT THIS!
UH-HUH.
TRYING TO BE A GENTLEMAN?
Heh
You gotta watch out for the nice ones!
CUT IT OUT, YOU GUYS!
Seriously!
BLUSH...
Any-way...
SADAKO... YOU'RE DOING AN AWESOME JOB...
Way to go!
WHA?!
THIS IS FOR YOU.
DRINK IT.
!
THANK YOU!

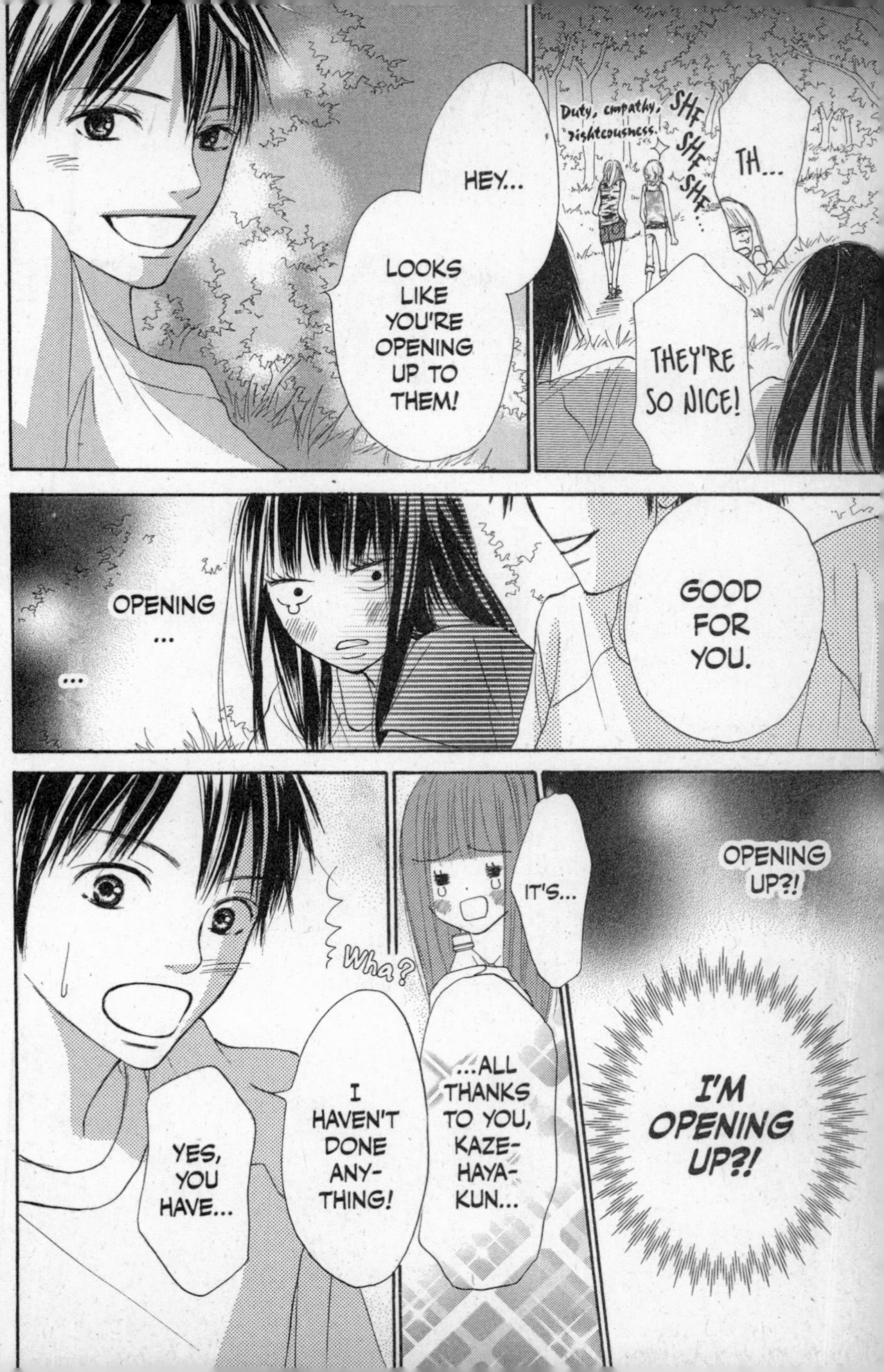
Duty, empathy, righteousness.
SHF SHF SHF...
TH...
THEY'RE SO NICE!
HEY...
LOOKS LIKE YOU'RE OPENING UP TO THEM!
GOOD FOR YOU.
OPENING...
...
OPENING UP?!
I'M OPENING UP?!
IT'S...
...ALL THANKS TO YOU, KAZE-HAYA-KUN...
Wha?
I HAVEN'T DONE ANY-THING!
YES, YOU HAVE...

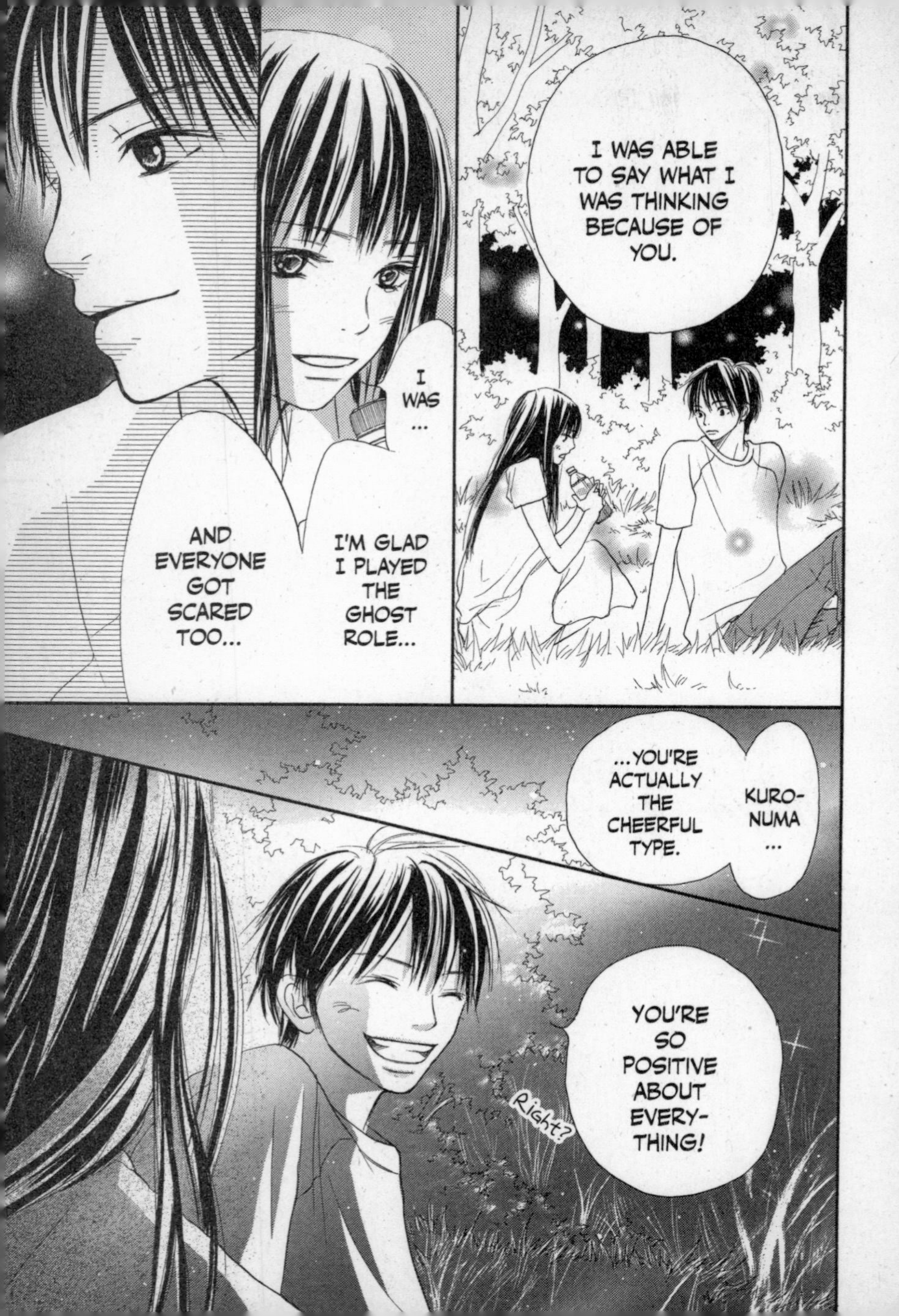
I WAS ABLE TO SAY WHAT I WAS THINKING BECAUSE OF YOU.
I WAS...
I'M GLAD I PLAYED THE GHOST ROLE...
AND EVERYONE GOT SCARED TOO...
KURO-NUMA...
...YOU'RE ACTUALLY THE CHEERFUL TYPE.
YOU'RE SO POSITIVE ABOUT EVERY-THING!
Right?

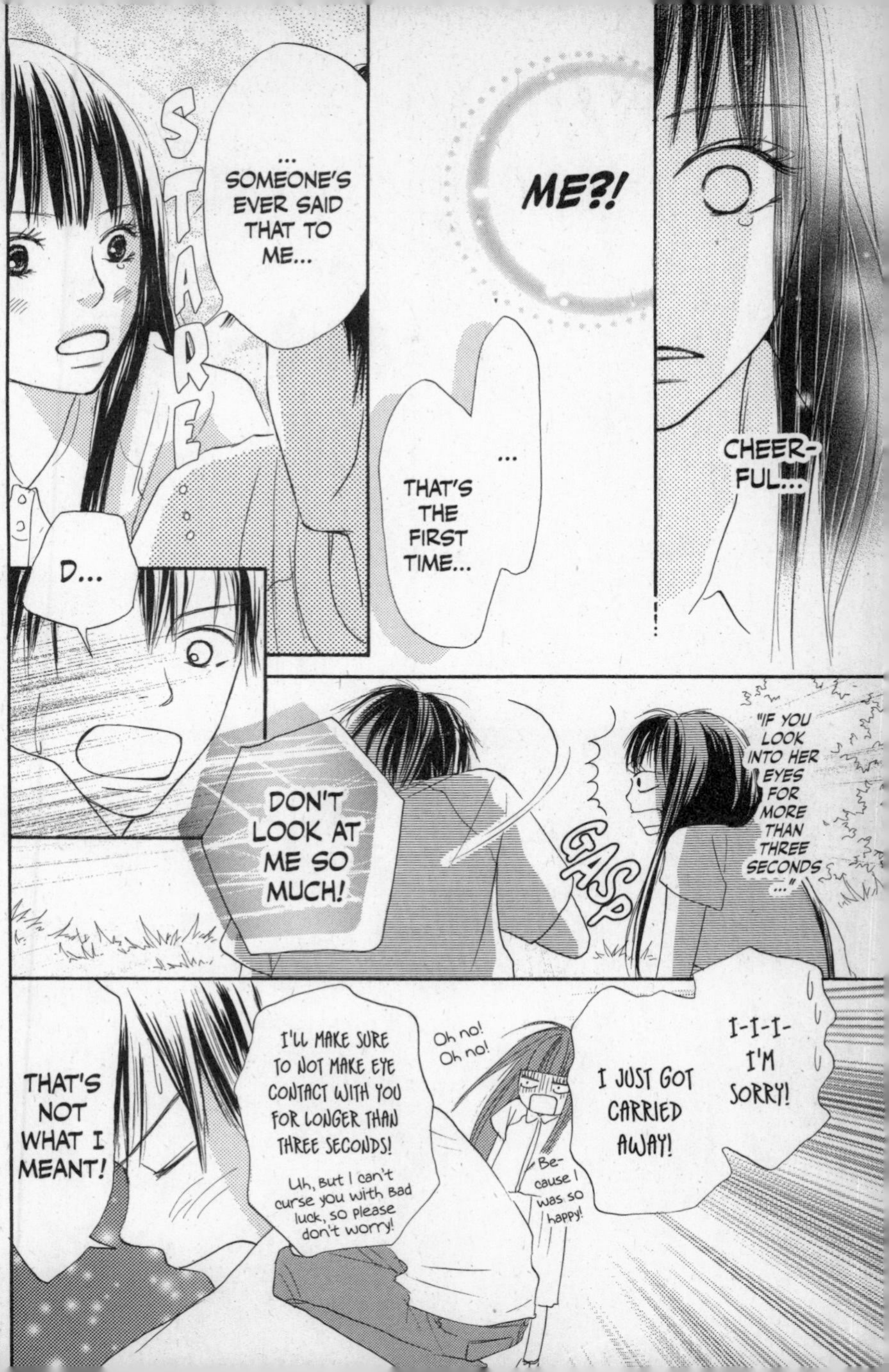
CHEER-FUL...
ME?!
... THAT'S THE FIRST TIME...
... SOMEONE'S EVER SAID THAT TO ME...
STARE
D...
DON'T LOOK AT ME SO MUCH!
GASP
"IF YOU LOOK INTO HER EYES FOR MORE THAN THREE SECONDS ..."
I-I-I-I'M SORRY!
I JUST GOT CARRIED AWAY!
Be-cause I was so happy!
Oh no! Oh no!
I'LL MAKE SURE TO NOT MAKE EYE CONTACT WITH YOU FOR LONGER THAN THREE SECONDS!
Uh, but I can't curse you with bad luck, so please don't worry!
THAT'S NOT WHAT I MEANT!

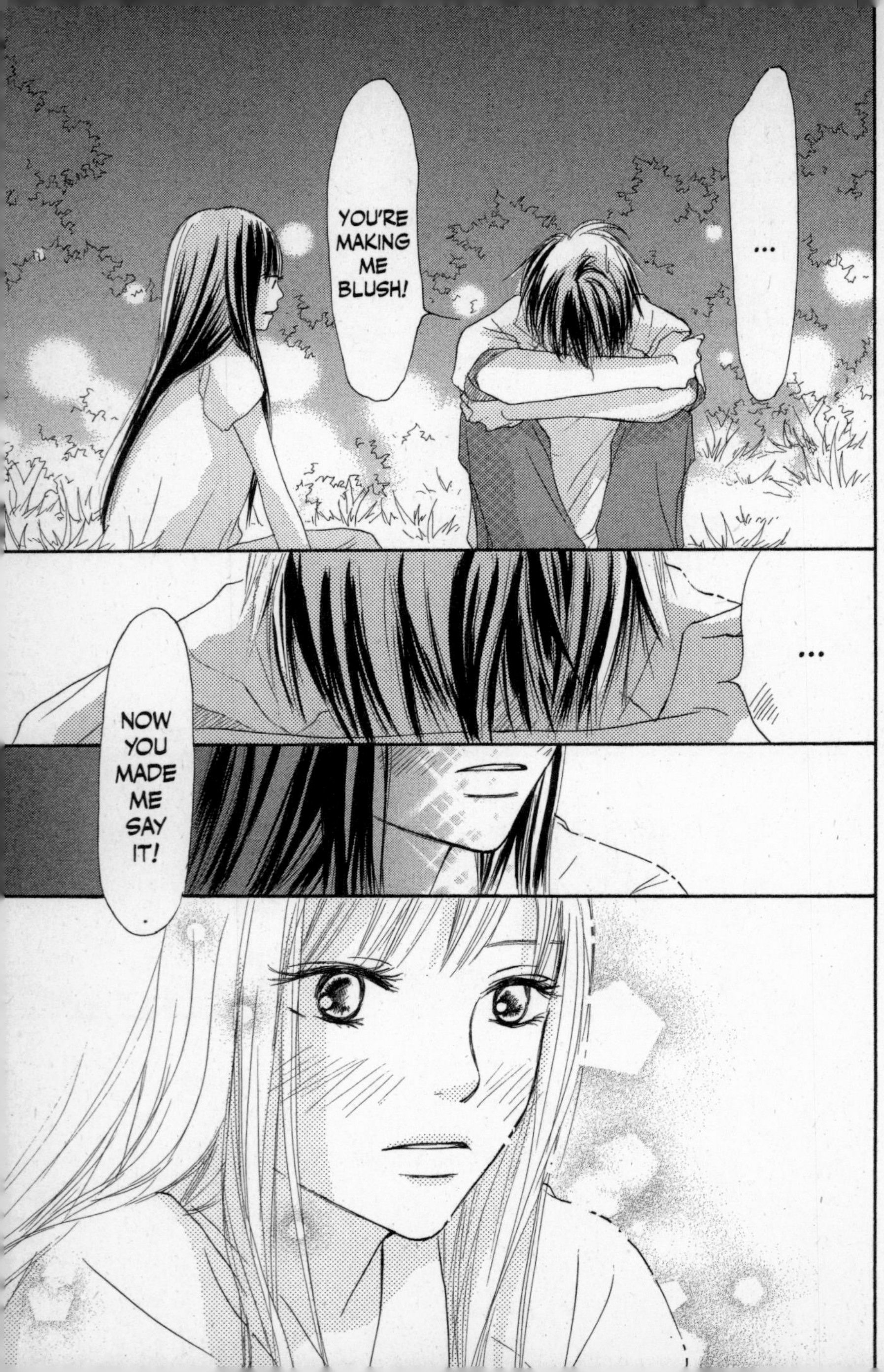
...
YOU'RE MAKING ME BLUSH!
...
NOW YOU MADE ME SAY IT!

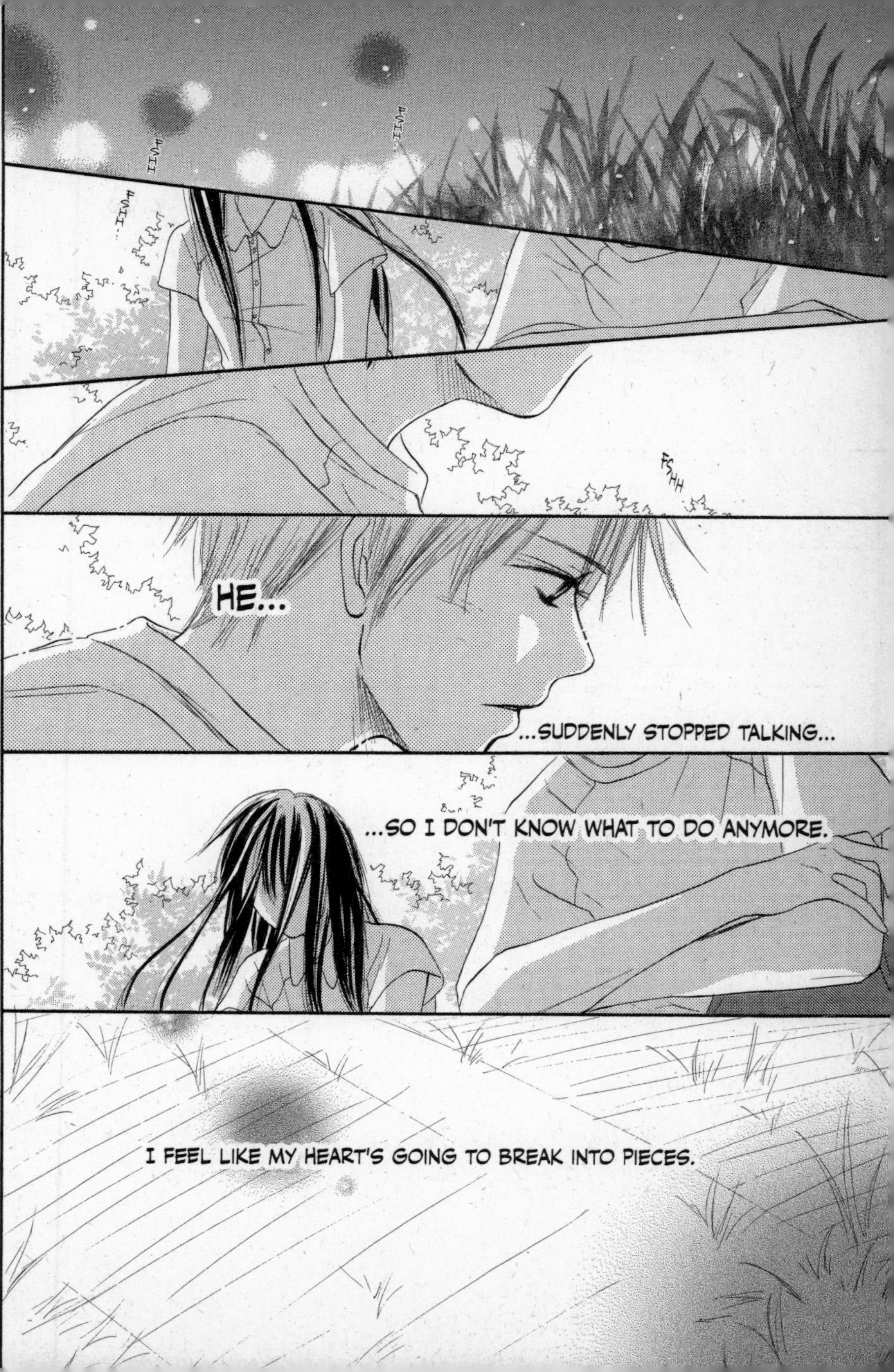
FSHH...
FSHH...
FSHH...
FSHH
HE...
...SUDDENLY STOPPED TALKING...
...SO I DON'T KNOW WHAT TO DO ANYMORE.
I FEEL LIKE MY HEART'S GOING TO BREAK INTO PIECES.

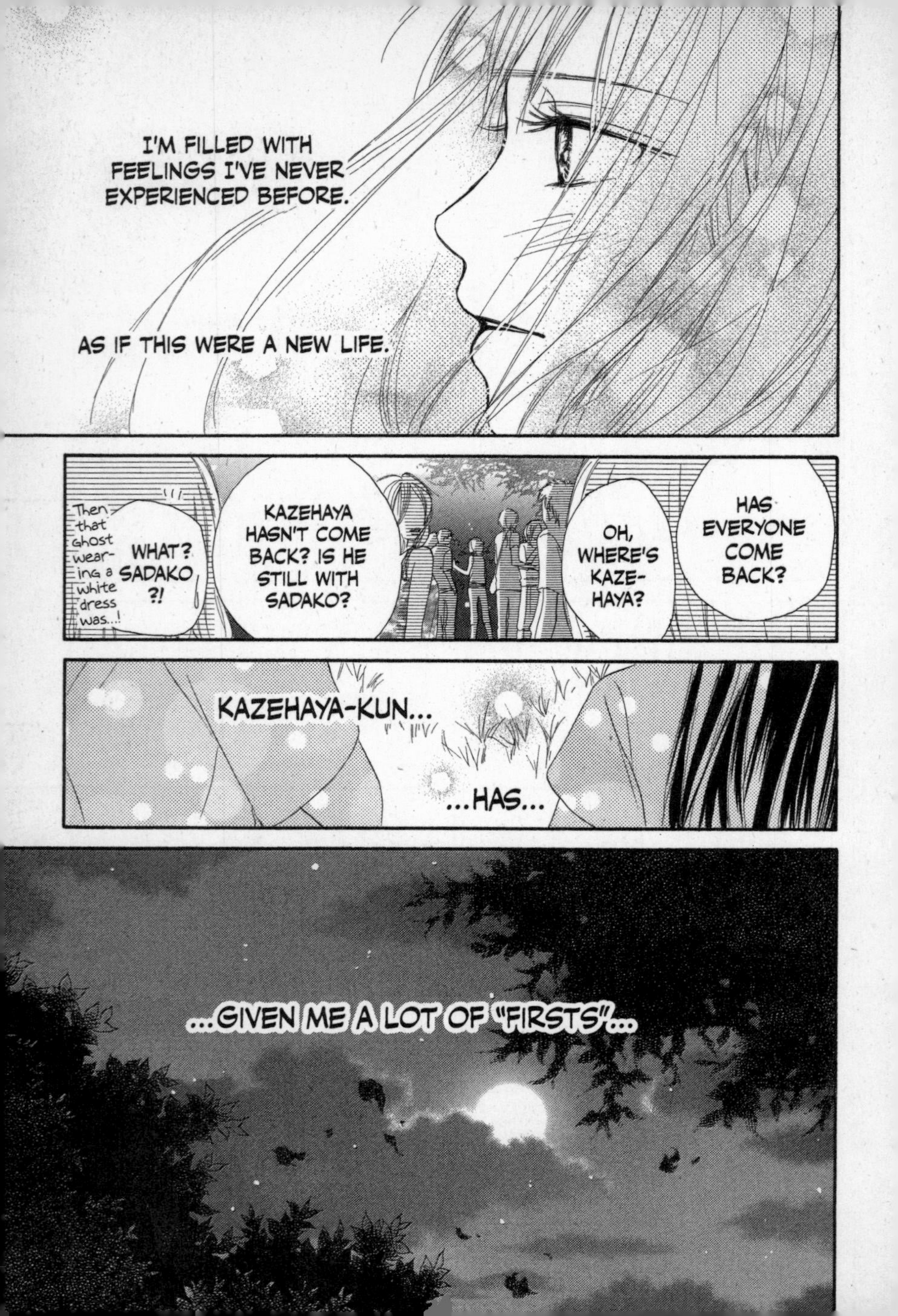
I'M FILLED WITH FEELINGS I'VE NEVER EXPERIENCED BEFORE.
AS IF THIS WERE A NEW LIFE.
HAS EVERYONE COME BACK?
OH, WHERE'S KAZE-HAYA?
KAZEHAYA HASN'T COME BACK? IS HE STILL WITH SADAKO?
WHAT? SADAKO?!
Then that ghost wearing a white dress was...!
KAZEHAYA-KUN...
...HAS...
...GIVEN ME A LOT OF "FIRSTS"...

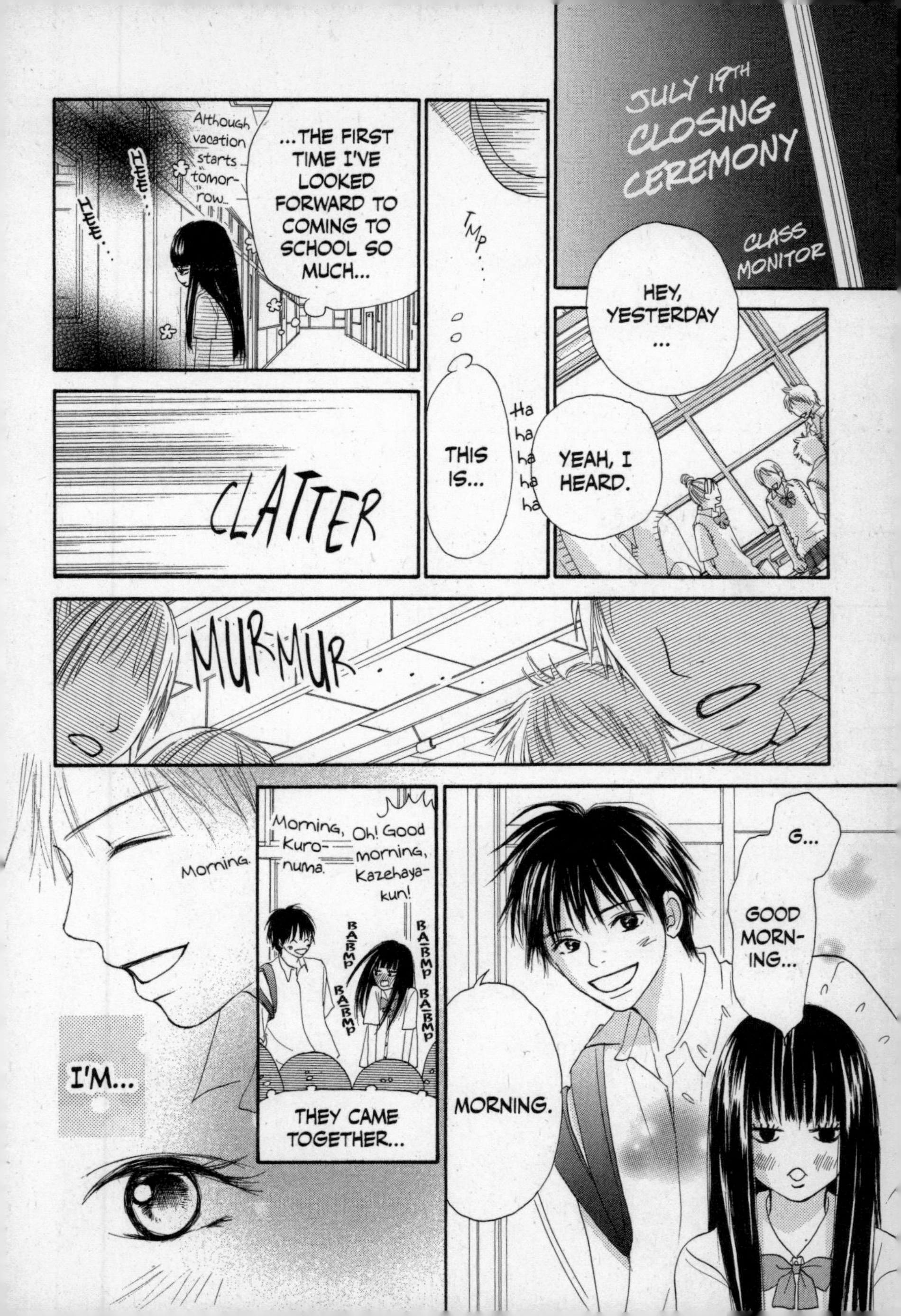
JULY 19TH
CLOSING CEREMONY
CLASS MONITOR
HEY, YESTERDAY...
YEAH, I HEARD.
TMP...
THIS IS...
Ha ha ha ha ha
Although vacation starts tomorrow...
...THE FIRST TIME I'VE LOOKED FORWARD TO COMING TO SCHOOL SO MUCH...
HEE... HEE...
CLATTER
MURMUR...
G...
GOOD MORNING...
MORNING.
Oh! Good morning, Kazehaya-kun!
Morning, Kuronuma.
BA-BMP BA-BMP
BA-BMP BA-BMP
THEY CAME TOGETHER...
Morning.
I'M...

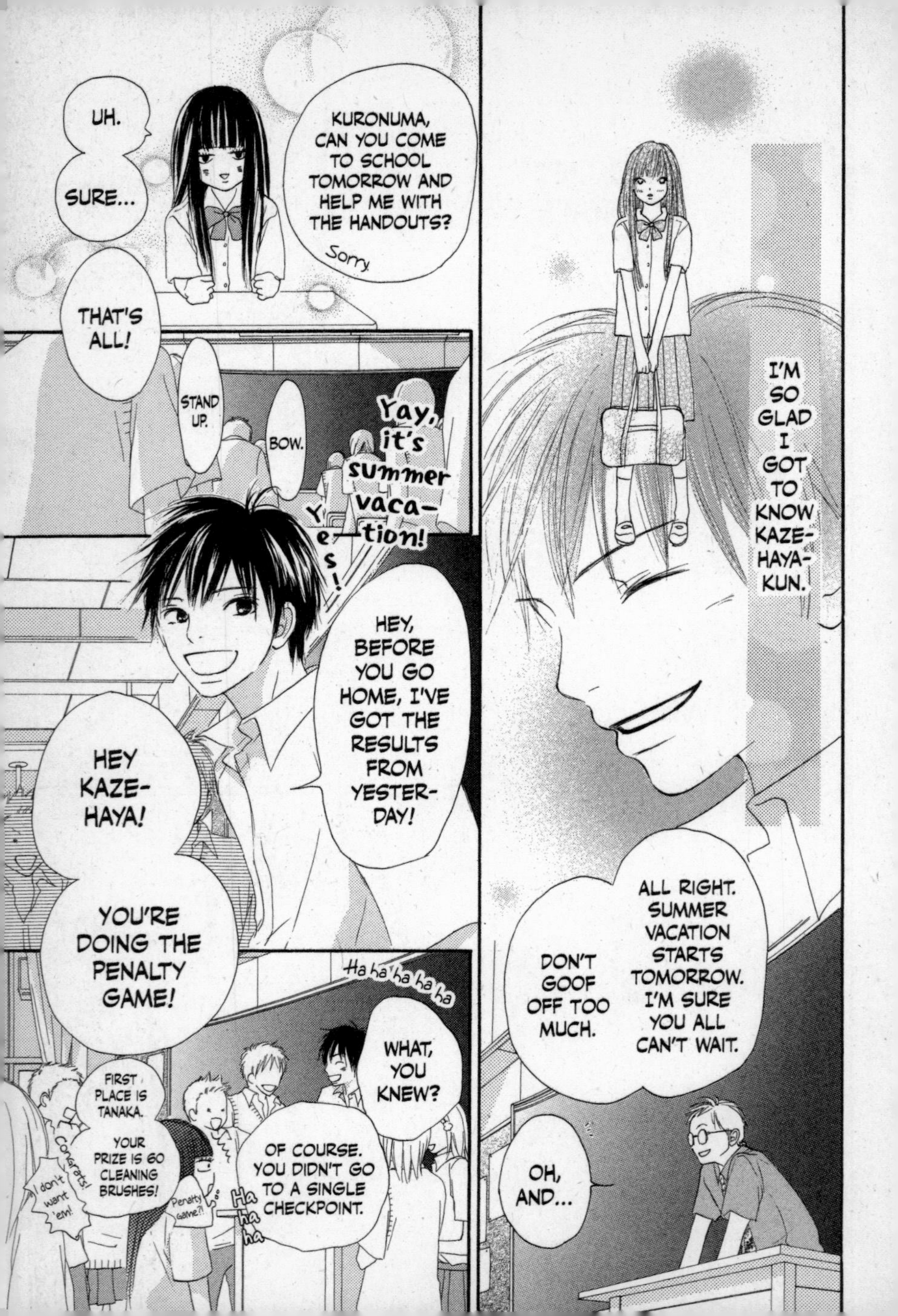
I'M SO GLAD I GOT TO KNOW KAZE-HAYA-KUN.
ALL RIGHT. SUMMER VACATION STARTS TOMORROW. I'M SURE YOU ALL CAN'T WAIT.
DON'T GOOF OFF TOO MUCH.
OH, AND...
KURONUMA, CAN YOU COME TO SCHOOL TOMORROW AND HELP ME WITH THE HANDOUTS?
Sorry
UH. SURE...
THAT'S ALL!
Yay, it's summer vacation!
Yes!
BOW.
STAND UP.
HEY, BEFORE YOU GO HOME, I'VE GOT THE RESULTS FROM YESTERDAY!
HEY KAZE-HAYA! YOU'RE DOING THE PENALTY GAME!
Ha ha ha ha ha
WHAT, YOU KNEW?
OF COURSE. YOU DIDN'T GO TO A SINGLE CHECKPOINT.
Ha ha ha
Penalty game?!
FIRST PLACE IS TANAKA. YOUR PRIZE IS 60 CLEANING BRUSHES!
Congrats!
I don't want 'em!

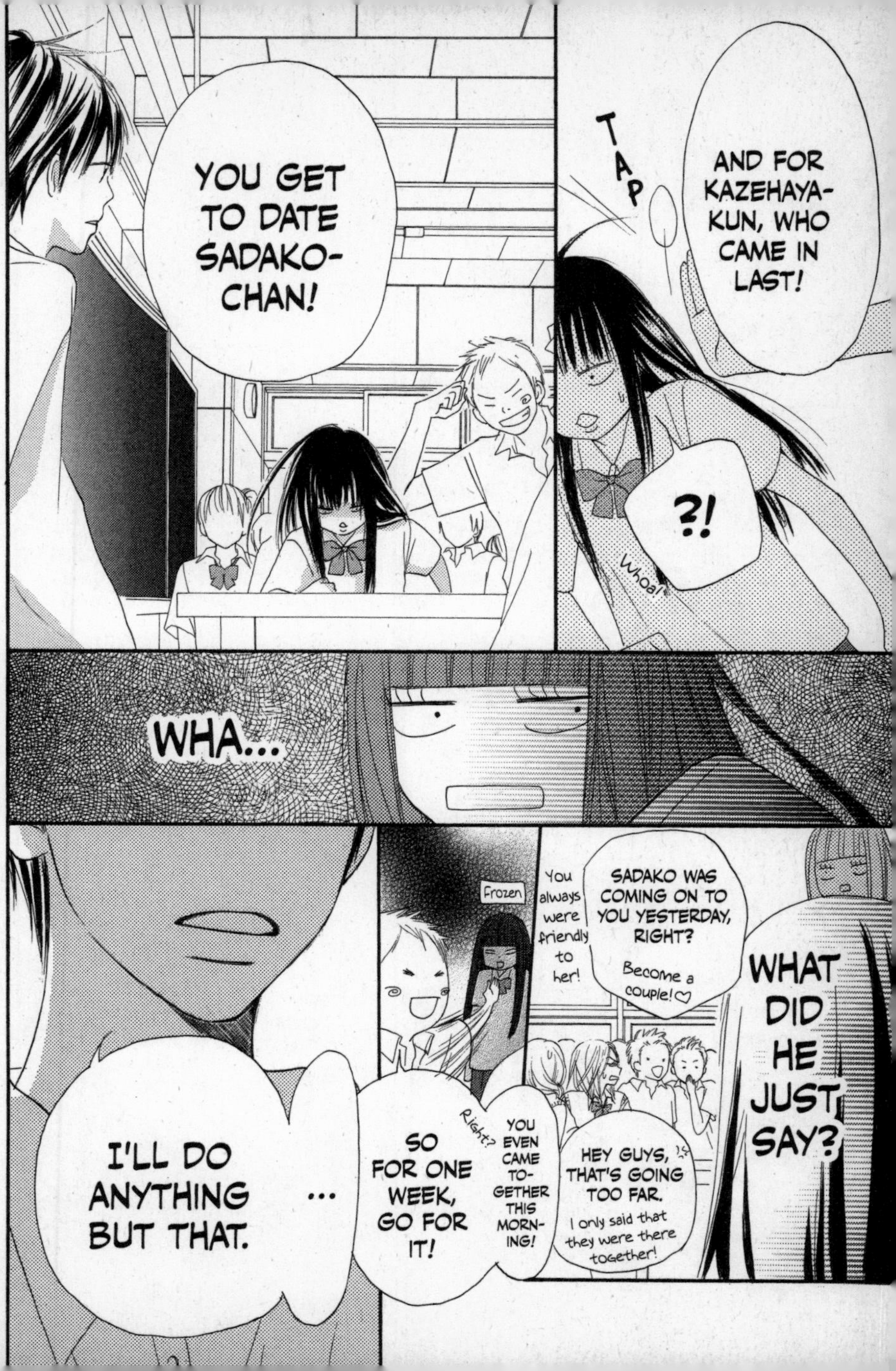
TAP
AND FOR KAZEHAYA-KUN, WHO CAME IN LAST!
?!
Whoa!
YOU GET TO DATE SADAKO-CHAN!
WHA...
WHAT DID HE JUST SAY?
SADAKO WAS COMING ON TO YOU YESTERDAY, RIGHT?
Become a couple!♡
You always were friendly to her!
Frozen
HEY GUYS, THAT'S GOING TOO FAR.
I only said that they were there together!
YOU EVEN CAME TO-GETHER THIS MORN-ING!
Right?
SO FOR ONE WEEK, GO FOR IT!
...
I'LL DO ANYTHING BUT THAT.

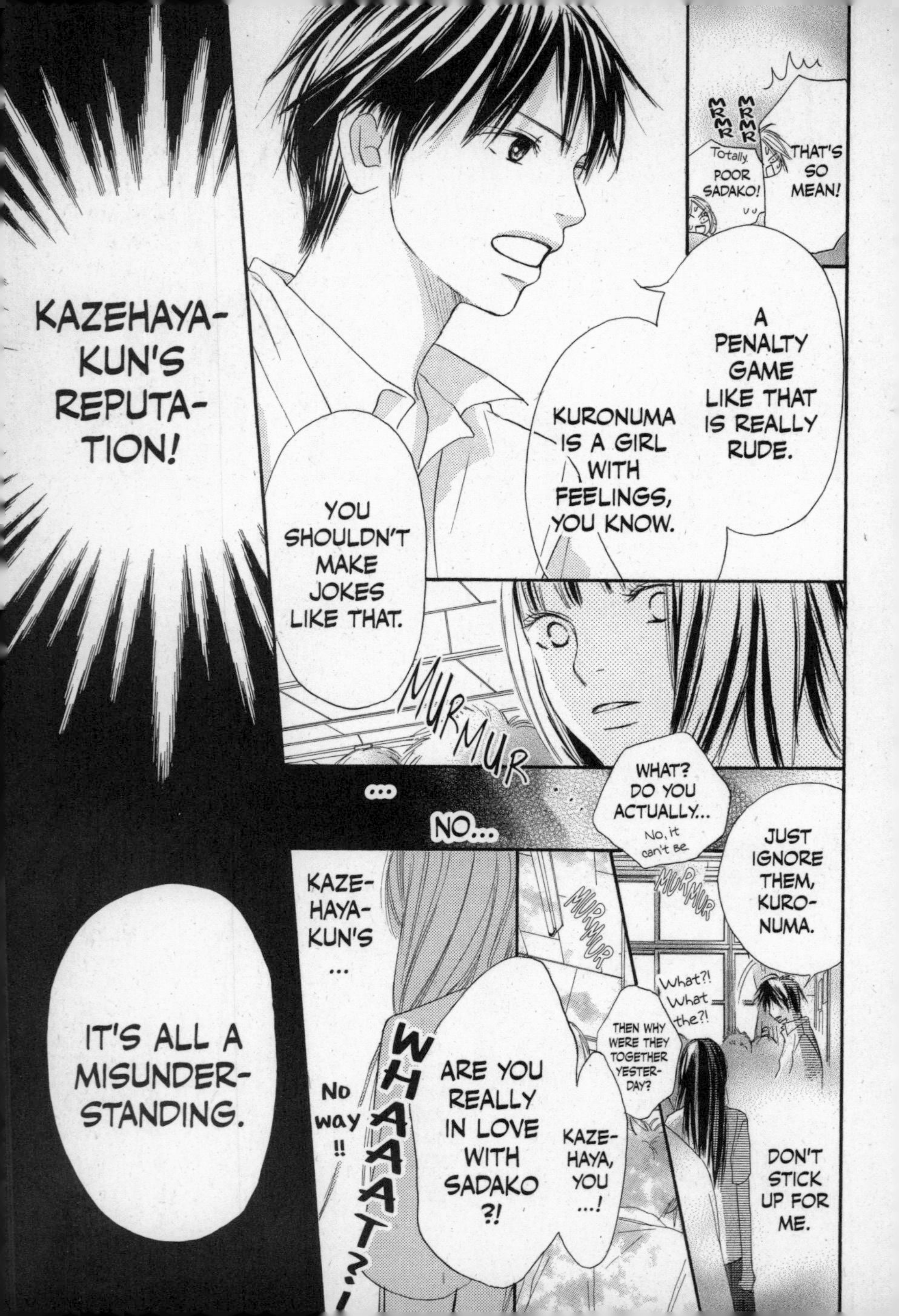
MRMR MRMR
Totally. POOR SADAKO!
THAT'S SO MEAN!
A PENALTY GAME LIKE THAT IS REALLY RUDE.
KURONUMA IS A GIRL WITH FEELINGS, YOU KNOW.
YOU SHOULDN'T MAKE JOKES LIKE THAT.
MURMUR
WHAT? DO YOU ACTUALLY...
No, it can't be.
JUST IGNORE THEM, KURONUMA.
DON'T STICK UP FOR ME.
MURMUR
What?! What the?!
THEN WHY WERE THEY TOGETHER YESTERDAY?
MURMUR
KAZEHAYA, YOU ...!
ARE YOU REALLY IN LOVE WITH SADAKO ?!
WHAAAT?!
No way !!
KAZEHAYA-KUN'S ...
KAZEHAYA-KUN'S REPUTATION!
...
NO...
IT'S ALL A MISUNDERSTANDING.

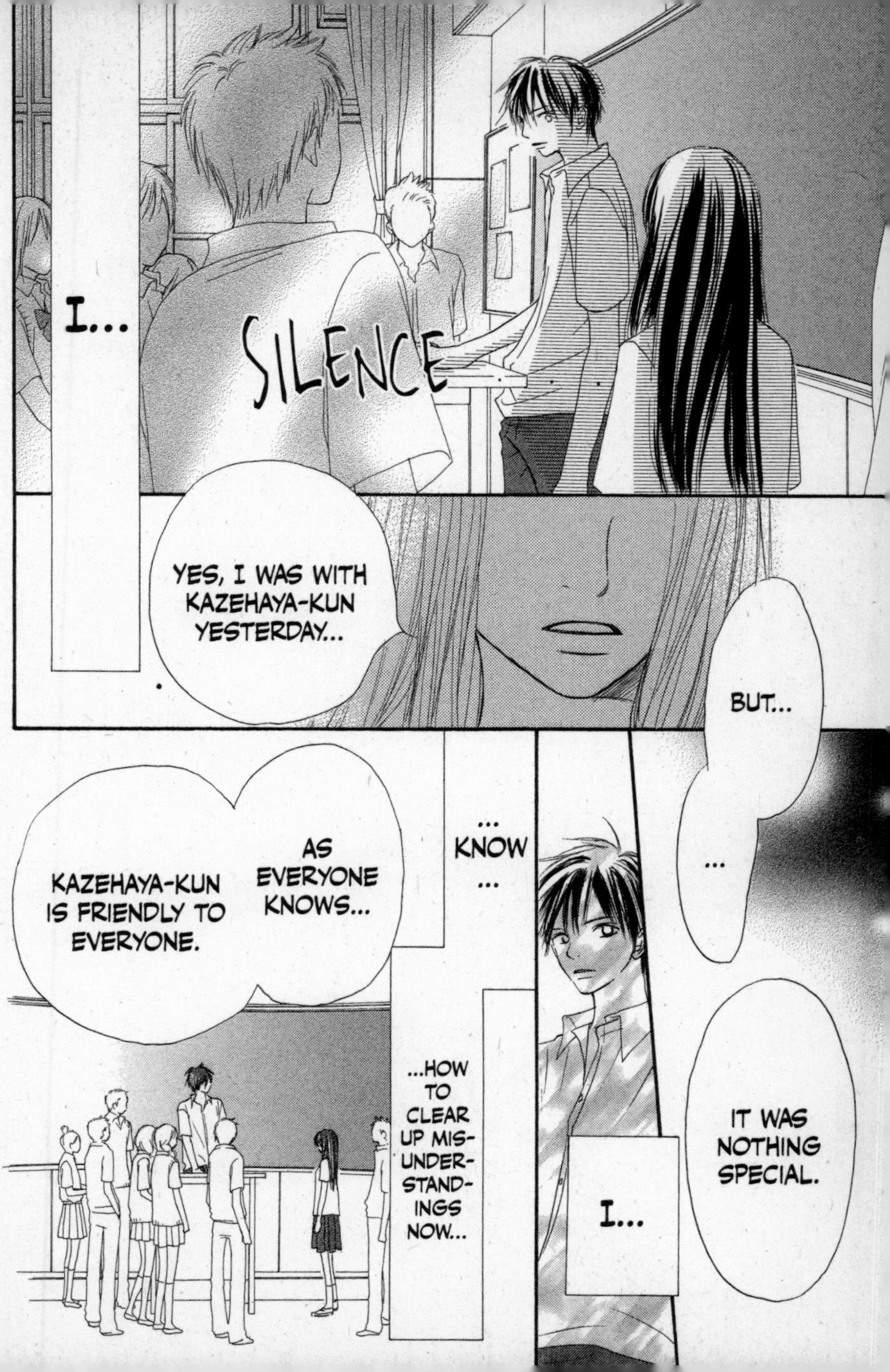
SILENCE
I...
YES, I WAS WITH KAZEHAYA-KUN YESTERDAY...
BUT...
...
IT WAS NOTHING SPECIAL.
I...
... KNOW ...
...HOW TO CLEAR UP MIS-UNDER-STAND-INGS NOW...
AS EVERYONE KNOWS...
KAZEHAYA-KUN IS FRIENDLY TO EVERYONE.

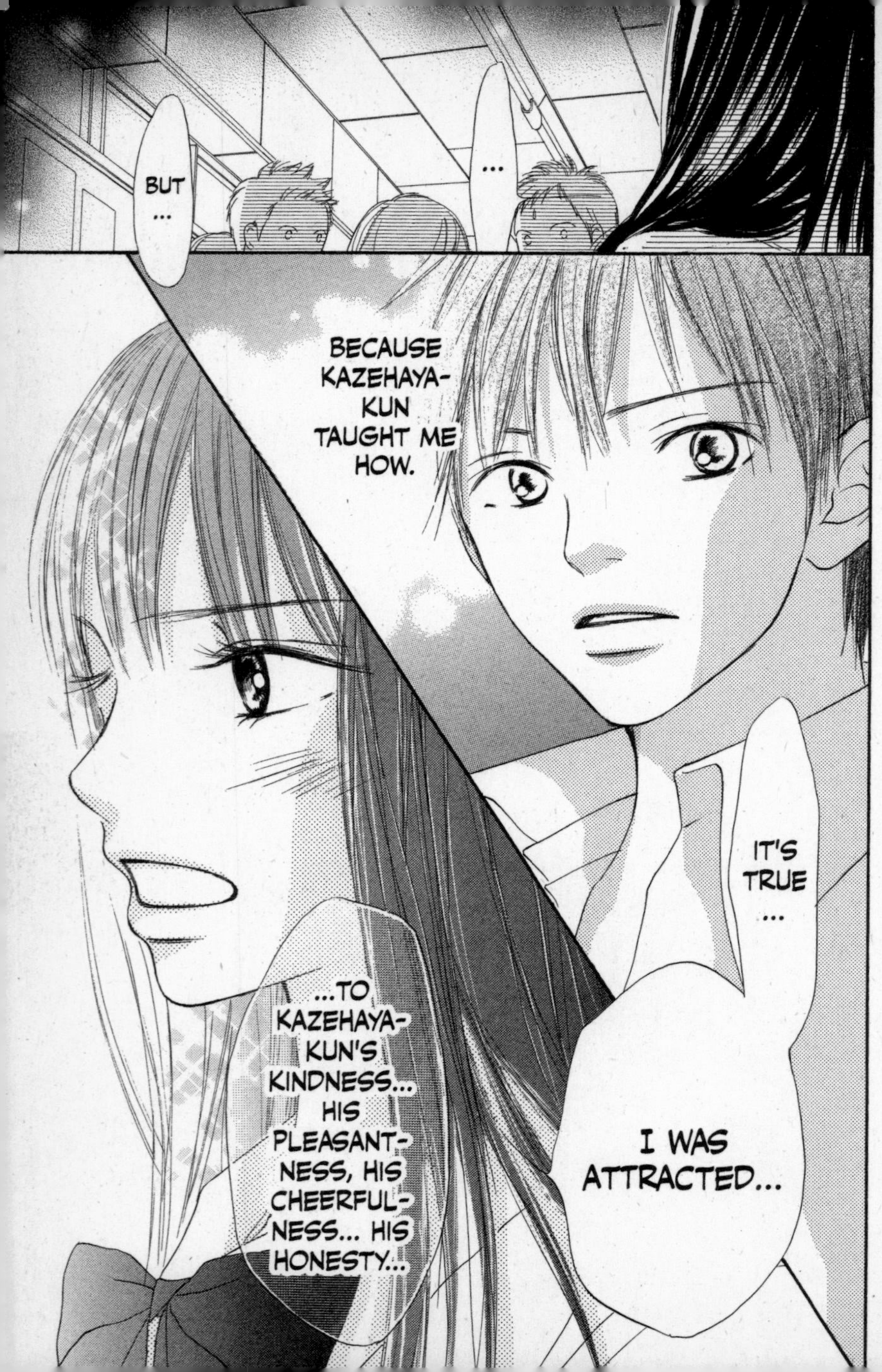
...
BUT ...
BECAUSE KAZEHAYA-KUN TAUGHT ME HOW.
IT'S TRUE ...
I WAS ATTRACTED...
...TO KAZEHAYA-KUN'S KINDNESS... HIS PLEASANT-NESS, HIS CHEERFUL-NESS... HIS HONESTY...

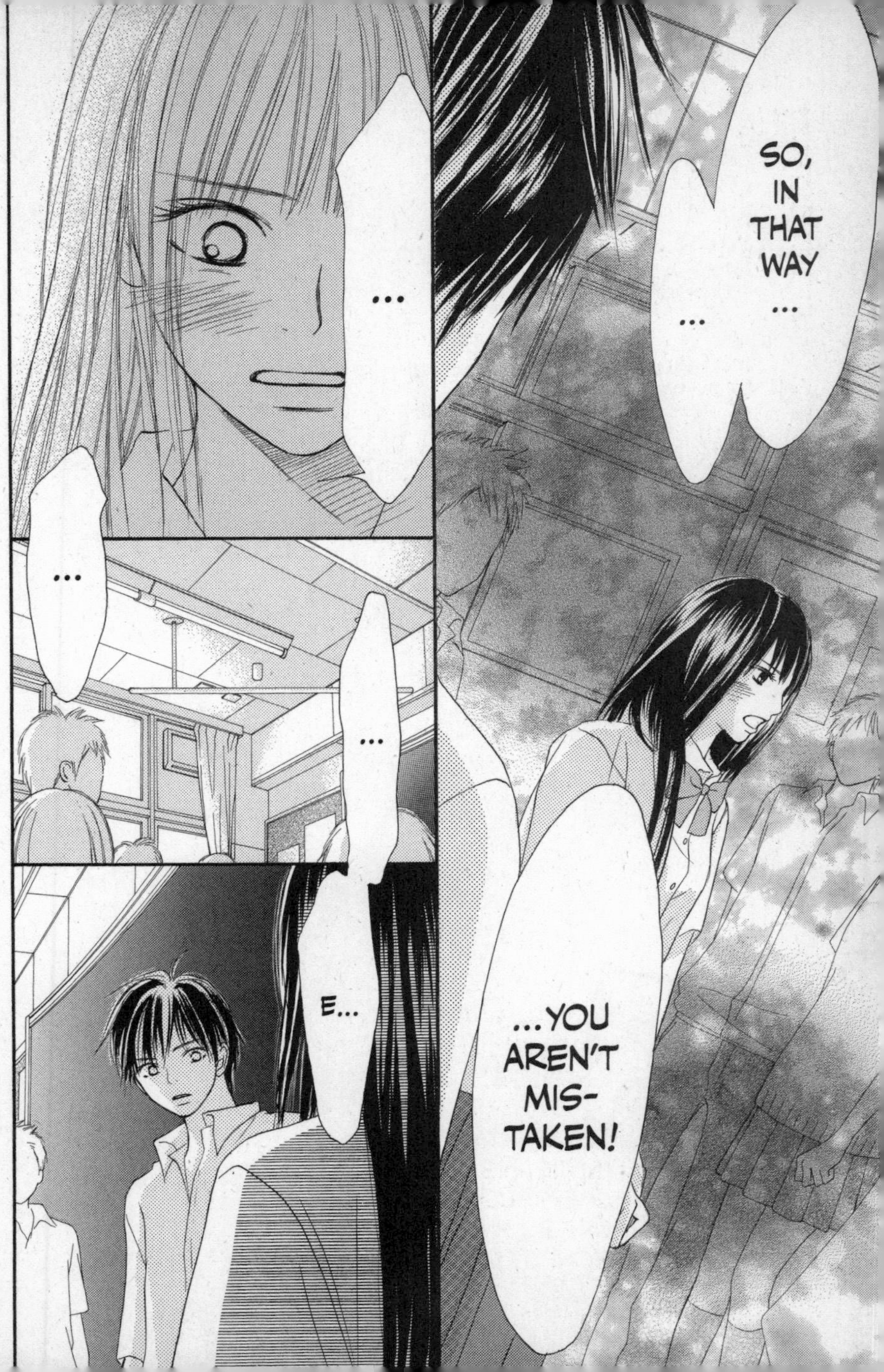
SO, IN THAT WAY ...
...
...YOU AREN'T MIS-TAKEN!
...
...
...
E...

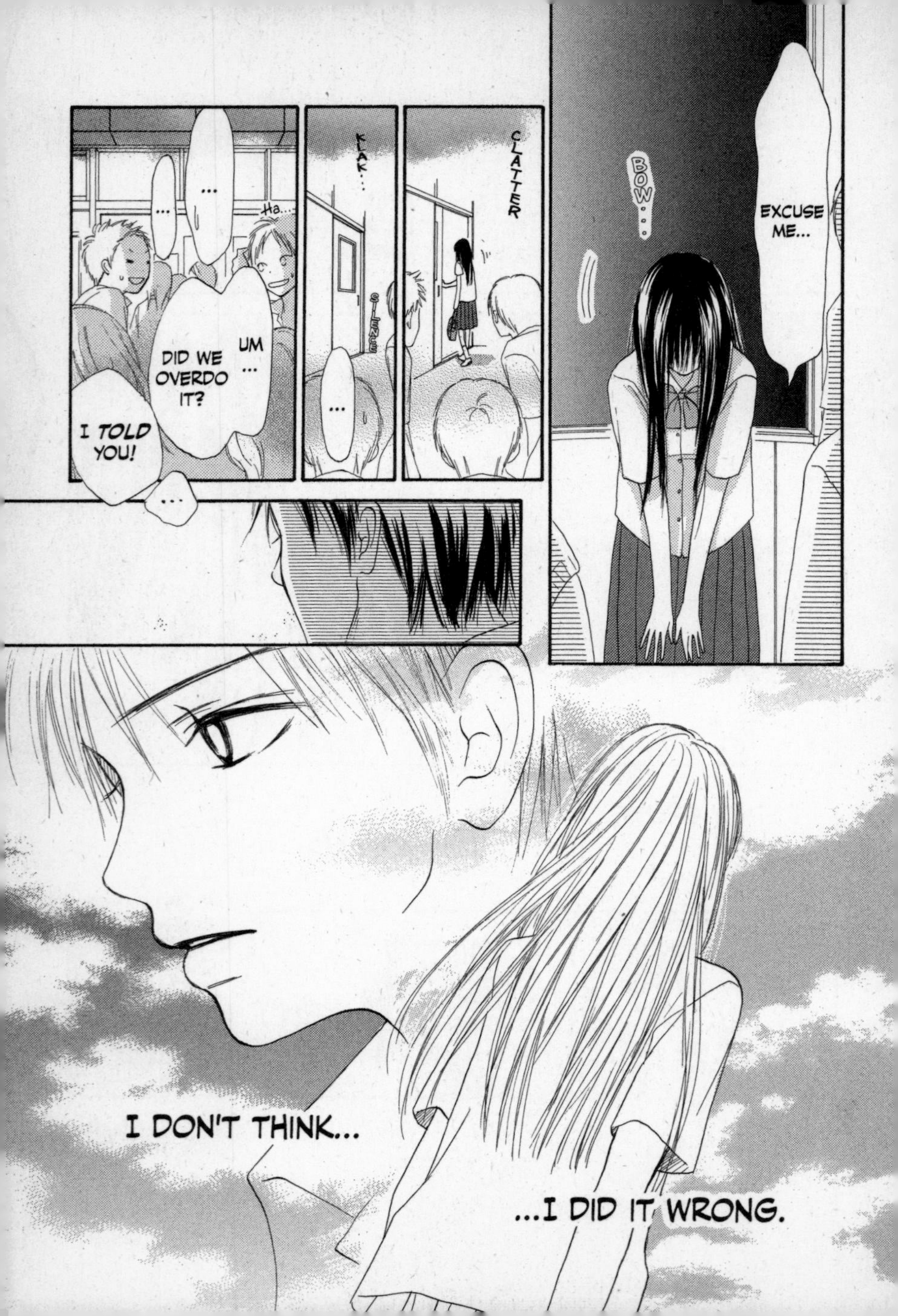
EXCUSE ME...
BOW...
CLATTER
KLAK...
SILENCE
...
Ha...
...
...
UM ...
DID WE OVERDO IT?
I TOLD YOU!
...
I DON'T THINK...
...I DID IT WRONG.

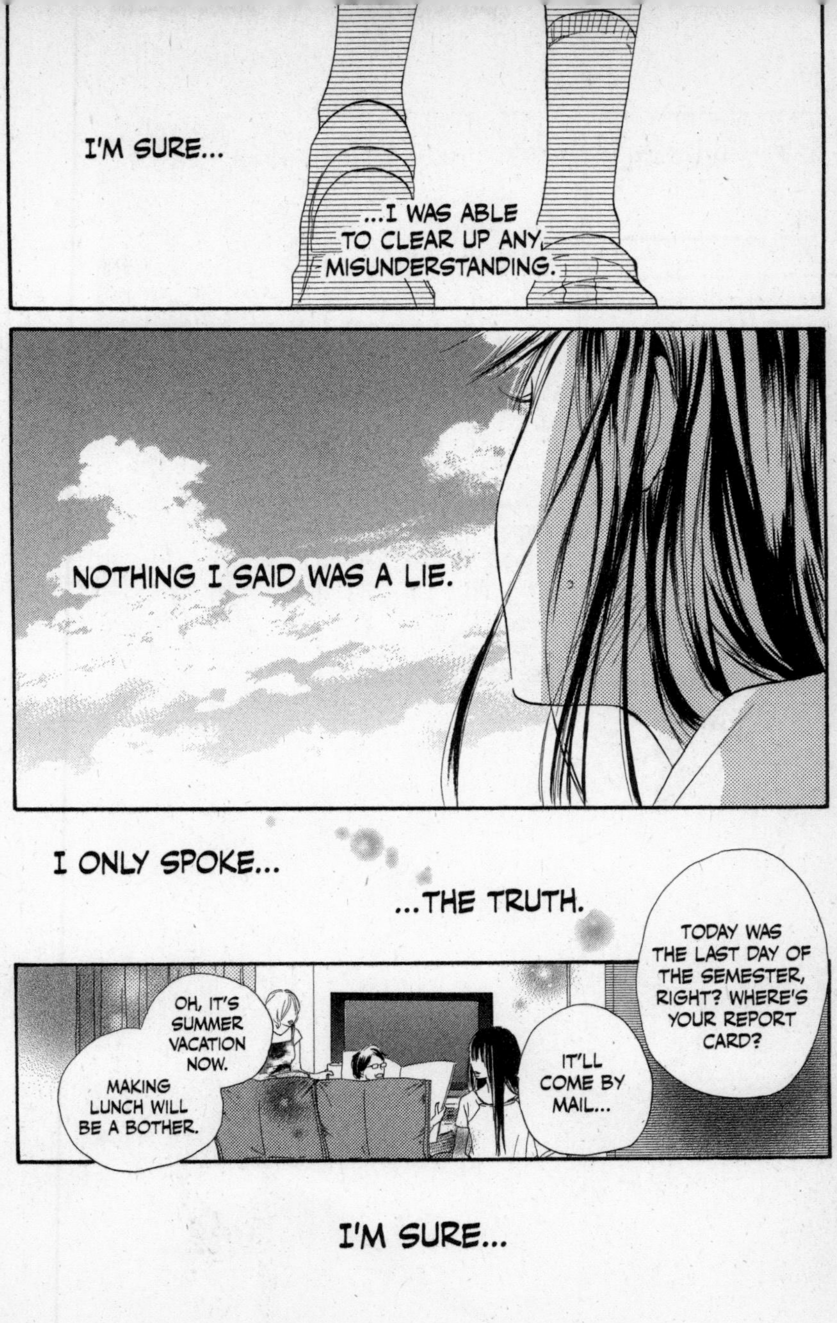
I'M SURE...
...I WAS ABLE TO CLEAR UP ANY MISUNDERSTANDING.
NOTHING I SAID WAS A LIE.
I ONLY SPOKE...
...THE TRUTH.
TODAY WAS THE LAST DAY OF THE SEMESTER, RIGHT? WHERE'S YOUR REPORT CARD?
IT'LL COME BY MAIL...
OH, IT'S SUMMER VACATION NOW.
MAKING LUNCH WILL BE A BOTHER.
I'M SURE...

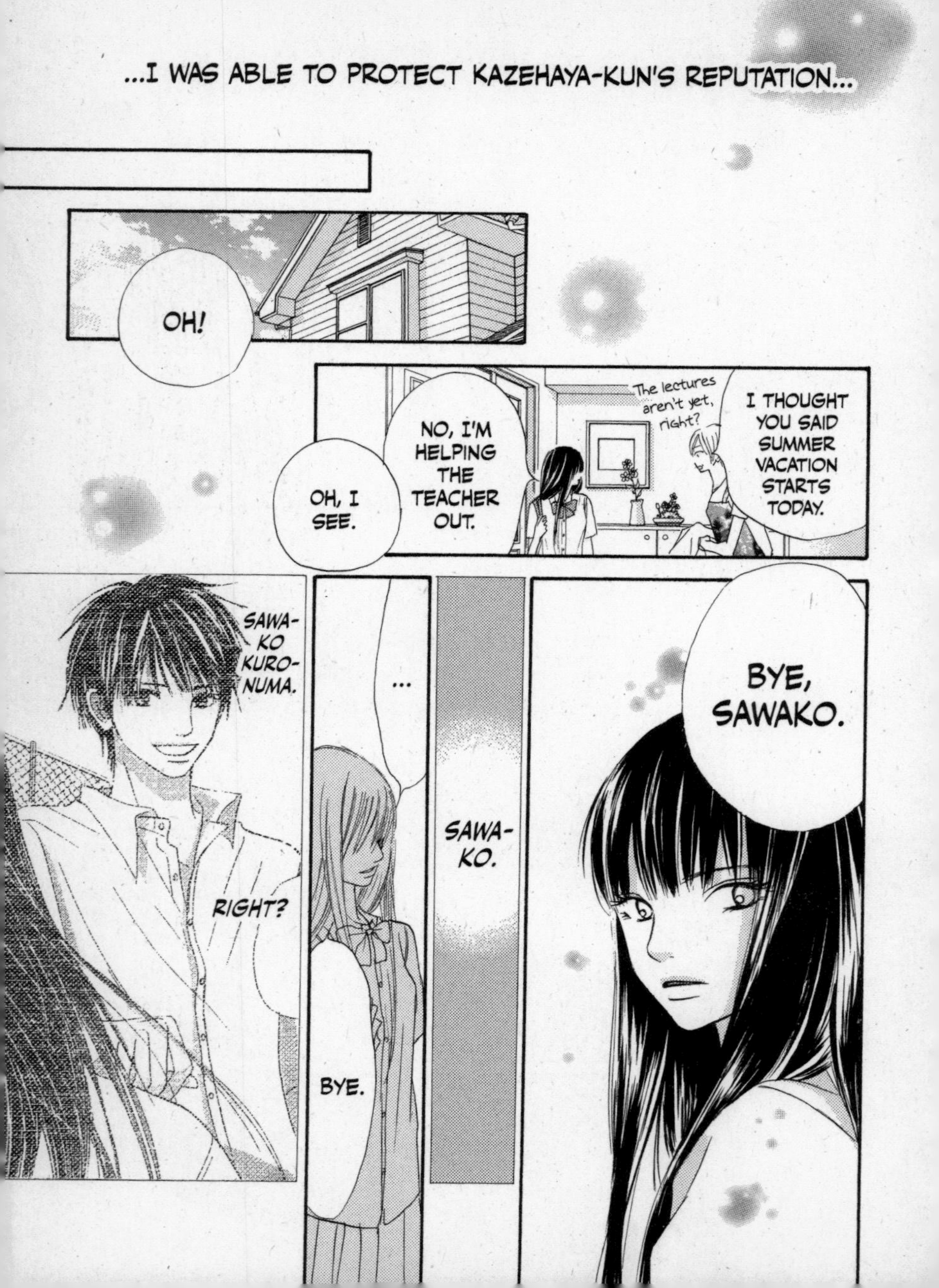
...I WAS ABLE TO PROTECT KAZEHAYA-KUN'S REPUTATION...
OH!
I THOUGHT YOU SAID SUMMER VACATION STARTS TODAY.
The lectures aren't yet, right?
NO, I'M HELPING THE TEACHER OUT.
OH, I SEE.
BYE, SAWAKO.
SAWA-KO.
...
BYE.
SAWA-KO KURO-NUMA.
RIGHT?

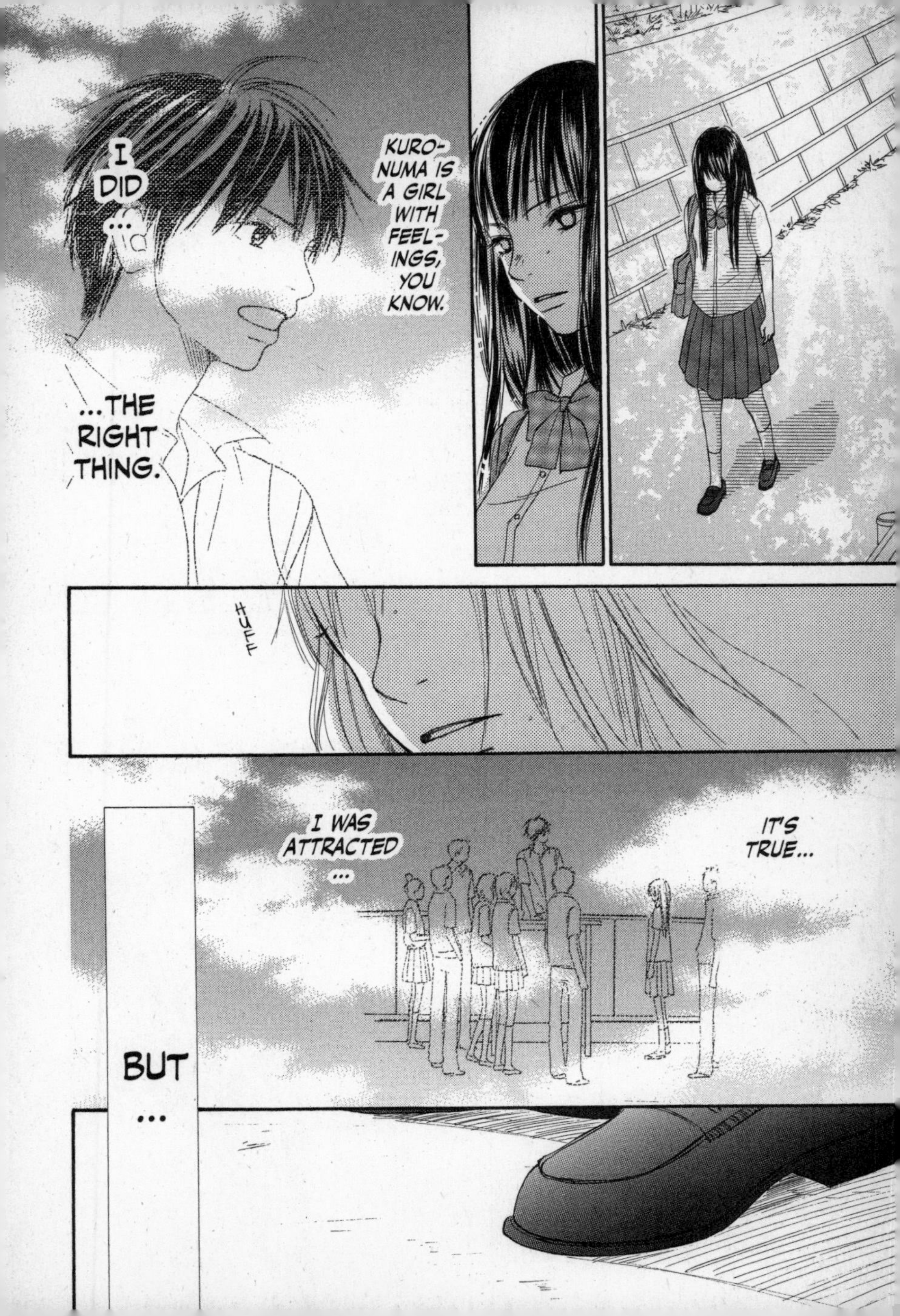
KURO-NUMA IS A GIRL WITH FEEL-INGS, YOU KNOW.
I DID...
...THE RIGHT THING.
HUFF
IT'S TRUE...
I WAS ATTRACTED...
BUT...

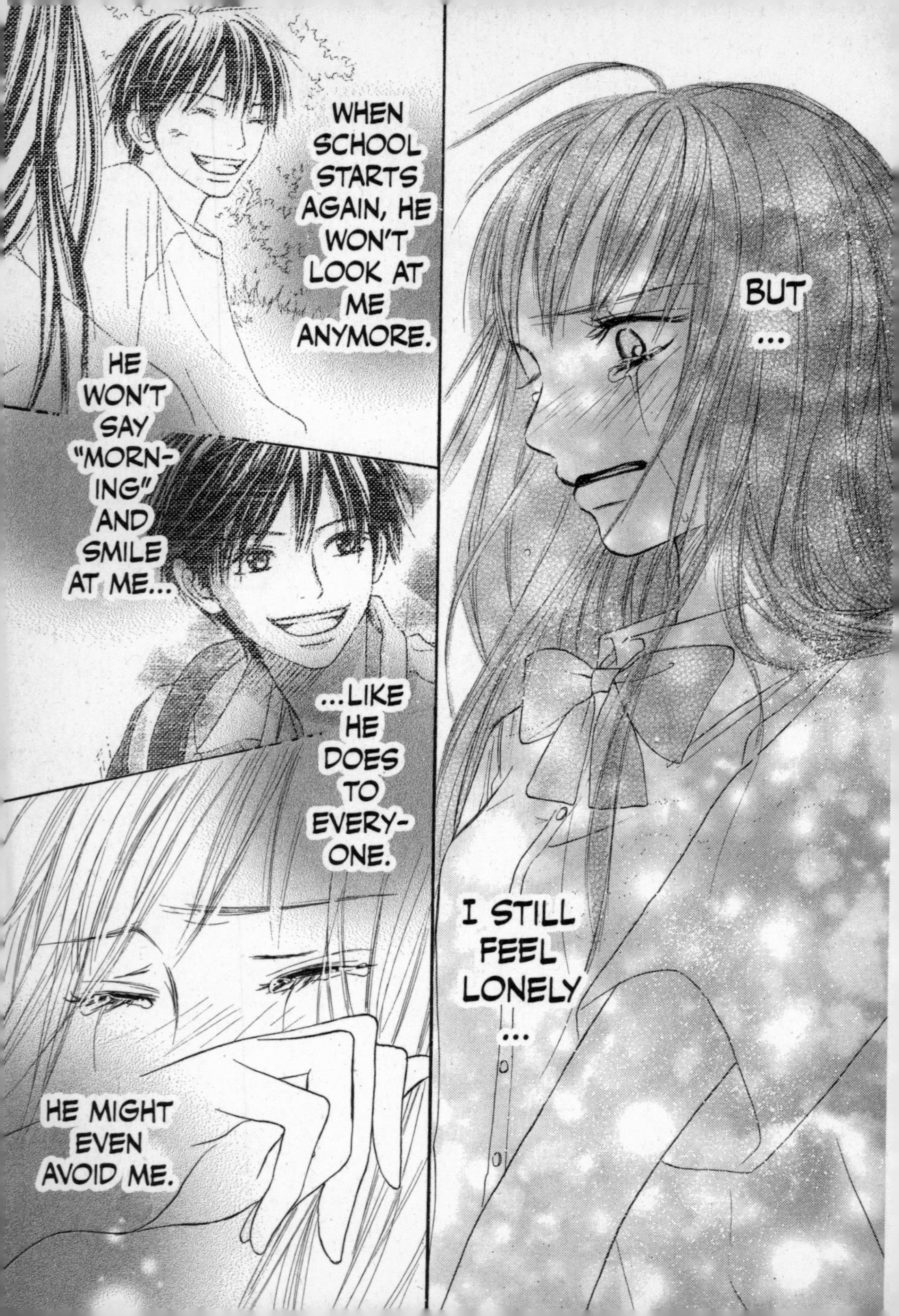
BUT ...
I STILL FEEL LONELY ...
WHEN SCHOOL STARTS AGAIN, HE WON'T LOOK AT ME ANYMORE.
HE WON'T SAY "MORNING" AND SMILE AT ME...
...LIKE HE DOES TO EVERYONE.
HE MIGHT EVEN AVOID ME.

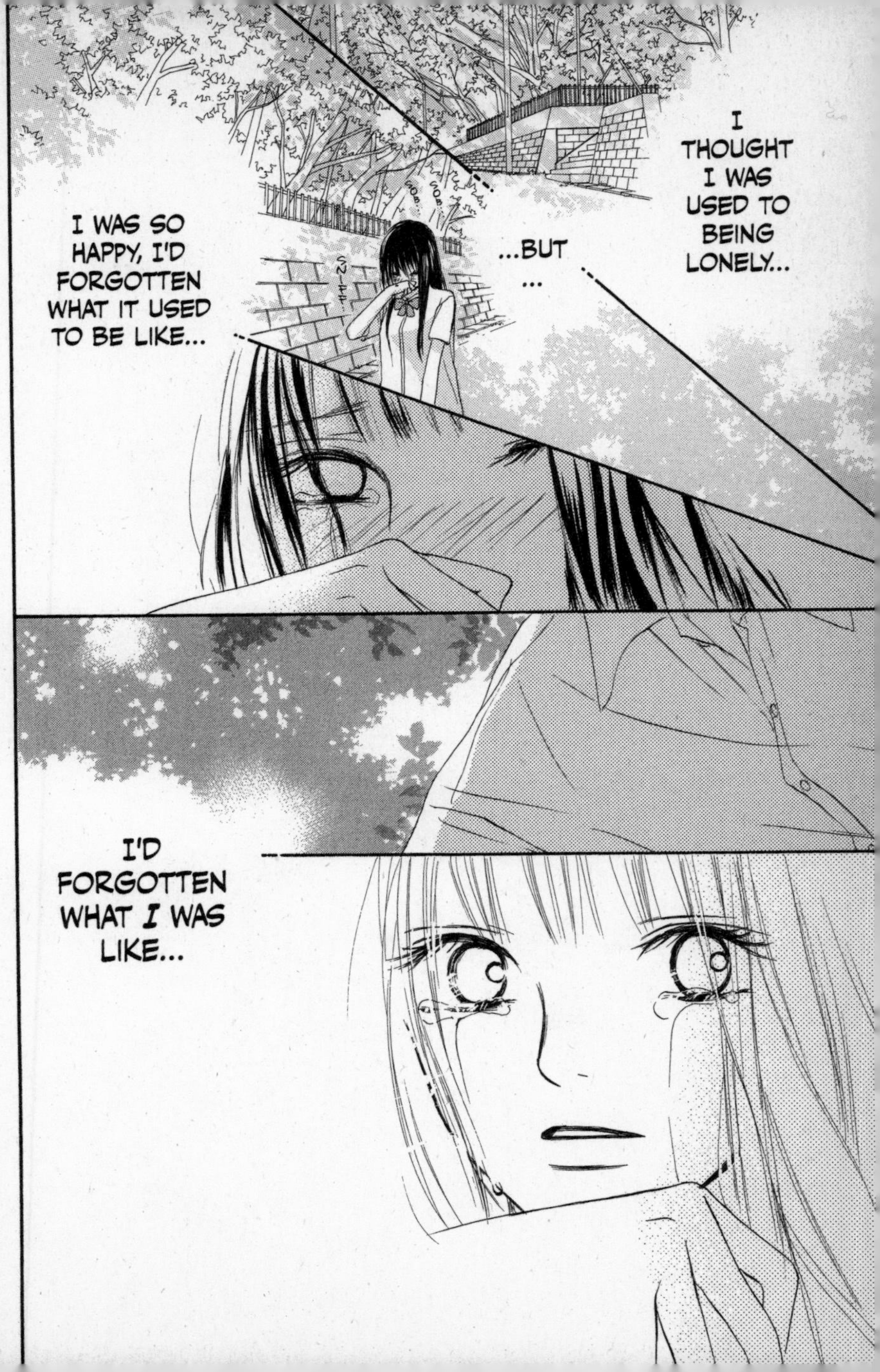
I THOUGHT I WAS USED TO BEING LONELY...
...BUT ...
I WAS SO HAPPY, I'D FORGOTTEN WHAT IT USED TO BE LIKE...
I'D FORGOTTEN WHAT I WAS LIKE...

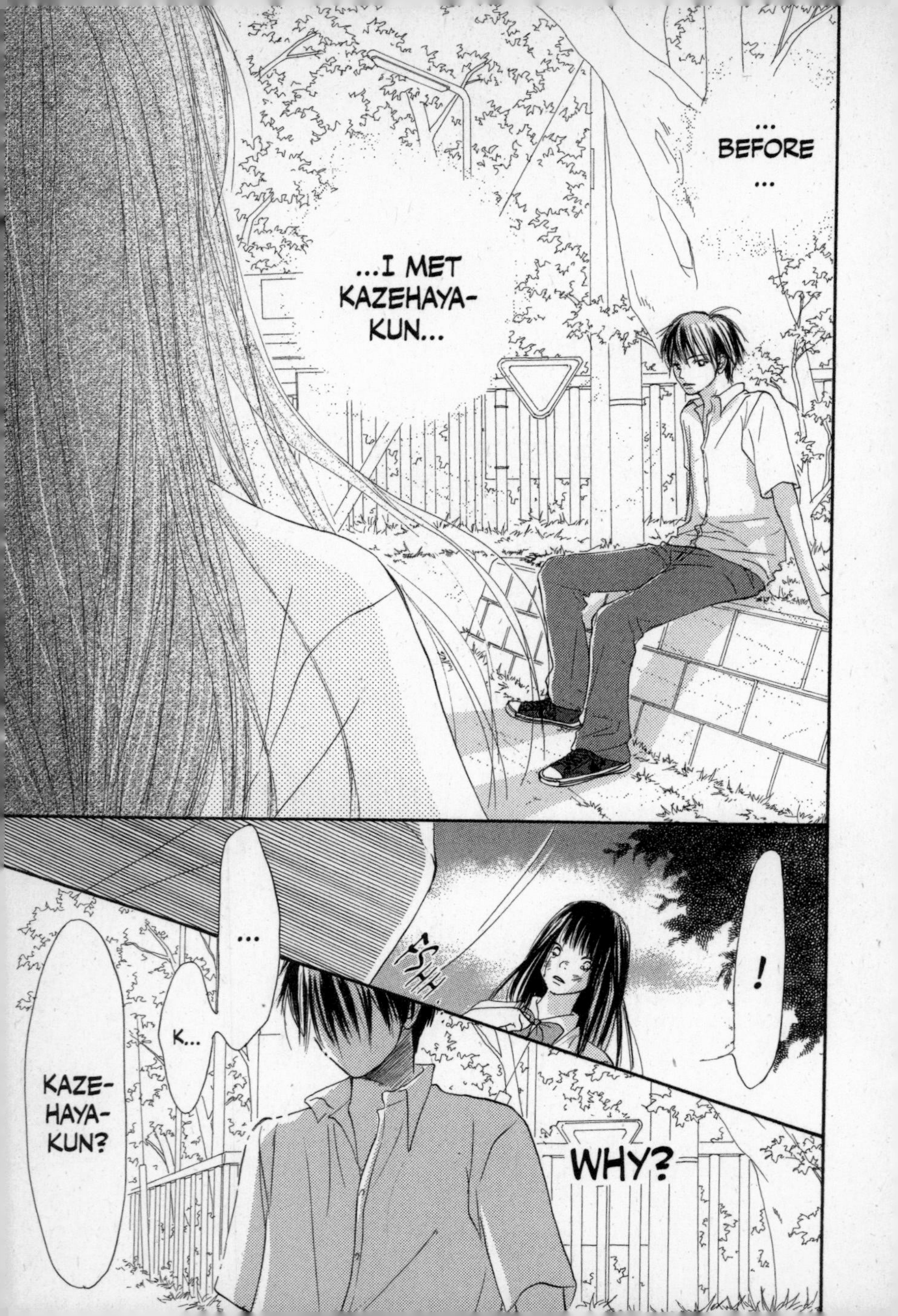
...BEFORE...
...I MET KAZEHAYA-KUN...
!
FSH
...
K...
KAZE-HAYA-KUN?
WHY?

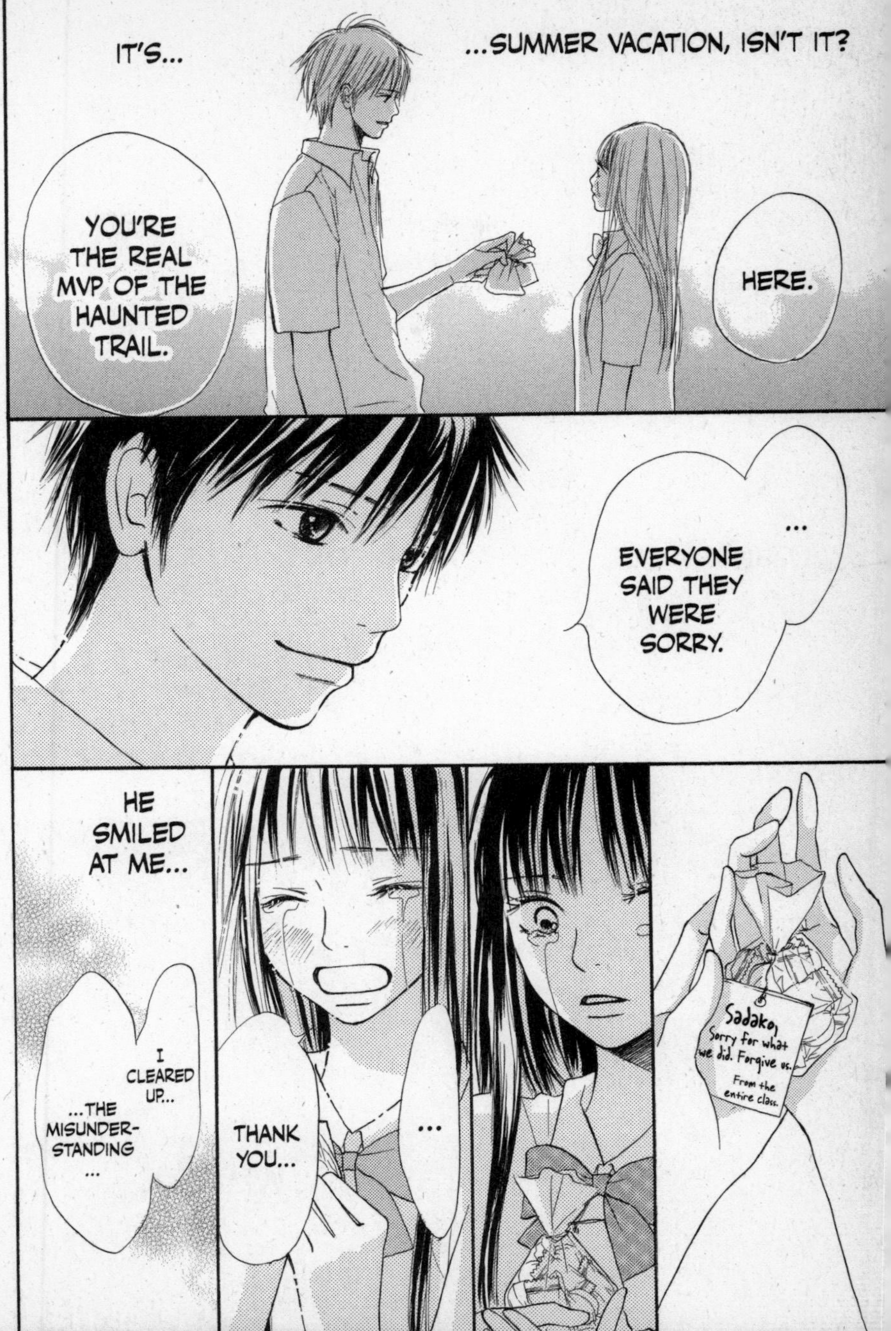
IT'S...
...SUMMER VACATION, ISN'T IT?
HERE.
YOU'RE THE REAL MVP OF THE HAUNTED TRAIL.
... EVERYONE SAID THEY WERE SORRY.
Sadako, Sorry for what we did. Forgive us. From the entire class.
...
HE SMILED AT ME...
THANK YOU...
I CLEARED UP... ...THE MISUNDER-STANDING ...

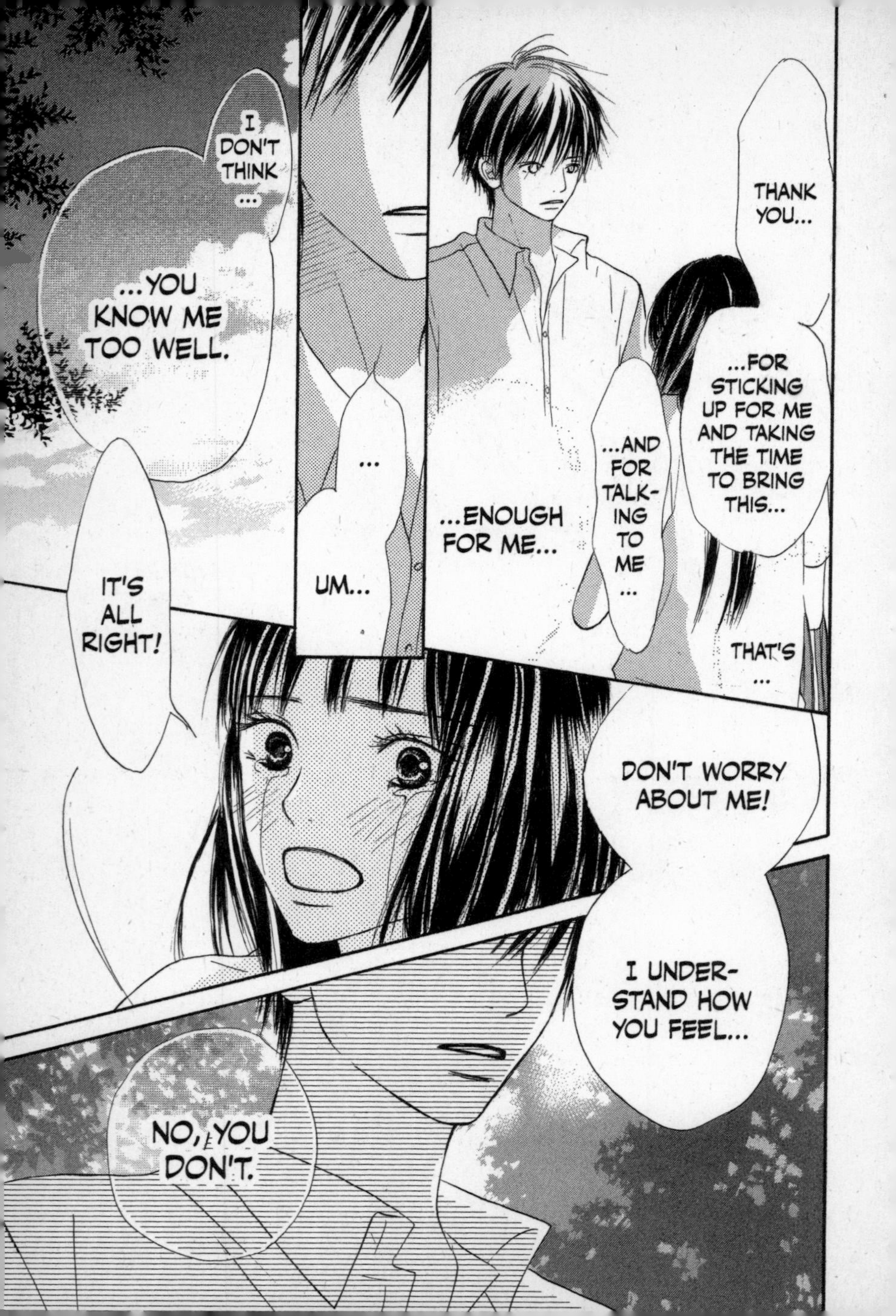
THANK YOU...
...FOR STICKING UP FOR ME AND TAKING THE TIME TO BRING THIS...
...AND FOR TALKING TO ME ...
THAT'S ...
...ENOUGH FOR ME...
...
UM...
I DON'T THINK ...
...YOU KNOW ME TOO WELL.
IT'S ALL RIGHT!
DON'T WORRY ABOUT ME!
I UNDER-STAND HOW YOU FEEL...
NO, YOU DON'T.

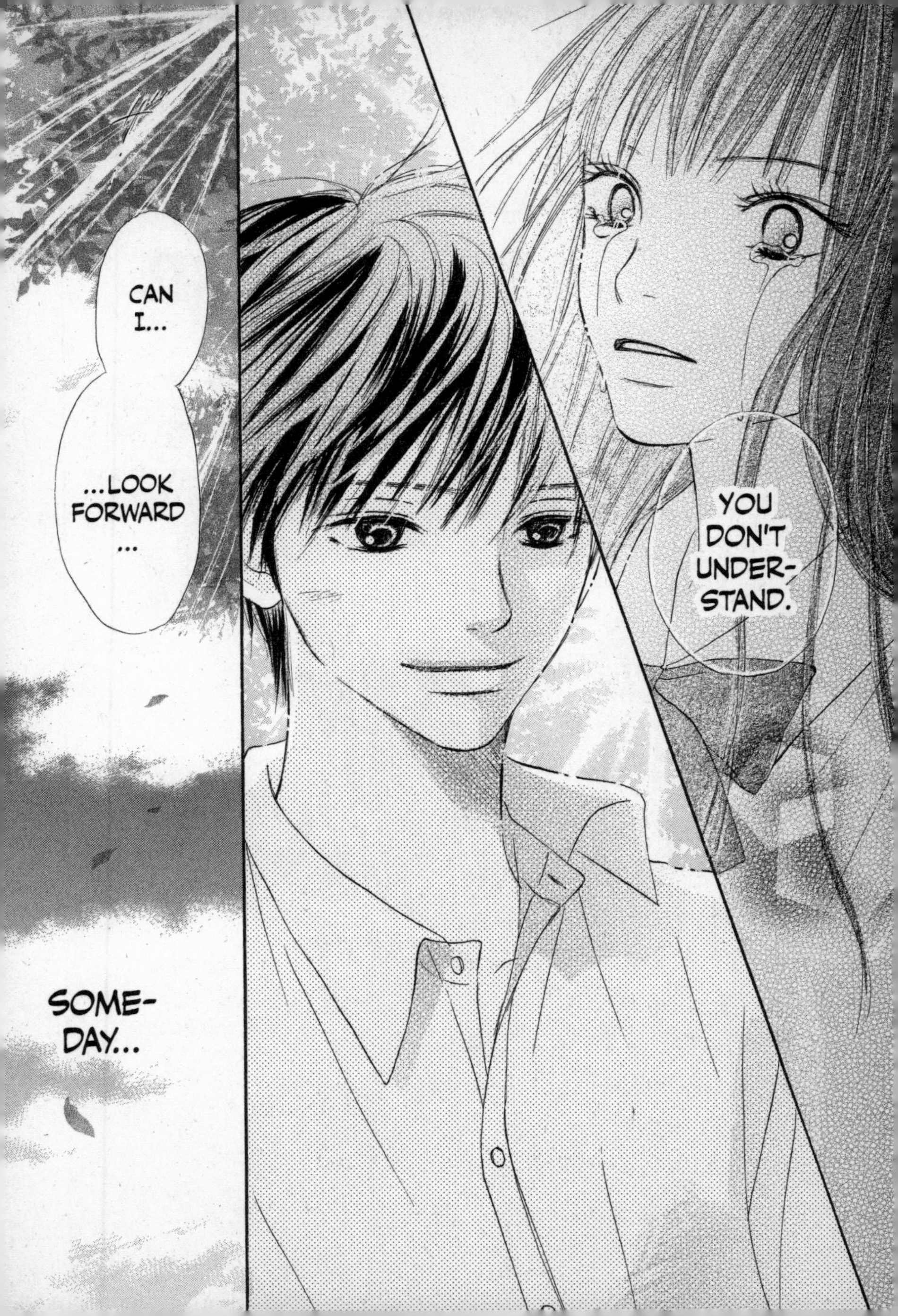
YOU DON'T UNDER-STAND.
CAN I...
...LOOK FORWARD ...
SOME-DAY...

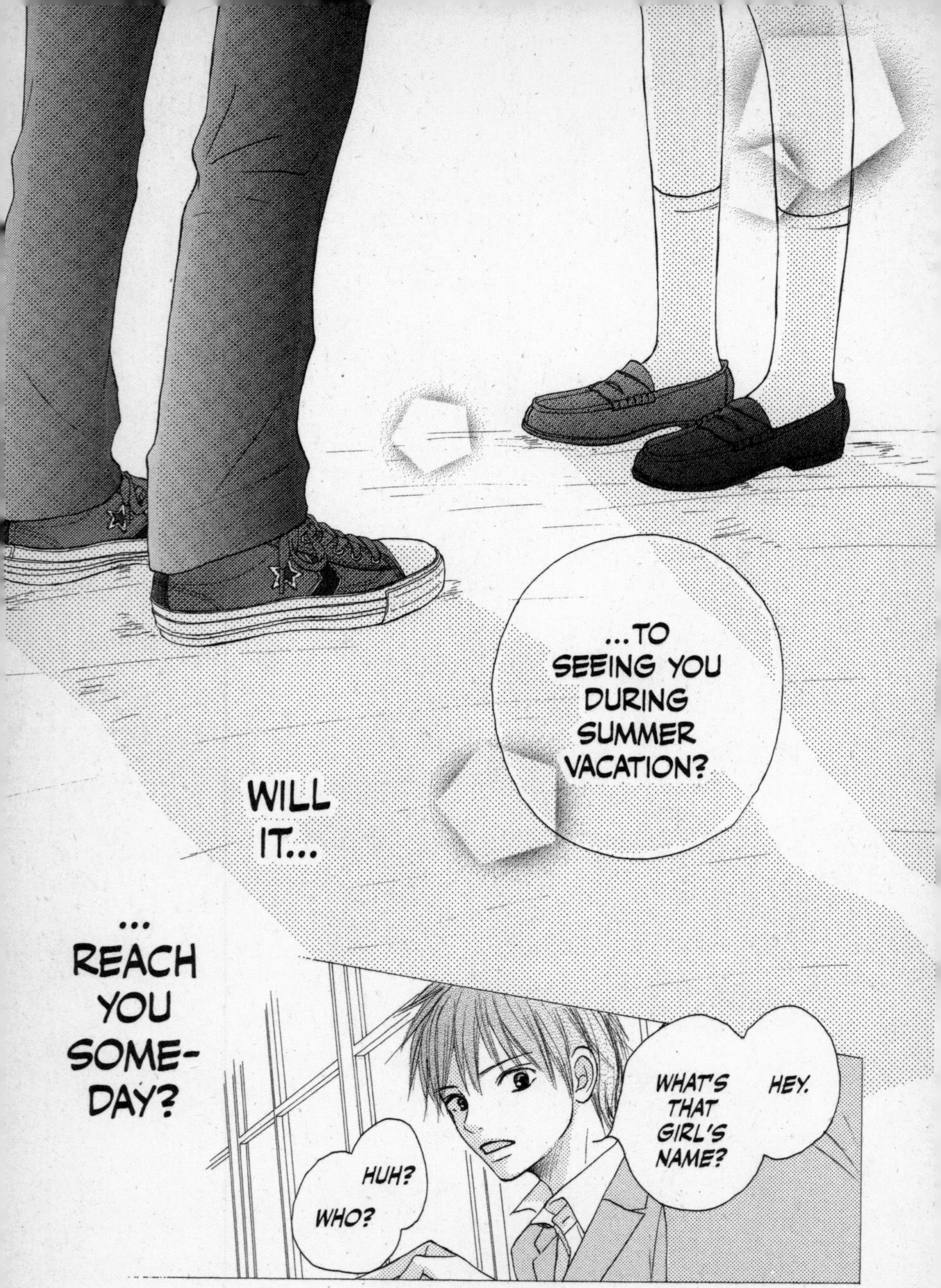
...TO SEEING YOU DURING SUMMER VACATION?
WILL IT...
...REACH YOU SOME-DAY?
HEY.
WHAT'S THAT GIRL'S NAME?
HUH?
WHO?

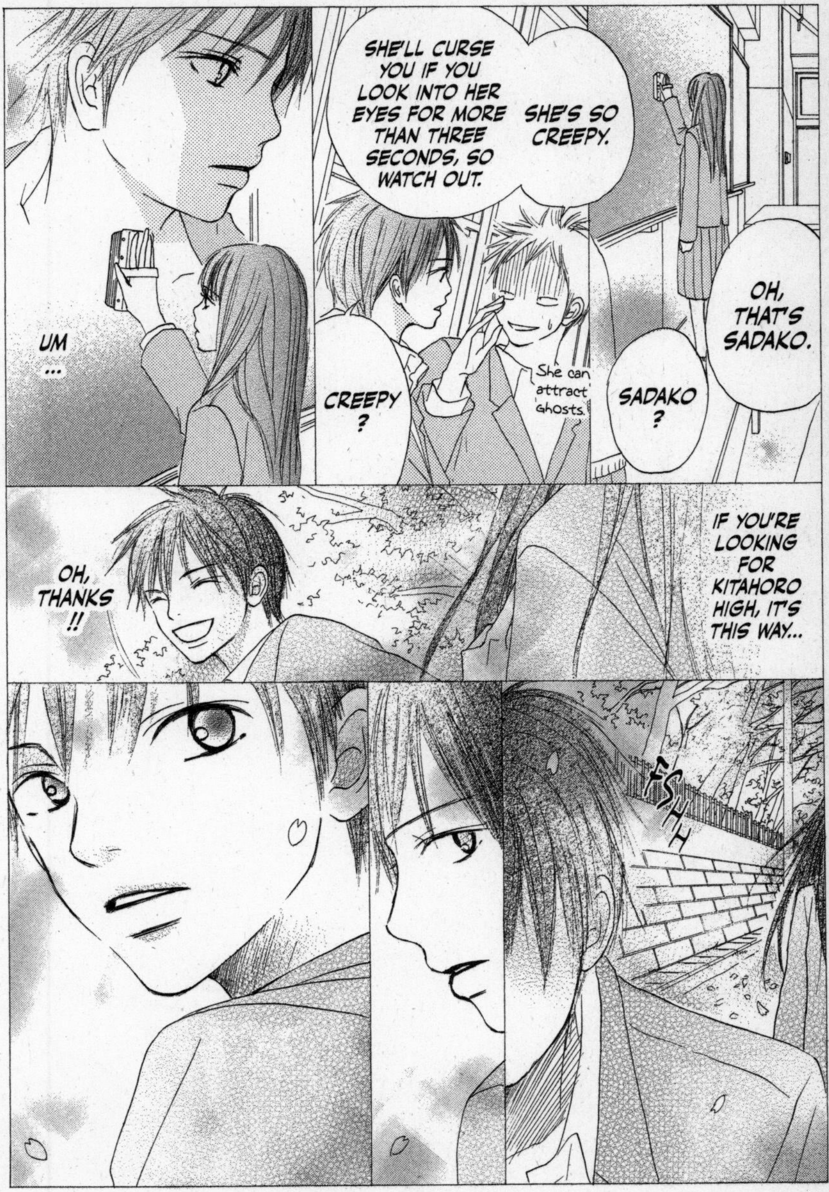
OH, THAT'S SADAKO.
SADAKO?
SHE'S SO CREEPY.
SHE'LL CURSE YOU IF YOU LOOK INTO HER EYES FOR MORE THAN THREE SECONDS, SO WATCH OUT.
She can attract ghosts.
CREEPY?
UM ...
IF YOU'RE LOOKING FOR KITAHORO HIGH, IT'S THIS WAY...
OH, THANKS!!
FSHH

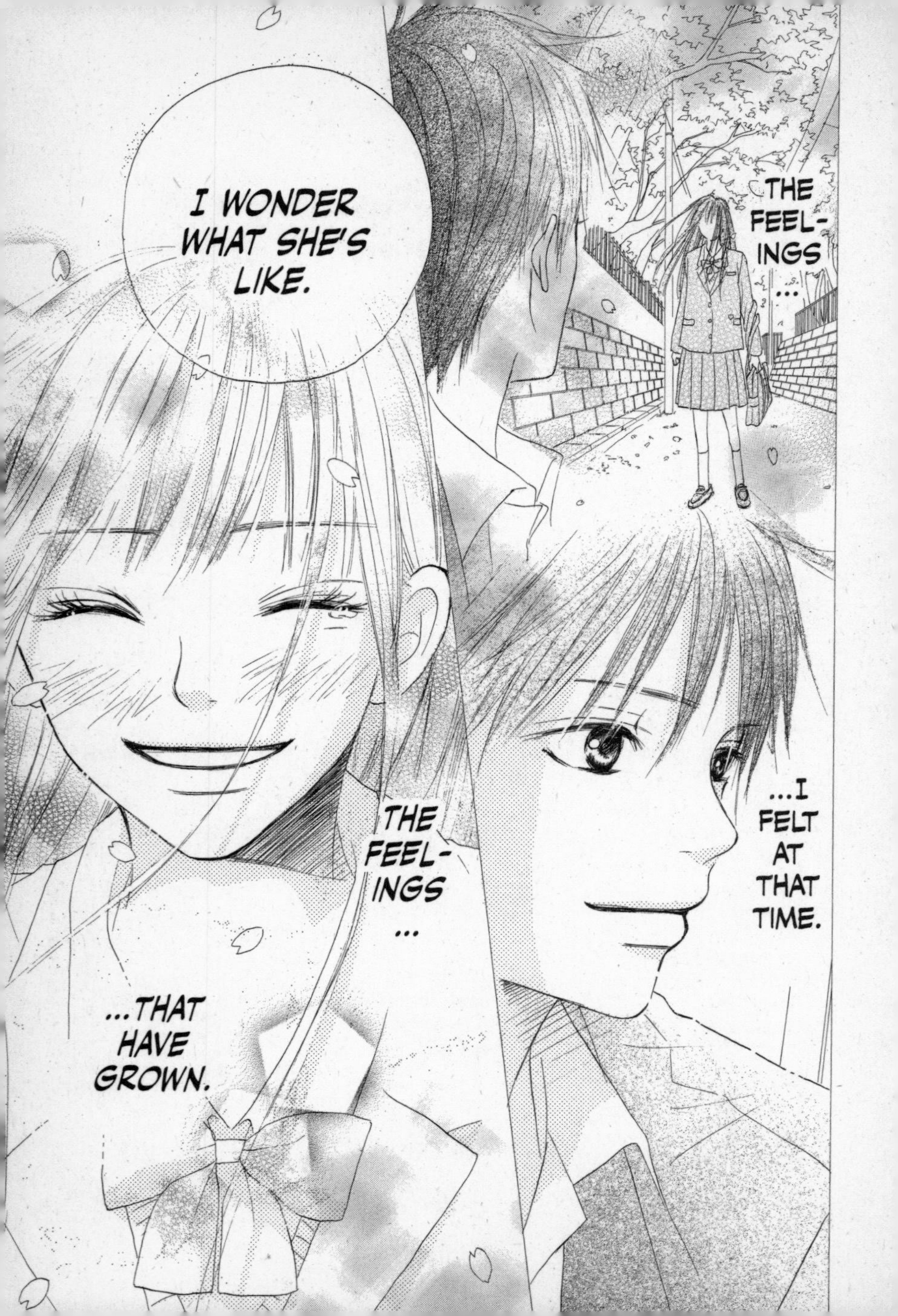
THE FEELINGS...
...I FELT AT THAT TIME.
I WONDER WHAT SHE'S LIKE.
THE FEELINGS...
...THAT HAVE GROWN.

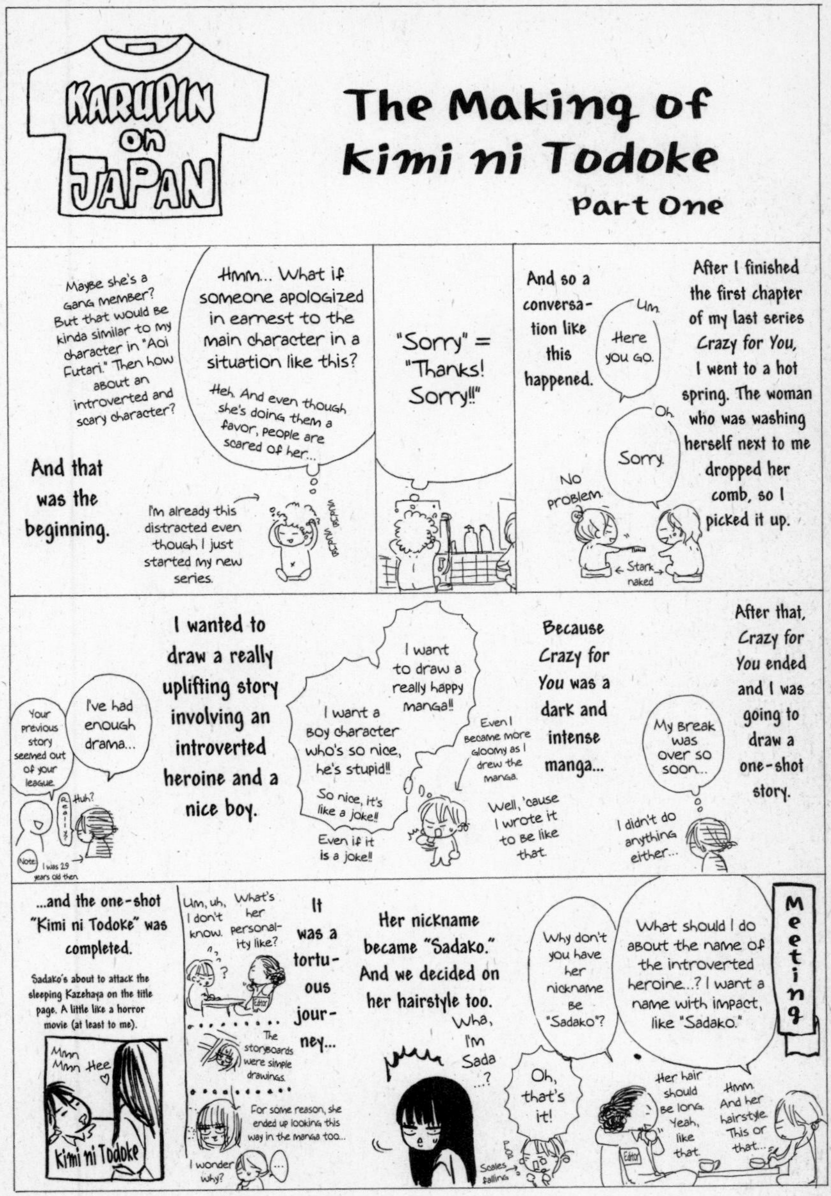
KARUPIN on JAPAN
The Making of Kimi ni Todoke
Part One
After I finished the first chapter of my last series Crazy for You, I went to a hot spring. The woman who was washing herself next to me dropped her comb, so I picked it up.
And so a conversation like this happened.
Um. Here you go.
Oh. Sorry.
No problem.
Stark naked
"Sorry" = "Thanks! Sorry!!"
Hmm... What if someone apologized in earnest to the main character in a situation like this?
Heh. And even though she's doing them a favor, people are scared of her...
Maybe she's a gang member? But that would be kinda similar to my character in "Aoi Futari." Then how about an introverted and scary character?
I'm already this distracted even though I just started my new series.
And that was the beginning.
After that, Crazy for You ended and I was going to draw a one-shot story.
My break was over so soon...
I didn't do anything either...
Because Crazy for You was a dark and intense manga...
Even I became more gloomy as I drew the manga.
Well, 'cause I wrote it to be like that.
I want to draw a really happy manga!!
I want a boy character who's so nice, he's stupid!!
So nice, it's like a joke!!
Even if it is a joke!!
I wanted to draw a really uplifting story involving an introverted heroine and a nice boy.
I've had enough drama...
Your previous story seemed out of your league.
Huh?
Really?
Note: I was 29 years old then.
Meeting
What should I do about the name of the introverted heroine...? I want a name with impact, like "Sadako."
Why don't you have her nickname be "Sadako"?
Oh, that's it!
Scales falling
Her hair should be long. Yeah, like that.
Hmm And her hairstyle This or that...
Editor
Her nickname became "Sadako." And we decided on her hairstyle too.
Wha, I'm Sada...?
It was a tortuous journey...
What's her personality like?
Um, uh, I don't know.
Editor
The storyboards were simple drawings.
For some reason, she ended up looking this way in the manga too...
I wonder why?
...
...and the one-shot "Kimi ni Todoke" was completed.
Sadako's about to attack the sleeping Kazehaya on the title page. A little like a horror movie (at least to me).
Mmn Mmn Hee
Kimi ni Todoke

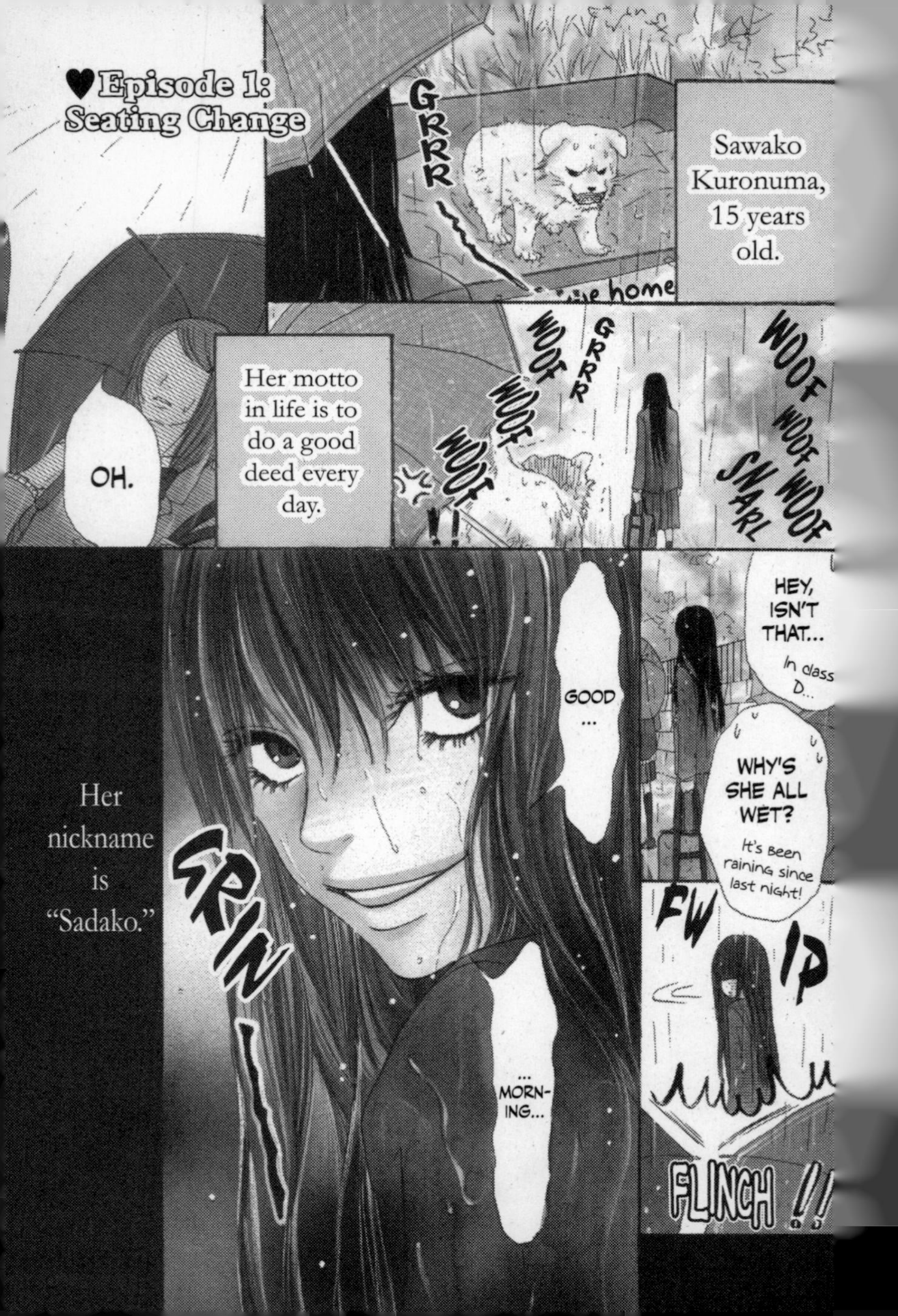
Sawako Kuronuma, 15 years old.
GRRR
WOOF WOOF WOOF SNARL
GRRR
WOOF WOOF WOOF
Her motto in life is to do a good deed every day.
♥Episode 1: Seating Change
OH.
HEY, ISN'T THAT...
In class D...
WHY'S SHE ALL WET?
It's Been raining since last night!
FW IP
FLINCH !!
GOOD ...
... MORNING...
GRIN
Her nickname is "Sadako."

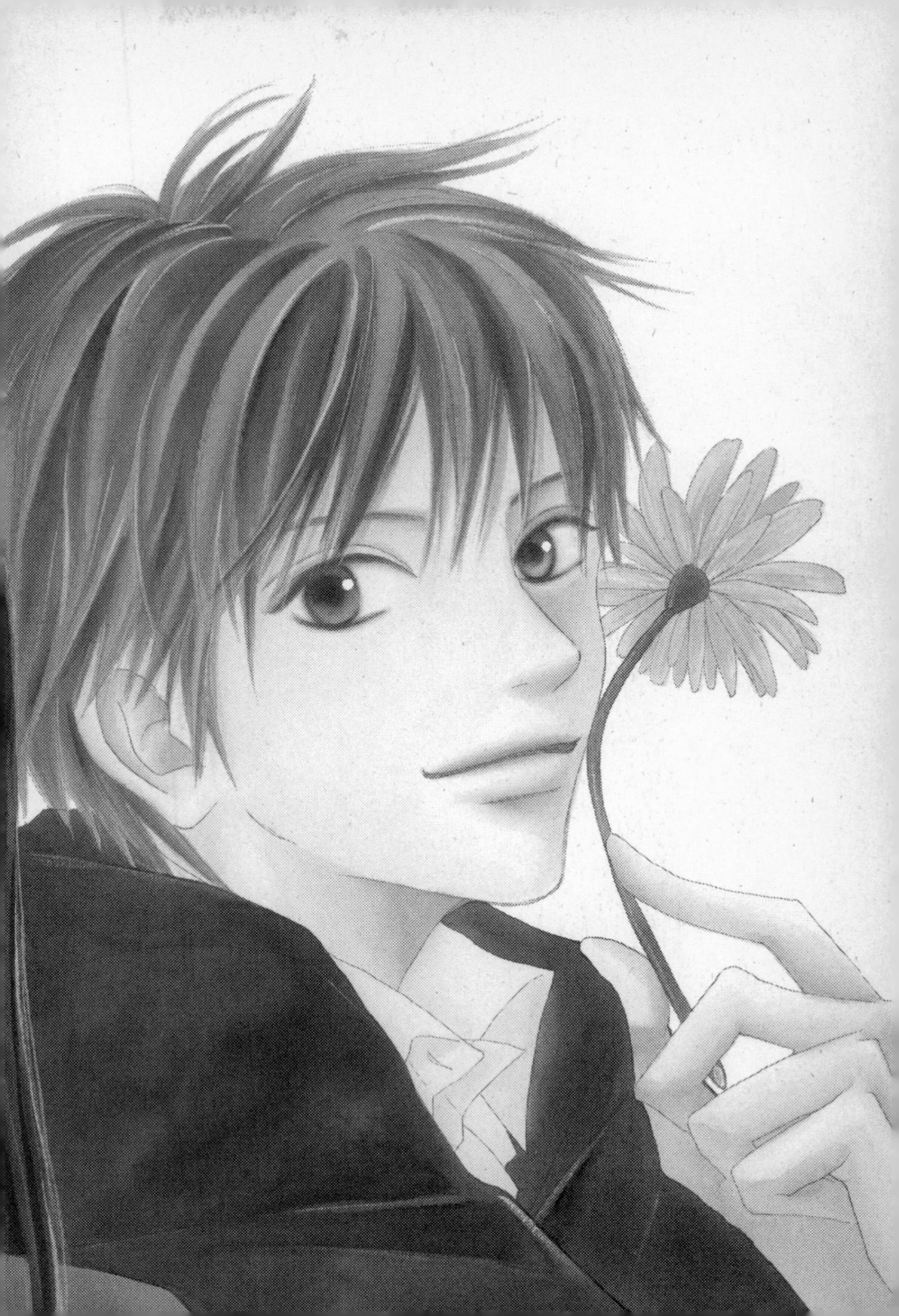

Episode 1: Seating Change

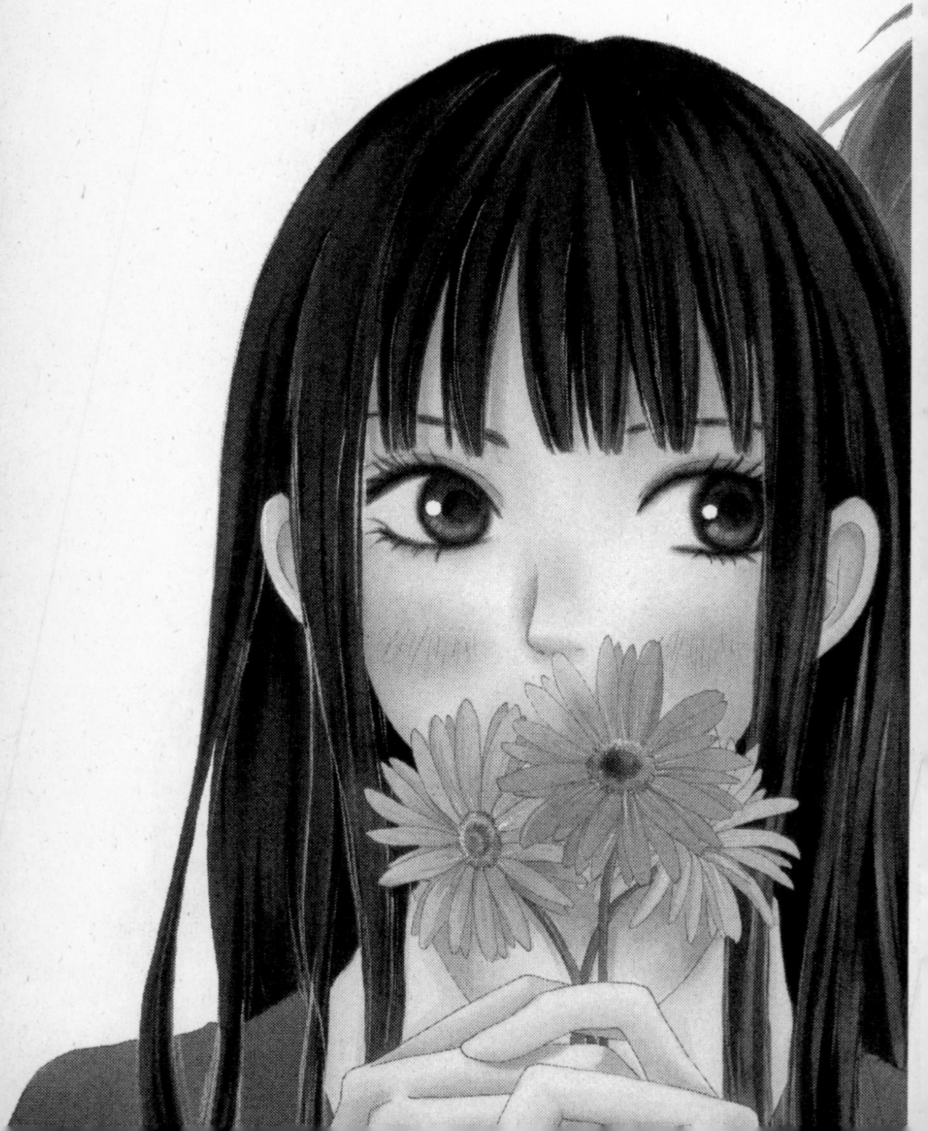

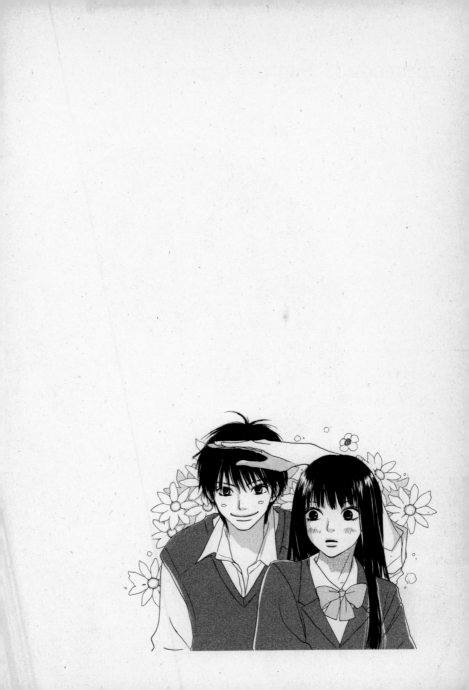

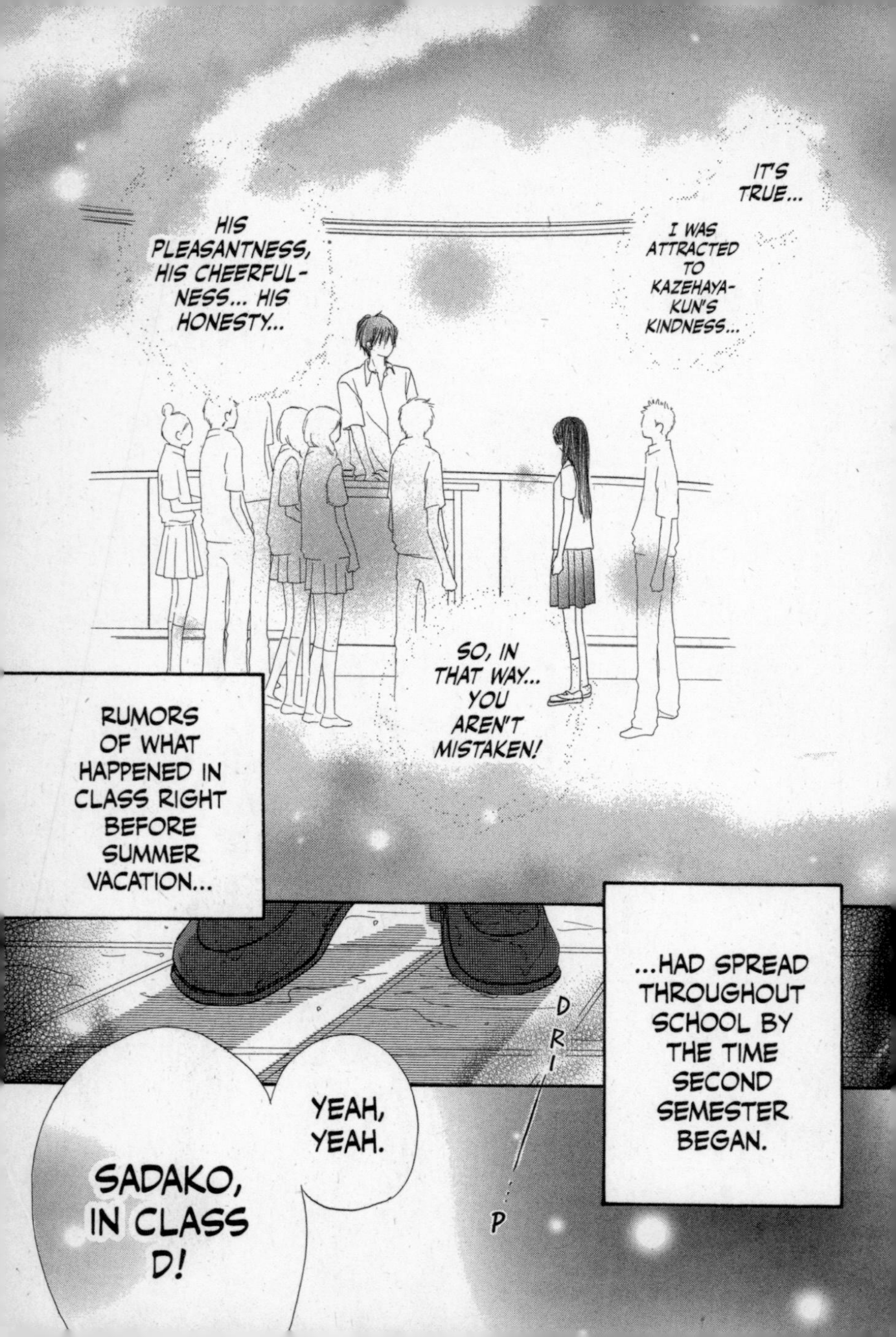
IT'S TRUE...
I WAS ATTRACTED TO KAZEHAYA-KUN'S KINDNESS...
HIS PLEASANTNESS, HIS CHEERFUL-NESS... HIS HONESTY...
SO, IN THAT WAY... YOU AREN'T MISTAKEN!
RUMORS OF WHAT HAPPENED IN CLASS RIGHT BEFORE SUMMER VACATION...
...HAD SPREAD THROUGHOUT SCHOOL BY THE TIME SECOND SEMESTER BEGAN.
DRI...P
YEAH, YEAH.
SADAKO, IN CLASS D!

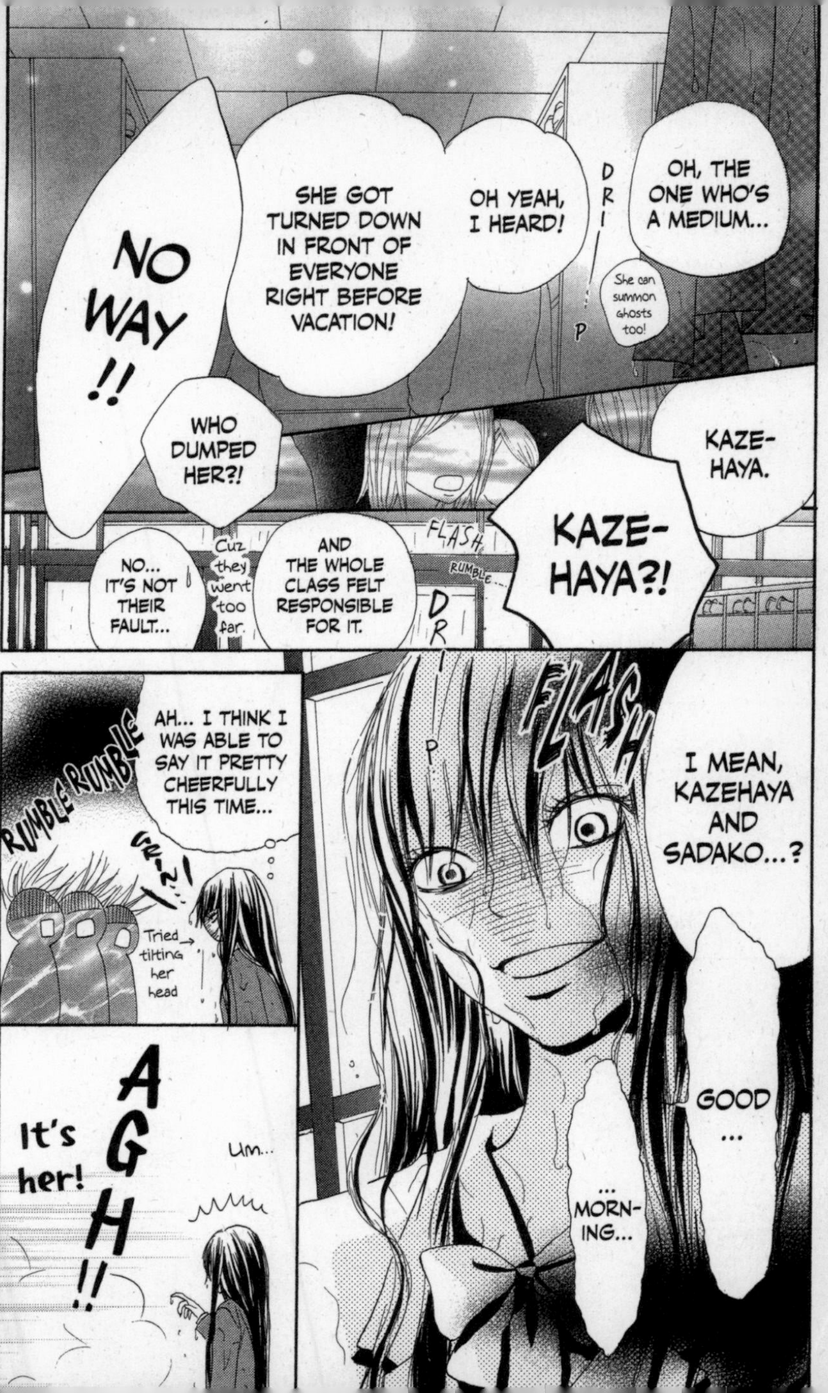
OH, THE ONE WHO'S A MEDIUM...
She can summon ghosts too!
DRIP
OH YEAH, I HEARD!
SHE GOT TURNED DOWN IN FRONT OF EVERYONE RIGHT BEFORE VACATION!
NO WAY!!
WHO DUMPED HER?!
KAZE-HAYA.
KAZE-HAYA?!
FLASH
RUMBLE...
DRIP
AND THE WHOLE CLASS FELT RESPONSIBLE FOR IT.
Cuz they went too far.
NO... IT'S NOT THEIR FAULT...
FLASH
DRIP
I MEAN, KAZEHAYA AND SADAKO...?
GOOD...
...MORNING...
AH... I THINK I WAS ABLE TO SAY IT PRETTY CHEERFULLY THIS TIME...
RUMBLE RUMBLE
GRIN!
Tried tilting her head
Um...
AGH!!
It's her!

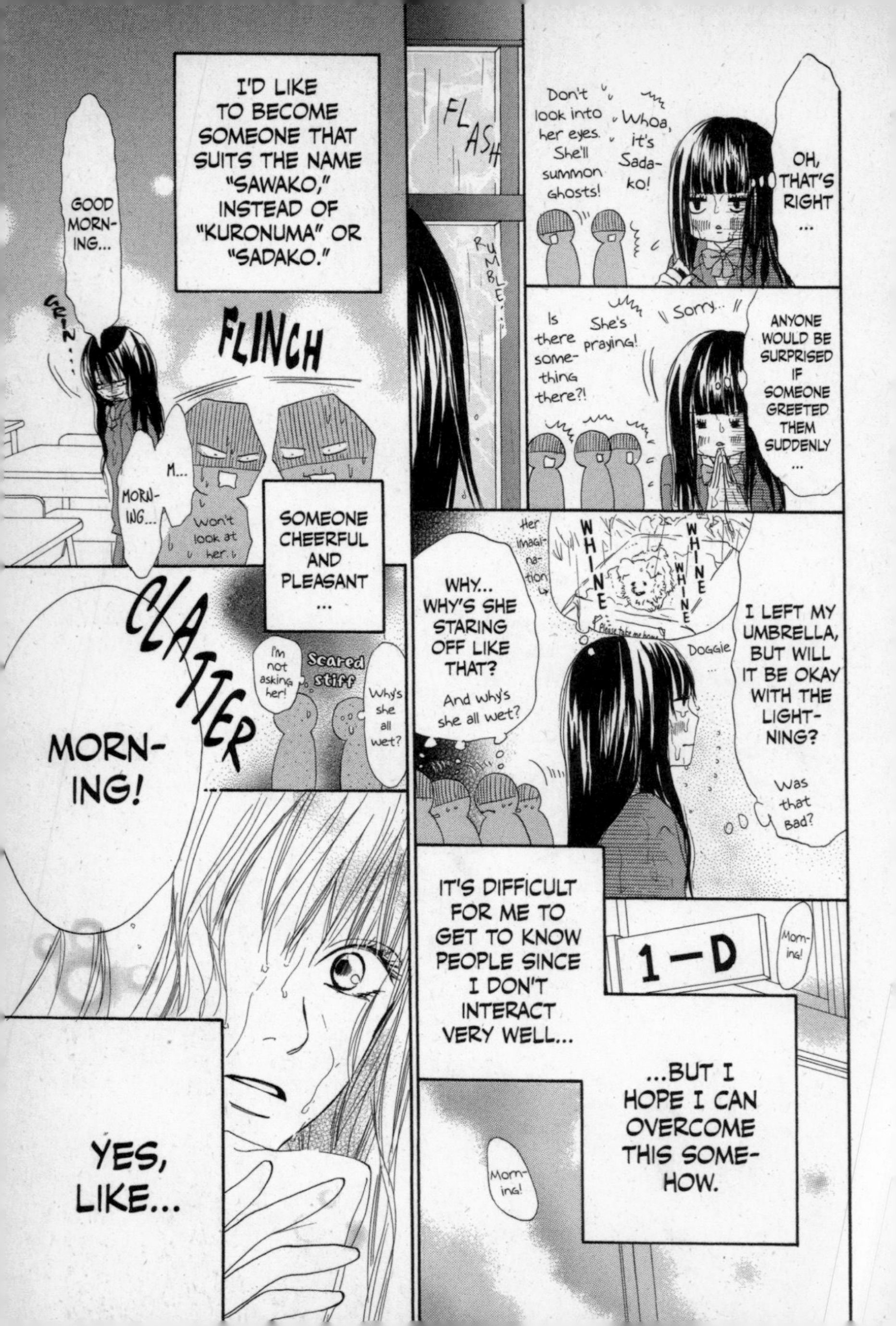
OH, THAT'S RIGHT...
Whoa, it's Sadako!
Don't look into her eyes. She'll summon ghosts!
ANYONE WOULD BE SURPRISED IF SOMEONE GREETED THEM SUDDENLY...
Sorry...
She's praying!
Is there something there?!
FLASH
RUMBLE...
I LEFT MY UMBRELLA, BUT WILL IT BE OKAY WITH THE LIGHTNING?
Was that bad?
Doggie...
WHINE
WHINE
Please take me home
Her imagination
WHY... WHY'S SHE STARING OFF LIKE THAT?
And why's she all wet?
IT'S DIFFICULT FOR ME TO GET TO KNOW PEOPLE SINCE I DON'T INTERACT VERY WELL...
1-D
Morn-ing!
...BUT I HOPE I CAN OVERCOME THIS SOMEHOW.
Morn-ing!
I'D LIKE TO BECOME SOMEONE THAT SUITS THE NAME "SAWAKO," INSTEAD OF "KURONUMA" OR "SADAKO."
GOOD MORNING...
GRIN...
FLINCH
M... MORNING...
Won't look at her.
SOMEONE CHEERFUL AND PLEASANT...
Scared stiff
Why's she all wet?
I'm not asking her!
CLATTER
MORNING!
YES, LIKE...

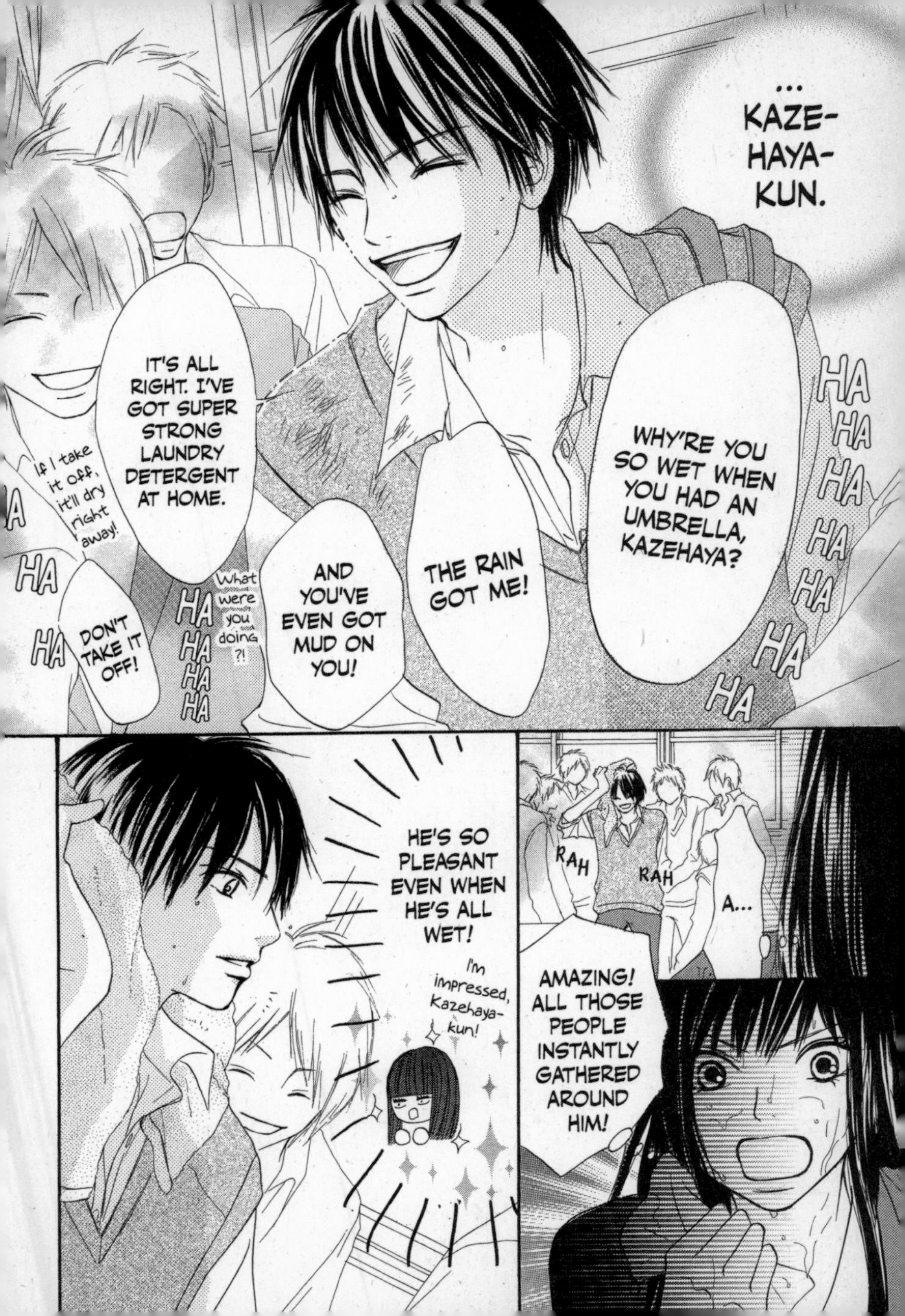
... KAZE-HAYA-KUN.
HA HA HA HA HA HA HA HA
WHY'RE YOU SO WET WHEN YOU HAD AN UMBRELLA, KAZEHAYA?
THE RAIN GOT ME!
AND YOU'VE EVEN GOT MUD ON YOU!
What were you doing?!
HA HA HA HA
IT'S ALL RIGHT. I'VE GOT SUPER STRONG LAUNDRY DETERGENT AT HOME.
If I take it off, it'll dry right away!
DON'T TAKE IT OFF!
A HA HA
RAH
RAH
A...
AMAZING! ALL THOSE PEOPLE INSTANTLY GATHERED AROUND HIM!
HE'S SO PLEASANT EVEN WHEN HE'S ALL WET!
I'm impressed, Kazehaya-kun!

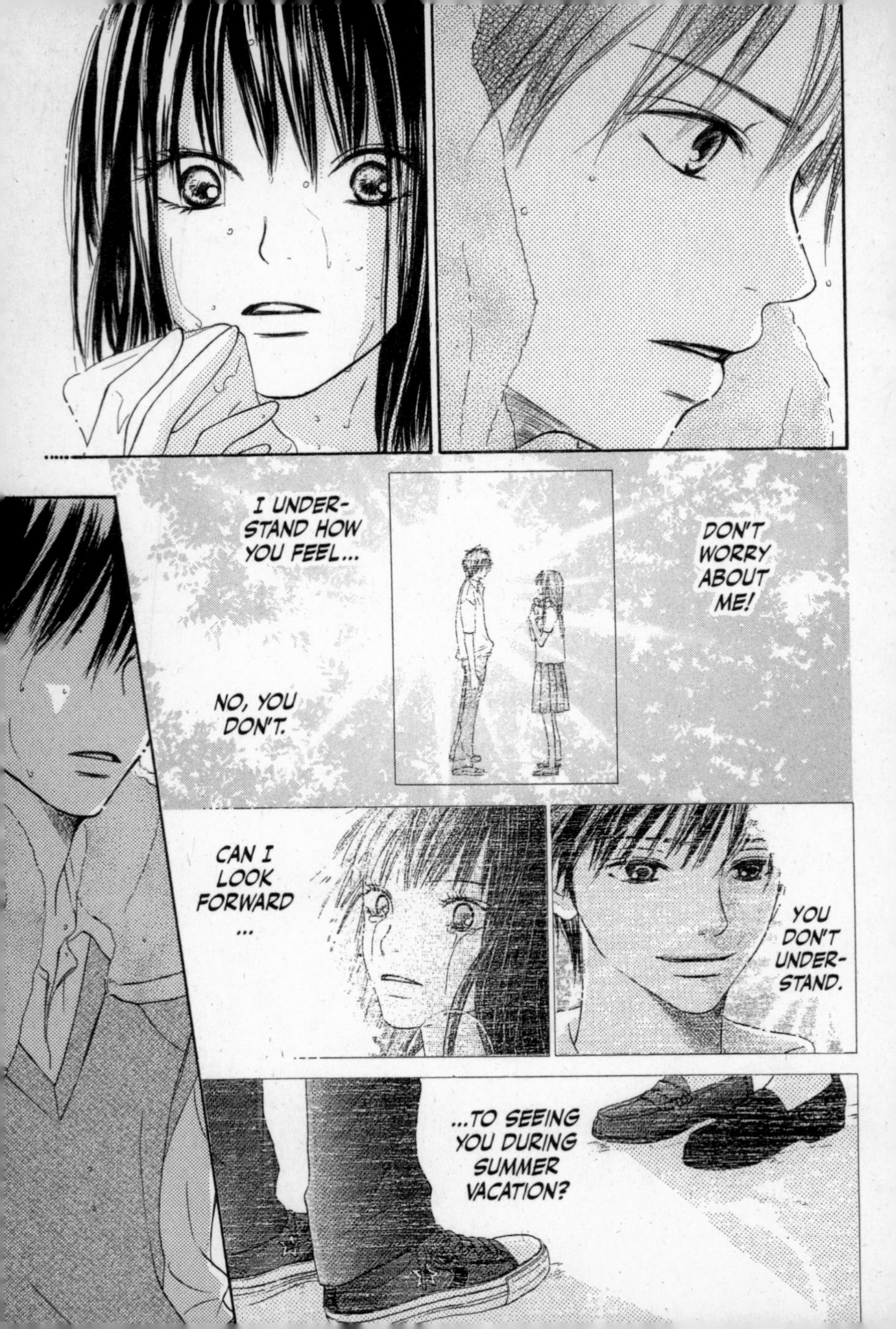
DON'T WORRY ABOUT ME!
I UNDER-STAND HOW YOU FEEL...
NO, YOU DON'T.
YOU DON'T UNDER-STAND.
CAN I LOOK FORWARD ...
...TO SEEING YOU DURING SUMMER VACATION?

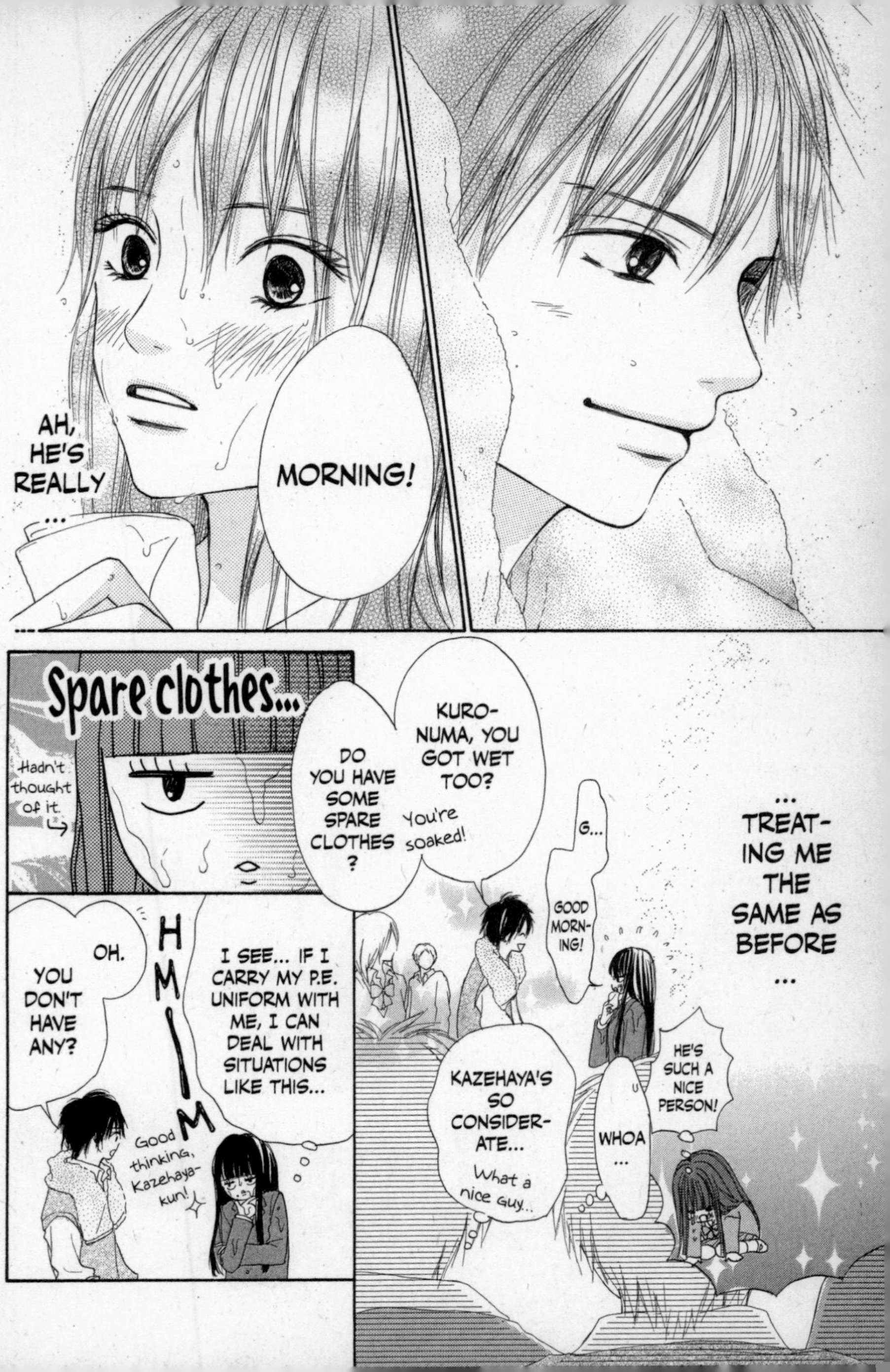

MORNING!
AH, HE'S REALLY ...
... TREATING ME THE SAME AS BEFORE ...
KURO-NUMA, YOU GOT WET TOO?
You're soaked!
G...
GOOD MORNING!
HE'S SUCH A NICE PERSON!
WHOA ...
KAZEHAYA'S SO CONSIDER-ATE...
What a nice guy...
DO YOU HAVE SOME SPARE CLOTHES?
Spare clothes...
Hadn't thought of it.
OH.
YOU DON'T HAVE ANY?
HMMM
I SEE... IF I CARRY MY P.E. UNIFORM WITH ME, I CAN DEAL WITH SITUATIONS LIKE THIS...
Good thinking, Kazehaya-kun!

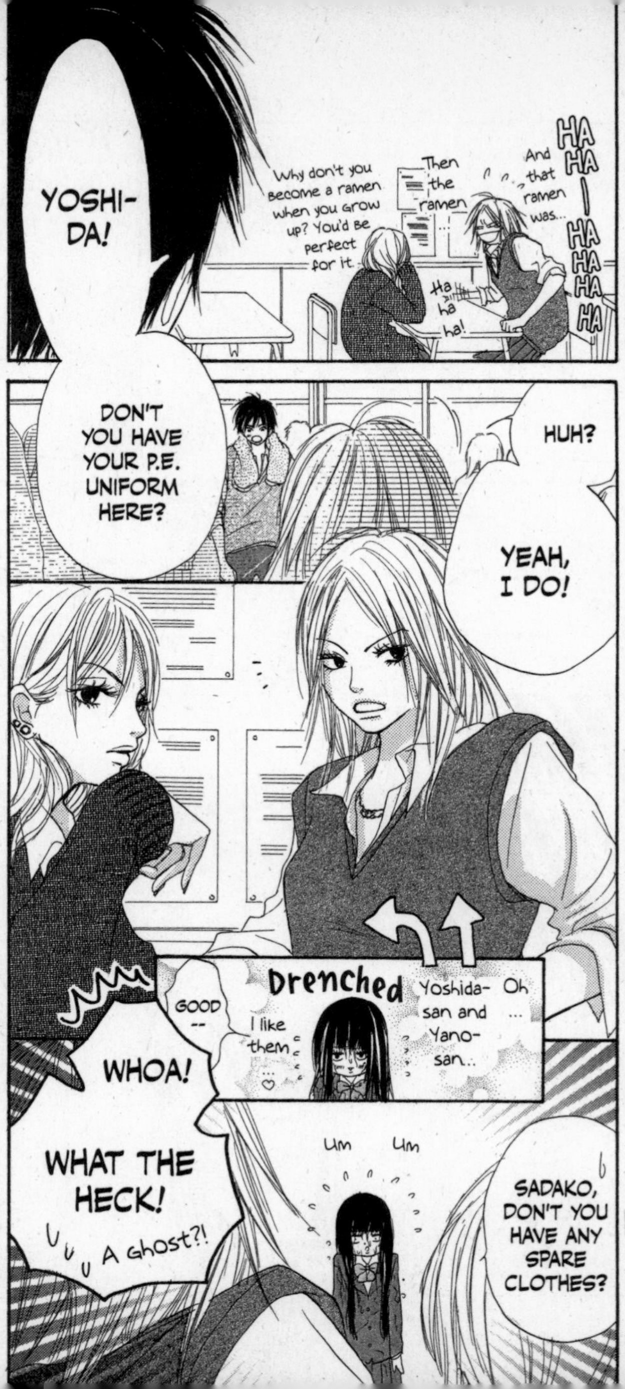
HA HA HA HA HA HA HA
And that ramen was...
Then the ramen...
Why don't you become a ramen when you grow up? You'd be perfect for it.
Ha ha ha!
YOSHI-DA!
DON'T YOU HAVE YOUR P.E. UNIFORM HERE?
HUH?
YEAH, I DO!
Oh...
Yoshida-san and Yano-san..
Drenched
I like them...♡
GOOD--
WHOA!
SADAKO, DON'T YOU HAVE ANY SPARE CLOTHES?
Um Um
WHAT THE HECK!
A Ghost?!

KARUPIN on JAPAN 2

In the spring, it's so lovely because the flower shops are all so colorful.
But if I buy flowers, they wither before my work deadline. (Both the flowers and me).
Even if it's just for a short time, if there're flowers in the room it makes the room more cheerful and I feel happy.
Though, right now there isn't a single flower in my place...
That's because I haven't gone out since my work was completed.
I'm writing this in my darkened room. Heh heh.
I'm looking forward to going to a flower shop when I have the time.

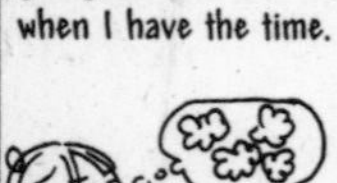

But I don't know much about flowers, so sadly, I can only draw something like this.

Oh, and during the winter, I forget about flowers completely! Yeah, that's how much I love flowers...

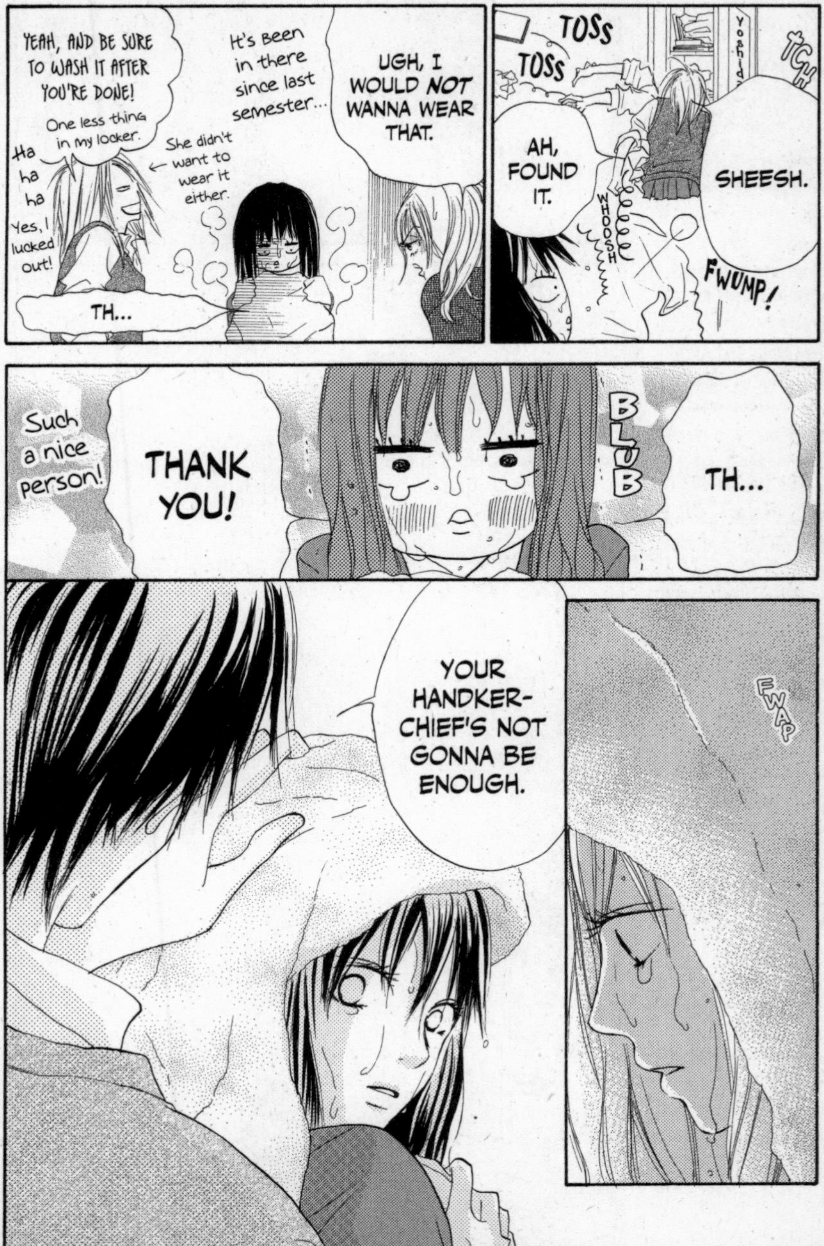
TCH
Yoshida
TOSS
TOSS
SHEESH.
AH, FOUND IT.
WHOOSH
FWUMP!
UGH, I WOULD NOT WANNA WEAR THAT.
It's been in there since last semester...
YEAH, AND BE SURE TO WASH IT AFTER YOU'RE DONE!
One less thing in my locker.
She didn't want to wear it either.
Ha ha ha
Yes, I lucked out!
TH...
TH...
BLUB
THANK YOU!
Such a nice person!
FWAP
YOUR HANDKER-CHIEF'S NOT GONNA BE ENOUGH.

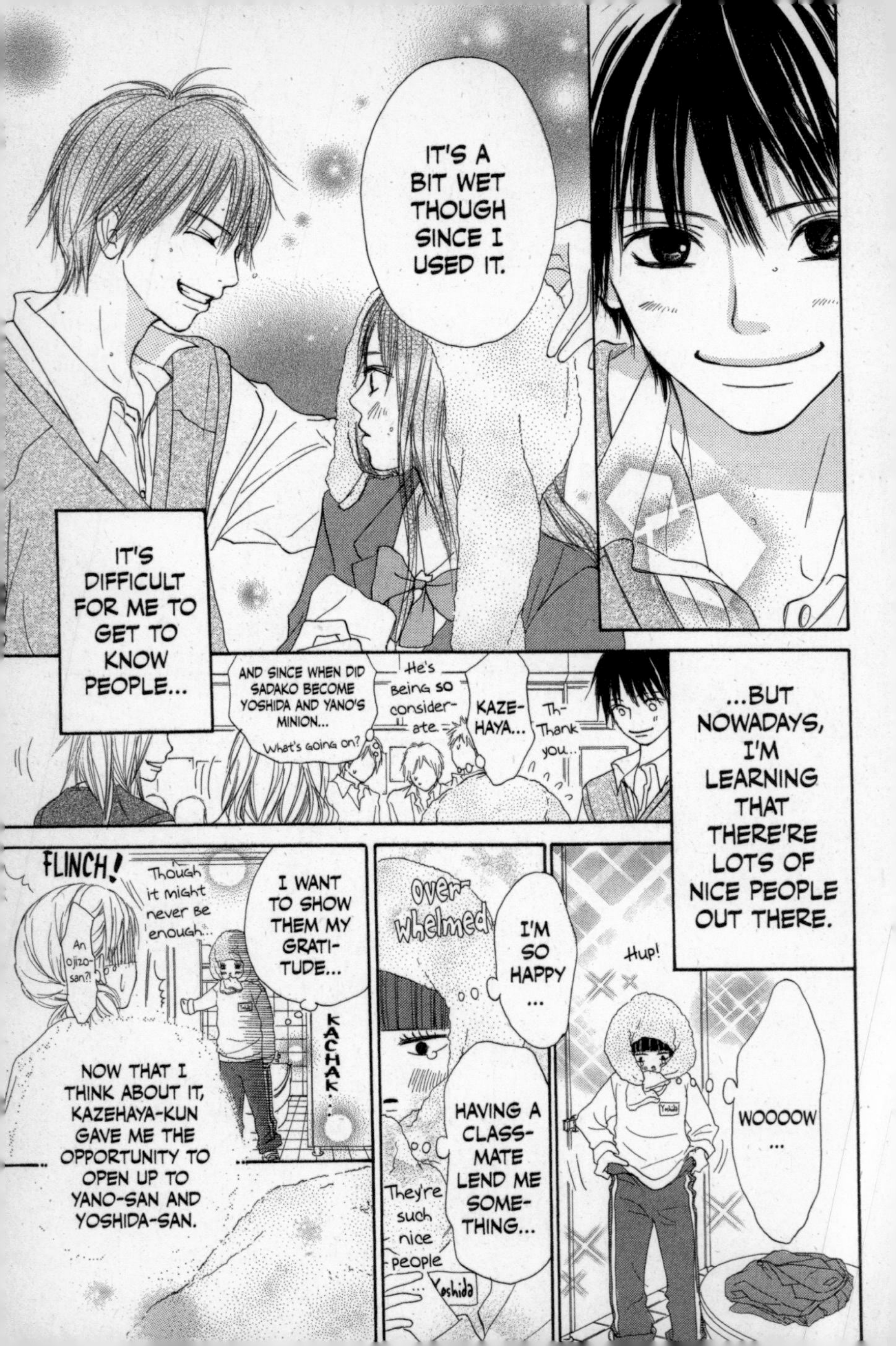
IT'S A BIT WET THOUGH SINCE I USED IT.
IT'S DIFFICULT FOR ME TO GET TO KNOW PEOPLE...
...BUT NOWADAYS, I'M LEARNING THAT THERE'RE LOTS OF NICE PEOPLE OUT THERE.
Th- Thank you...
KAZE-HAYA...
He's being so consider-ate.
AND SINCE WHEN DID SADAKO BECOME YOSHIDA AND YANO'S MINION...
What's going on?
Hup!
WOOOOW...
over-whelmed
I'M SO HAPPY...
HAVING A CLASS-MATE LEND ME SOME-THING...
They're such nice people...
Yoshida
I WANT TO SHOW THEM MY GRATI-TUDE...
KACHAK...
Though it might never be enough...
FLINCH!
An ojizo-san?!
NOW THAT I THINK ABOUT IT, KAZEHAYA-KUN GAVE ME THE OPPORTUNITY TO OPEN UP TO YANO-SAN AND YOSHIDA-SAN.

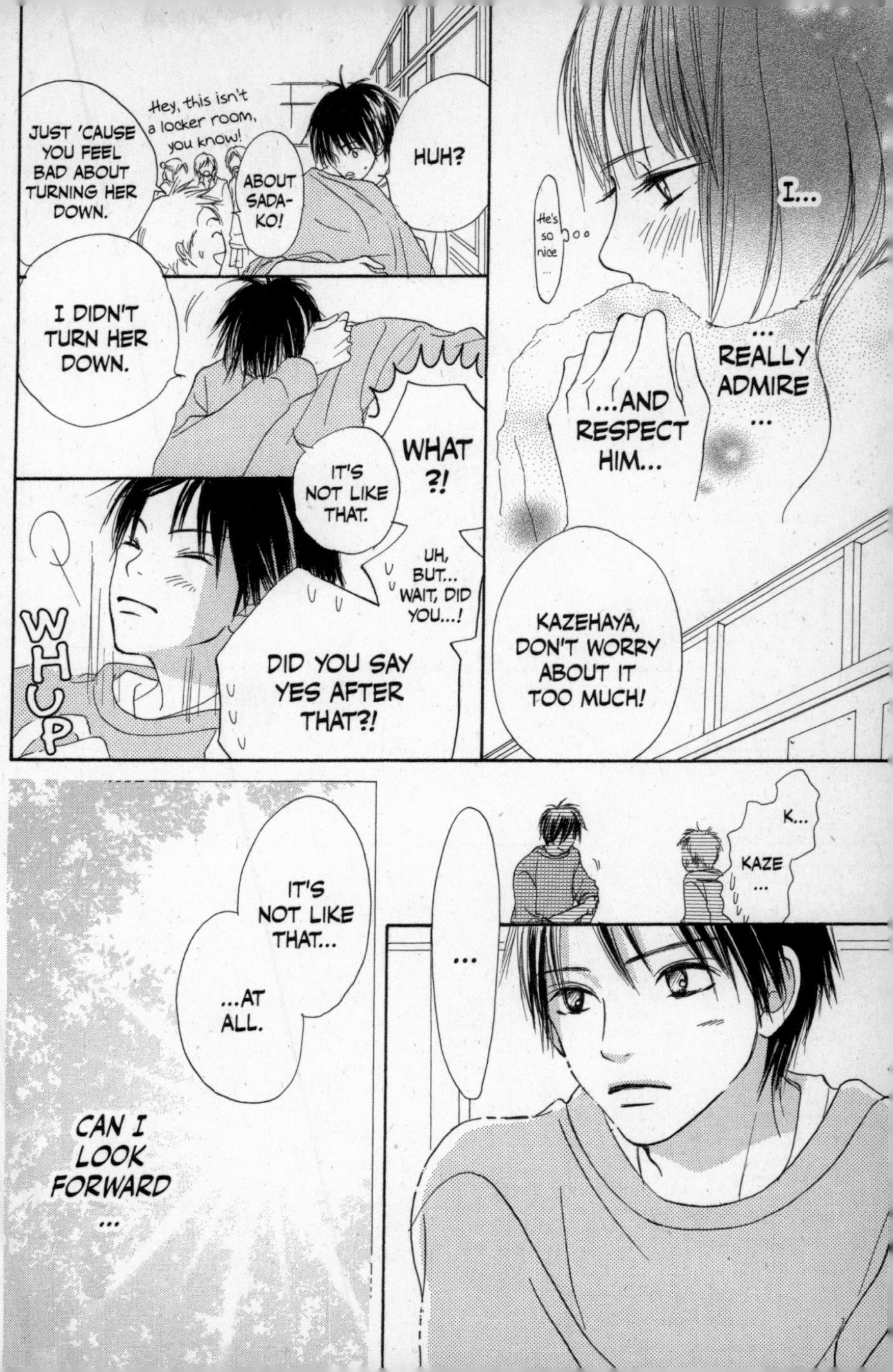
I...
He's so nice...
...REALLY ADMIRE...
...AND RESPECT HIM...
KAZEHAYA, DON'T WORRY ABOUT IT TOO MUCH!
HUH?
ABOUT SADAKO!
Hey, this isn't a locker room, you know!
JUST 'CAUSE YOU FEEL BAD ABOUT TURNING HER DOWN.
I DIDN'T TURN HER DOWN.
WHAT ?!
IT'S NOT LIKE THAT.
UH, BUT... WAIT, DID YOU...!
DID YOU SAY YES AFTER THAT?!
WHUP
K... KAZE...
...
IT'S NOT LIKE THAT... ...AT ALL.
CAN I LOOK FORWARD ...

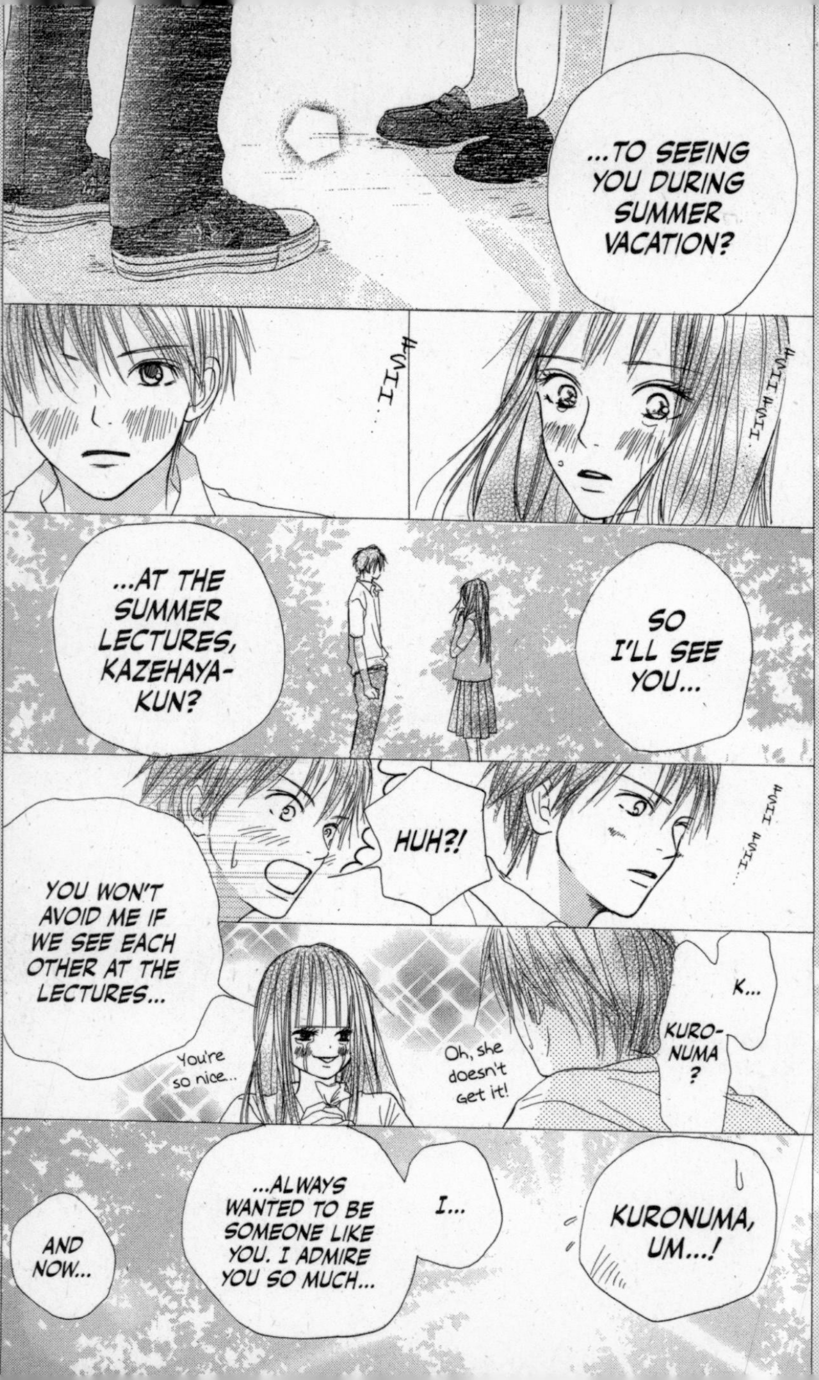
...TO SEEING YOU DURING SUMMER VACATION?
FSH FSH...
FSH...
SO I'LL SEE YOU...
...AT THE SUMMER LECTURES, KAZEHAYA-KUN?
FSH FSH...
HUH?!
YOU WON'T AVOID ME IF WE SEE EACH OTHER AT THE LECTURES...
K...
KURO-NUMA?
Oh, she doesn't get it!
You're so nice...
KURONUMA, UM...!
I...
...ALWAYS WANTED TO BE SOMEONE LIKE YOU. I ADMIRE YOU SO MUCH...
AND NOW...

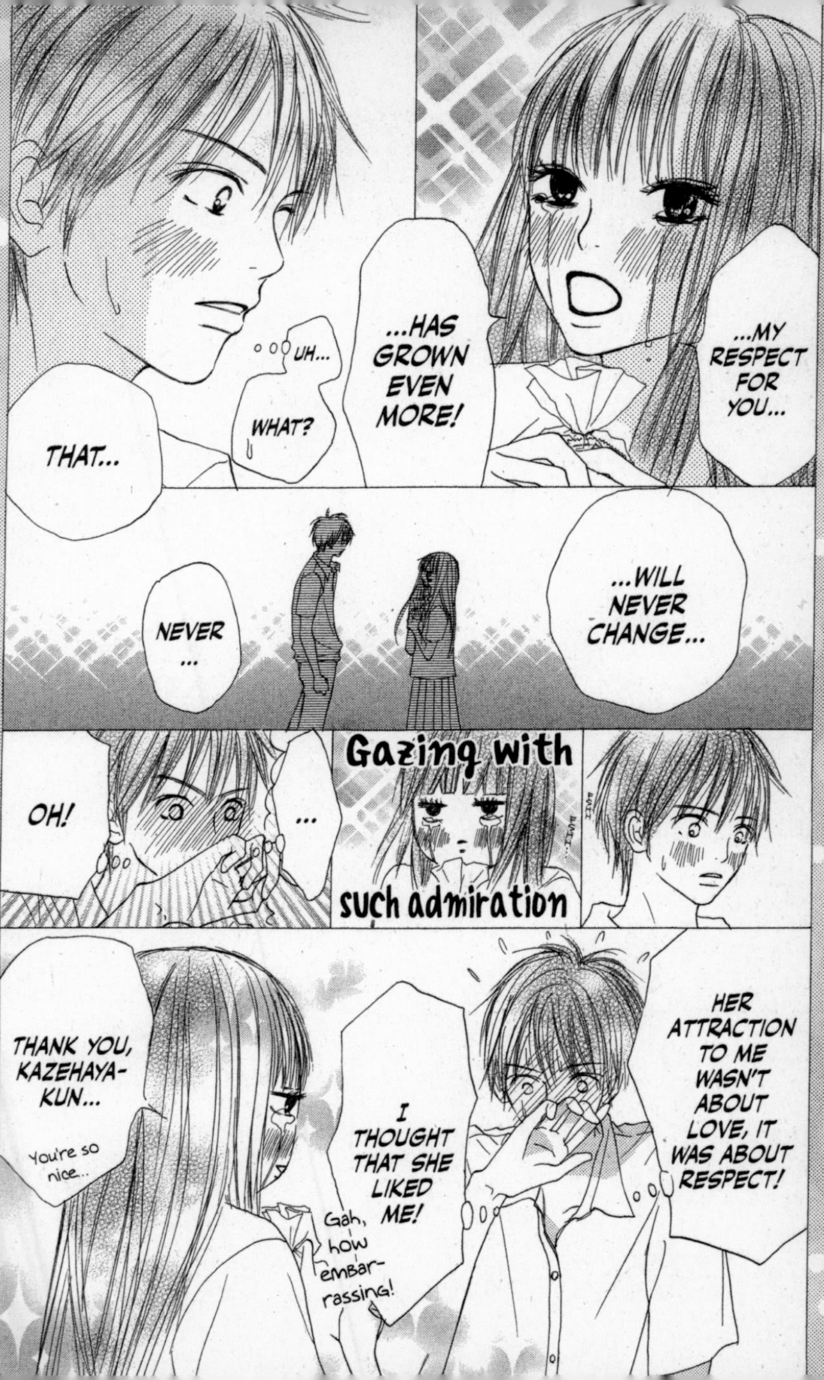
...MY RESPECT FOR YOU...
...HAS GROWN EVEN MORE!
UH...
WHAT?
THAT...
...WILL NEVER CHANGE...
NEVER ...
Gazing with such admiration
...
OH!
HER ATTRACTION TO ME WASN'T ABOUT LOVE, IT WAS ABOUT RESPECT!
I THOUGHT THAT SHE LIKED ME!
Gah, how embarrassing!
THANK YOU, KAZEHAYA-KUN...
You're so nice...

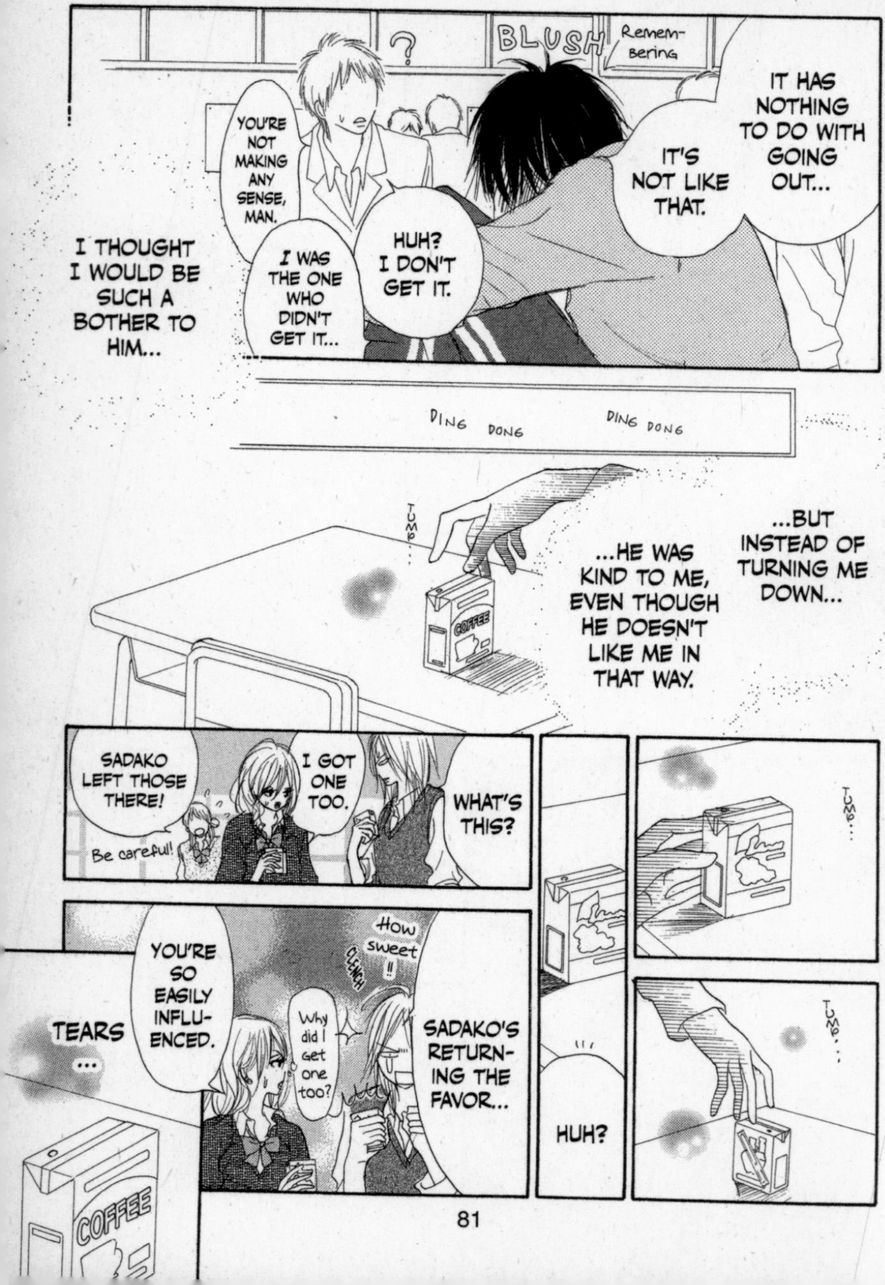
IT HAS NOTHING TO DO WITH GOING OUT...
IT'S NOT LIKE THAT.
Remem-bering
BLUSH
?
YOU'RE NOT MAKING ANY SENSE, MAN.
HUH? I DON'T GET IT.
I WAS THE ONE WHO DIDN'T GET IT...
I THOUGHT I WOULD BE SUCH A BOTHER TO HIM...
DING DONG DING DONG
...BUT INSTEAD OF TURNING ME DOWN...
...HE WAS KIND TO ME, EVEN THOUGH HE DOESN'T LIKE ME IN THAT WAY.
TUMP...
COFFEE
TUMP...
TUMP...
HUH?
WHAT'S THIS?
I GOT ONE TOO.
SADAKO LEFT THOSE THERE!
Be careful!
SADAKO'S RETURNING THE FAVOR...
How sweet!!
CLENCH
Why did I get one too?
YOU'RE SO EASILY INFLUENCED.
TEARS...
COFFEE

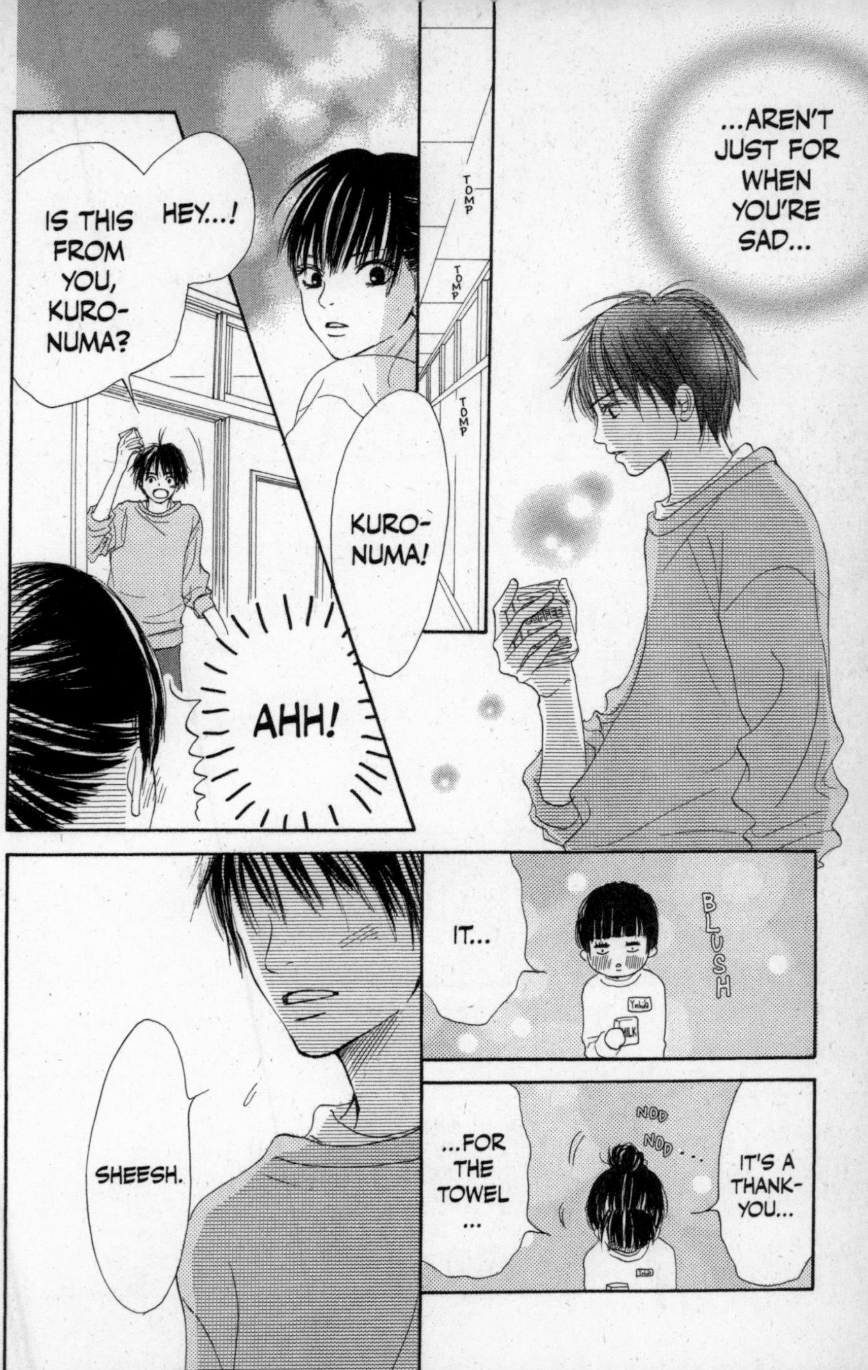
...AREN'T JUST FOR WHEN YOU'RE SAD...
TOMP
TOMP
TOMP
KURO-NUMA!
AHH!
HEY...!
IS THIS FROM YOU, KURO-NUMA?
IT...
BLUSH
NOD
NOD . . .
IT'S A THANK-YOU...
...FOR THE TOWEL ...
SHEESH.

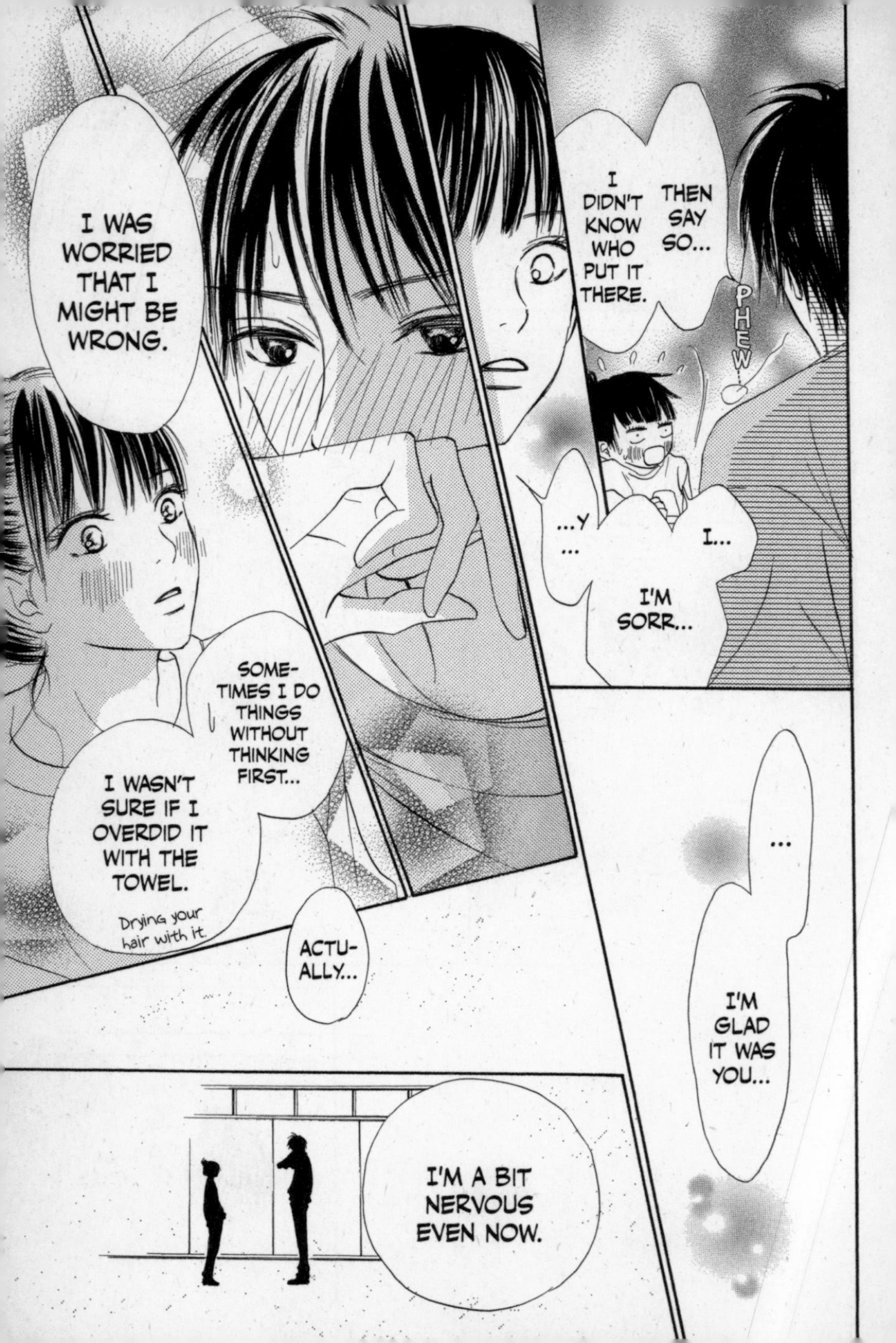
THEN SAY SO...
I DIDN'T KNOW WHO PUT IT THERE.
PHEW
I...
I'M SORR...
...Y...
I WAS WORRIED THAT I MIGHT BE WRONG.
SOME-TIMES I DO THINGS WITHOUT THINKING FIRST...
I WASN'T SURE IF I OVERDID IT WITH THE TOWEL.
Drying your hair with it.
...
I'M GLAD IT WAS YOU...
ACTU-ALLY...
I'M A BIT NERVOUS EVEN NOW.

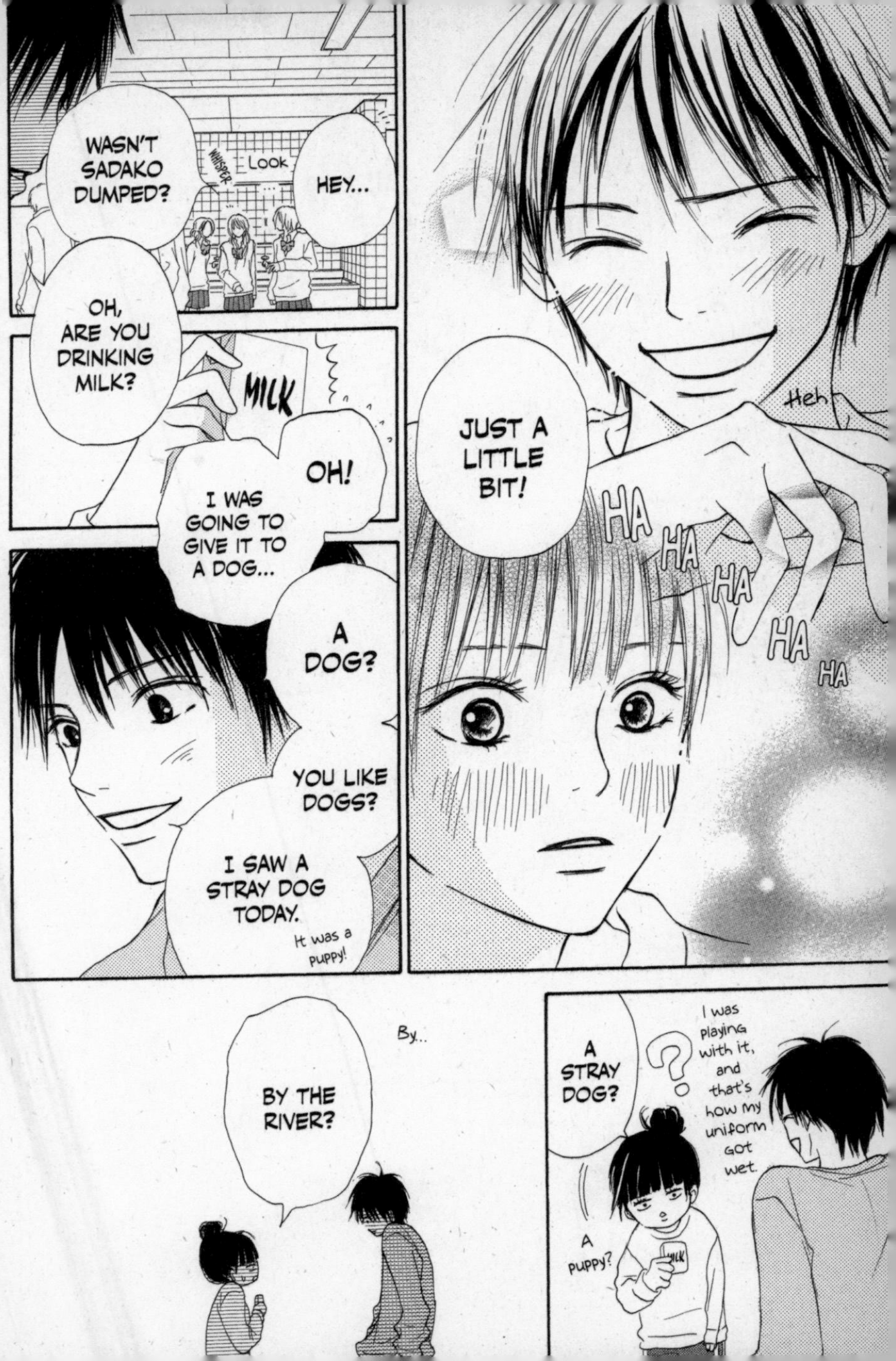
Heh
JUST A LITTLE BIT!
HA HA HA HA HA
WASN'T SADAKO DUMPED?
WHISPER
Look
HEY...
OH, ARE YOU DRINKING MILK?
MILK
OH!
I WAS GOING TO GIVE IT TO A DOG...
A DOG?
YOU LIKE DOGS?
I SAW A STRAY DOG TODAY.
It was a puppy!
A STRAY DOG?
I was playing with it, and that's how my uniform got wet.
A puppy?
By...
BY THE RIVER?

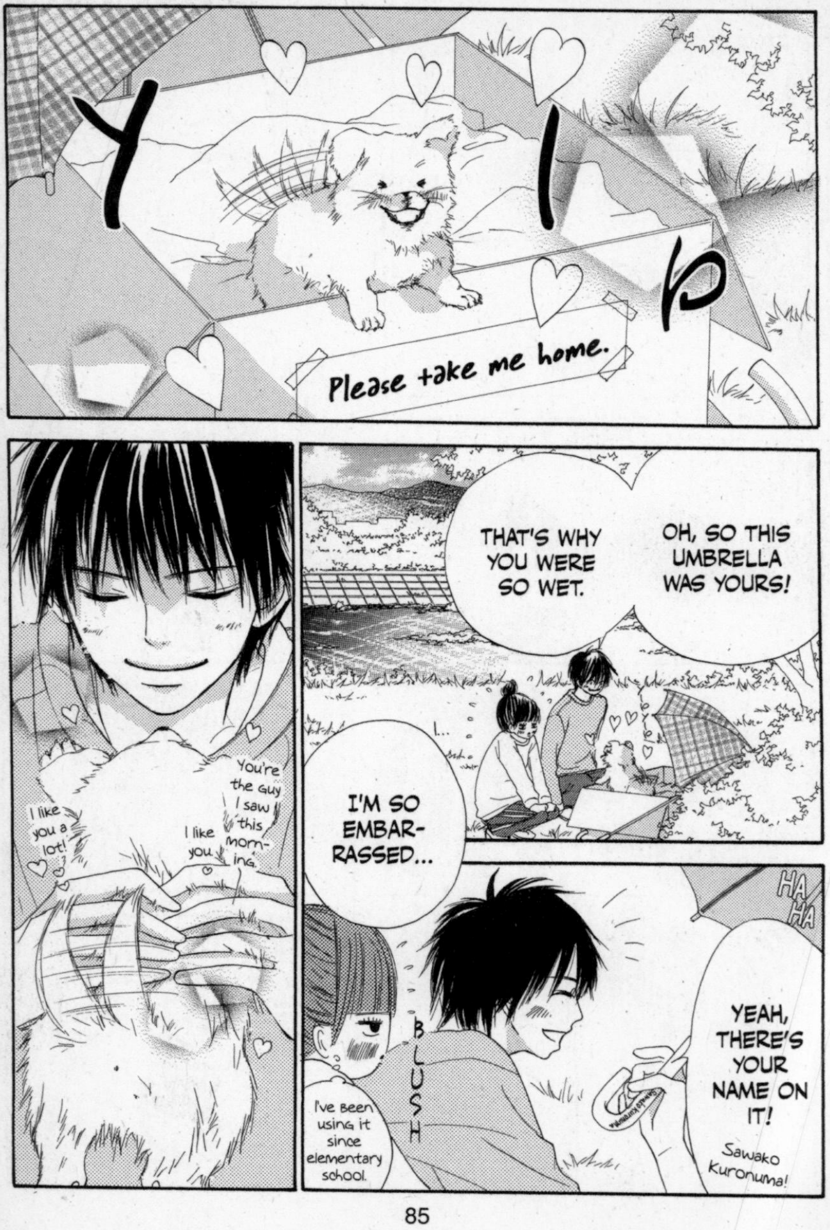
YIP
Please take me home.
OH, SO THIS UMBRELLA WAS YOURS!
THAT'S WHY YOU WERE SO WET.
I...
I'M SO EMBAR-RASSED...
HA HA
YEAH, THERE'S YOUR NAME ON IT!
Sawako Kuronuma!
BLUSH
I've been using it since elementary school.
You're the Guy I saw this morn-ing.
I like you.
I like you a lot!

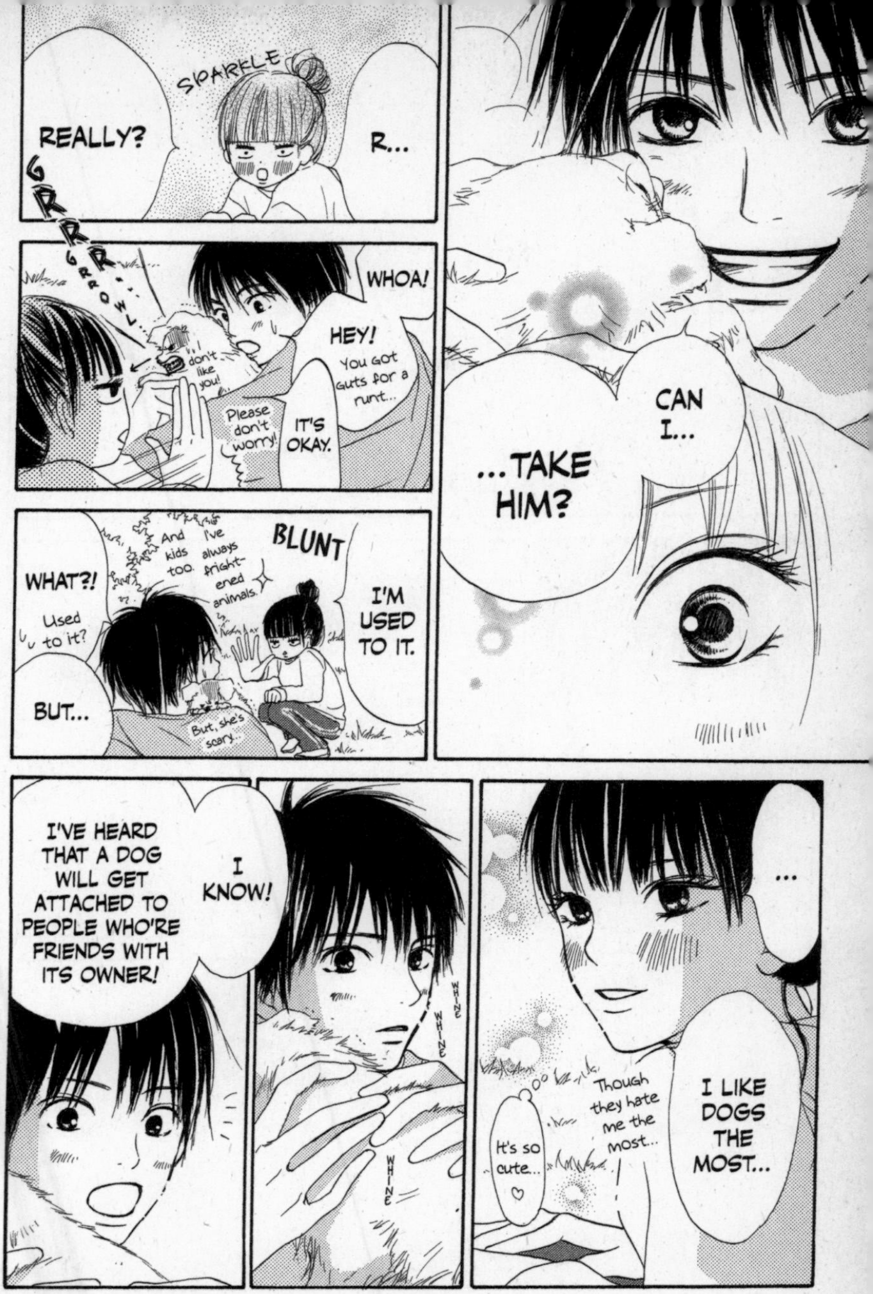
CAN I...
...TAKE HIM?
R...
SPARKLE
REALLY?
GRRRR...
WHOA!
HEY!
You got guts for a runt...
IT'S OKAY.
Please don't worry!
GRRROWL...
I don't like you!
I'M USED TO IT.
BLUNT
I've always fright-ened animals.
And kids too.
WHAT?!
Used to it?
BUT...
But, she's scary...
...
I LIKE DOGS THE MOST...
Though they hate me the most...
It's so cute... ♡
WHINE
WHINE
WHINE
I KNOW!
I'VE HEARD THAT A DOG WILL GET ATTACHED TO PEOPLE WHO'RE FRIENDS WITH ITS OWNER!

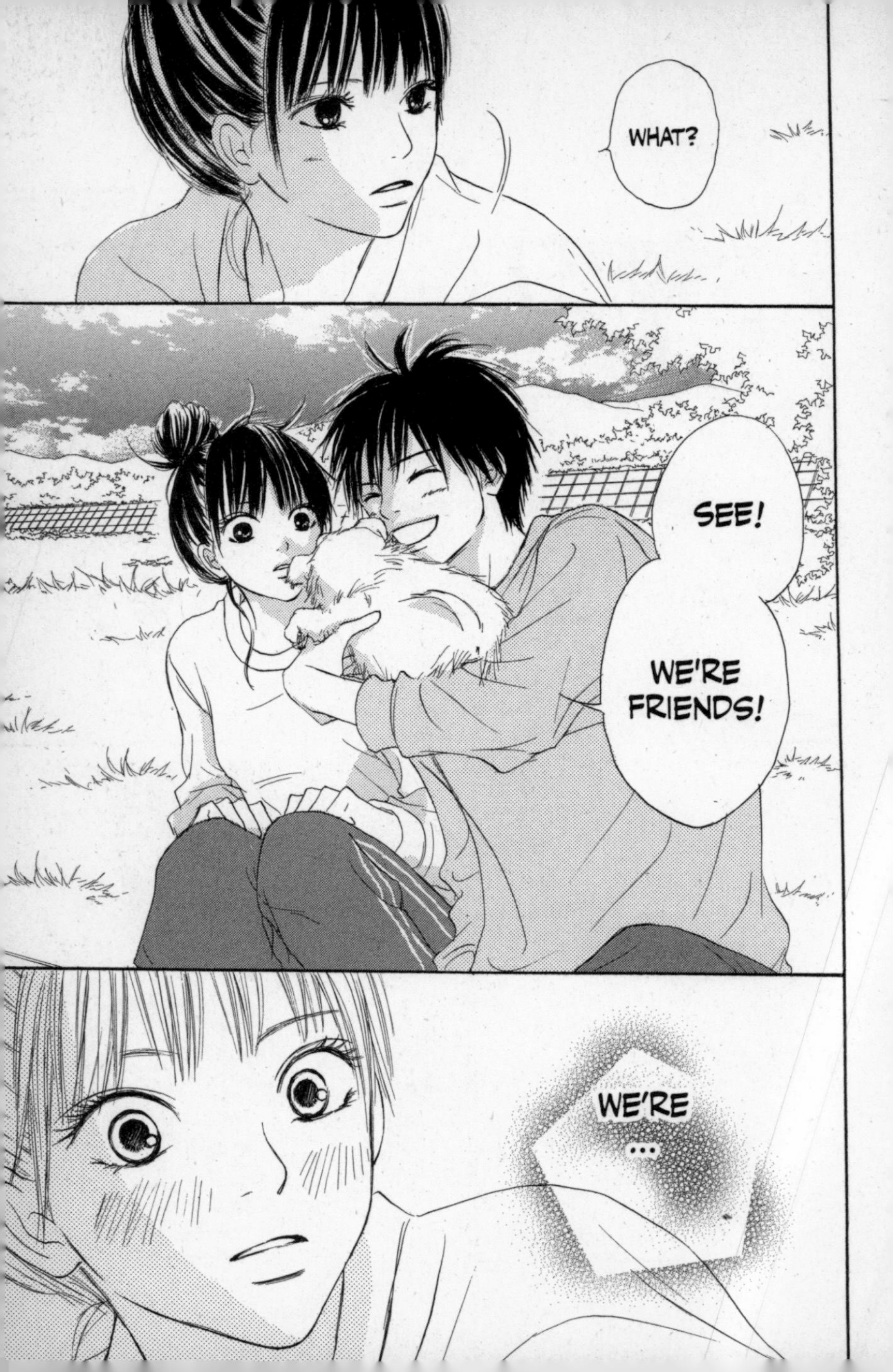
WHAT?
SEE!
WE'RE FRIENDS!
WE'RE ...

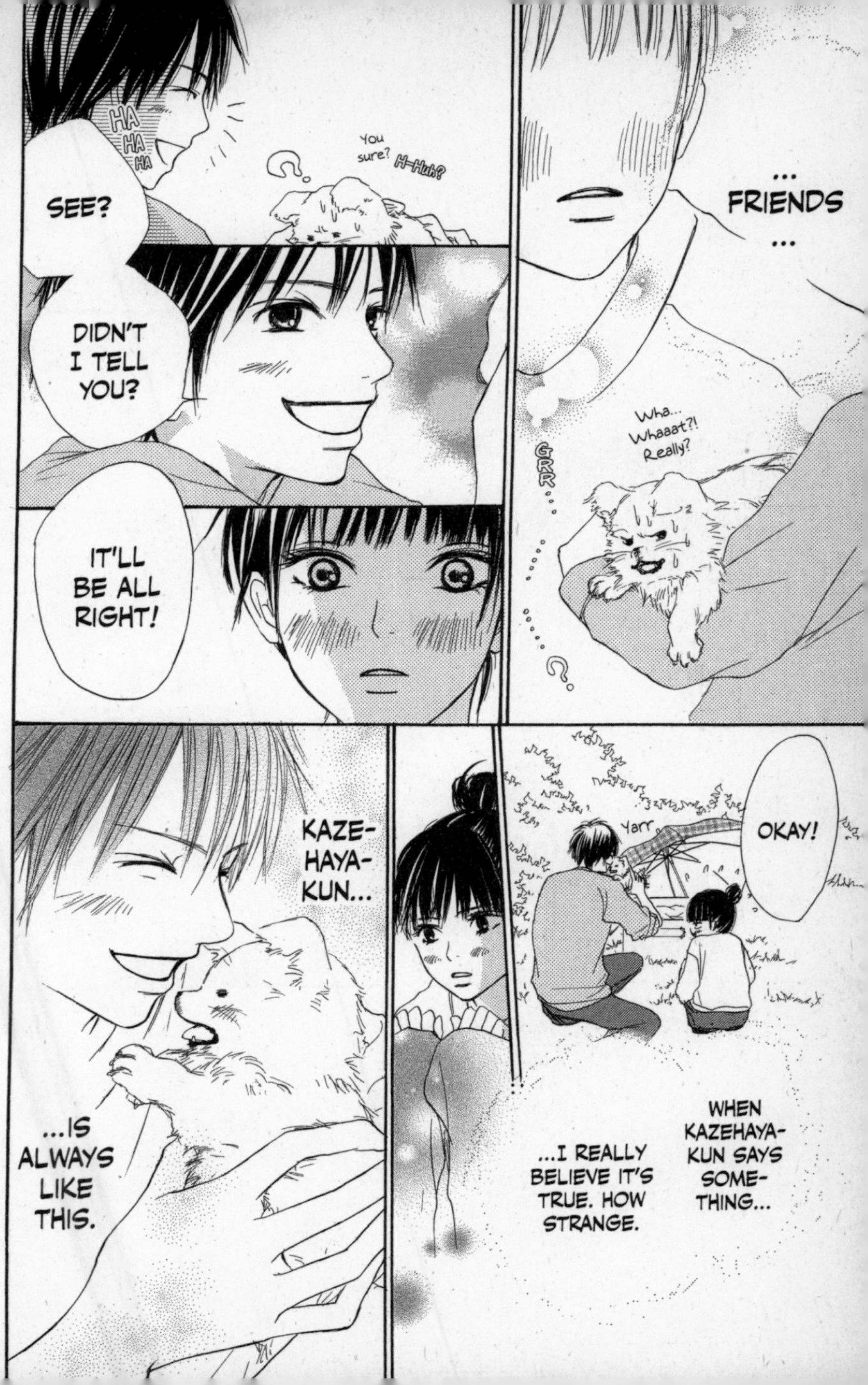
...FRIENDS...
Wha... Whaaat?! Really?
GRR...
?
HA HA HA
SEE?
You sure? H-Huh?
?
DIDN'T I TELL YOU?
IT'LL BE ALL RIGHT!
OKAY!
Yarr
WHEN KAZEHAYA-KUN SAYS SOME-THING...
...I REALLY BELIEVE IT'S TRUE. HOW STRANGE.
KAZE-HAYA-KUN...
...IS ALWAYS LIKE THIS.

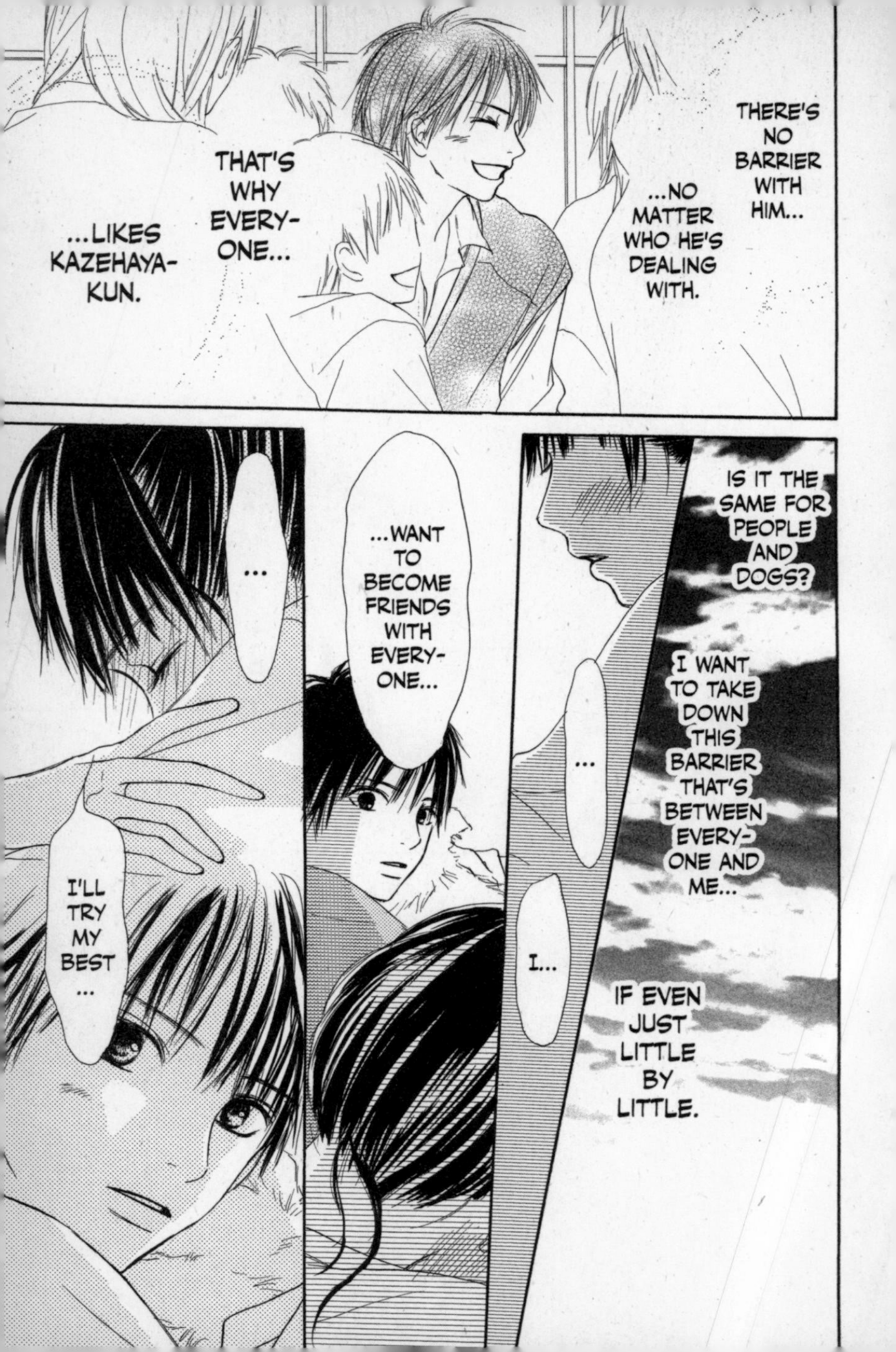
THERE'S NO BARRIER WITH HIM...
...NO MATTER WHO HE'S DEALING WITH.
THAT'S WHY EVERY-ONE...
...LIKES KAZEHAYA-KUN.
IS IT THE SAME FOR PEOPLE AND DOGS?
I WANT TO TAKE DOWN THIS BARRIER THAT'S BETWEEN EVERY-ONE AND ME...
...
I...
IF EVEN JUST LITTLE BY LITTLE.
...WANT TO BECOME FRIENDS WITH EVERY-ONE...
...
I'LL TRY MY BEST ...

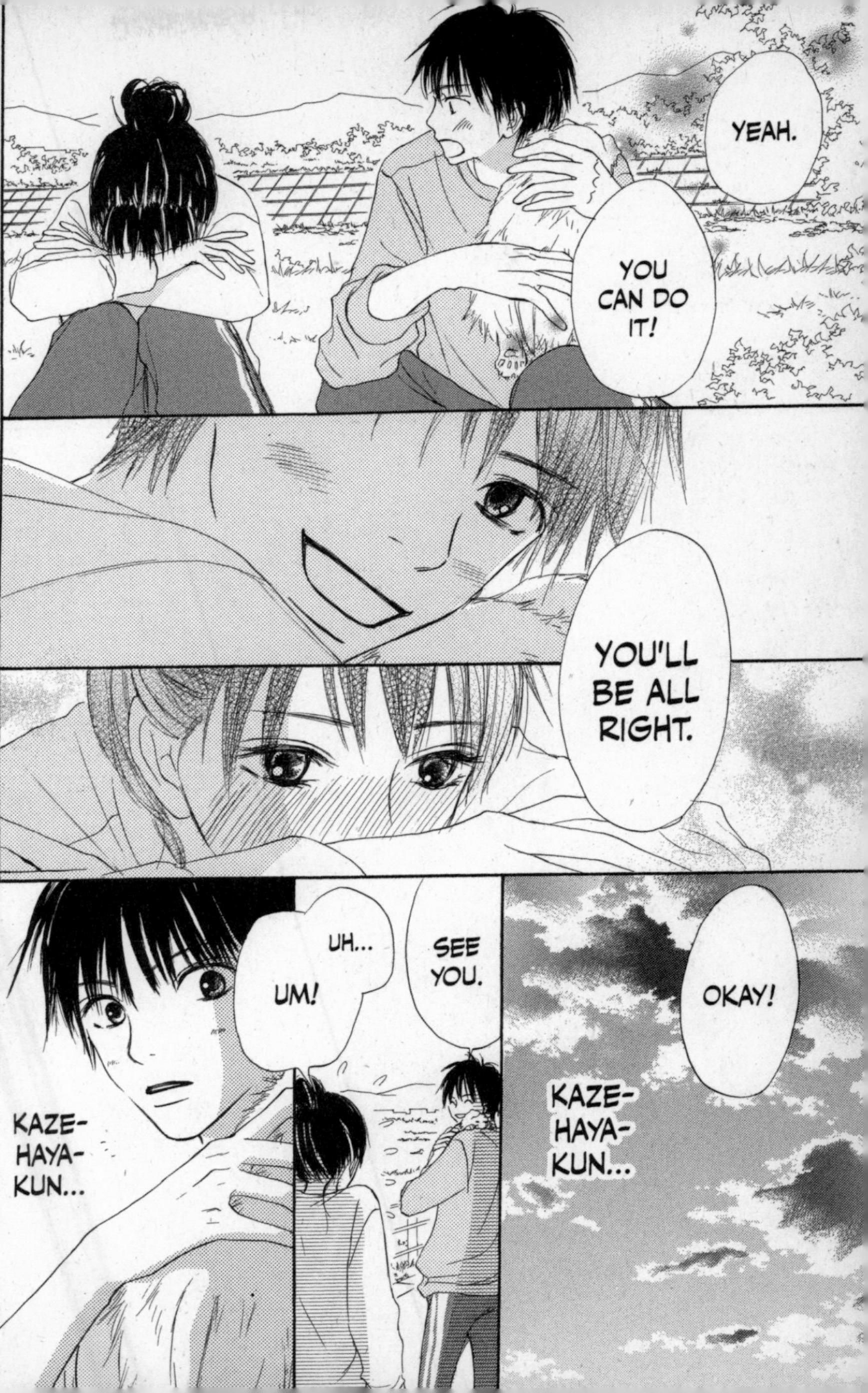
YEAH.
YOU CAN DO IT!
YOU'LL BE ALL RIGHT.
OKAY!
KAZE-HAYA-KUN...
SEE YOU.
UH...
UM!
KAZE-HAYA-KUN...

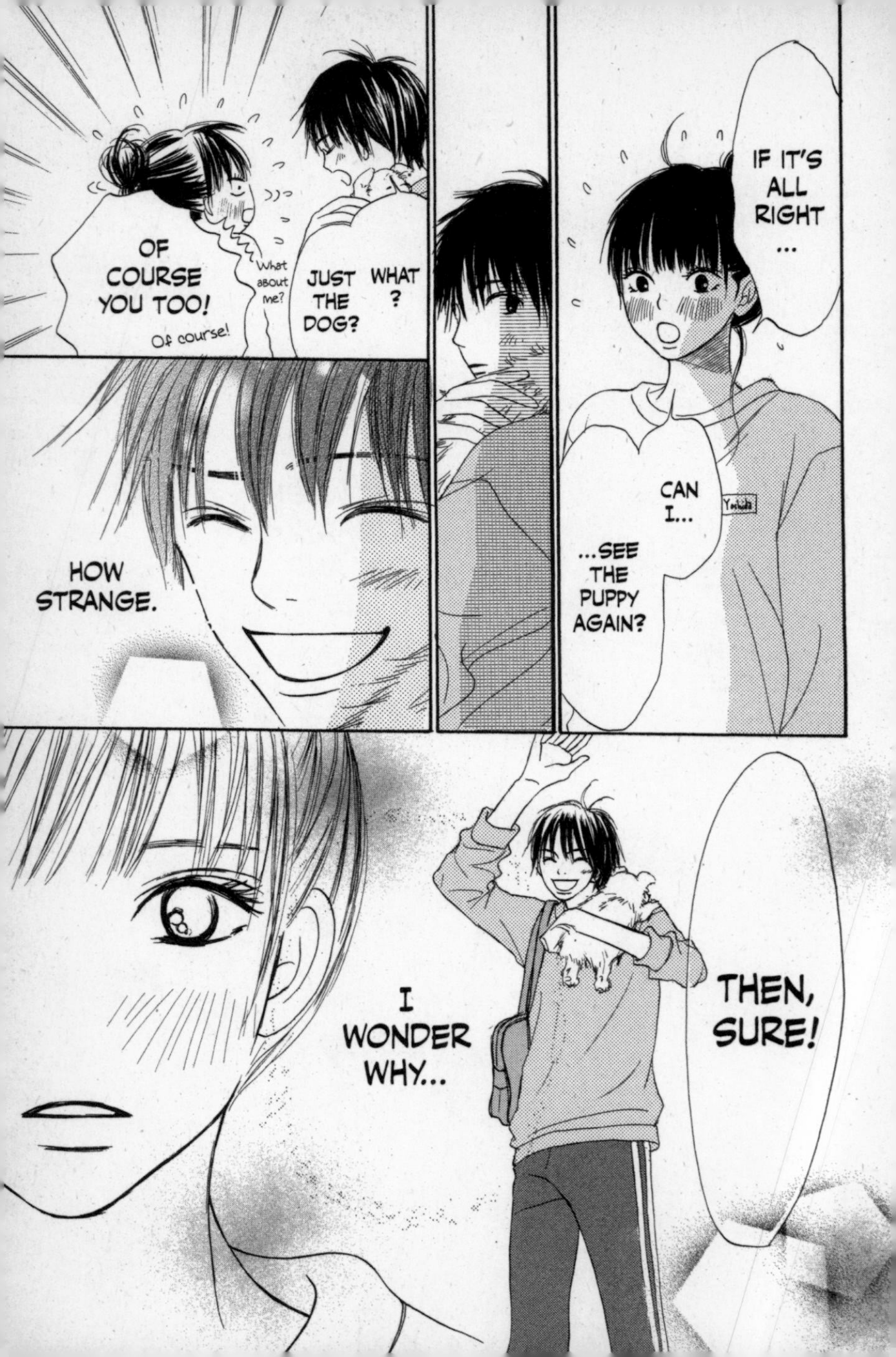
IF IT'S ALL RIGHT ...
CAN I...
...SEE THE PUPPY AGAIN?
WHAT?
JUST THE DOG?
What about me?
OF COURSE YOU TOO!
Of course!
HOW STRANGE.
THEN, SURE!
I WONDER WHY...

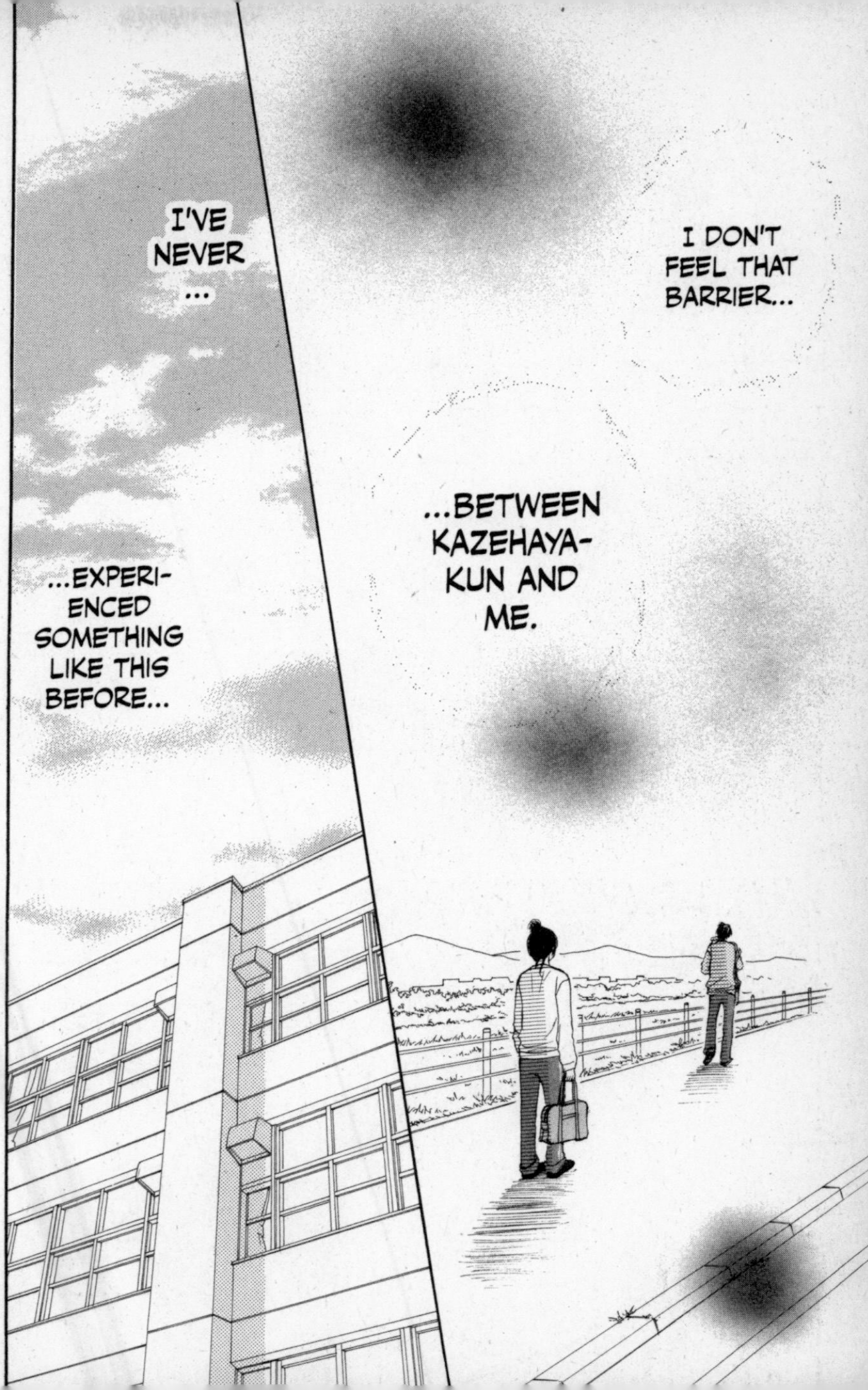
I DON'T FEEL THAT BARRIER...
...BETWEEN KAZEHAYA-KUN AND ME.
I'VE NEVER ...
...EXPERIENCED SOMETHING LIKE THIS BEFORE...

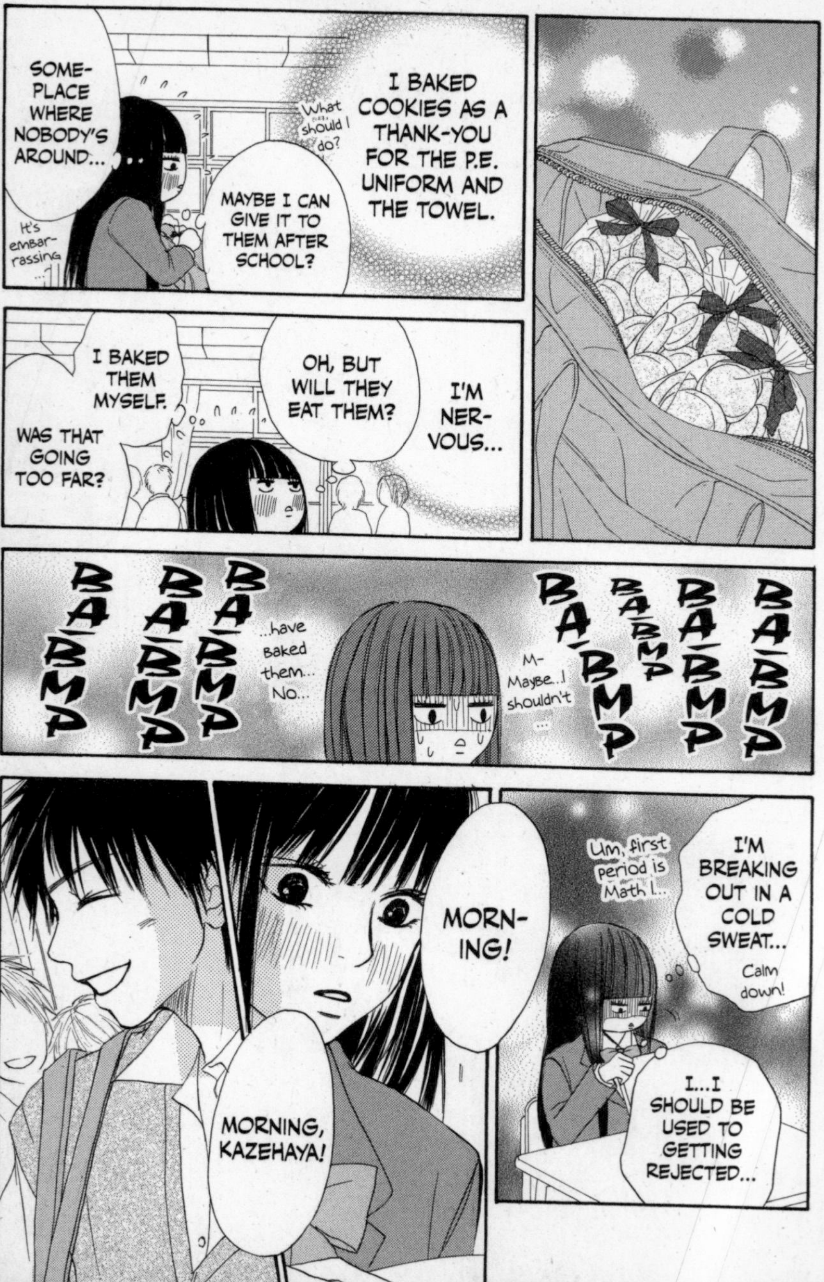
I BAKED COOKIES AS A THANK-YOU FOR THE P.E. UNIFORM AND THE TOWEL.
What should I do?
MAYBE I CAN GIVE IT TO THEM AFTER SCHOOL?
SOME-PLACE WHERE NOBODY'S AROUND...
It's embar-rassing...
I'M NER-VOUS...
OH, BUT WILL THEY EAT THEM?
I BAKED THEM MYSELF.
WAS THAT GOING TOO FAR?
BA-BMP
BA-BMP
BA-BMP
BA-BMP
M-Maybe...I shouldn't...
...have baked them... No...
BA-BMP
BA-BMP
BA-BMP
I'M BREAKING OUT IN A COLD SWEAT...
Um, first period is Math I...
Calm down!
I...I SHOULD BE USED TO GETTING REJECTED...
MORN-ING!
MORNING, KAZEHAYA!

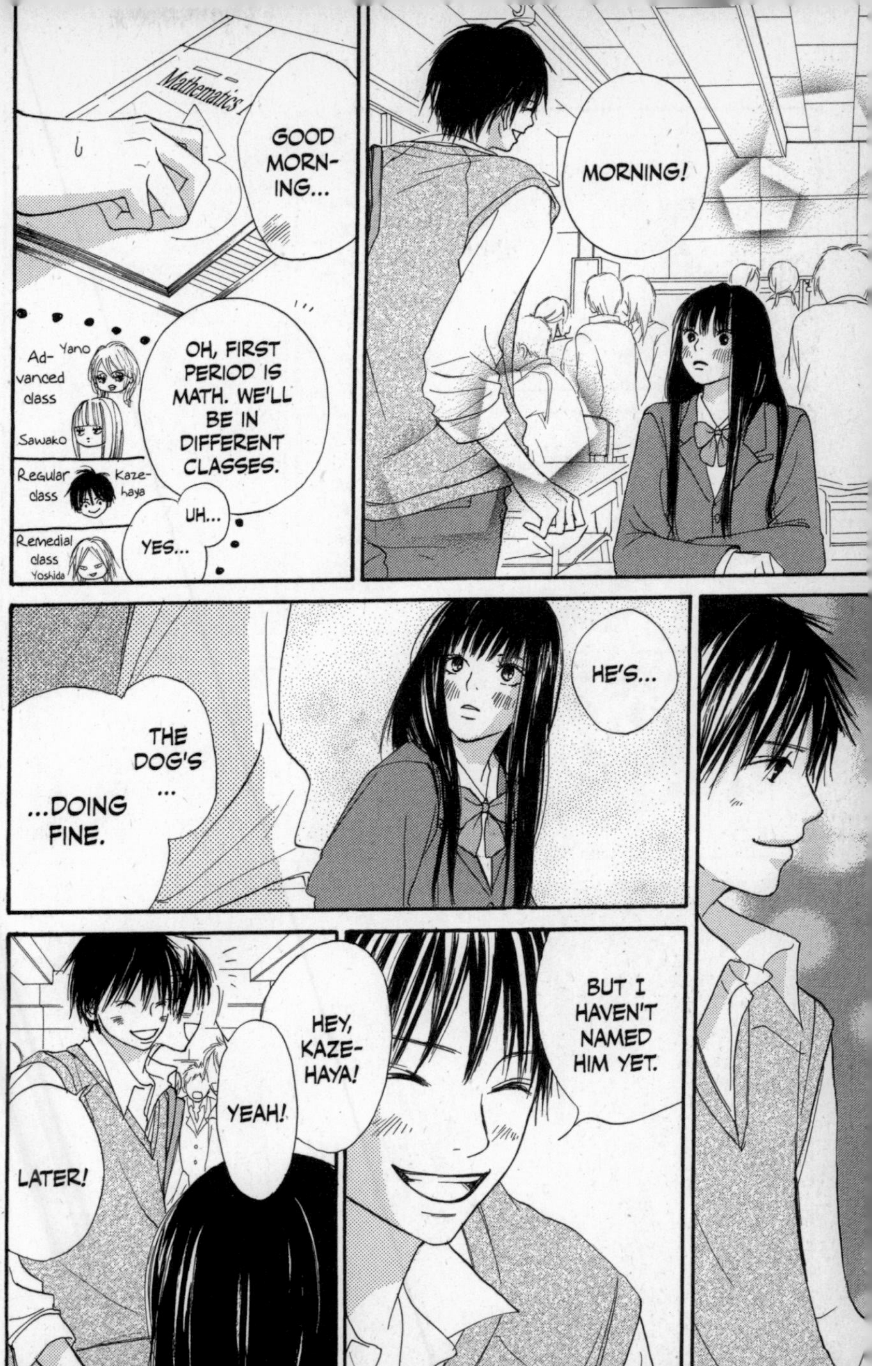
MORNING!
GOOD MORNING-ING...
OH, FIRST PERIOD IS MATH. WE'LL BE IN DIFFERENT CLASSES.
Mathematics
Yano
Advanced class
Sawako
Regular class
Kazehaya
Remedial class
Yoshida
UH...
YES...
HE'S...
THE DOG'S ...
...DOING FINE.
BUT I HAVEN'T NAMED HIM YET.
HEY, KAZE-HAYA!
YEAH!
LATER!

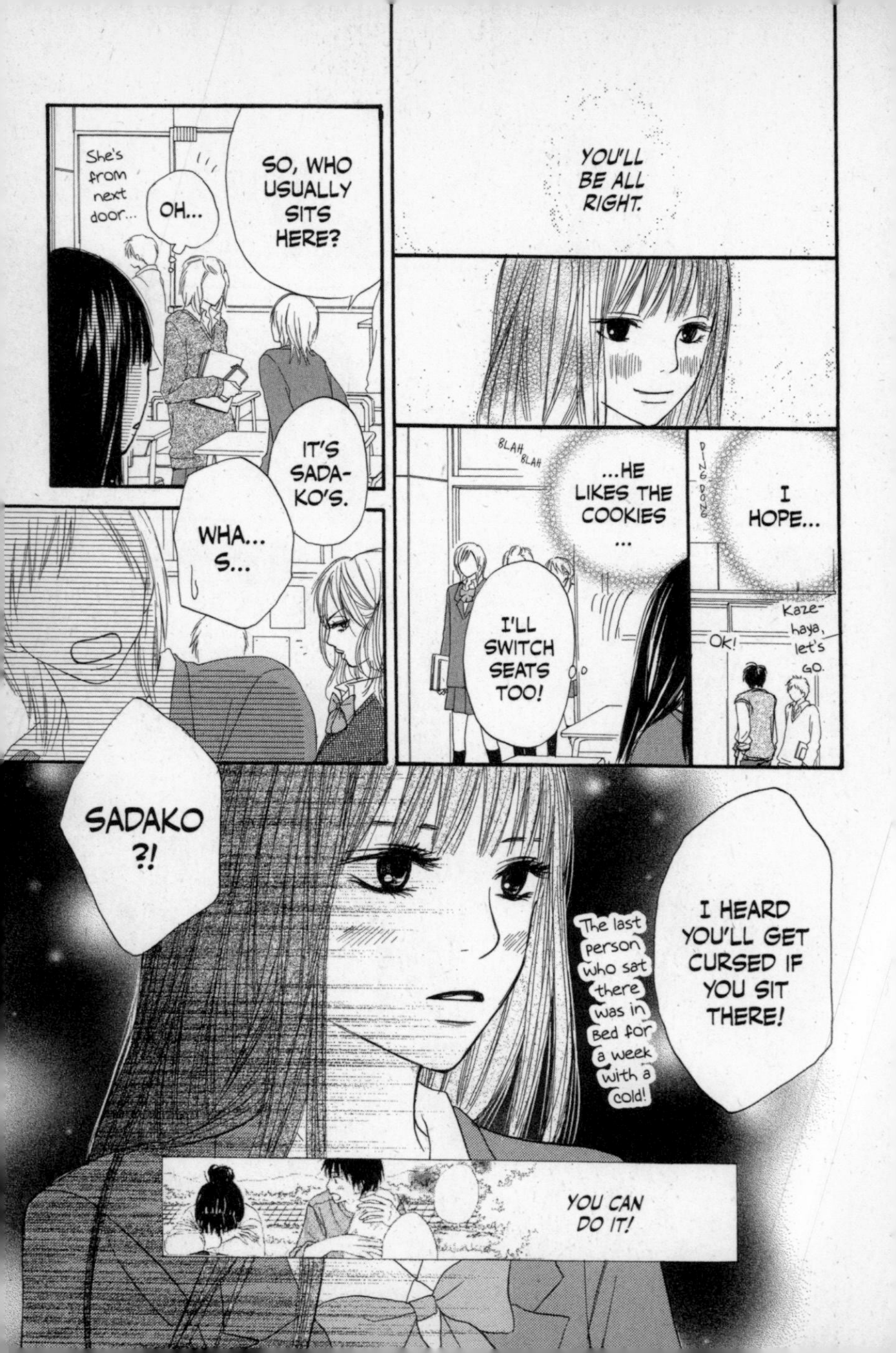
YOU'LL BE ALL RIGHT.
I HOPE...
DING DONG
Kaze-haya, let's GO.
OK!
...HE LIKES THE COOKIES ...
BLAH BLAH
I'LL SWITCH SEATS TOO!
SO, WHO USUALLY SITS HERE?
OH...
She's from next door...
IT'S SADA-KO'S.
WHA... S...
SADAKO ?!
I HEARD YOU'LL GET CURSED IF YOU SIT THERE!
The last person who sat there was in Bed for a week with a cold!
YOU CAN DO IT!

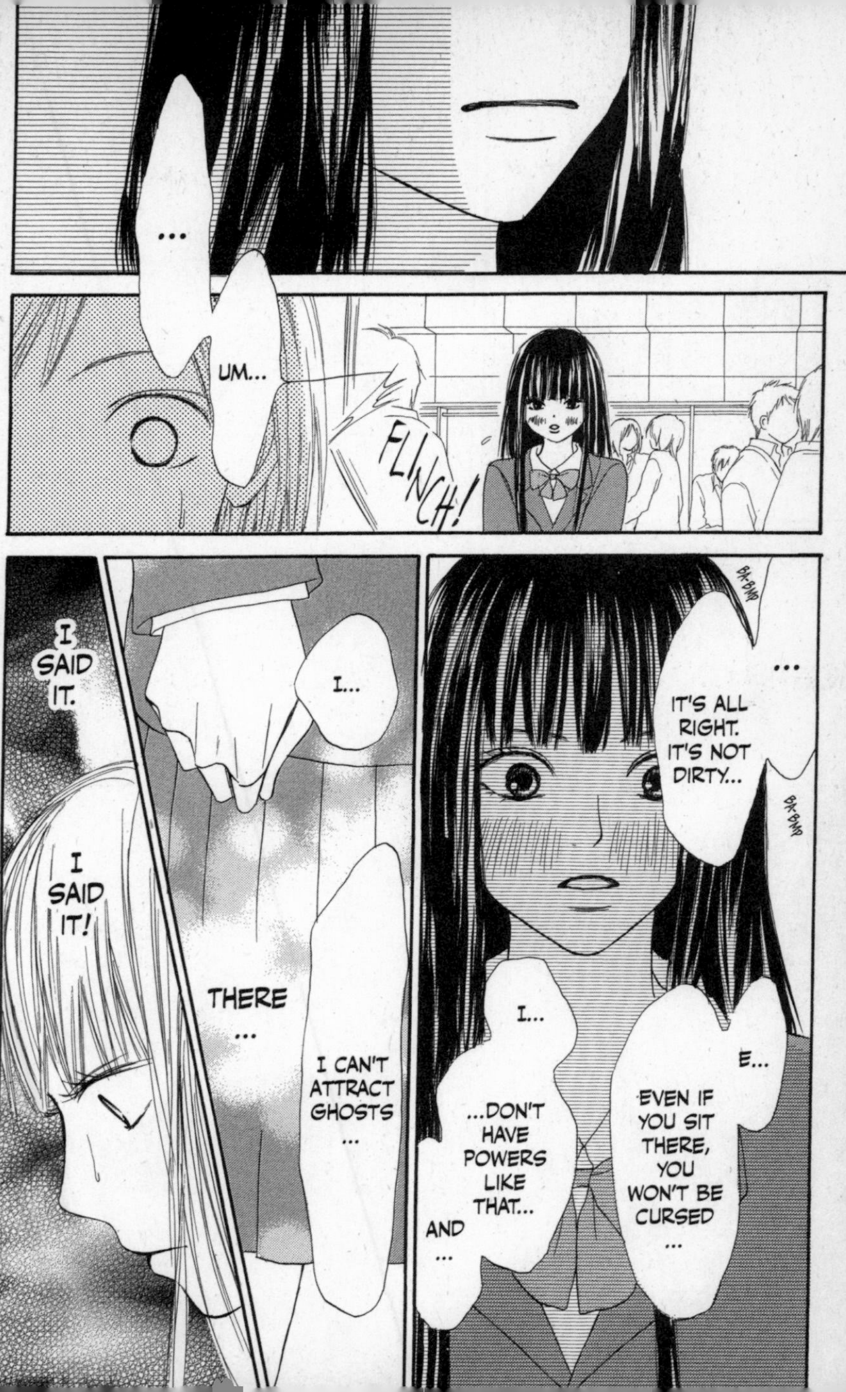
...
UM...
FLINCH!
...
IT'S ALL RIGHT. IT'S NOT DIRTY...
E...
EVEN IF YOU SIT THERE, YOU WON'T BE CURSED ...
I...
...DON'T HAVE POWERS LIKE THAT...
AND ...
I...
I CAN'T ATTRACT GHOSTS ...
THERE ...
I SAID IT.
I SAID IT!

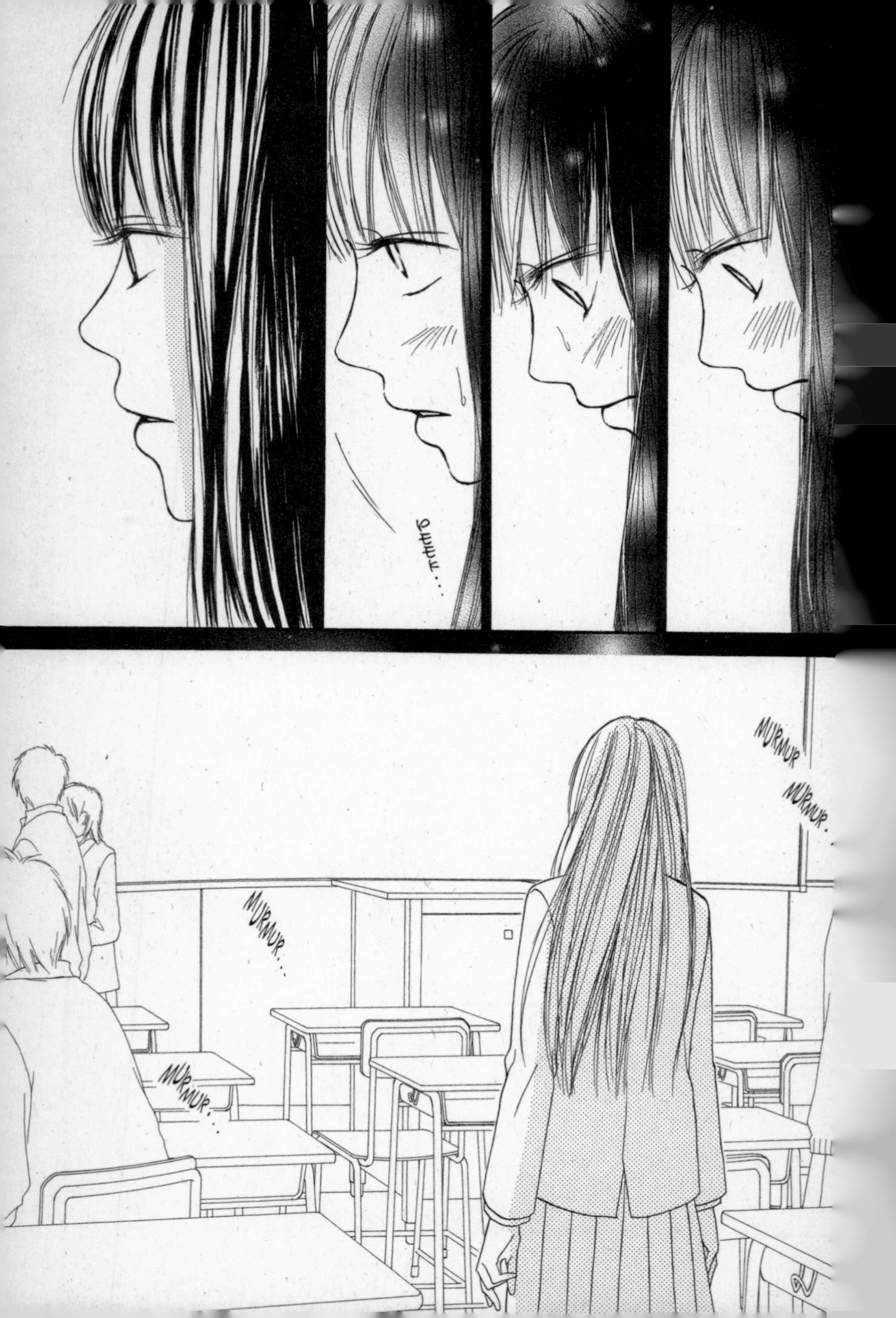
MURMUR
MURMUR...
MURMUR...
MURMUR...

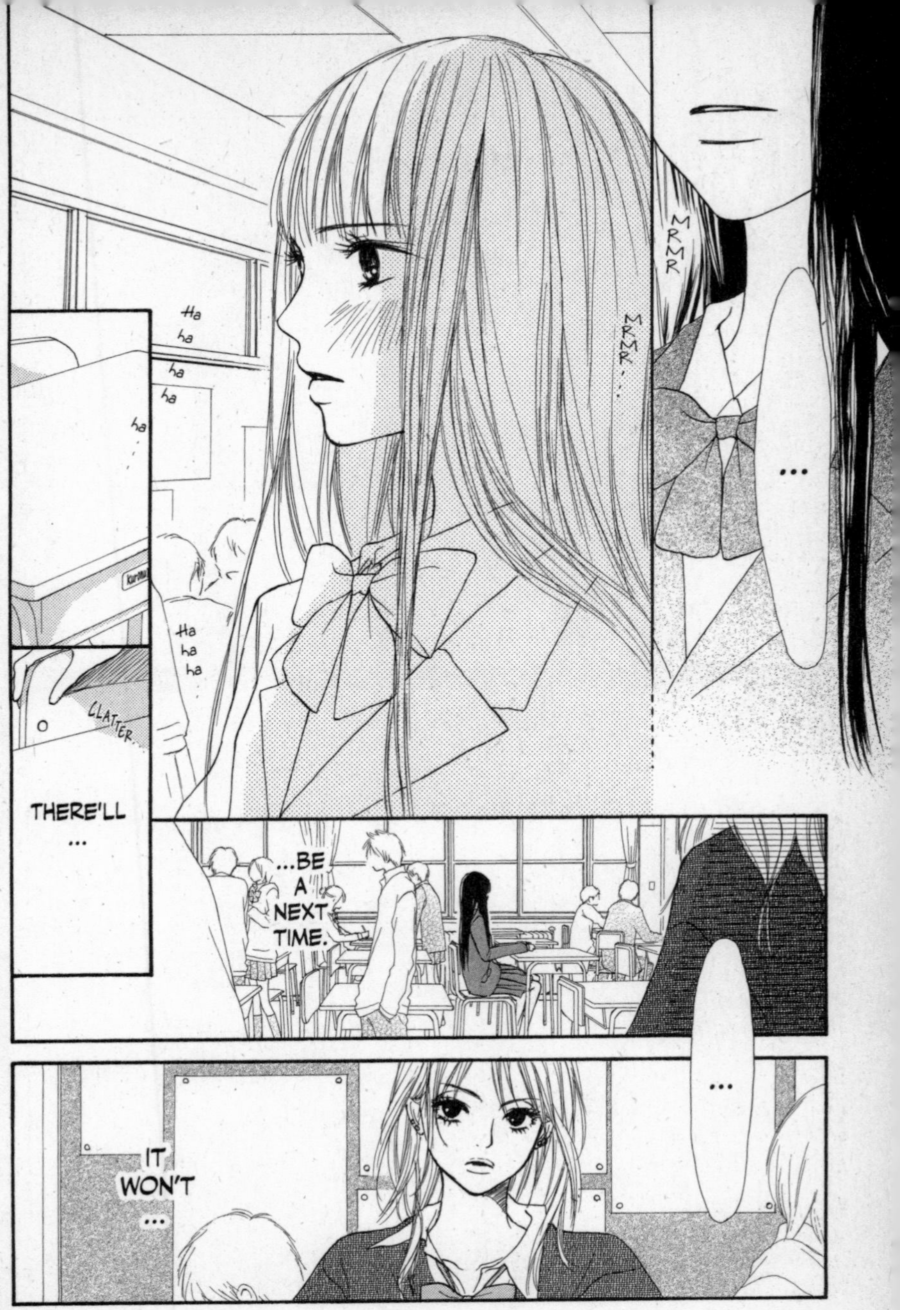
MRMR
MRMR...
...
Ha ha ha ha ha...
Ha ha ha
CLATTER
THERE'LL ...
...BE A NEXT TIME.
...
IT WON'T ...

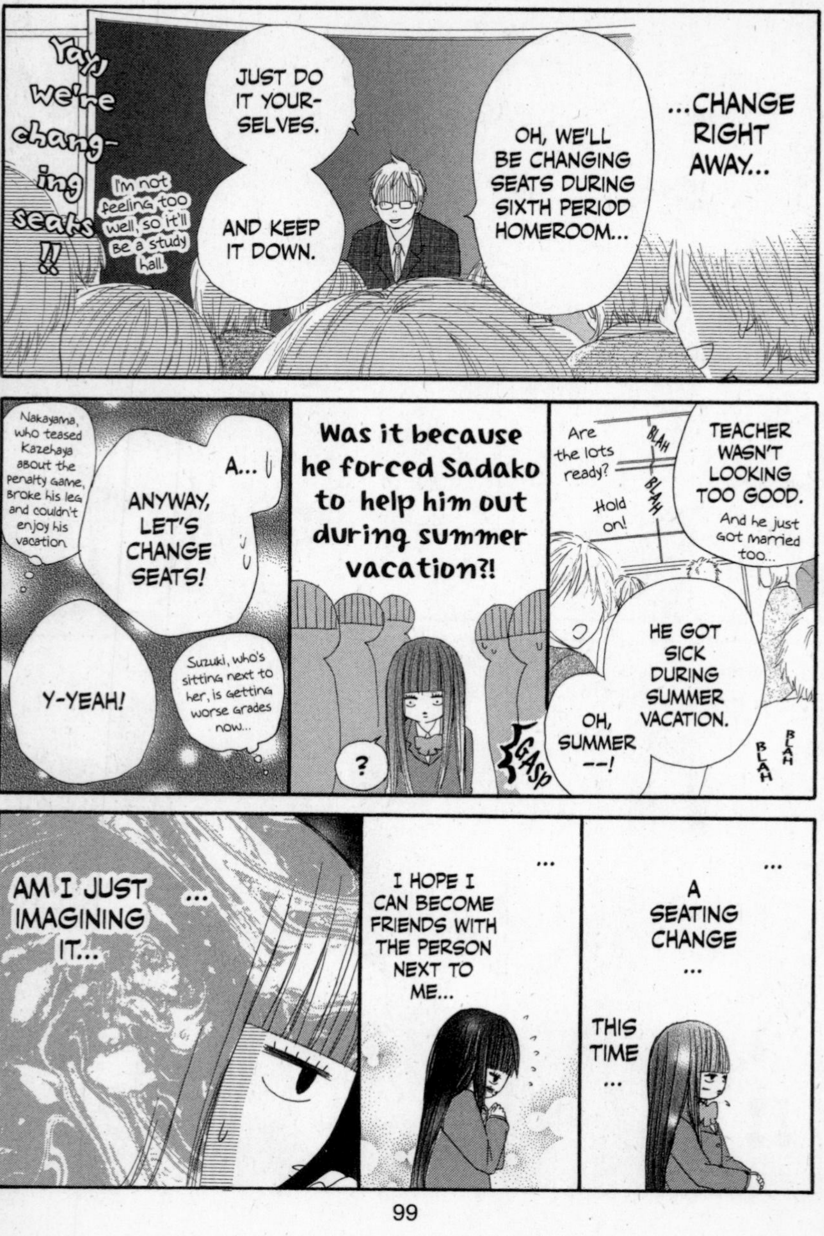
...CHANGE RIGHT AWAY...
OH, WE'LL BE CHANGING SEATS DURING SIXTH PERIOD HOMEROOM...
JUST DO IT YOURSELVES.
AND KEEP IT DOWN.
I'm not feeling too well, so it'll be a study hall.
Yay, we're chang-ing seats!!
TEACHER WASN'T LOOKING TOO GOOD.
And he just got married too...
Are the lots ready?
BLAH
BLAH
Hold on!
HE GOT SICK DURING SUMMER VACATION.
BLAH BLAH
OH, SUMMER--!
GASP
Was it because he forced Sadako to help him out during summer vacation?!
?
A...
ANYWAY, LET'S CHANGE SEATS!
Nakayama, who teased Kazehaya about the penalty game, broke his leg and couldn't enjoy his vacation.
Suzuki, who's sitting next to her, is getting worse grades now...
Y-YEAH!
...
A SEATING CHANGE ...
THIS TIME ...
...
I HOPE I CAN BECOME FRIENDS WITH THE PERSON NEXT TO ME...
...
AM I JUST IMAGINING IT...

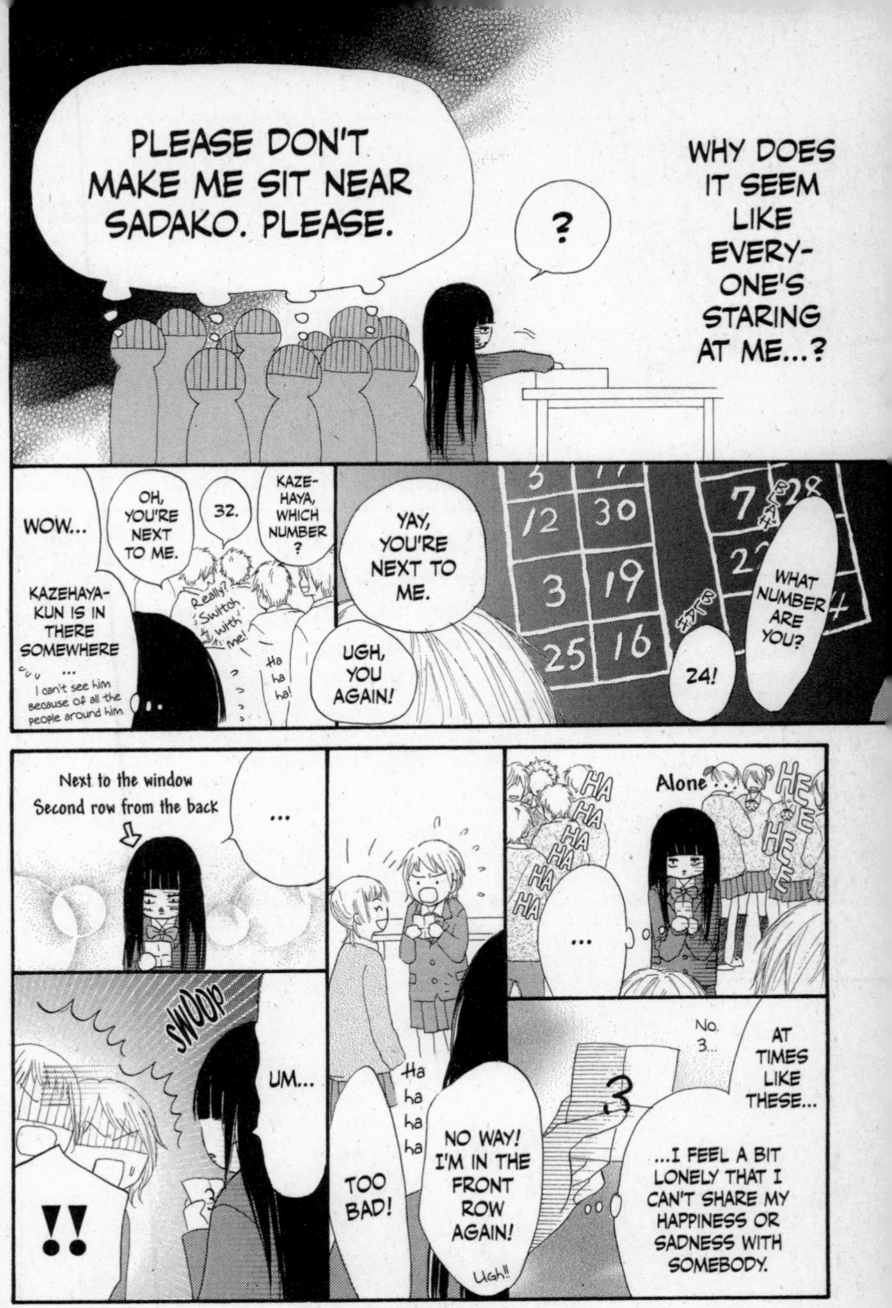

WHY DOES IT SEEM LIKE EVERY-ONE'S STARING AT ME...?
?
PLEASE DON'T MAKE ME SIT NEAR SADAKO. PLEASE.
WHAT NUMBER ARE YOU?
24!
YAY, YOU'RE NEXT TO ME.
UGH, YOU AGAIN!
KAZE-HAYA, WHICH NUMBER ?
32.
OH, YOU'RE NEXT TO ME.
Really? Switch with me!
Ha ha ha!
WOW...
KAZEHAYA-KUN IS IN THERE SOMEWHERE ...
I can't see him because of all the people around him.
HEE HEE
Alone
HA HA HA HA HA HA
...
No. 3...
AT TIMES LIKE THESE...
3
...I FEEL A BIT LONELY THAT I CAN'T SHARE MY HAPPINESS OR SADNESS WITH SOMEBODY.
NO WAY! I'M IN THE FRONT ROW AGAIN!
Ha ha ha ha
TOO BAD!
Ugh!!
...
Next to the window
Second row from the back
SWOOP
UM...
!!

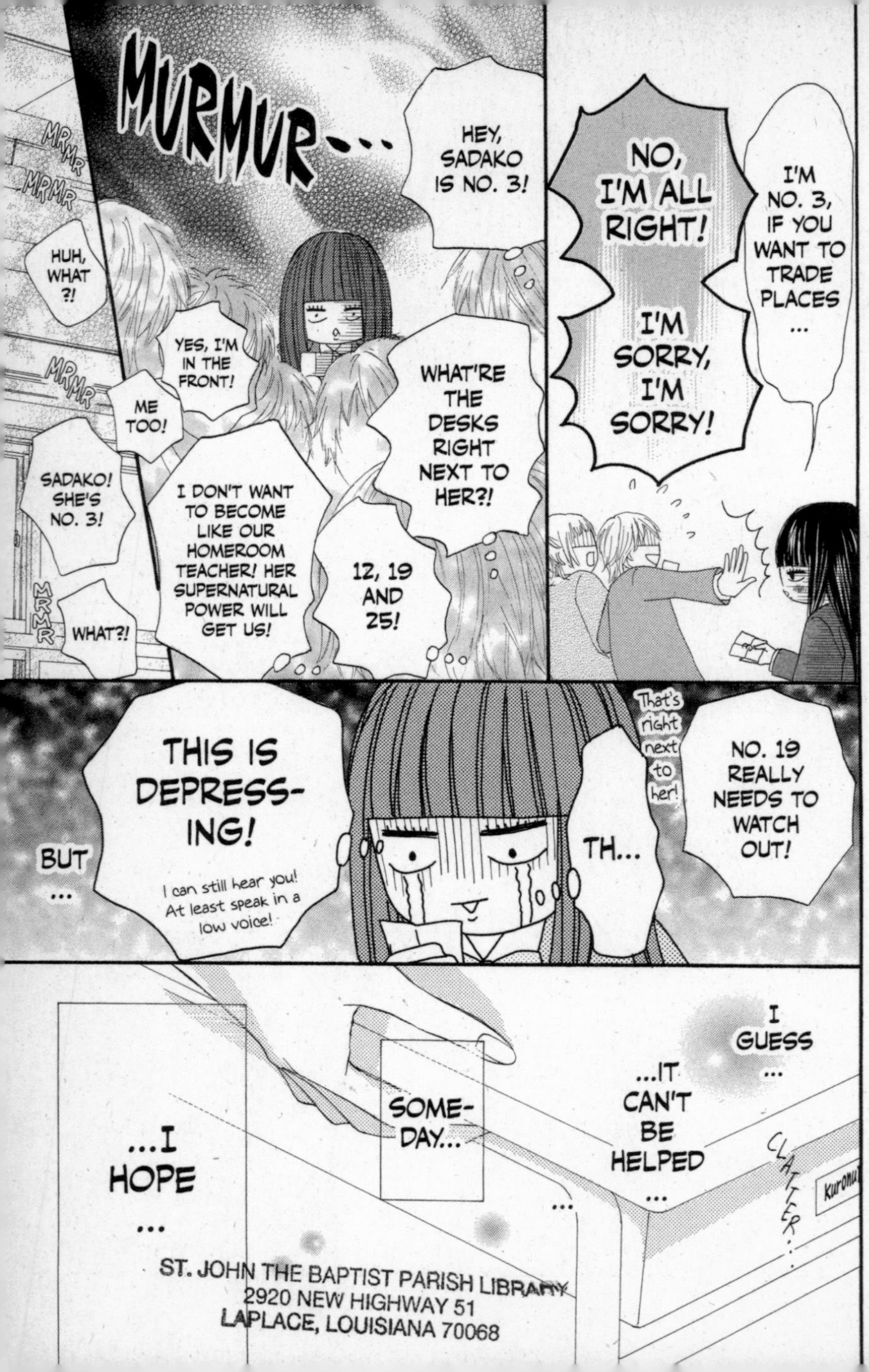
I'M NO. 3, IF YOU WANT TO TRADE PLACES...
NO, I'M ALL RIGHT!
I'M SORRY, I'M SORRY!
MURMUR...
HEY, SADAKO IS NO. 3!
WHAT'RE THE DESKS RIGHT NEXT TO HER?!
12, 19 AND 25!
I DON'T WANT TO BECOME LIKE OUR HOMEROOM TEACHER! HER SUPERNATURAL POWER WILL GET US!
YES, I'M IN THE FRONT!
ME TOO!
MRMR
MRMR
HUH, WHAT ?!
MRMR
SADAKO! SHE'S NO. 3!
MRMR
WHAT?!
NO. 19 REALLY NEEDS TO WATCH OUT!
That's right next to her!
TH...
THIS IS DEPRESS-ING!
I can still hear you! At least speak in a low voice!
BUT...
I GUESS...
...IT CAN'T BE HELPED...
CLATTER...
SOME-DAY...
...I HOPE...

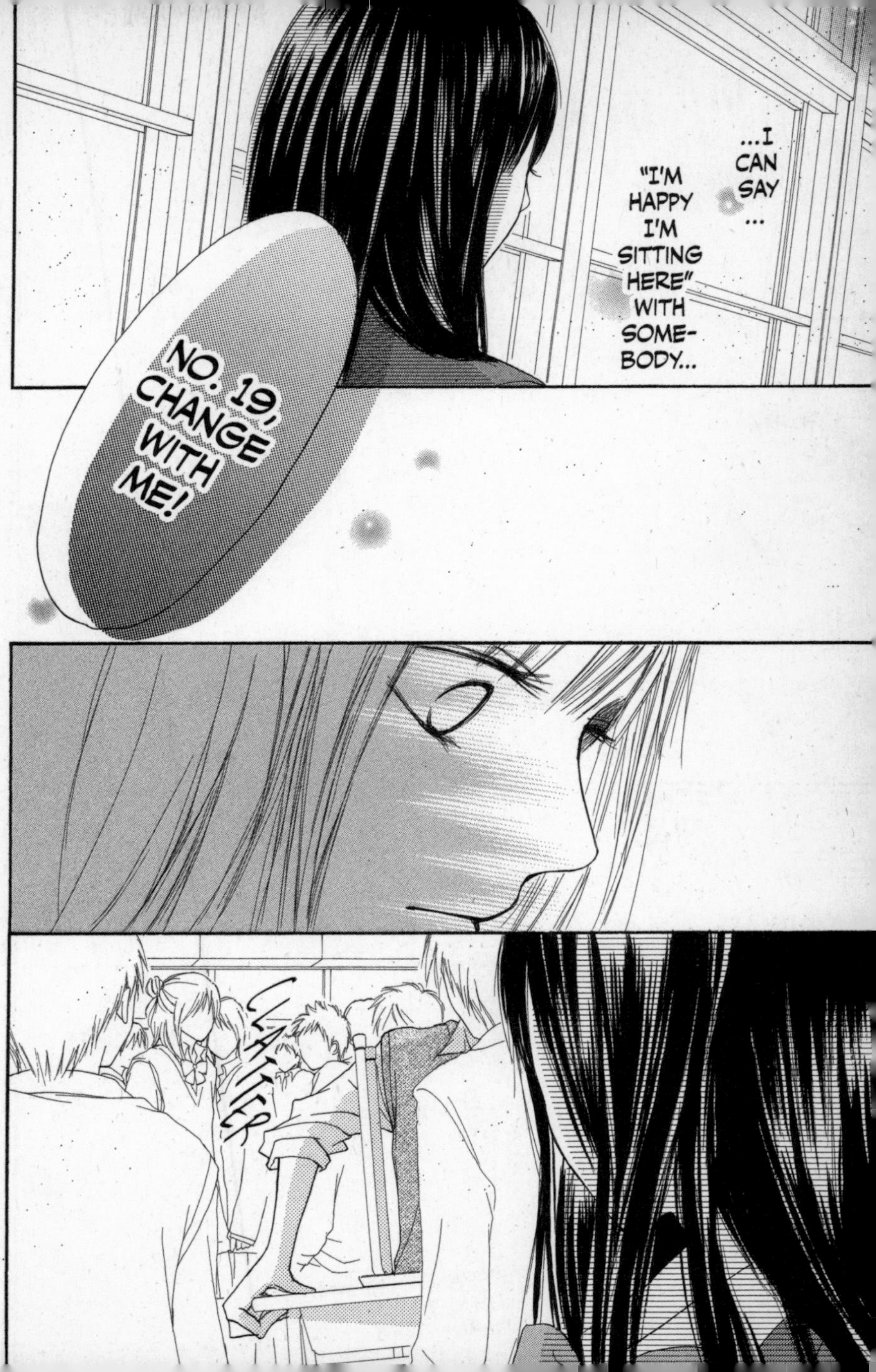
...I CAN SAY ...
"I'M HAPPY I'M SITTING HERE" WITH SOME-BODY...
NO. 19, CHANGE WITH ME!
CLATTER

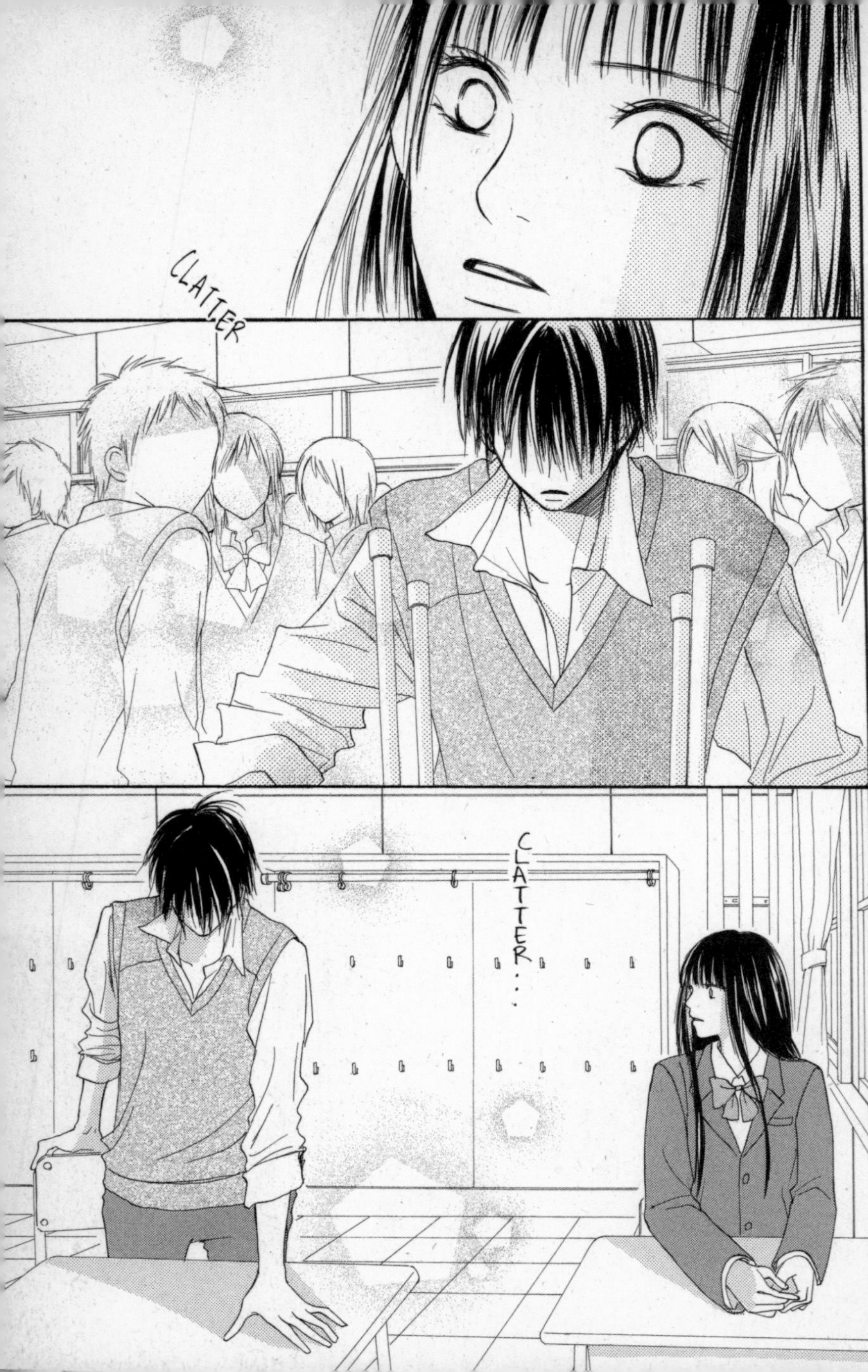
CLATTER
CLATTER...

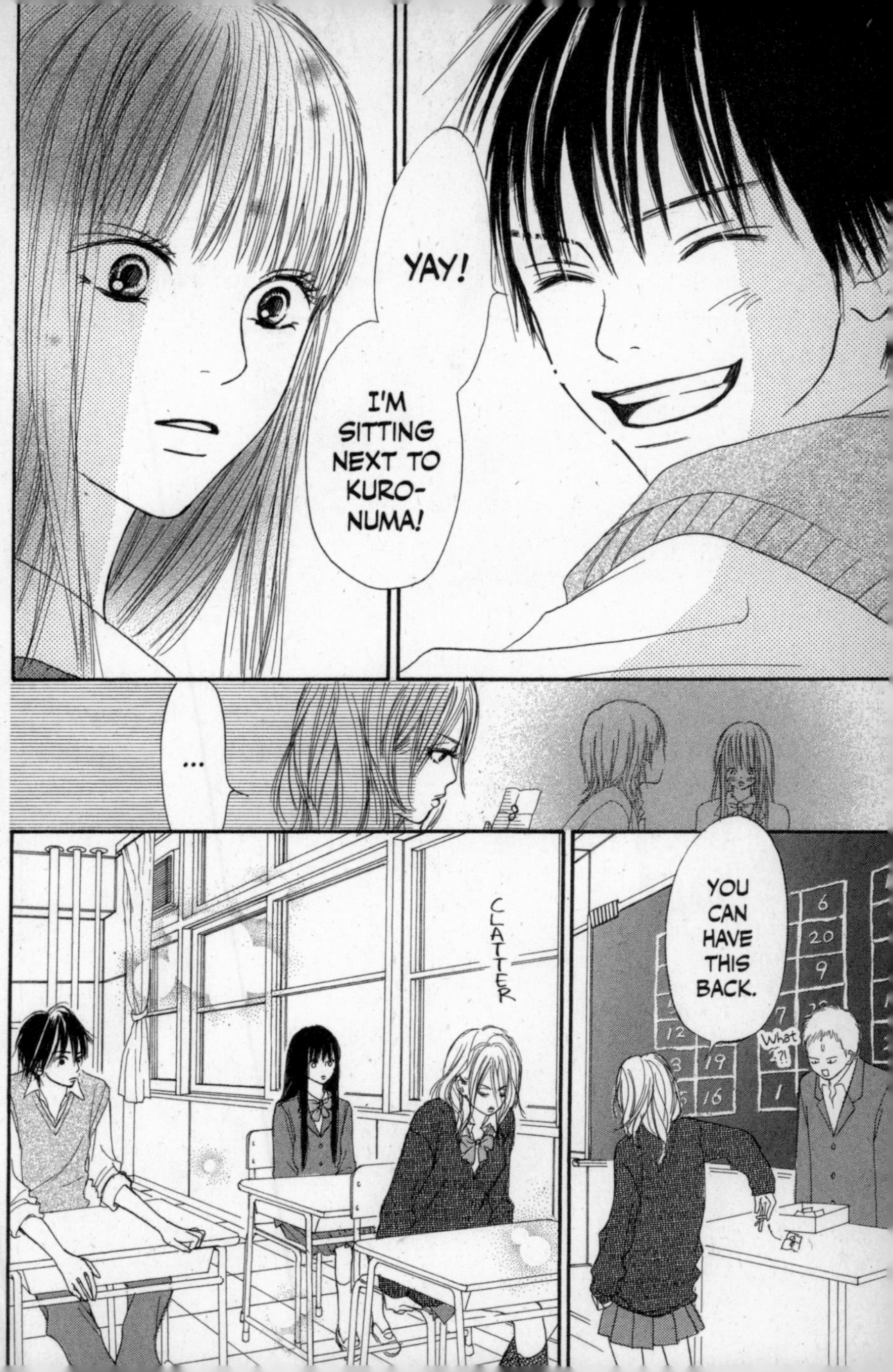
YAY!
I'M SITTING NEXT TO KURO-NUMA!
...
YOU CAN HAVE THIS BACK.
What ?!
CLATTER

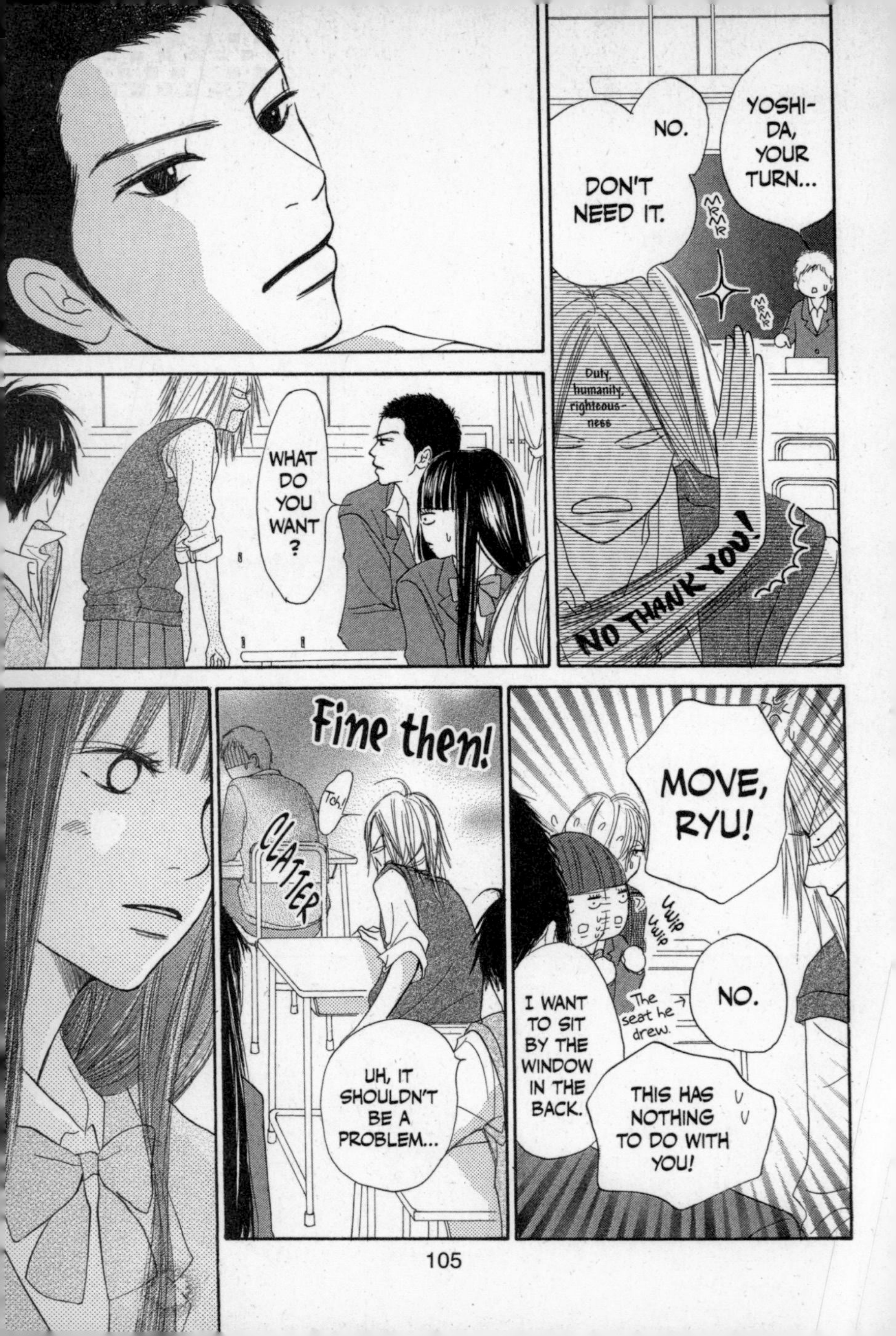
YOSHIDA, YOUR TURN...
NO.
DON'T NEED IT.
MRMR
MRMR
Duty, humanity, righteousness
NO THANK YOU!
WHAT DO YOU WANT?
MOVE, RYU!
Uwip uwip
NO.
The seat he drew.
I WANT TO SIT BY THE WINDOW IN THE BACK.
THIS HAS NOTHING TO DO WITH YOU!
Fine then!
Tch!
CLATTER
UH, IT SHOULDN'T BE A PROBLEM...

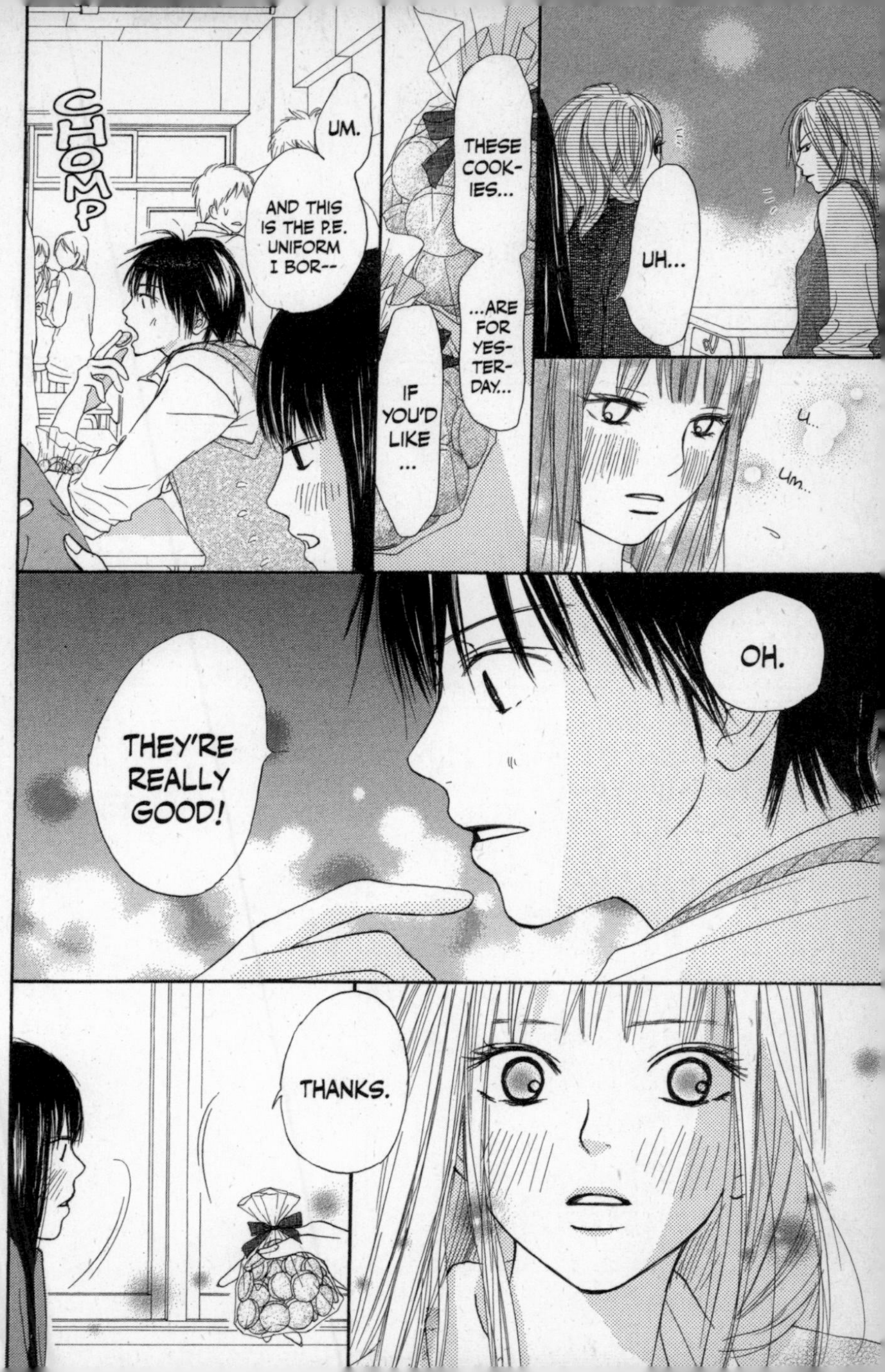
UH...
u..
um..
THESE COOKIES...
...ARE FOR YESTERDAY...
IF YOU'D LIKE ...
UM.
AND THIS IS THE P.E. UNIFORM I BOR--
CHOMP
OH.
THEY'RE REALLY GOOD!
THANKS.

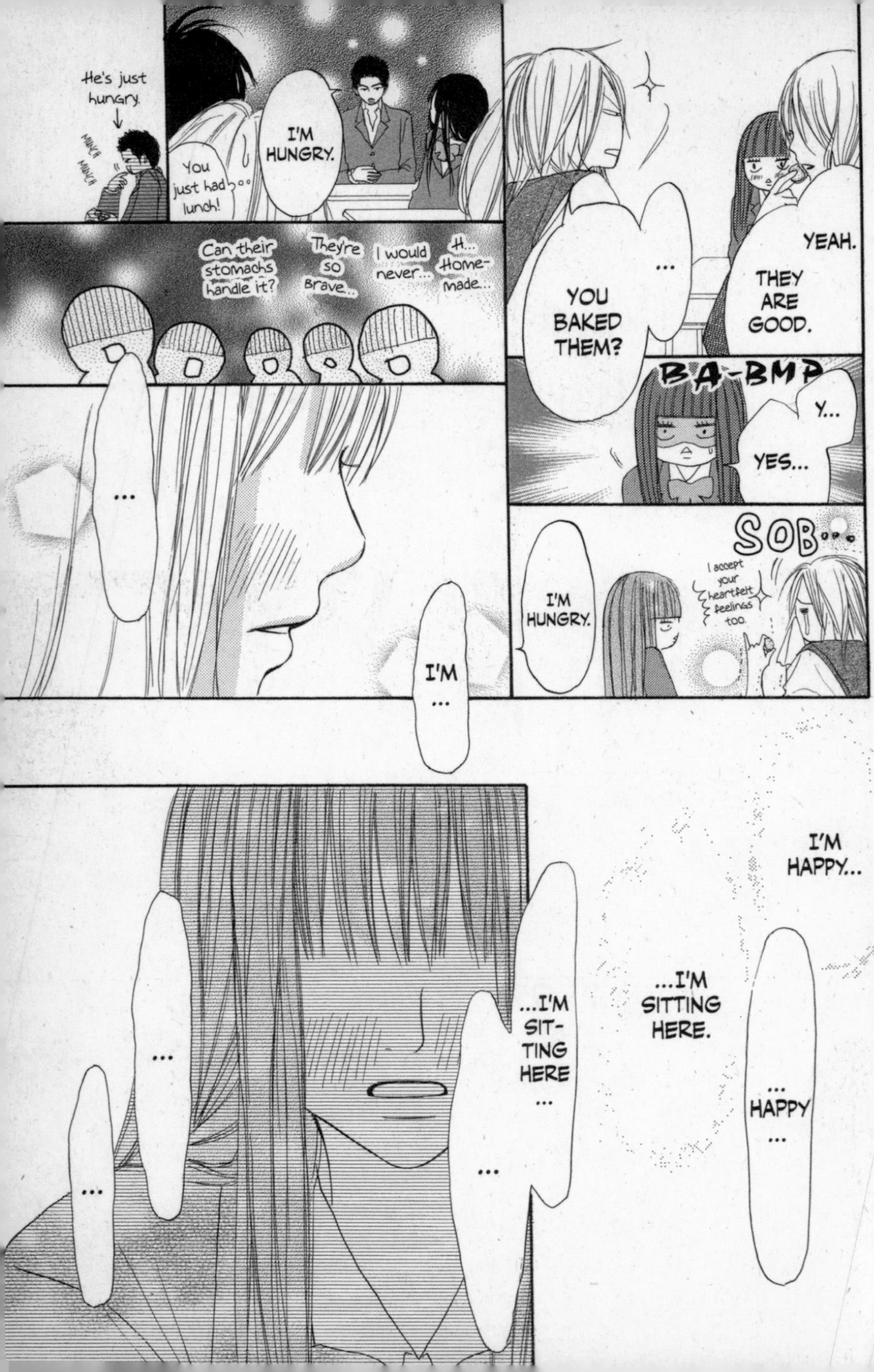
YEAH.
THEY ARE GOOD.
... YOU BAKED THEM?
I'M HUNGRY.
You just had lunch!
He's just hungry.
MUNCH MUNCH
BA-BMP
Y... YES...
H... Home-made...
I would never...
They're so brave...
Can their stomachs handle it?
SOB...
I accept your heartfelt feelings too.
I'M HUNGRY.
I'M ...
...
I'M HAPPY...
... HAPPY ...
...I'M SITTING HERE.
...I'M SIT-TING HERE ...
...
...
...

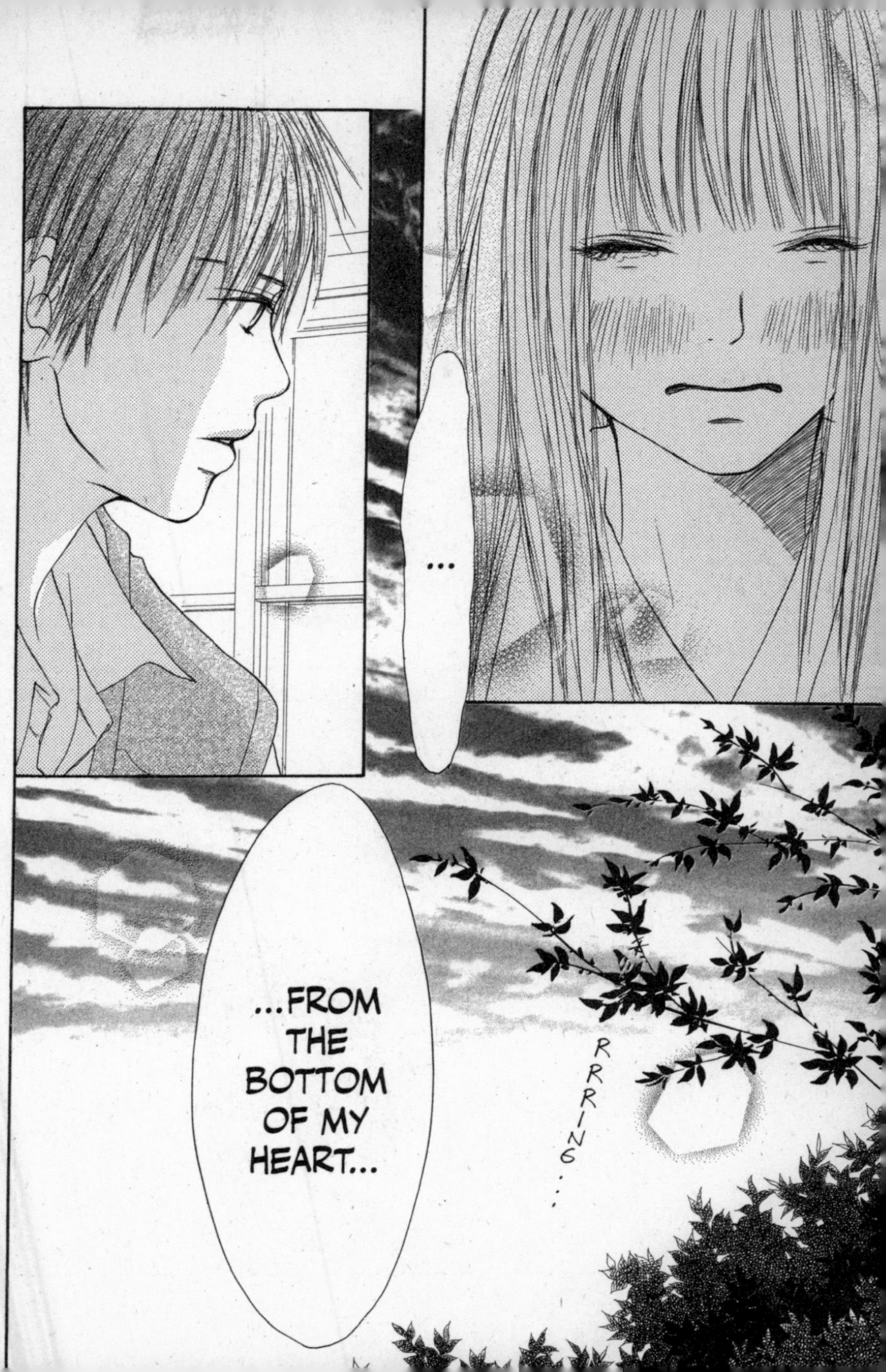
...
...FROM THE BOTTOM OF MY HEART...
RRRING...

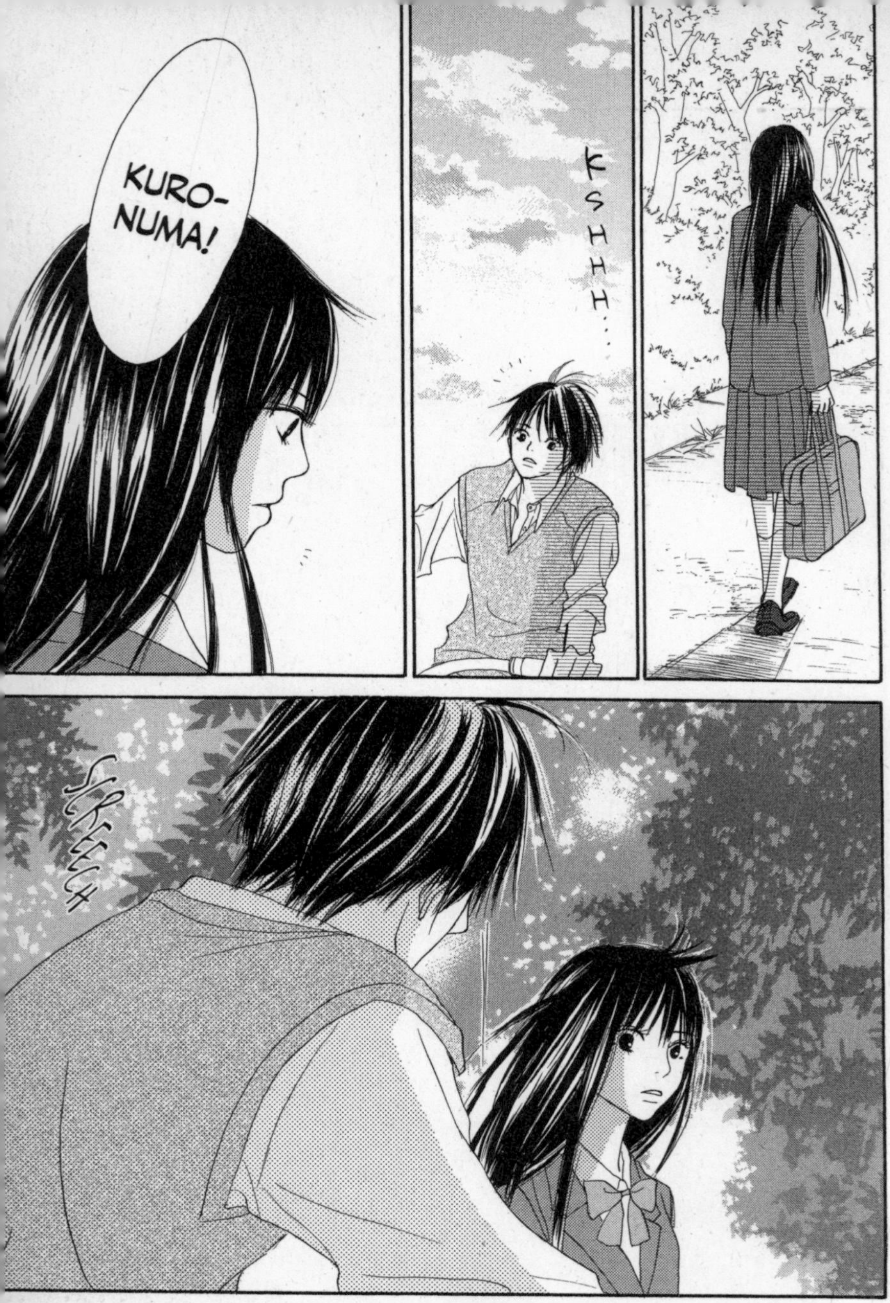
KSHHH...
KURO-NUMA!
SKREECH

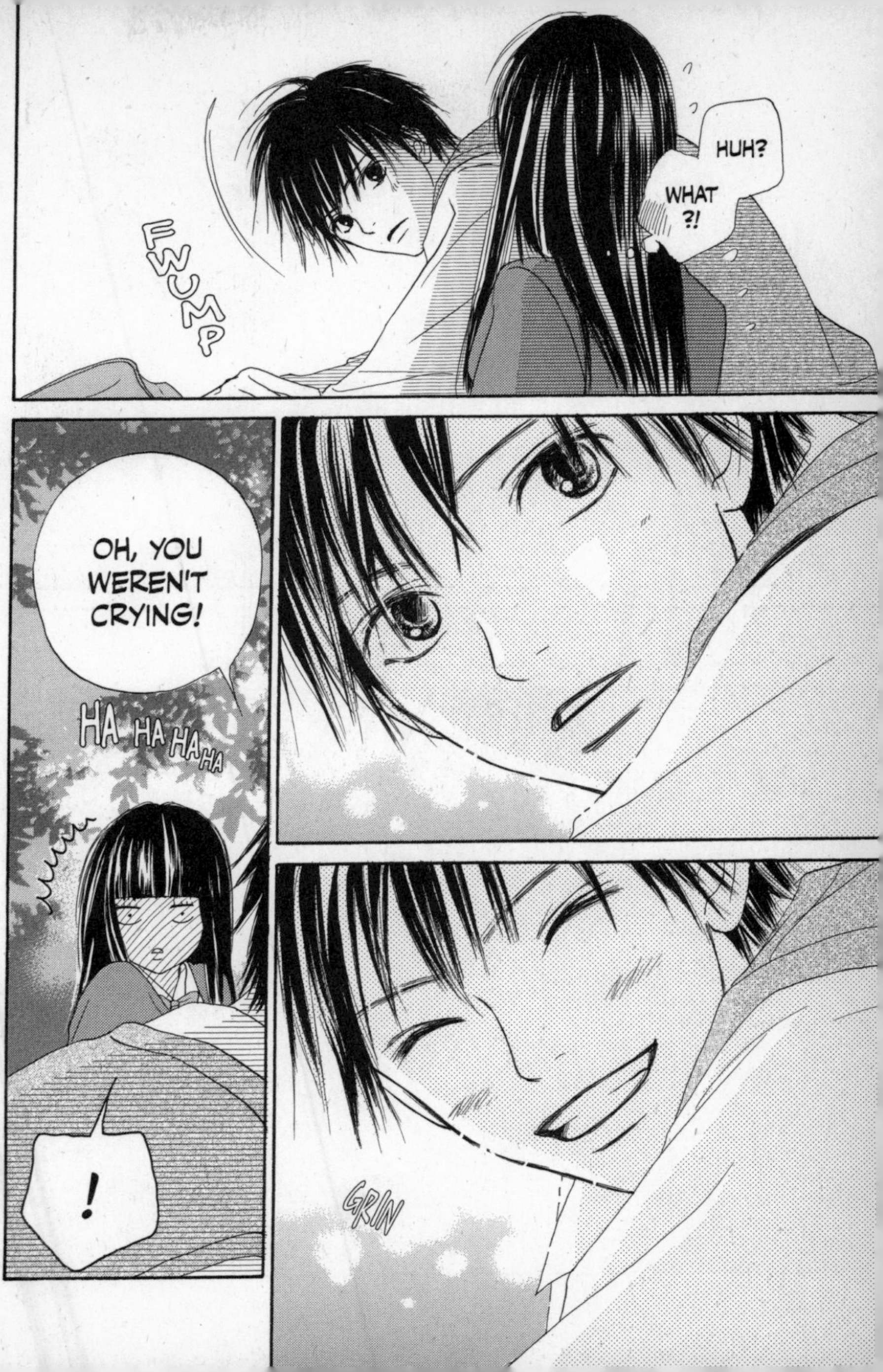
HUH?
WHAT ?!
FWUMP
GRIN
OH, YOU WEREN'T CRYING!
HA HA HA HA
!

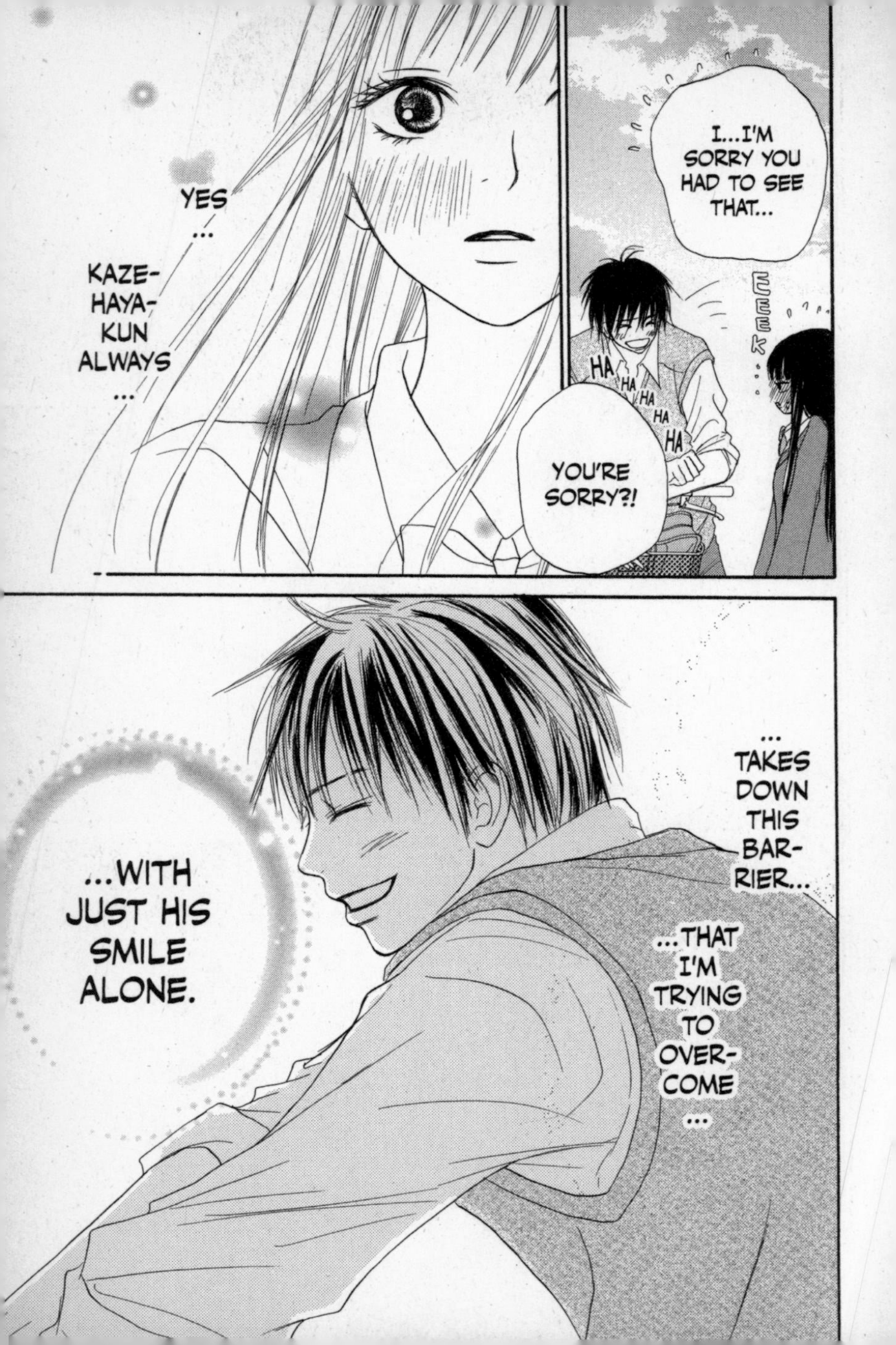
I...I'M SORRY YOU HAD TO SEE THAT...
EEEK...
HA HA HA HA HA HA
YOU'RE SORRY?!
YES...
KAZEHAYA-KUN ALWAYS...
...TAKES DOWN THIS BARRIER...
...THAT I'M TRYING TO OVERCOME...
...WITH JUST HIS SMILE ALONE.

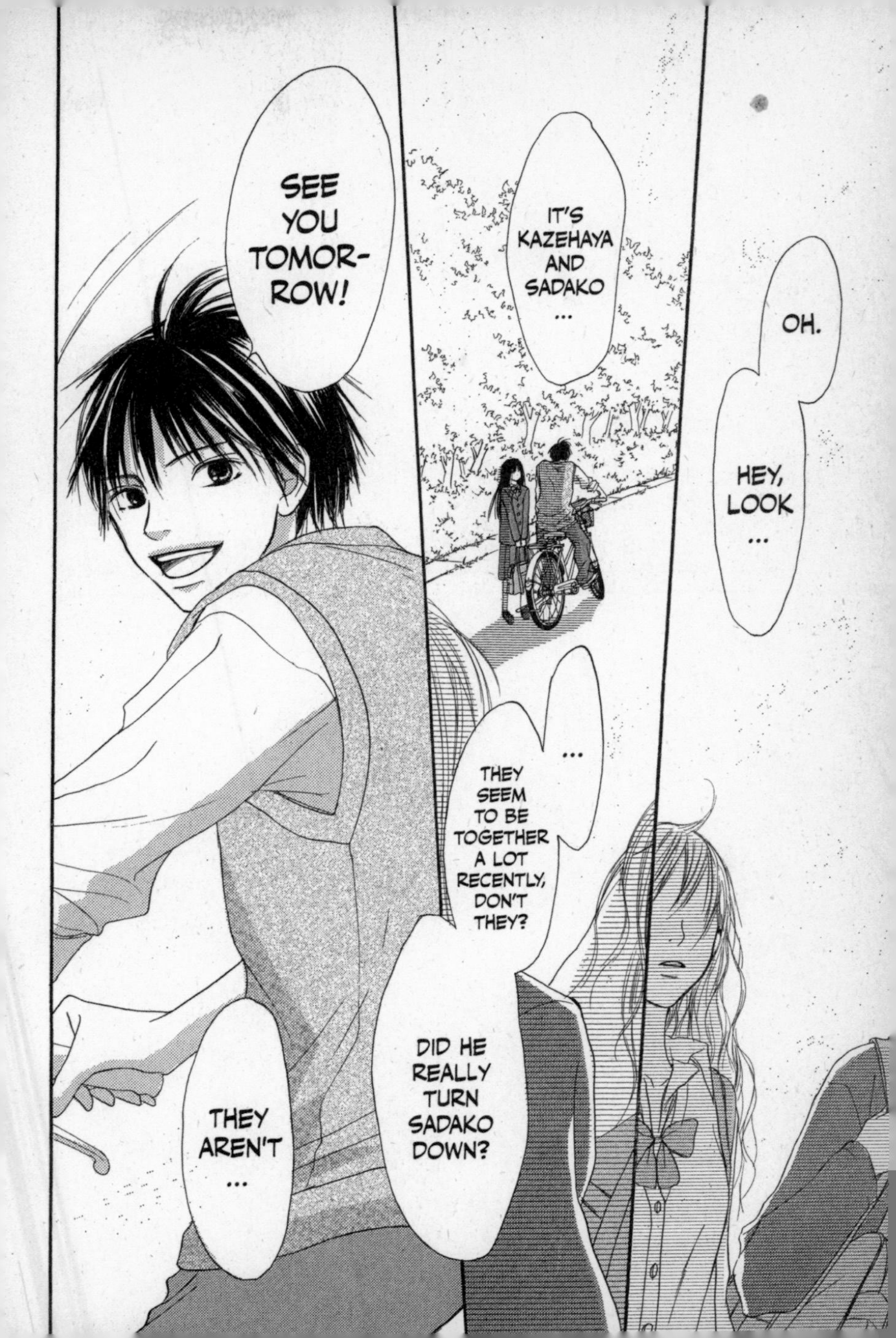

OH.
HEY, LOOK ...
IT'S KAZEHAYA AND SADAKO ...
... THEY SEEM TO BE TOGETHER A LOT RECENTLY, DON'T THEY?
DID HE REALLY TURN SADAKO DOWN?
SEE YOU TOMOR-ROW!
THEY AREN'T ...

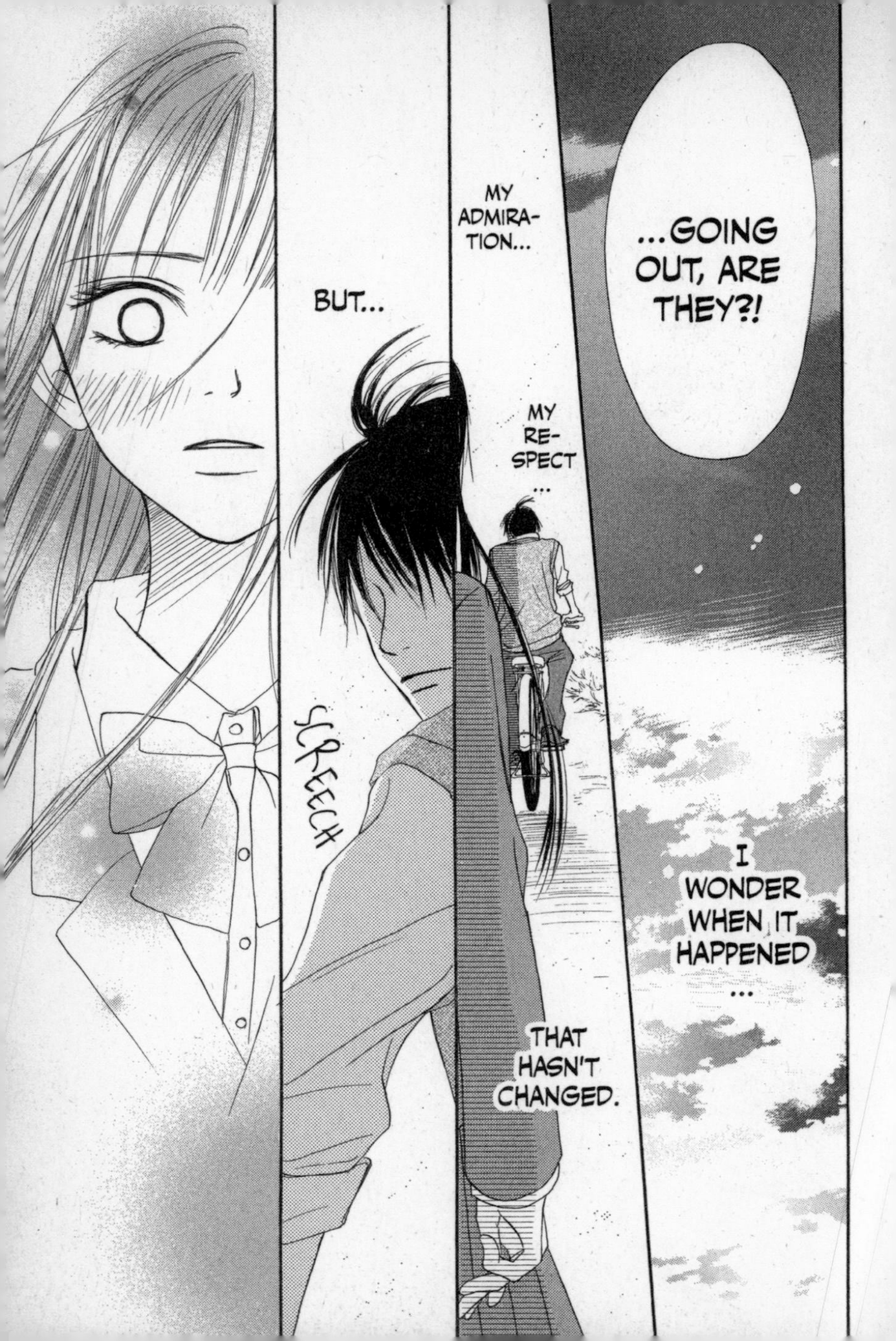
...GOING OUT, ARE THEY?!
I WONDER WHEN IT HAPPENED ...
MY ADMIRA-TION...
MY RE-SPECT ...
THAT HASN'T CHANGED.
BUT...
SCREECH

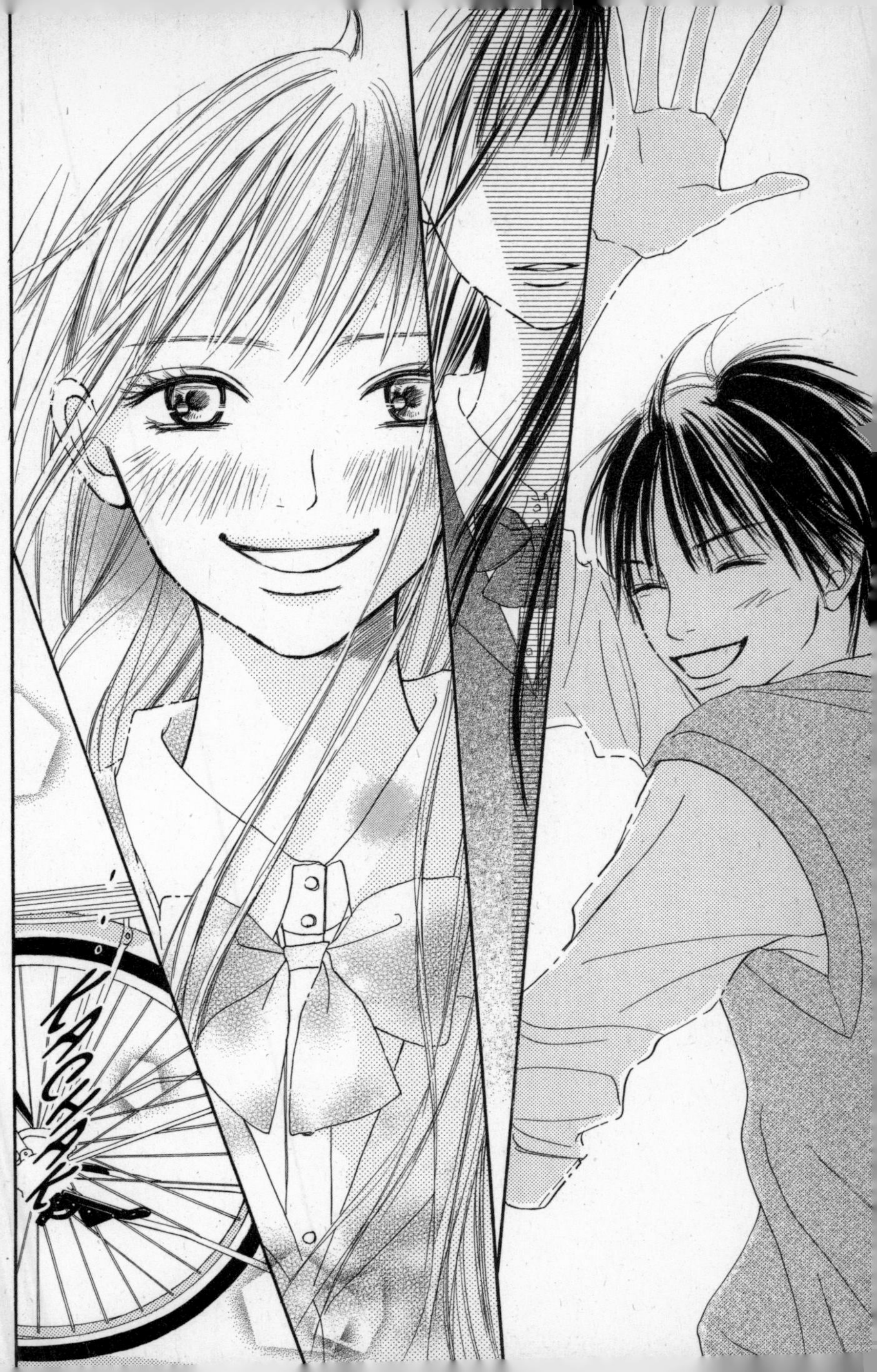
KACHAK

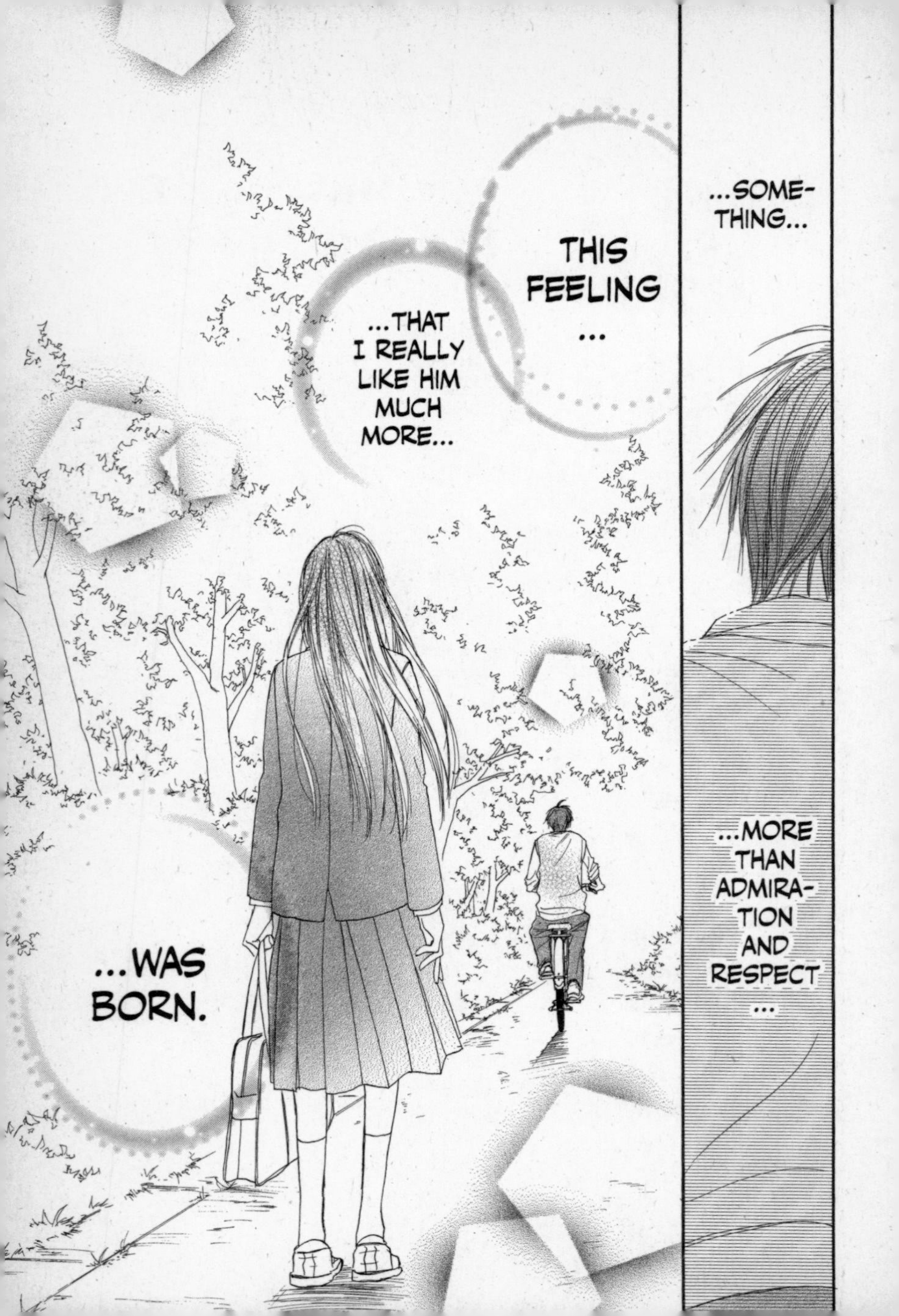
...SOME-THING...
...MORE THAN ADMIRA-TION AND RESPECT...
THIS FEELING...
...THAT I REALLY LIKE HIM MUCH MORE...
...WAS BORN.

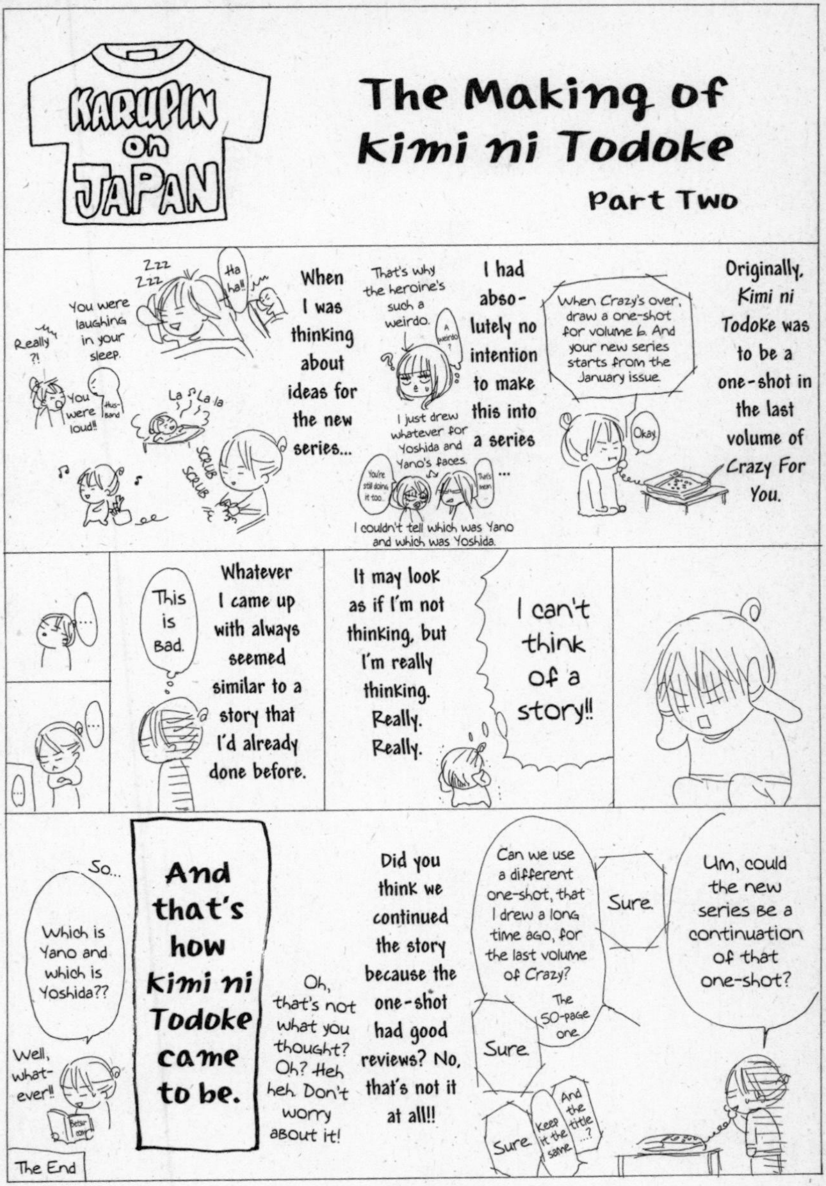

The Making of Kimi ni Todoke
Part Two
KARUPIN on JAPAN
Originally, Kimi ni Todoke was to be a one-shot in the last volume of Crazy For You.
When Crazy's over, draw a one-shot for volume 6. And your new series starts from the January issue.
Okay.
I had absolutely no intention to make this into a series...
That's why the heroine's such a weirdo.
A weirdo?
I just drew whatever for Yoshida and Yano's faces.
You're still doing it too...
That's mean.
I couldn't tell which was Yano and which was Yoshida.
When I was thinking about ideas for the new series...
Ha ha!!
Zzz Zzz
You were laughing in your sleep.
Really?!
You were loud!!
Hus-band
La La la
SCRUB SCRUB
I can't think of a story!!
It may look as if I'm not thinking, but I'm really thinking. Really. Really.
Whatever I came up with always seemed similar to a story that I'd already done before.
This is Bad.
...
...
...
Um, could the new series be a continuation of that one-shot?
Can we use a different one-shot, that I drew a long time ago, for the last volume of Crazy?
Sure.
The 50-page one.
Sure.
And the title...?
Keep it the same.
Sure.
Did you think we continued the story because the one-shot had good reviews? No, that's not it at all!!
Oh, that's not what you thought? Oh? Heh heh. Don't worry about it!
And that's how Kimi ni Todoke came to be.
So...
Which is Yano and which is Yoshida??
Well, whatever!!
The End

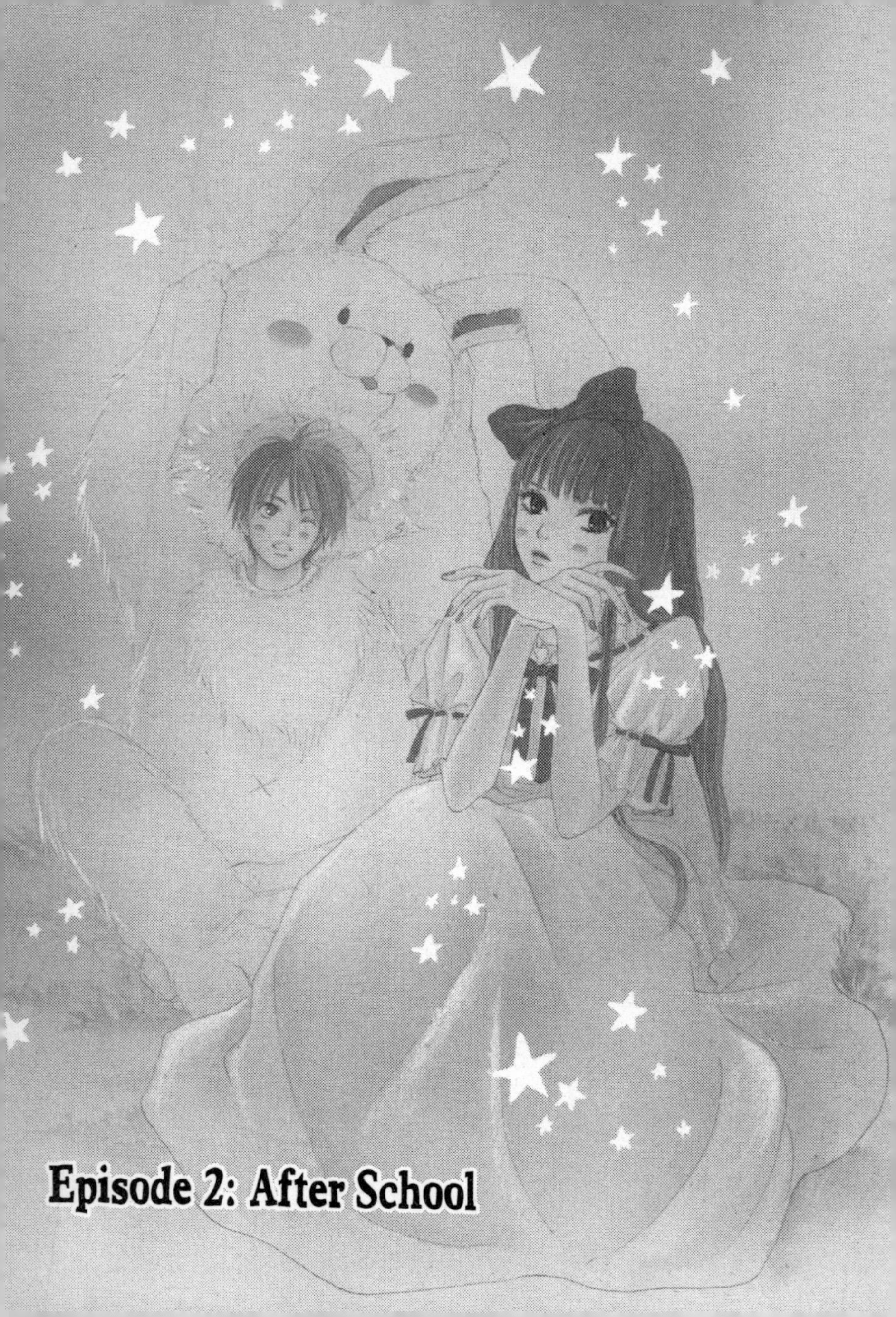

Episode 2: After School

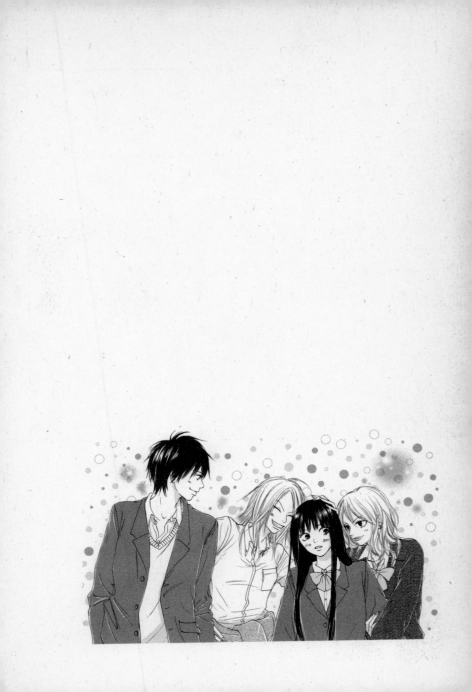

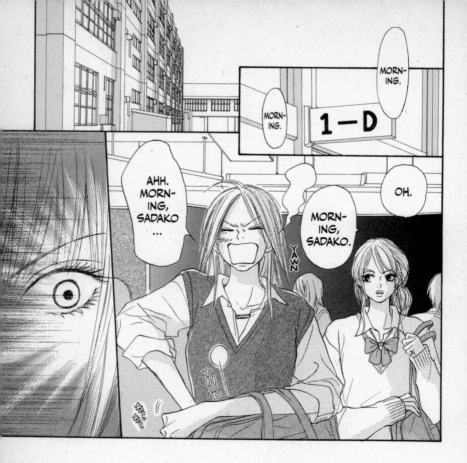

MORN-
ING.

MORN-
ING.

1—D

OH.

AHH.
MORN-
ING,
SADAKO
...

MORN-
ING,
SADAKO.

YAWN

THUD

SCRITCH
SCRITCH

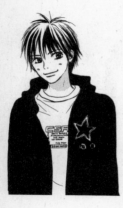

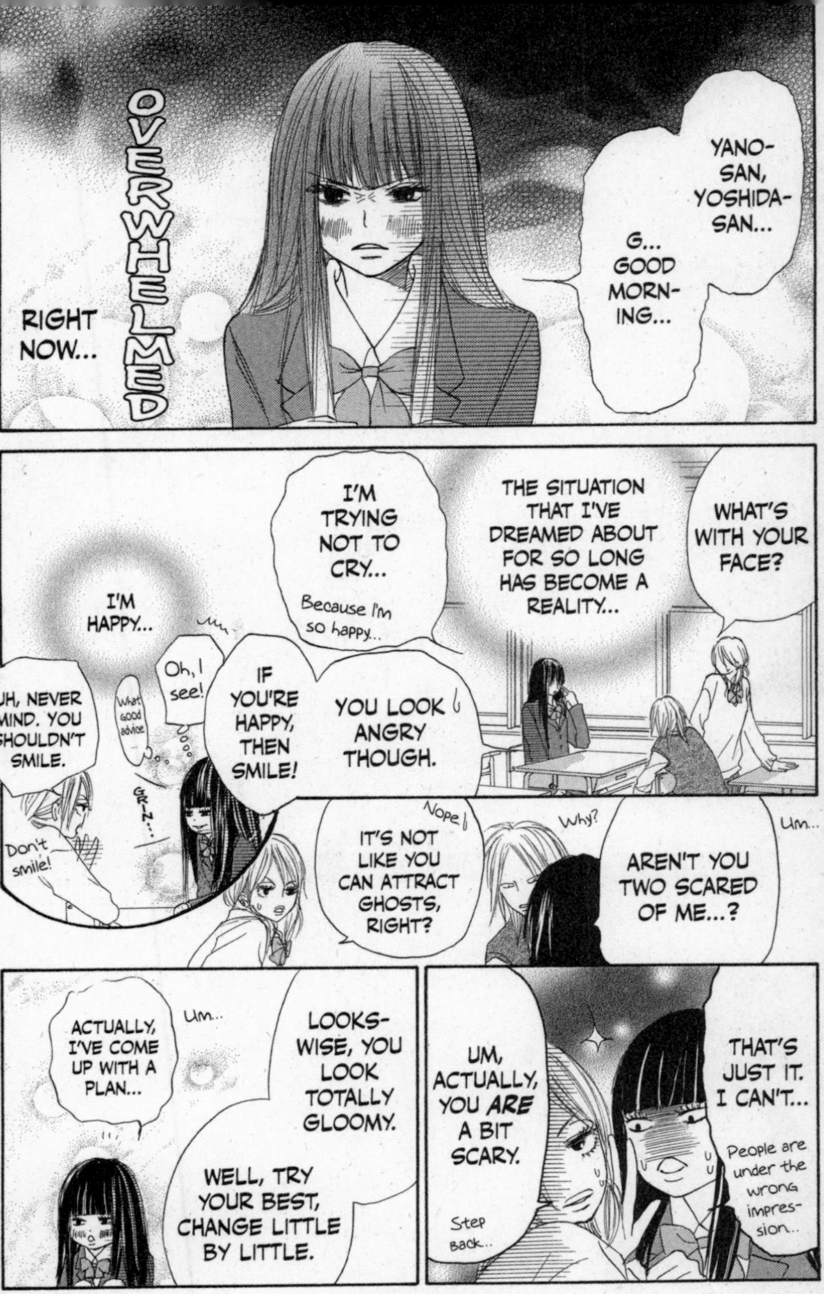
YANO-SAN, YOSHIDA-SAN...
G... GOOD MORNING...
OVERWHELMED
RIGHT NOW...
WHAT'S WITH YOUR FACE?
THE SITUATION THAT I'VE DREAMED ABOUT FOR SO LONG HAS BECOME A REALITY...
I'M TRYING NOT TO CRY...
Because I'm so happy...
I'M HAPPY...
YOU LOOK ANGRY THOUGH.
IF YOU'RE HAPPY, THEN SMILE!
Oh, I see!
What good advice...
GRIN...
UH, NEVER MIND. YOU SHOULDN'T SMILE.
Don't smile!
Um...
AREN'T YOU TWO SCARED OF ME...?
Why?
Nope!
IT'S NOT LIKE YOU CAN ATTRACT GHOSTS, RIGHT?
THAT'S JUST IT. I CAN'T...
People are under the wrong impression...
UM, ACTUALLY, YOU *ARE* A BIT SCARY.
Step back...
LOOKS-WISE, YOU LOOK TOTALLY GLOOMY.
WELL, TRY YOUR BEST, CHANGE LITTLE BY LITTLE.
Um...
ACTUALLY, I'VE COME UP WITH A PLAN...

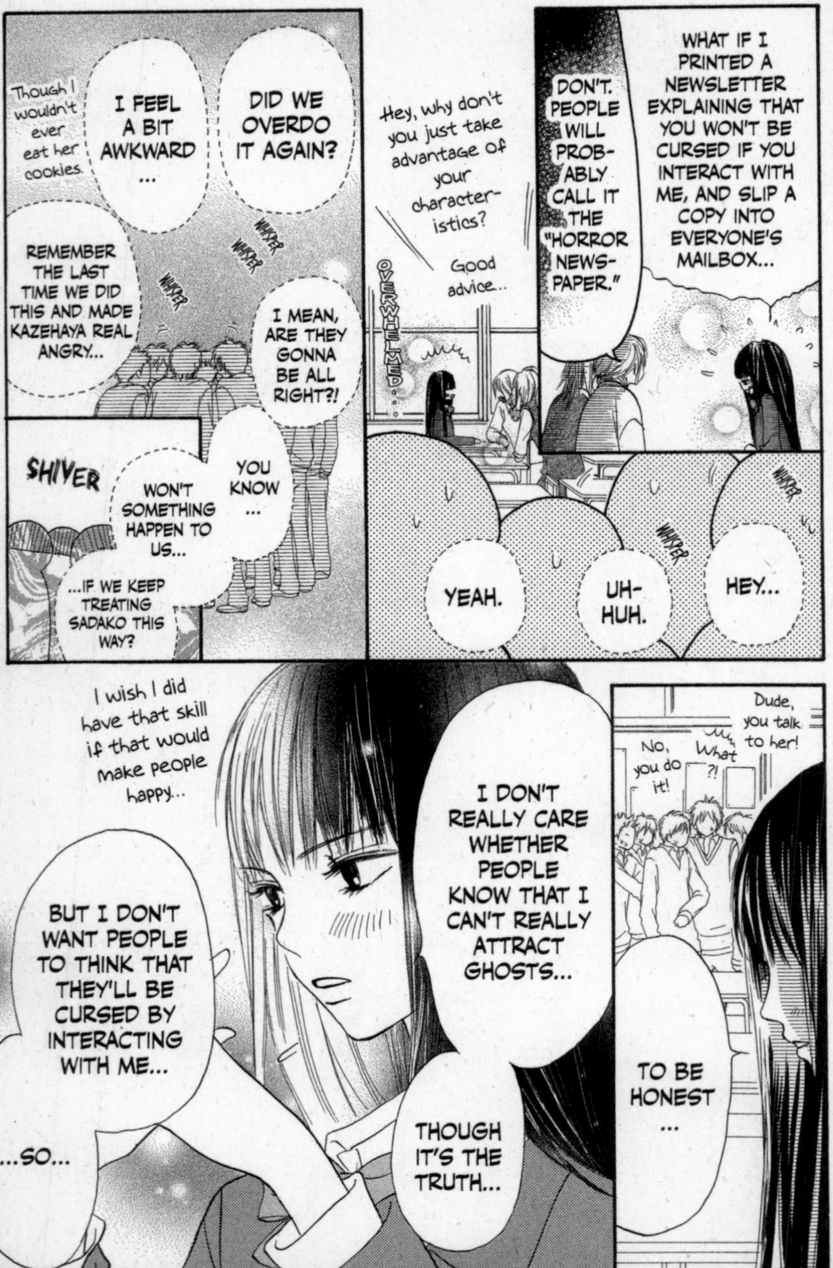
WHAT IF I PRINTED A NEWSLETTER EXPLAINING THAT YOU WON'T BE CURSED IF YOU INTERACT WITH ME, AND SLIP A COPY INTO EVERYONE'S MAILBOX...
DON'T. PEOPLE WILL PROBABLY CALL IT THE "HORROR NEWSPAPER."
Hey, why don't you just take advantage of your characteristics?
Good advice...
OVERWHELMED...
DID WE OVERDO IT AGAIN?
I FEEL A BIT AWKWARD...
Though I wouldn't ever eat her cookies.
WHISPER
WHISPER
WHISPER
REMEMBER THE LAST TIME WE DID THIS AND MADE KAZEHAYA REAL ANGRY...
I MEAN, ARE THEY GONNA BE ALL RIGHT?!
WHISPER
WHISPER
HEY...
UH-HUH.
YEAH.
SHIVER
YOU KNOW...
WON'T SOMETHING HAPPEN TO US...
...IF WE KEEP TREATING SADAKO THIS WAY?
Dude, you talk to her!
What?!
No, you do it!
TO BE HONEST...
I DON'T REALLY CARE WHETHER PEOPLE KNOW THAT I CAN'T REALLY ATTRACT GHOSTS...
THOUGH IT'S THE TRUTH...
I wish I did have that skill if that would make people happy...
BUT I DON'T WANT PEOPLE TO THINK THAT THEY'LL BE CURSED BY INTERACTING WITH ME...
...SO...

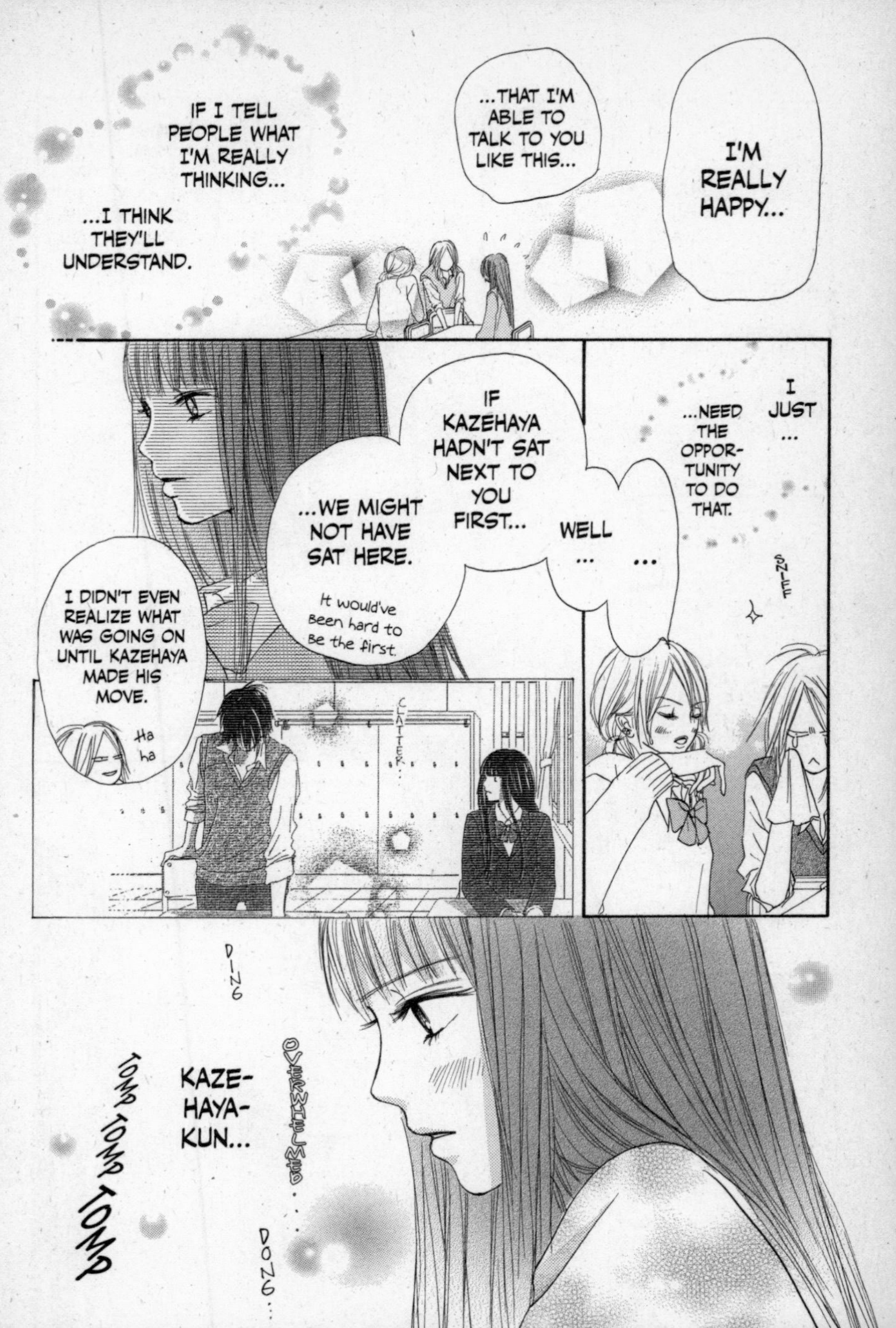
I'M REALLY HAPPY...
...THAT I'M ABLE TO TALK TO YOU LIKE THIS...
IF I TELL PEOPLE WHAT I'M REALLY THINKING...
...I THINK THEY'LL UNDERSTAND.
...
I JUST ...
...NEED THE OPPORTUNITY TO DO THAT.
SNIFF
WELL ... ...
IF KAZEHAYA HADN'T SAT NEXT TO YOU FIRST...
...WE MIGHT NOT HAVE SAT HERE.
It would've been hard to be the first.
I DIDN'T EVEN REALIZE WHAT WAS GOING ON UNTIL KAZEHAYA MADE HIS MOVE.
Ha ha
CLATTER...
DING
KAZE-HAYA-KUN...
OVERWHELMED...
DONG...
TOMP TOMP TOMP TOMP

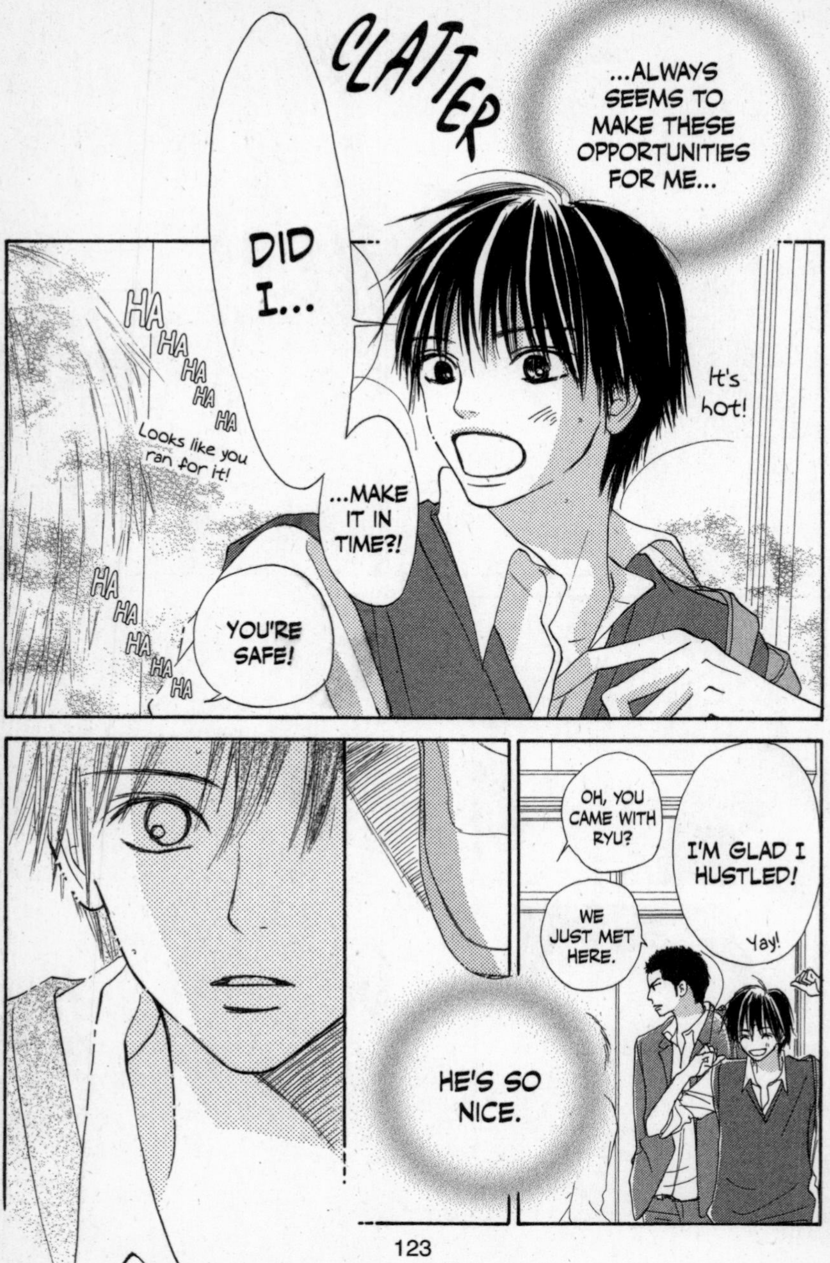
...ALWAYS SEEMS TO MAKE THESE OPPORTUNITIES FOR ME...
CLATTER
DID I...
It's hot!
...MAKE IT IN TIME?!
HA HA HA HA HA
Looks like you ran for it!
YOU'RE SAFE!
HA HA HA HA HA
I'M GLAD I HUSTLED!
Yay!
OH, YOU CAME WITH RYU?
WE JUST MET HERE.
HE'S SO NICE.

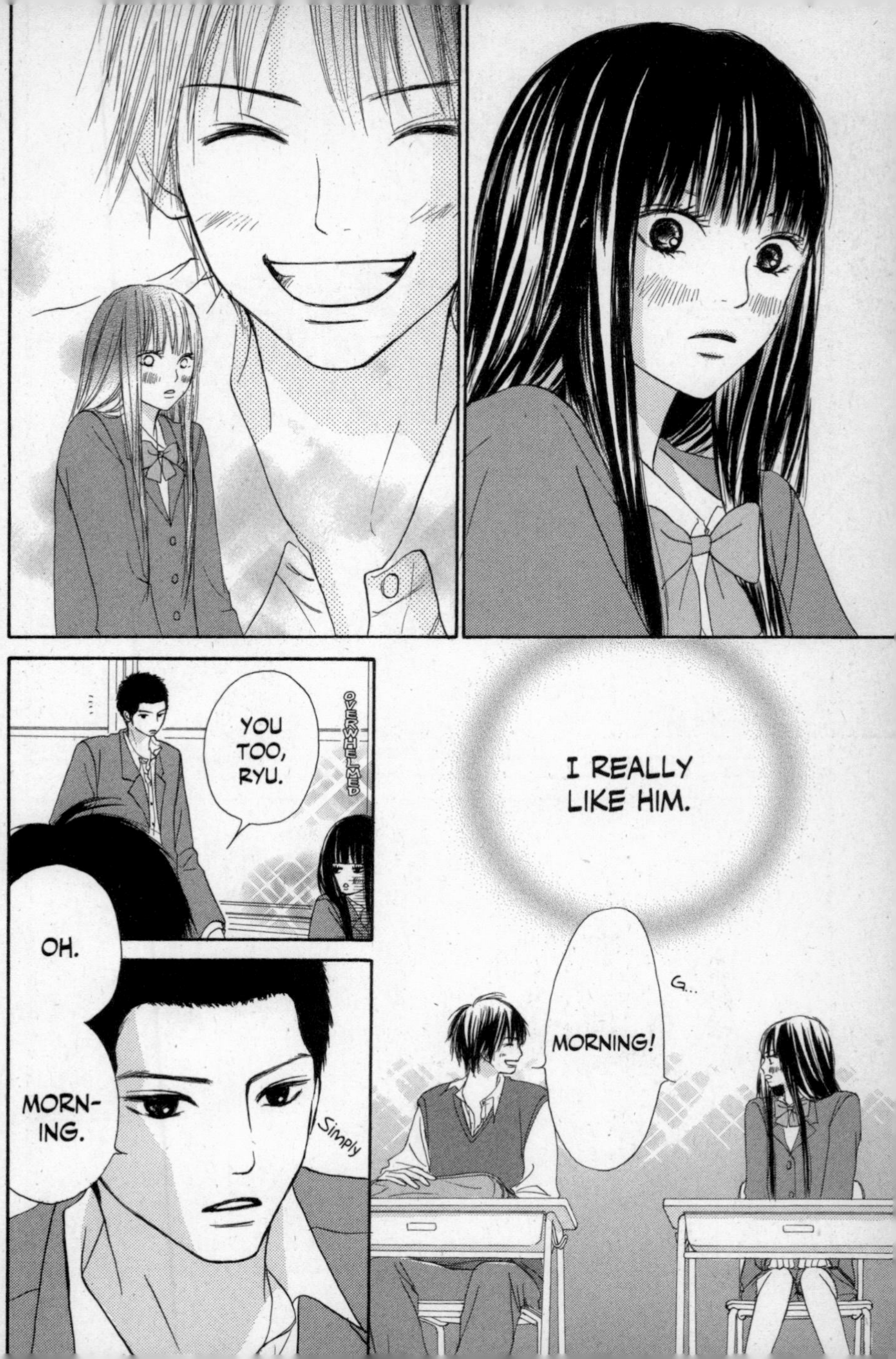
I REALLY LIKE HIM.
G...
MORNING!
YOU TOO, RYU.
OVERWHELMED
OH.
MORNING.
Simply

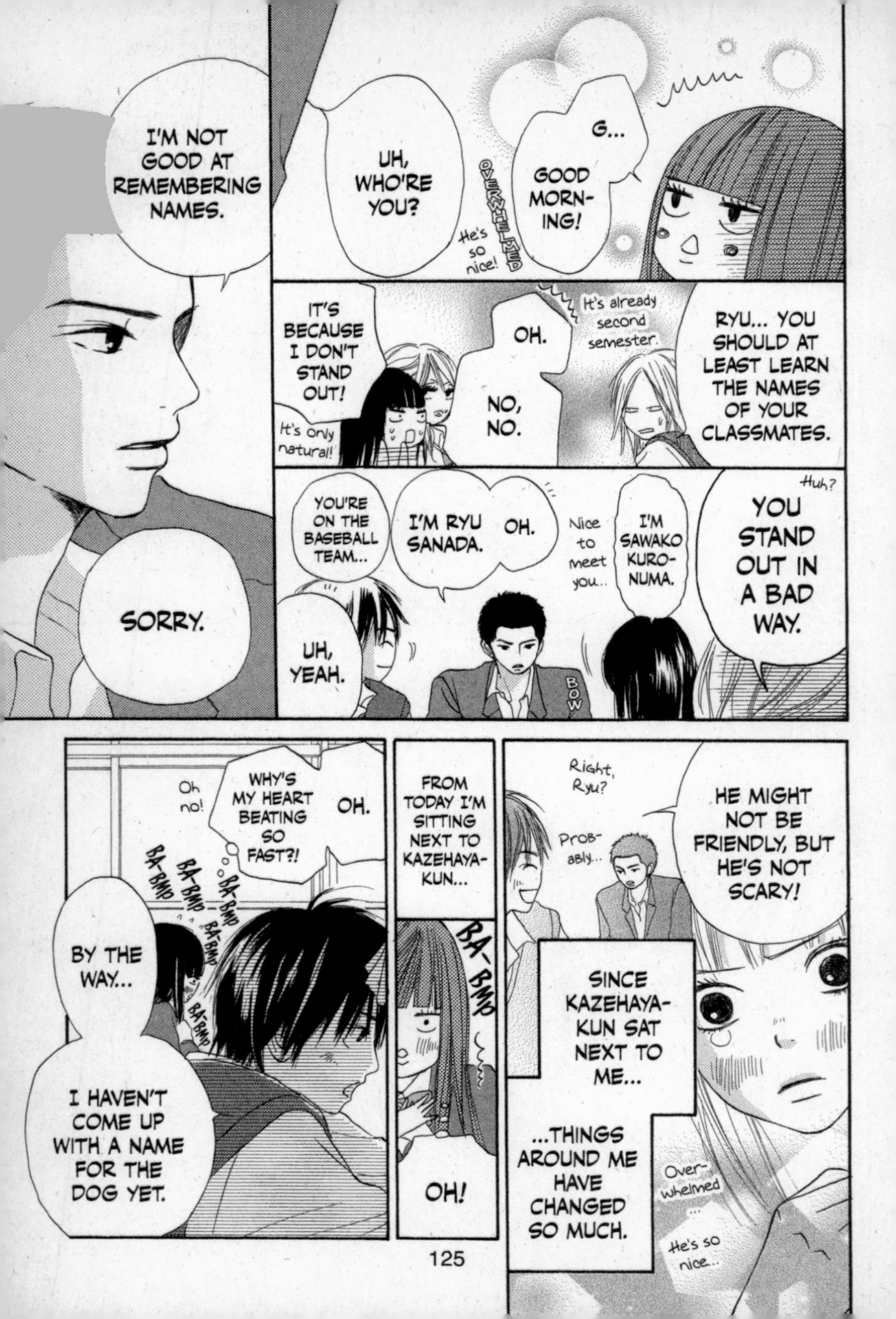
G...
GOOD MORNING!
OVERWHELMED
He's so nice!
UH, WHO'RE YOU?
RYU... YOU SHOULD AT LEAST LEARN THE NAMES OF YOUR CLASSMATES.
It's already second semester.
OH.
NO, NO.
IT'S BECAUSE I DON'T STAND OUT!
It's only natural!
Huh?
YOU STAND OUT IN A BAD WAY.
I'M SAWAKO KURONUMA.
Nice to meet you...
BOW
OH.
I'M RYU SANADA.
YOU'RE ON THE BASEBALL TEAM...
UH, YEAH.
I'M NOT GOOD AT REMEMBERING NAMES.
SORRY.
HE MIGHT NOT BE FRIENDLY, BUT HE'S NOT SCARY!
Right, Ryu?
Probably...
SINCE KAZEHAYA-KUN SAT NEXT TO ME...
...THINGS AROUND ME HAVE CHANGED SO MUCH.
Overwhelmed...
He's so nice...
FROM TODAY I'M SITTING NEXT TO KAZEHAYA-KUN...
BA-BMP
OH!
OH.
WHY'S MY HEART BEATING SO FAST?!
Oh no!
BA-BMP BA-BMP BA-BMP BA-BMP BA-BMP
BY THE WAY...
I HAVEN'T COME UP WITH A NAME FOR THE DOG YET.

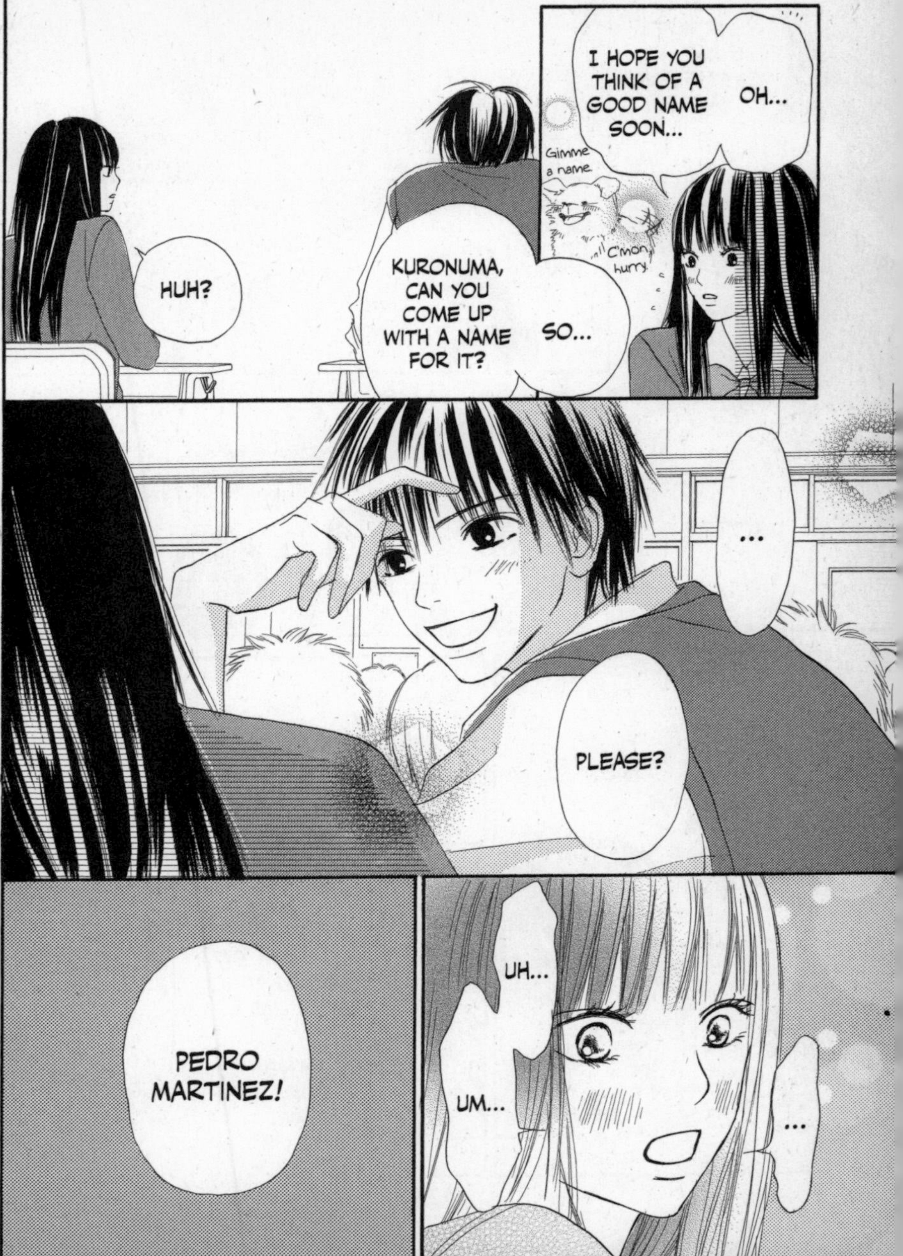

I HOPE YOU THINK OF A GOOD NAME SOON...
OH...
Gimme a name.
C'mon, hurry.
SO...
KURONUMA, CAN YOU COME UP WITH A NAME FOR IT?
HUH?
...
PLEASE?
...
UH...
UM...
PEDRO MARTINEZ!

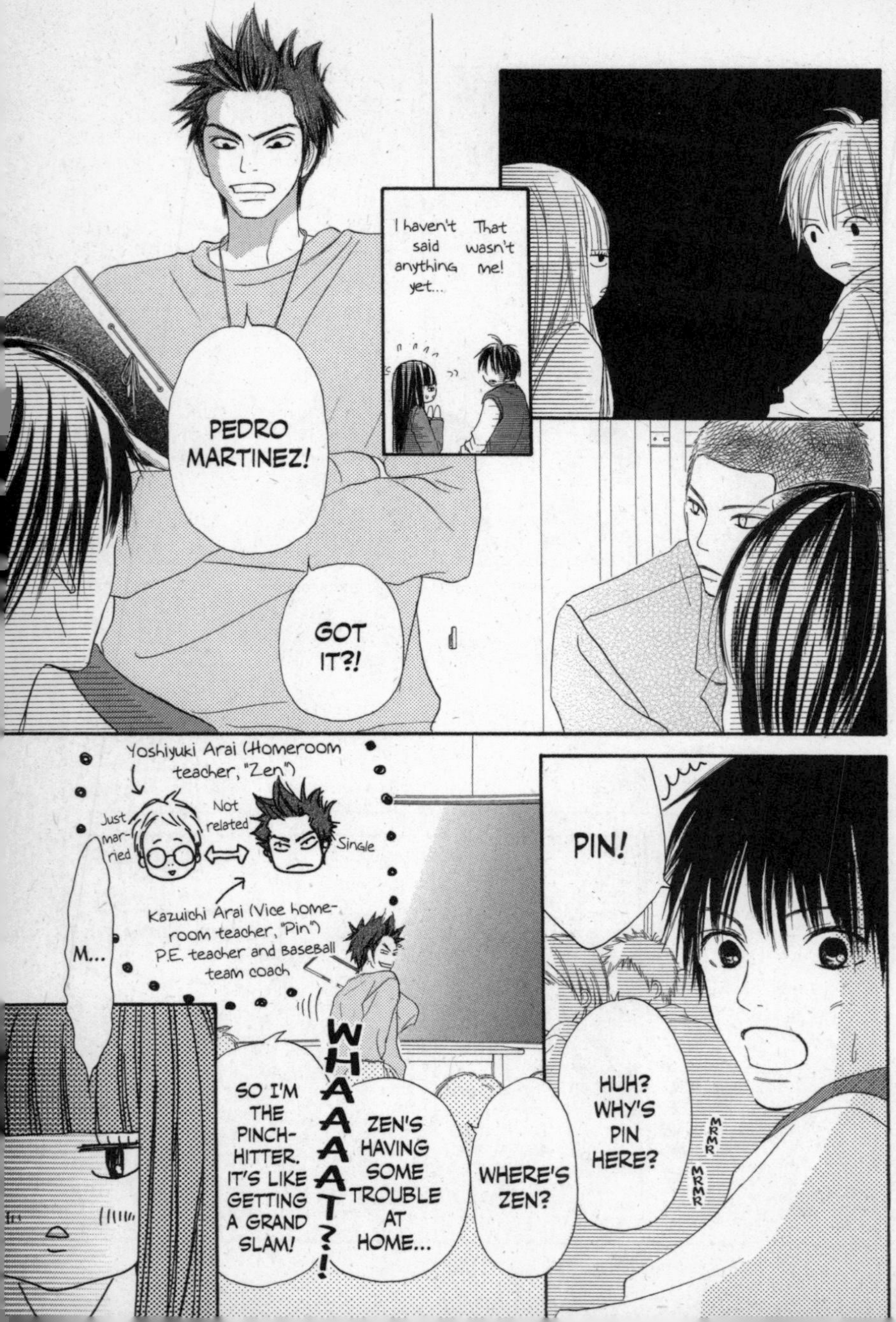
That wasn't me!
I haven't said anything yet...
PEDRO MARTINEZ!
GOT IT?!
PIN!
HUH? WHY'S PIN HERE?
MRMR MRMR
WHERE'S ZEN?
ZEN'S HAVING SOME TROUBLE AT HOME...
WHAAAAAT?!
SO I'M THE PINCH-HITTER. IT'S LIKE GETTING A GRAND SLAM!
Yoshiyuki Arai (Homeroom teacher, "Zen")
Just married
Not related
Single
Kazuichi Arai (Vice homeroom teacher, "Pin") P.E. teacher and baseball team coach
M...

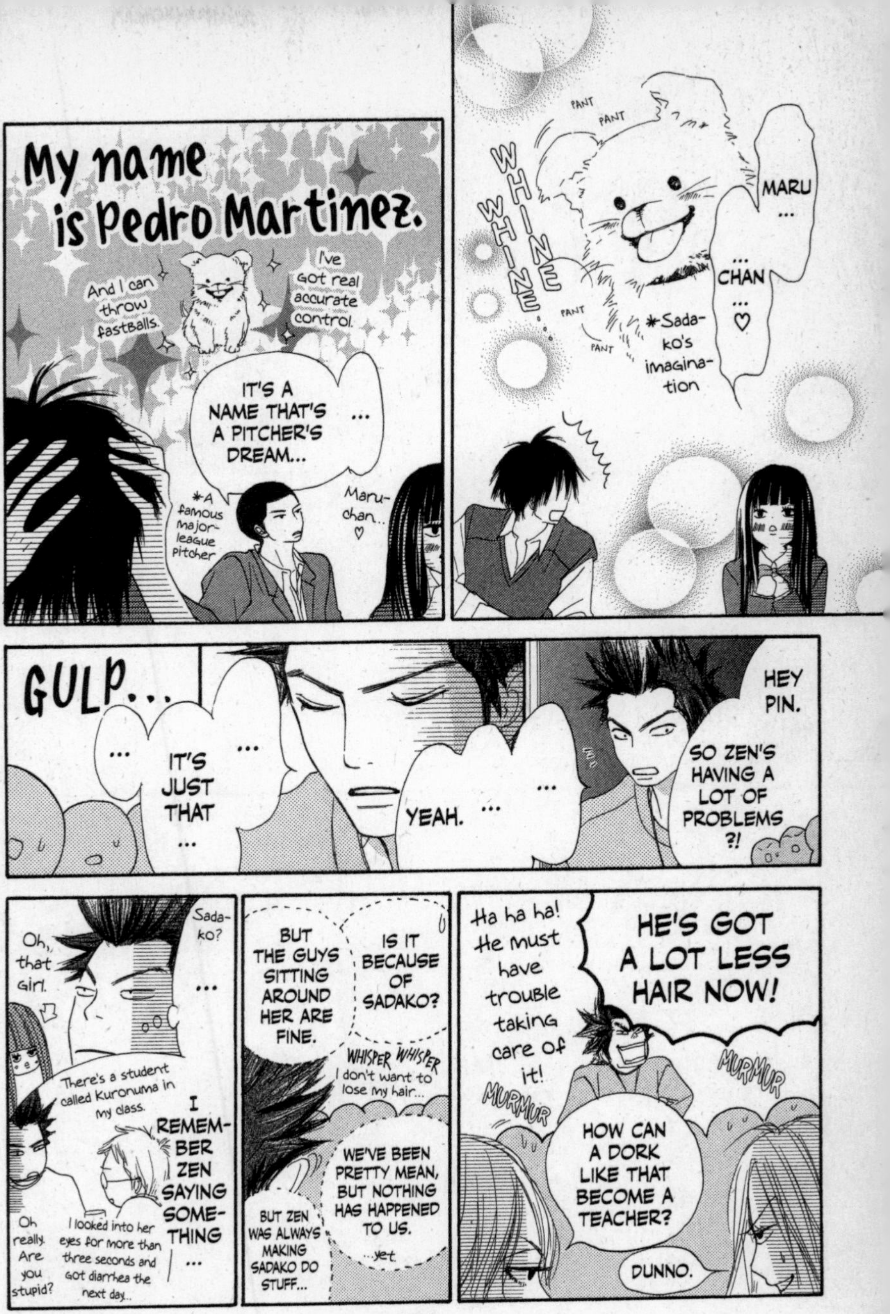
PANT PANT
WHINE WHINE
MARU ...
... CHAN ... ♡
*Sadako's imagination
PANT PANT
My name is Pedro Martinez.
I've got real accurate control.
And I can throw fastballs.
IT'S A NAME THAT'S A PITCHER'S DREAM... ...
Maru-chan... ♡
*A famous major-league pitcher
HEY PIN.
SO ZEN'S HAVING A LOT OF PROBLEMS?!
... YEAH. ...
... IT'S JUST THAT ... ...
GULP...
HE'S GOT A LOT LESS HAIR NOW!
Ha ha ha! He must have trouble taking care of it!
MURMUR
MURMUR
HOW CAN A DORK LIKE THAT BECOME A TEACHER?
DUNNO.
IS IT BECAUSE OF SADAKO?
BUT THE GUYS SITTING AROUND HER ARE FINE.
WHISPER WHISPER
I don't want to lose my hair...
WE'VE BEEN PRETTY MEAN, BUT NOTHING HAS HAPPENED TO US.
...yet.
BUT ZEN WAS ALWAYS MAKING SADAKO DO STUFF...
Sadako?
Oh, that girl.
...
There's a student called Kuronuma in my class.
I REMEMBER ZEN SAYING SOMETHING ...
I looked into her eyes for more than three seconds and got diarrhea the next day...
Oh really. Are you stupid?

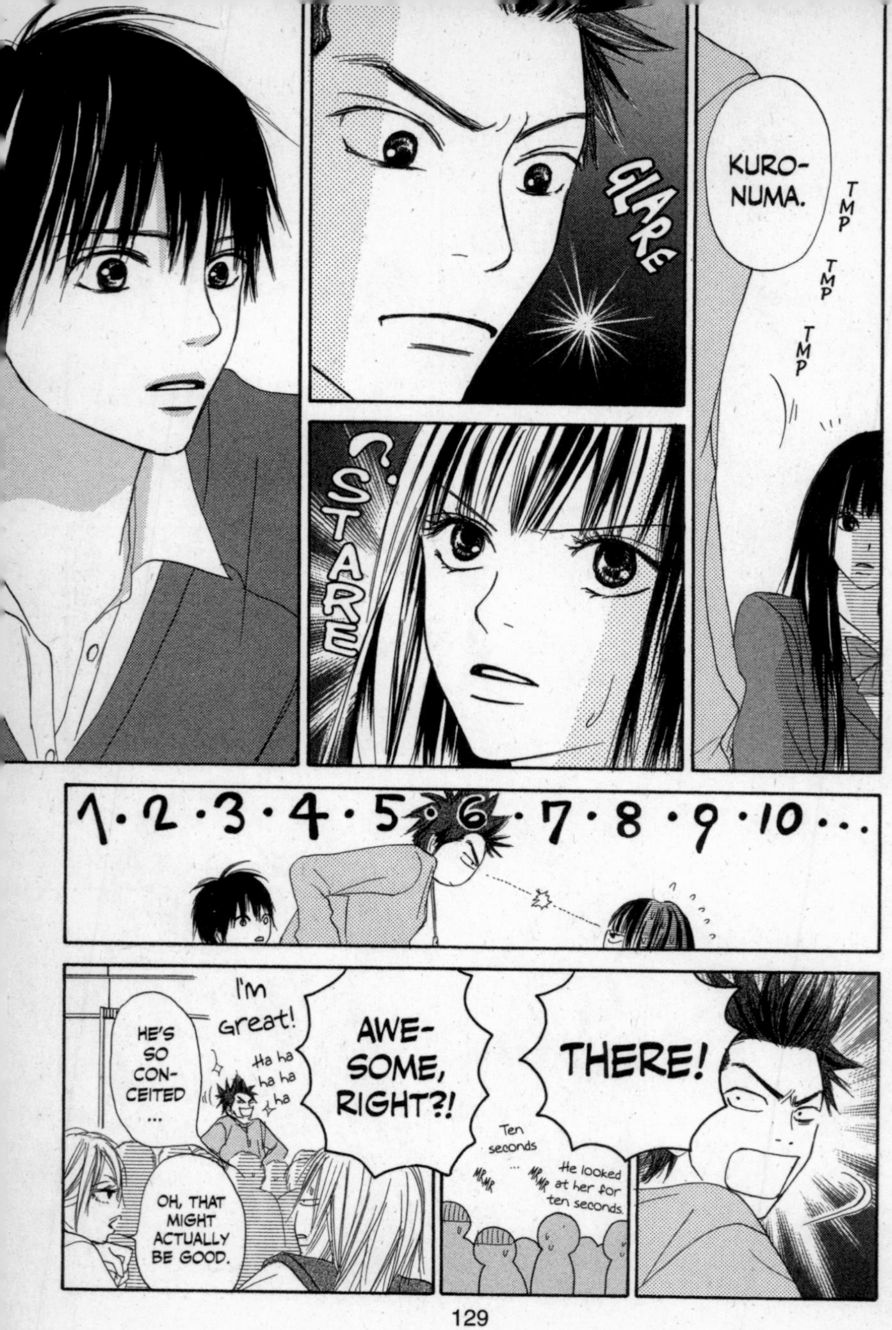
KURO-NUMA.
TMP
TMP
TMP
GLARE
?
STARE
1·2·3·4·5·6·7·8·9·10…
THERE!
AWE-SOME, RIGHT?!
Ten seconds …
He looked at her for ten seconds.
MR MR
MR MR
I'm Great!
Ha ha ha ha ha
HE'S SO CON-CEITED …
OH, THAT MIGHT ACTUALLY BE GOOD.

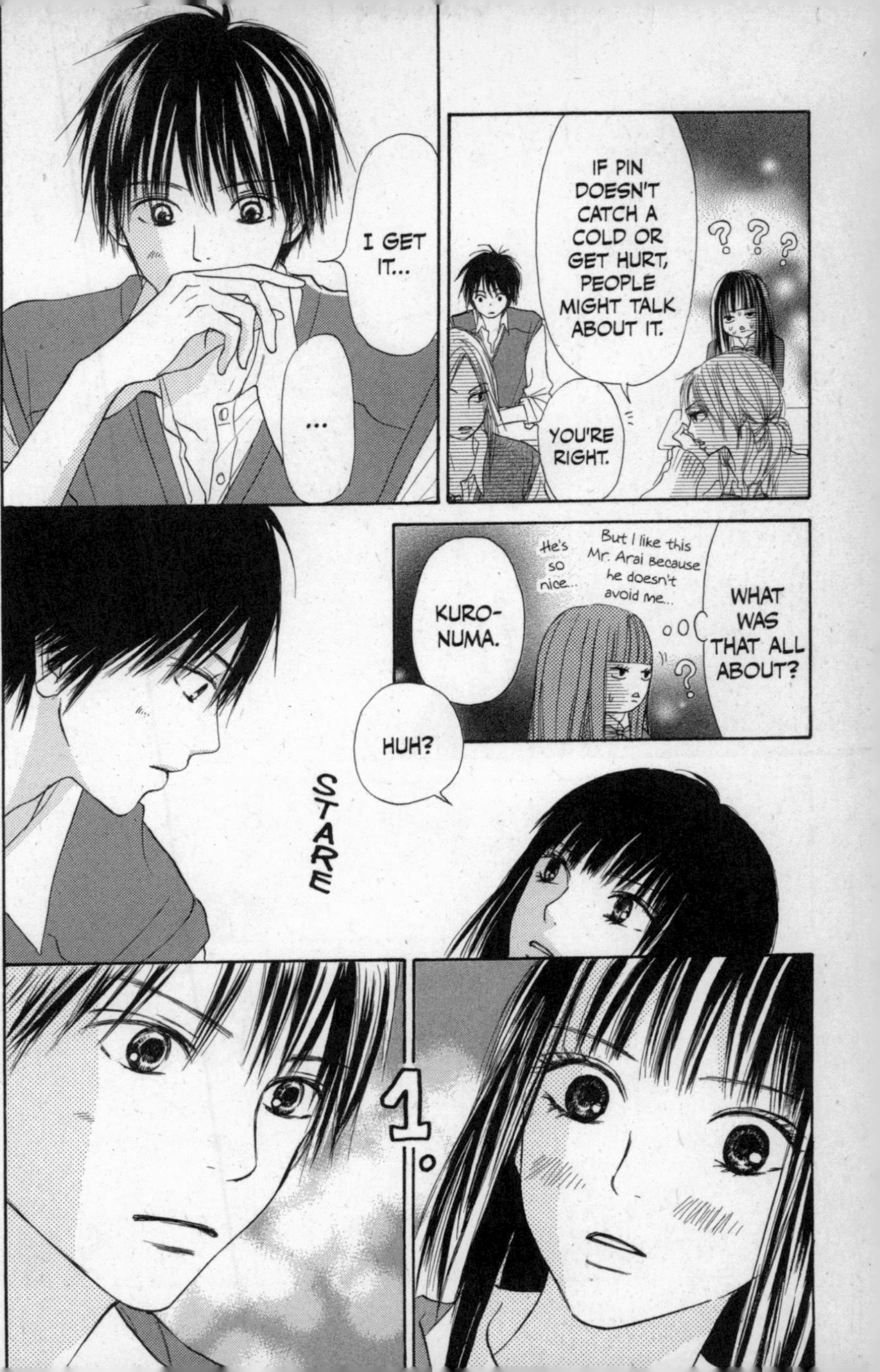
IF PIN DOESN'T CATCH A COLD OR GET HURT, PEOPLE MIGHT TALK ABOUT IT.
YOU'RE RIGHT.
I GET IT...
...
WHAT WAS THAT ALL ABOUT?
But I like this Mr. Arai because he doesn't avoid me...
He's so nice...
KURO-NUMA.
HUH?
STARE

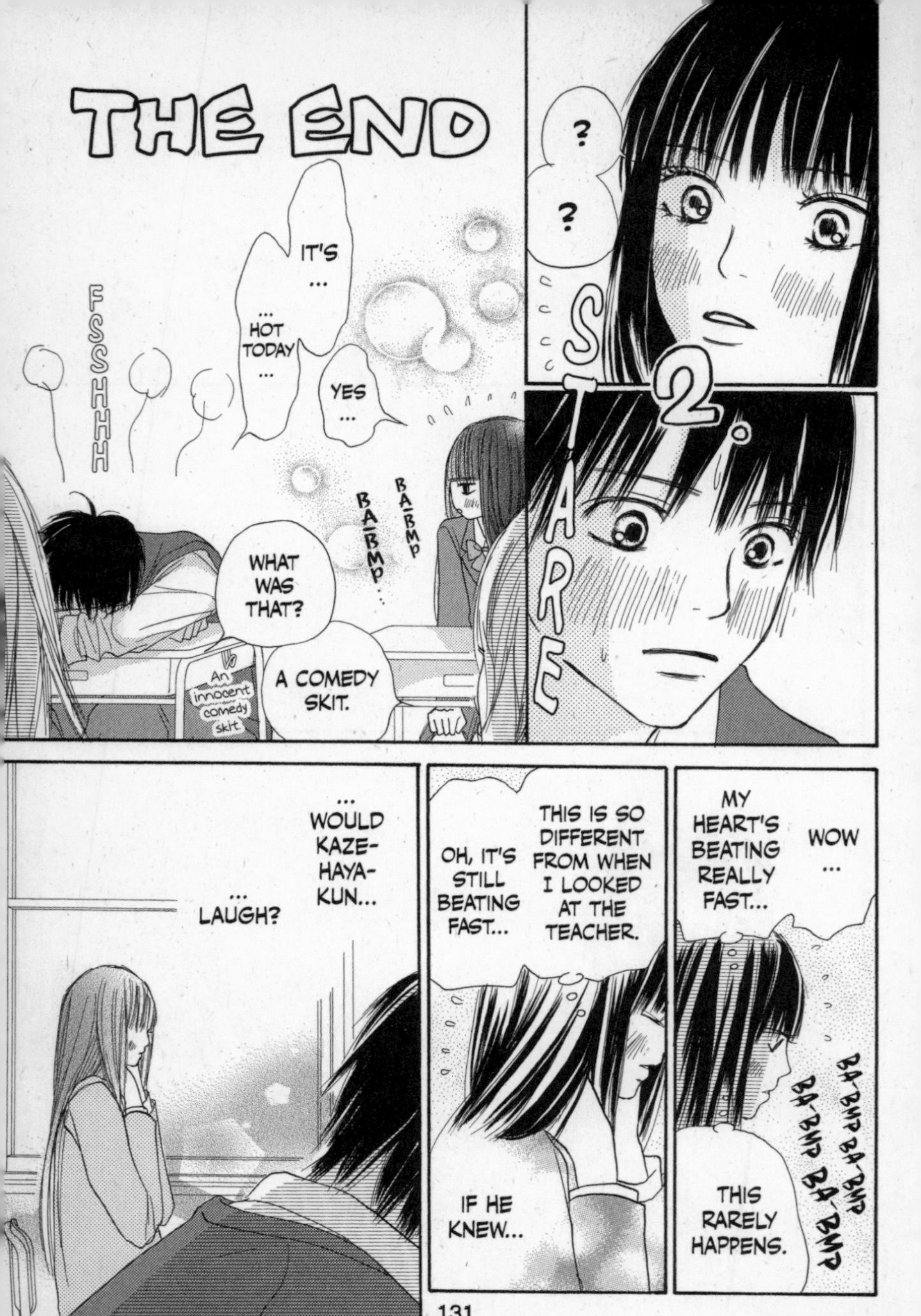
? ?
STARE
2
THE END
IT'S ...
... HOT TODAY ...
YES ...
FSSHHH
BA-BMP BA-BMP...
WHAT WAS THAT?
A COMEDY SKIT.
An innocent comedy skit.
WOW ...
MY HEART'S BEATING REALLY FAST...
THIS RARELY HAPPENS.
BA-BMP BA-BMP BA-BMP BA-BMP
THIS IS SO DIFFERENT FROM WHEN I LOOKED AT THE TEACHER.
OH, IT'S STILL BEATING FAST...
IF HE KNEW...
... WOULD KAZE-HAYA-KUN...
... LAUGH?

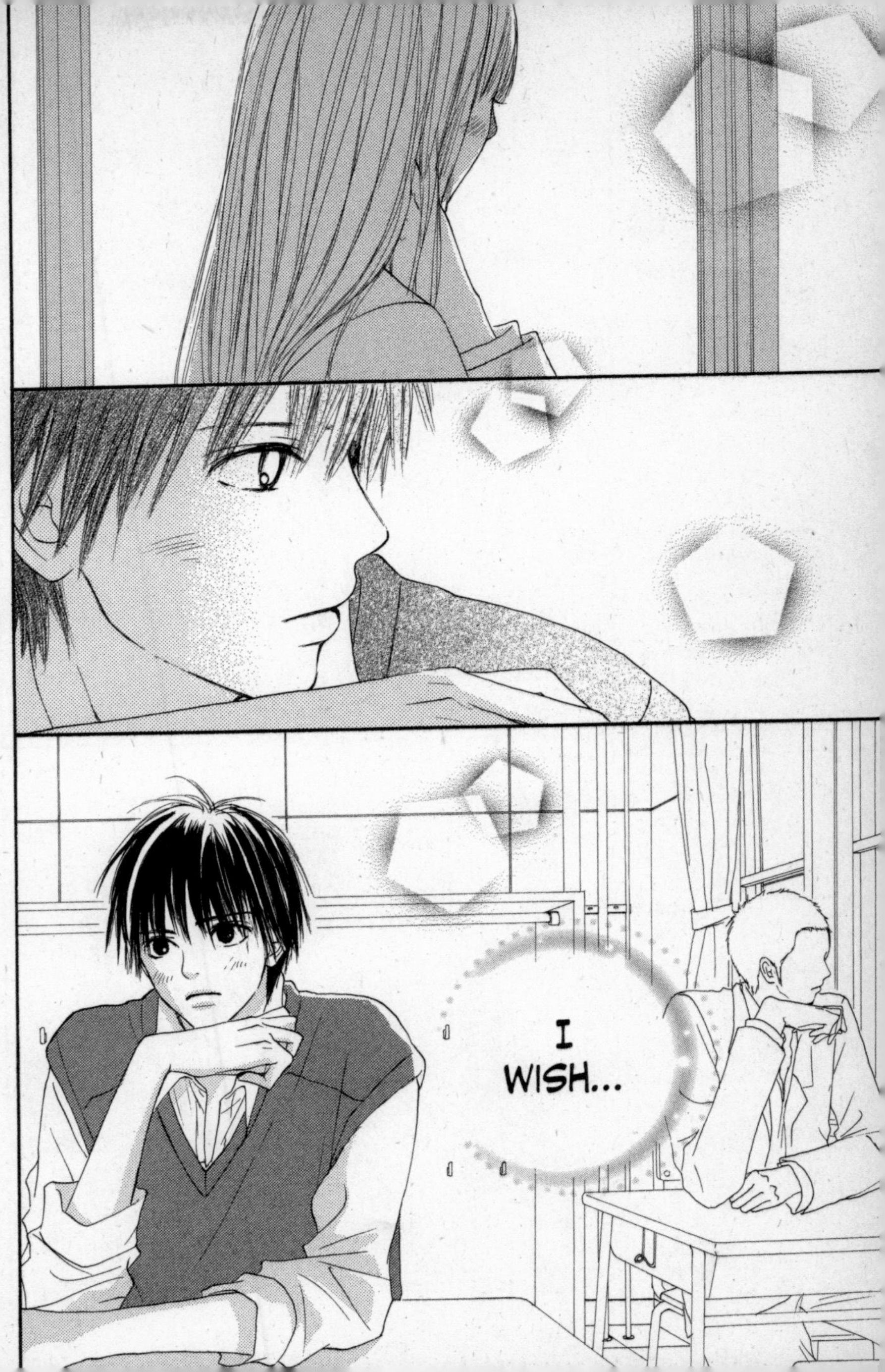
I WISH...

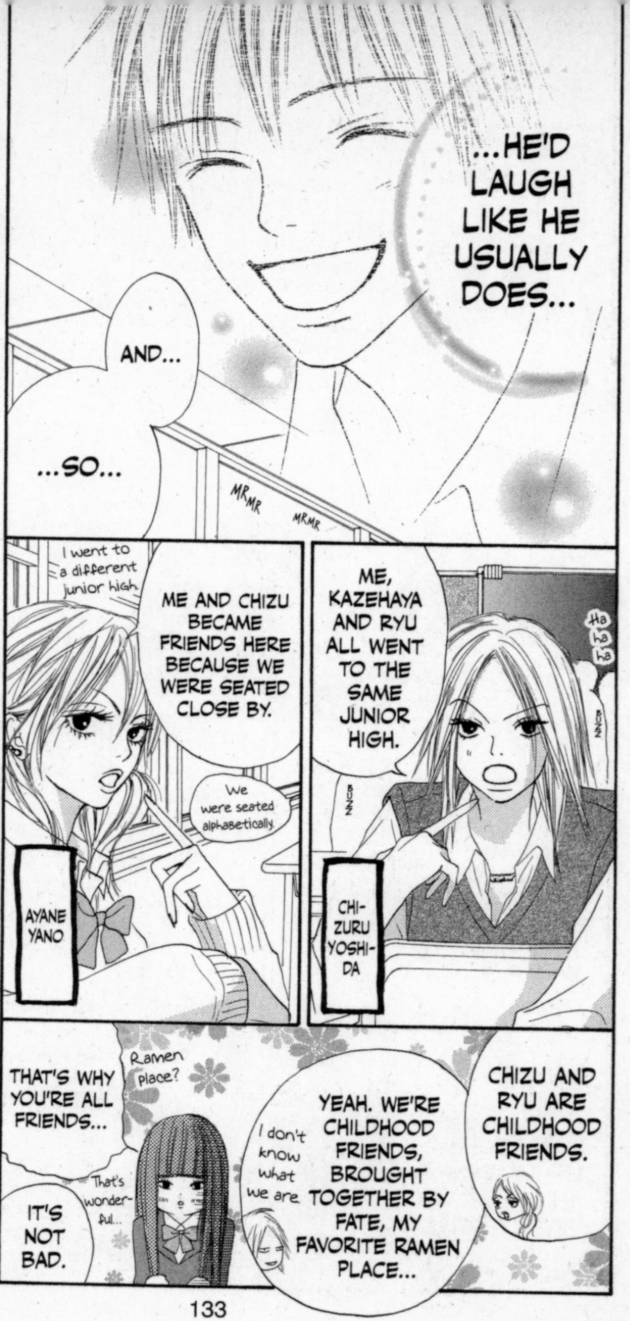
...HE'D LAUGH LIKE HE USUALLY DOES...
AND...
...SO...
MRMR
MRMR
ME, KAZEHAYA AND RYU ALL WENT TO THE SAME JUNIOR HIGH.
Ha ha ha
BUZZ
BUZZ
CHI-ZURU YOSHI-DA
I went to a different junior high.
ME AND CHIZU BECAME FRIENDS HERE BECAUSE WE WERE SEATED CLOSE BY.
We were seated alphabetically.
AYANE YANO
CHIZU AND RYU ARE CHILDHOOD FRIENDS.
YEAH. WE'RE CHILDHOOD FRIENDS, BROUGHT TOGETHER BY FATE, MY FAVORITE RAMEN PLACE...
I don't know what we are.
Ramen place?
THAT'S WHY YOU'RE ALL FRIENDS...
That's wonderful...
IT'S NOT BAD.

KARUPIN on JAPAN 3

Nowadays, time passes by in chunks of one month, so one year goes by really, really fast!

I'm really bad at using my time wisely, so I never get anything accomplished. A year will go by without me doing anything.

Like video games. I can't play anymore! I wish I could make time for them somehow...

Future aspiration

Playing video games as much as I want with Kazune Kawahara.

Let's play when we're old and have the time...

...

If only I could do my storyboards faster...

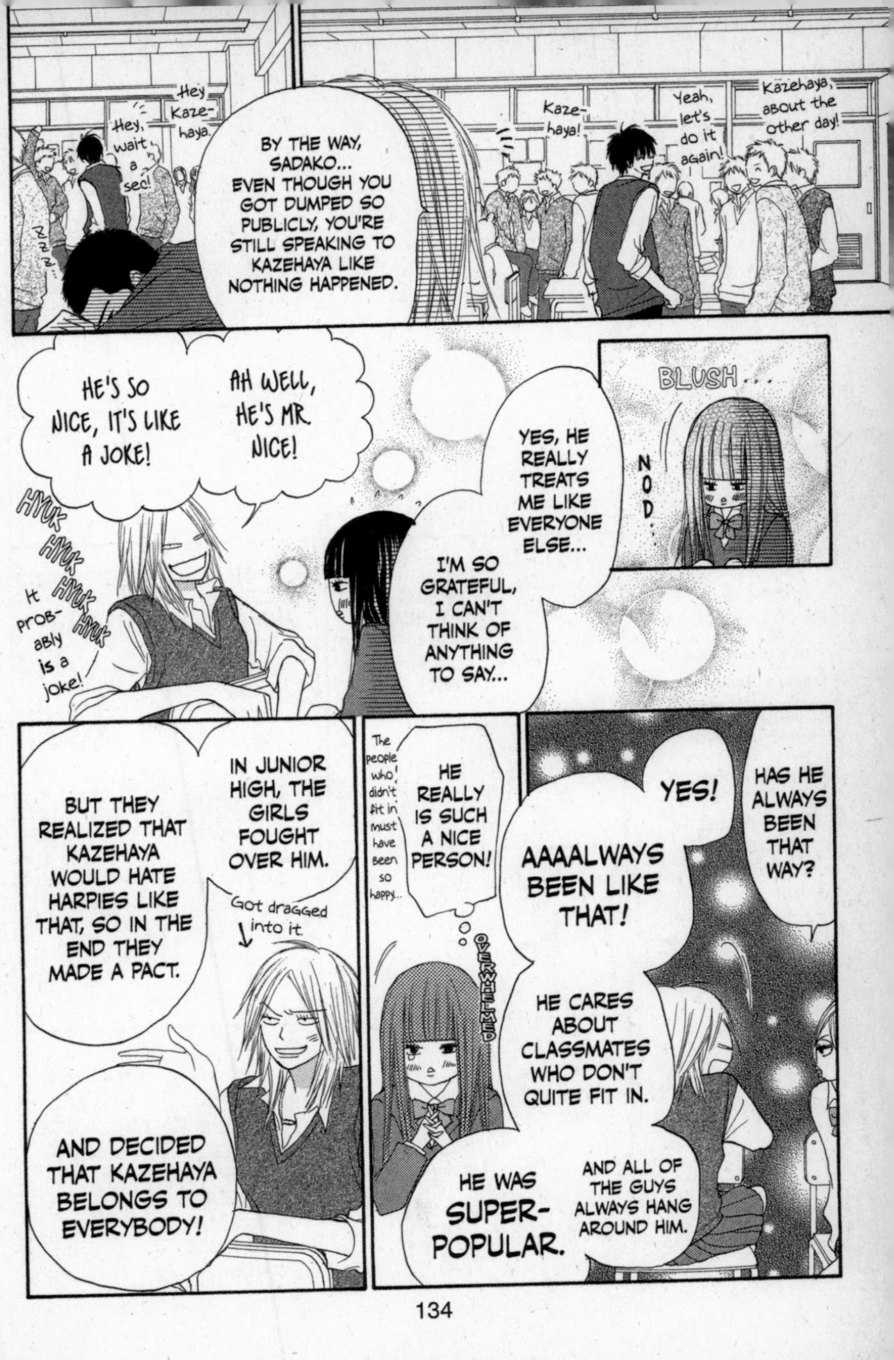
Kazehaya, about the other day!
Yeah, let's do it again!
Kaze-haya!
BY THE WAY, SADAKO... EVEN THOUGH YOU GOT DUMPED SO PUBLICLY, YOU'RE STILL SPEAKING TO KAZEHAYA LIKE NOTHING HAPPENED.
Hey Kaze-haya.
Hey, wait a sec!
ZZZ
BLUSH...
NOD...
YES, HE REALLY TREATS ME LIKE EVERYONE ELSE...
I'M SO GRATEFUL, I CAN'T THINK OF ANYTHING TO SAY...
AH WELL, HE'S MR. NICE!
HE'S SO NICE, IT'S LIKE A JOKE!
HYUK HYUK HYUK HYUK
It probably is a joke!
HAS HE ALWAYS BEEN THAT WAY?
YES!
AAAALWAYS BEEN LIKE THAT!
HE CARES ABOUT CLASSMATES WHO DON'T QUITE FIT IN.
AND ALL OF THE GUYS ALWAYS HANG AROUND HIM.
HE WAS SUPER-POPULAR.
HE REALLY IS SUCH A NICE PERSON!
The people who didn't fit in must have been so happy...
OVERWHELMED
IN JUNIOR HIGH, THE GIRLS FOUGHT OVER HIM.
BUT THEY REALIZED THAT KAZEHAYA WOULD HATE HARPIES LIKE THAT, SO IN THE END THEY MADE A PACT.
Got dragged into it.
AND DECIDED THAT KAZEHAYA BELONGS TO EVERYBODY!

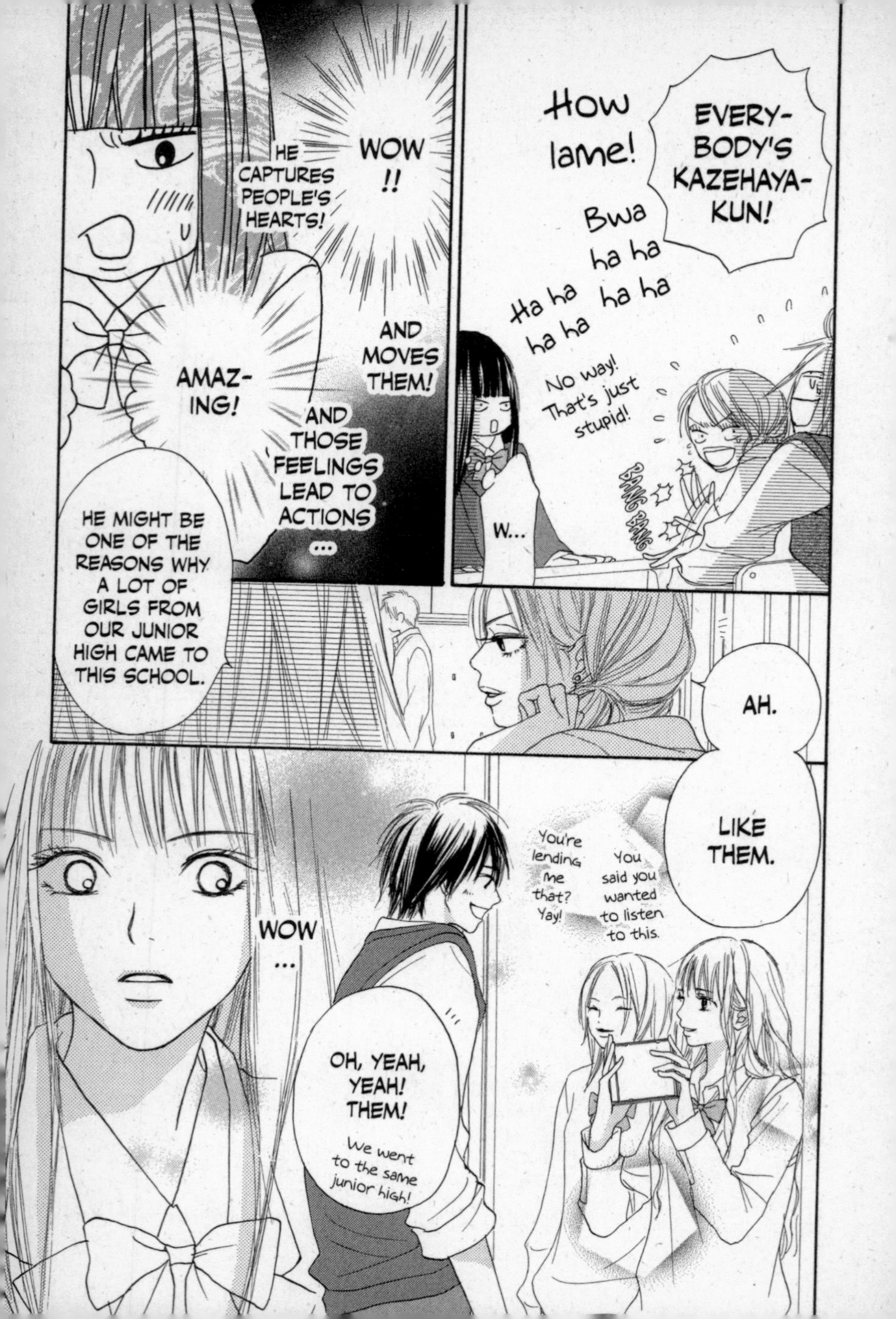

EVERY-BODY'S KAZEHAYA-KUN!
How lame!
Bwa ha ha ha ha
Ha ha ha ha
No way! That's just stupid!
BANG BANG
W...
WOW !!
HE CAPTURES PEOPLE'S HEARTS!
AND MOVES THEM!
AMAZ-ING!
AND THOSE FEELINGS LEAD TO ACTIONS ...
HE MIGHT BE ONE OF THE REASONS WHY A LOT OF GIRLS FROM OUR JUNIOR HIGH CAME TO THIS SCHOOL.
AH.
LIKE THEM.
You said you wanted to listen to this.
You're lending me that? Yay!
OH, YEAH, YEAH! THEM!
We went to the same junior high!
WOW ...

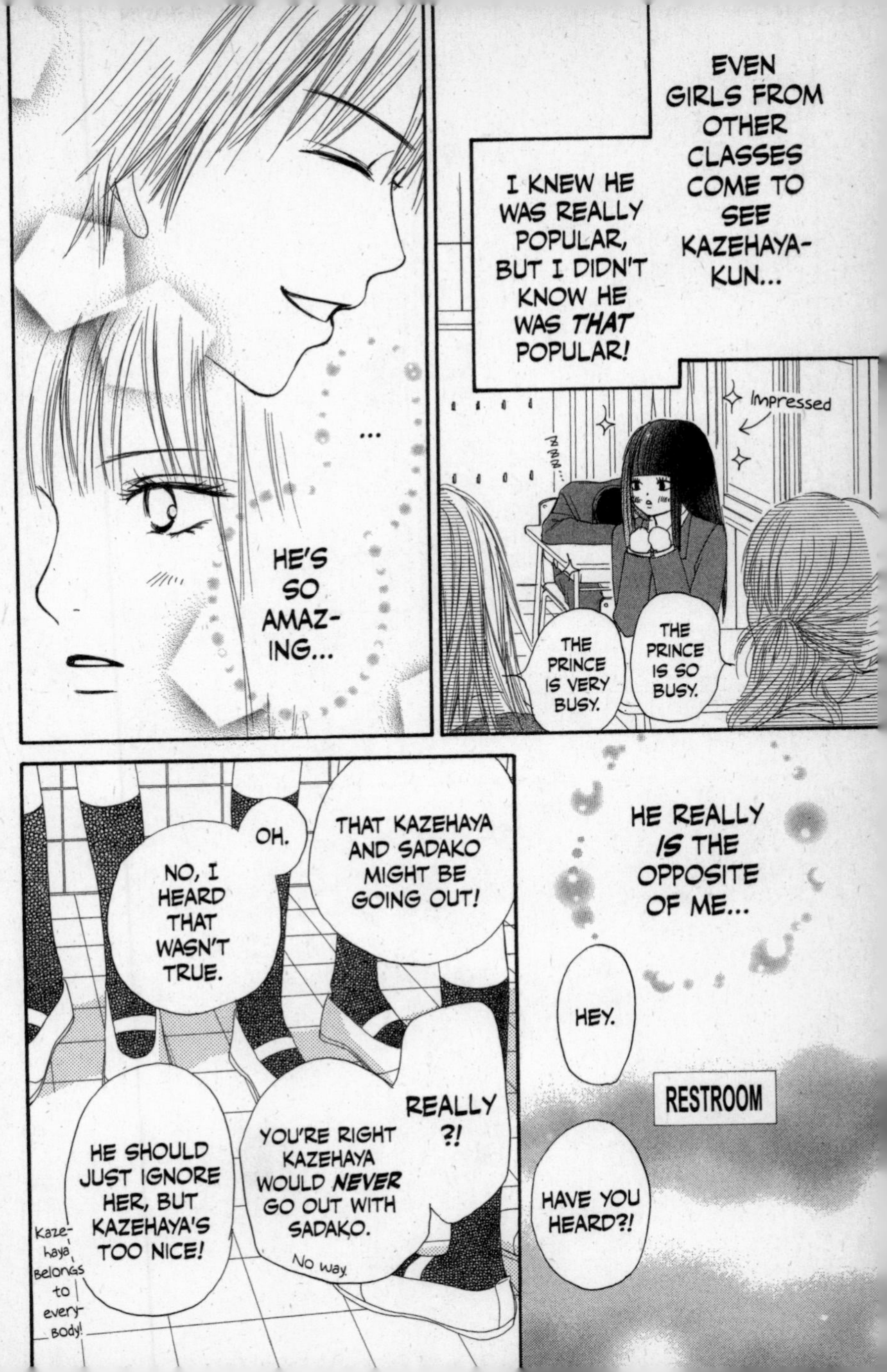
EVEN GIRLS FROM OTHER CLASSES COME TO SEE KAZEHAYA-KUN...
I KNEW HE WAS REALLY POPULAR, BUT I DIDN'T KNOW HE WAS *THAT* POPULAR!
Impressed
THE PRINCE IS SO BUSY.
THE PRINCE IS VERY BUSY.
...
HE'S SO AMAZ-ING...
HE REALLY *IS* THE OPPOSITE OF ME...
HEY.
RESTROOM
HAVE YOU HEARD?!
THAT KAZEHAYA AND SADAKO MIGHT BE GOING OUT!
OH.
NO, I HEARD THAT WASN'T TRUE.
REALLY ?!
YOU'RE RIGHT KAZEHAYA WOULD *NEVER* GO OUT WITH SADAKO.
No way.
HE SHOULD JUST IGNORE HER, BUT KAZEHAYA'S TOO NICE!
Kaze-haya belongs to every-body!

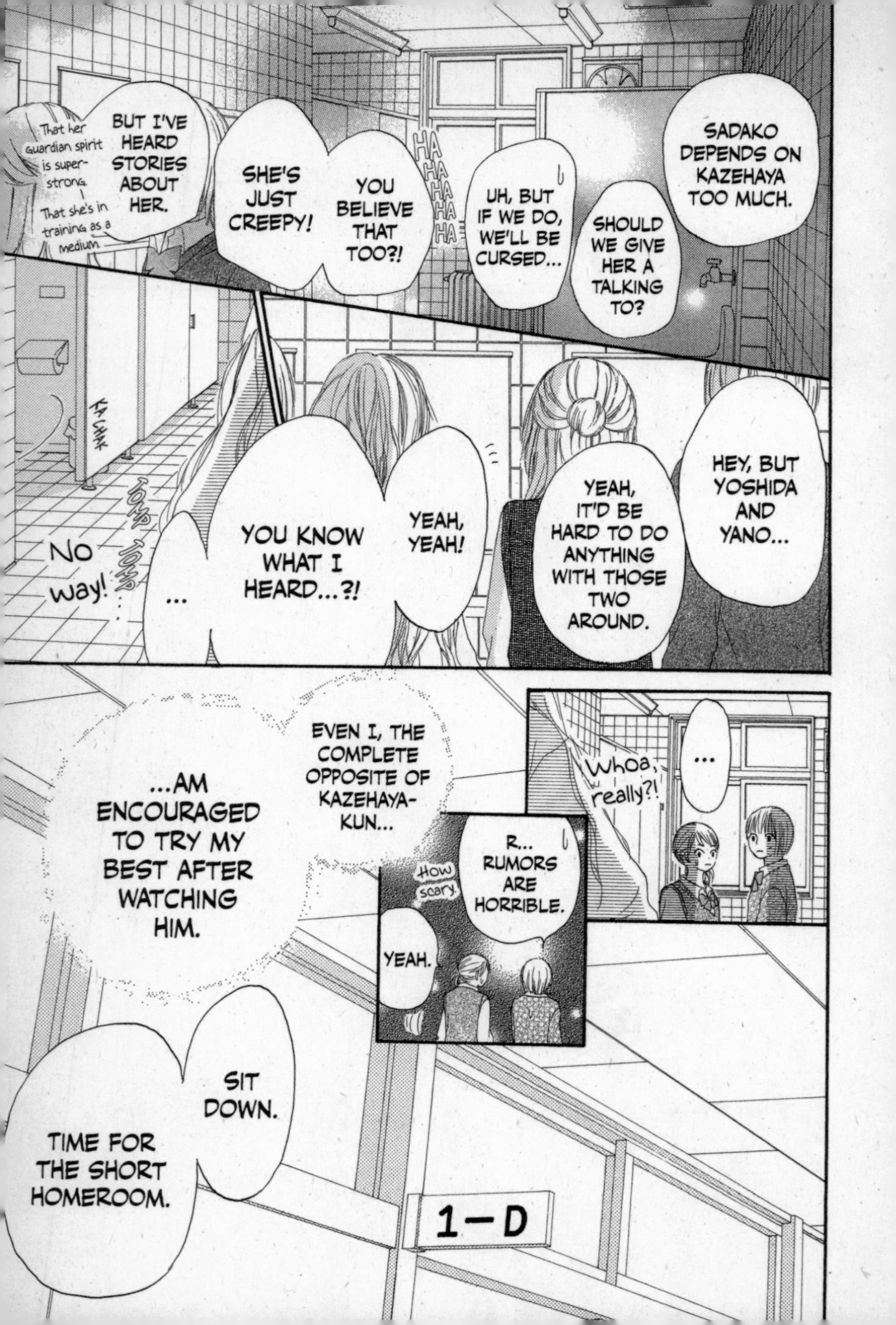
SADAKO DEPENDS ON KAZEHAYA TOO MUCH.
SHOULD WE GIVE HER A TALKING TO?
UH, BUT IF WE DO, WE'LL BE CURSED...
HA HA HA HA HA HA
YOU BELIEVE THAT TOO?!
SHE'S JUST CREEPY!
BUT I'VE HEARD STORIES ABOUT HER.
That her Guardian spirit is super-strong. That she's in training as a medium.
HEY, BUT YOSHIDA AND YANO...
YEAH, IT'D BE HARD TO DO ANYTHING WITH THOSE TWO AROUND.
YEAH, YEAH!
YOU KNOW WHAT I HEARD...?!
...
No way!
TOMP TOMP
KA CHAK
...
Whoa, really?!
R... RUMORS ARE HORRIBLE.
How scary.
YEAH.
EVEN I, THE COMPLETE OPPOSITE OF KAZEHAYA-KUN...
...AM ENCOURAGED TO TRY MY BEST AFTER WATCHING HIM.
1-D
SIT DOWN.
TIME FOR THE SHORT HOMEROOM.

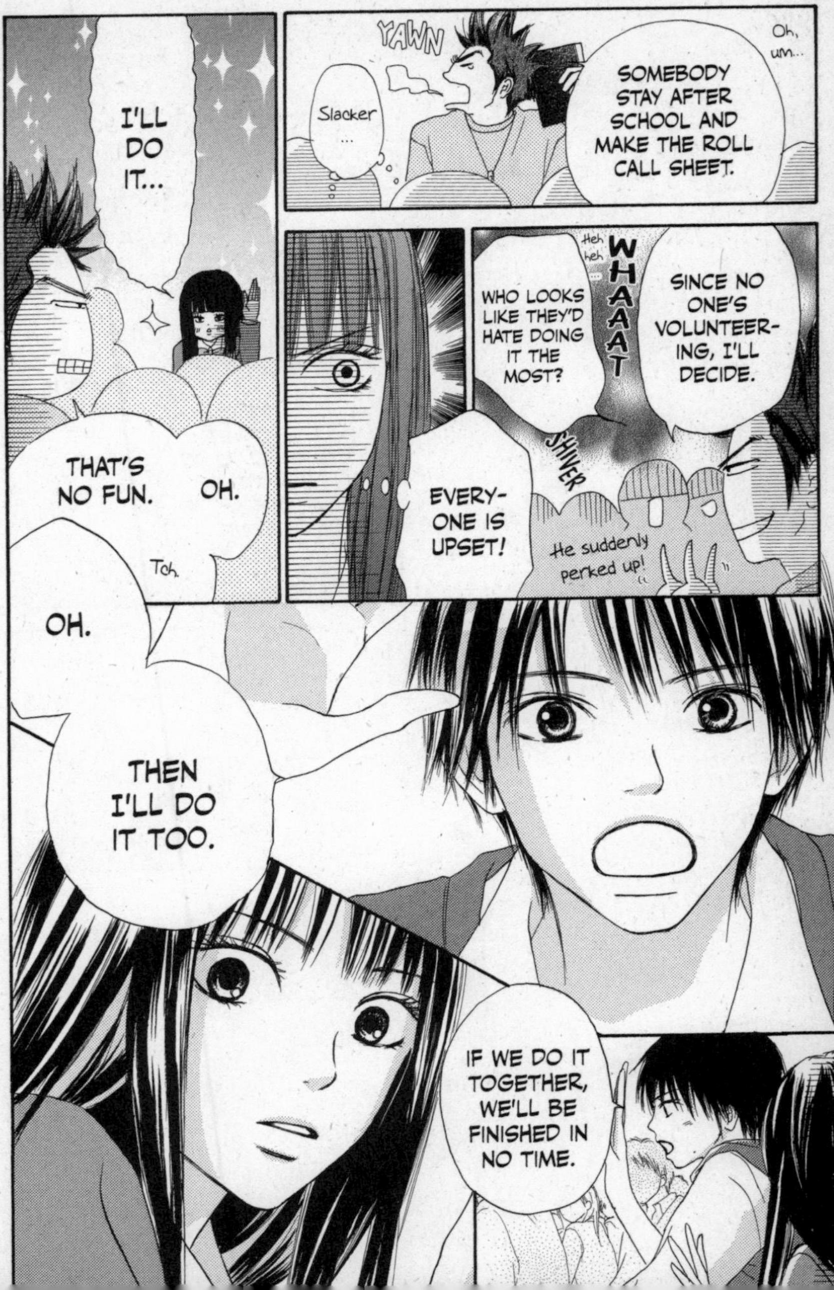
Oh, um...
SOMEBODY STAY AFTER SCHOOL AND MAKE THE ROLL CALL SHEET.
YAWN
Slacker ...
SINCE NO ONE'S VOLUNTEER-ING, I'LL DECIDE.
WHAAAT
Heh heh ...
WHO LOOKS LIKE THEY'D HATE DOING IT THE MOST?
SHIVER
He suddenly perked up!
EVERY-ONE IS UPSET!
I'LL DO IT...
OH.
THAT'S NO FUN.
Tch.
OH.
THEN I'LL DO IT TOO.
IF WE DO IT TOGETHER, WE'LL BE FINISHED IN NO TIME.

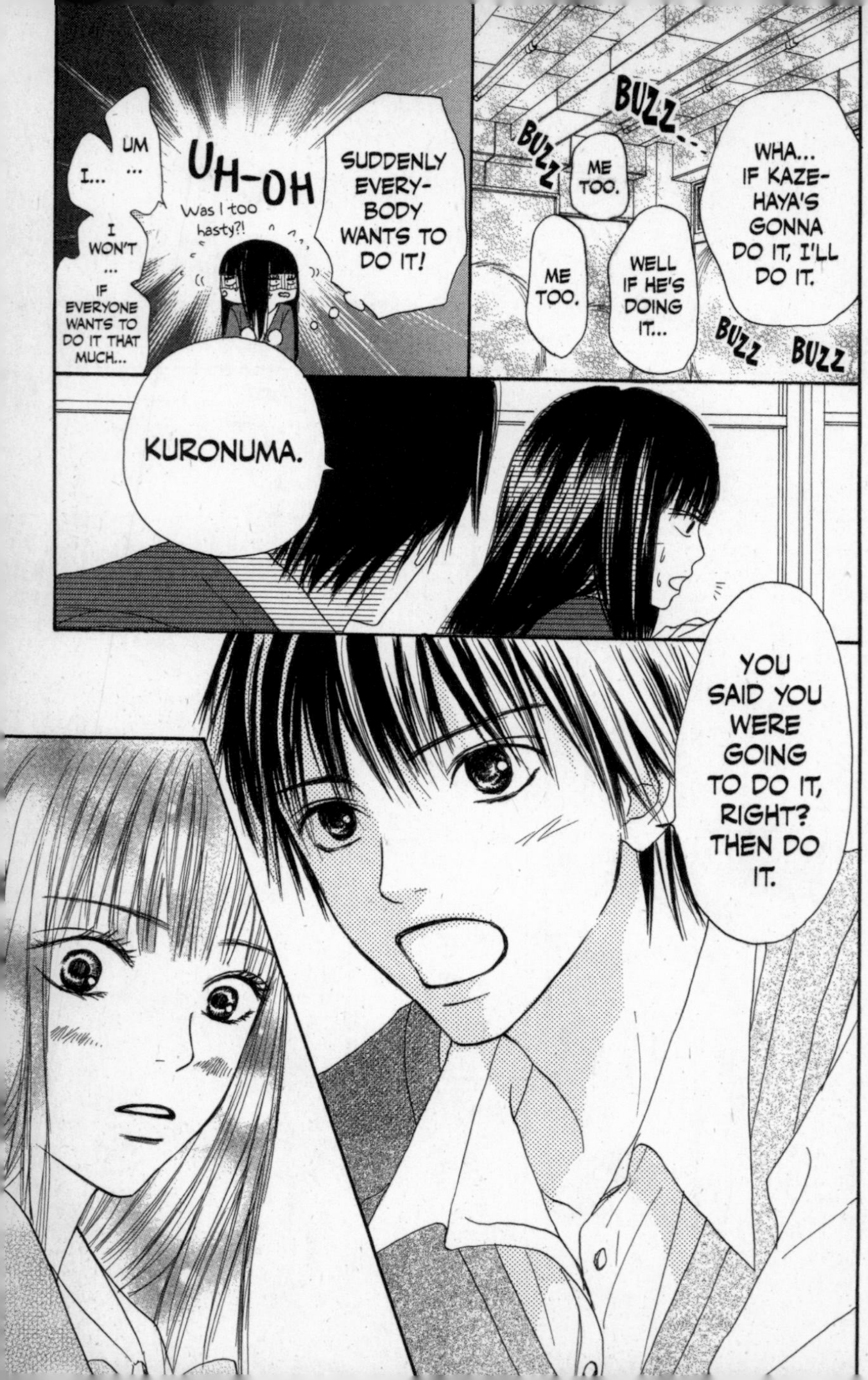
BUZZ...
WHA... IF KAZE-HAYA'S GONNA DO IT, I'LL DO IT.
BUZZ
ME TOO.
WELL IF HE'S DOING IT...
ME TOO.
BUZZ BUZZ
SUDDENLY EVERY-BODY WANTS TO DO IT!
UH-OH
Was I too hasty?!
UM ...
I...
I WON'T ... IF EVERYONE WANTS TO DO IT THAT MUCH...
KURONUMA.
YOU SAID YOU WERE GOING TO DO IT, RIGHT? THEN DO IT.

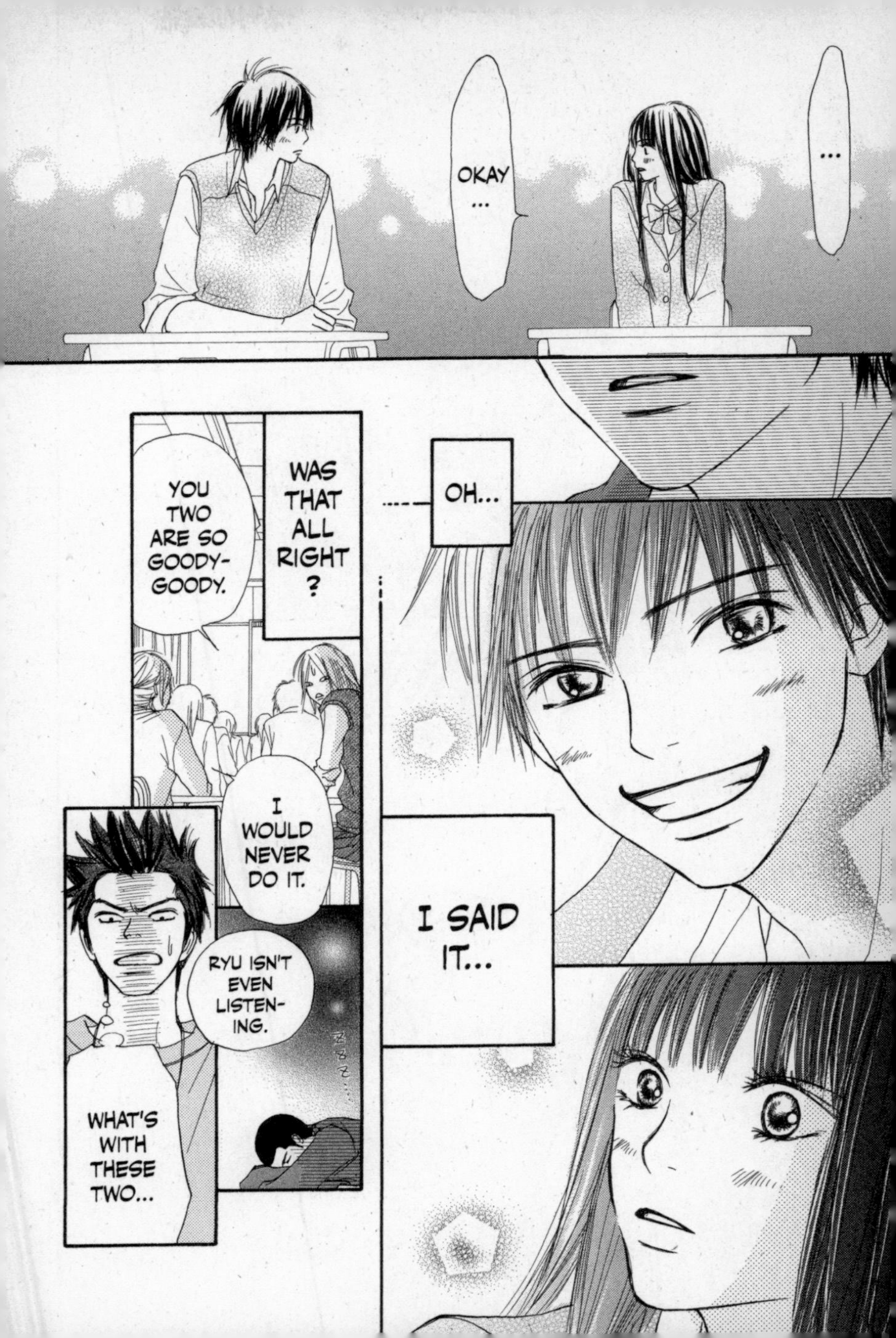
...
OKAY ...
OH...
I SAID IT...
WAS THAT ALL RIGHT ?
YOU TWO ARE SO GOODY-GOODY.
I WOULD NEVER DO IT.
RYU ISN'T EVEN LISTEN-ING.
ZZZ...
WHAT'S WITH THESE TWO...

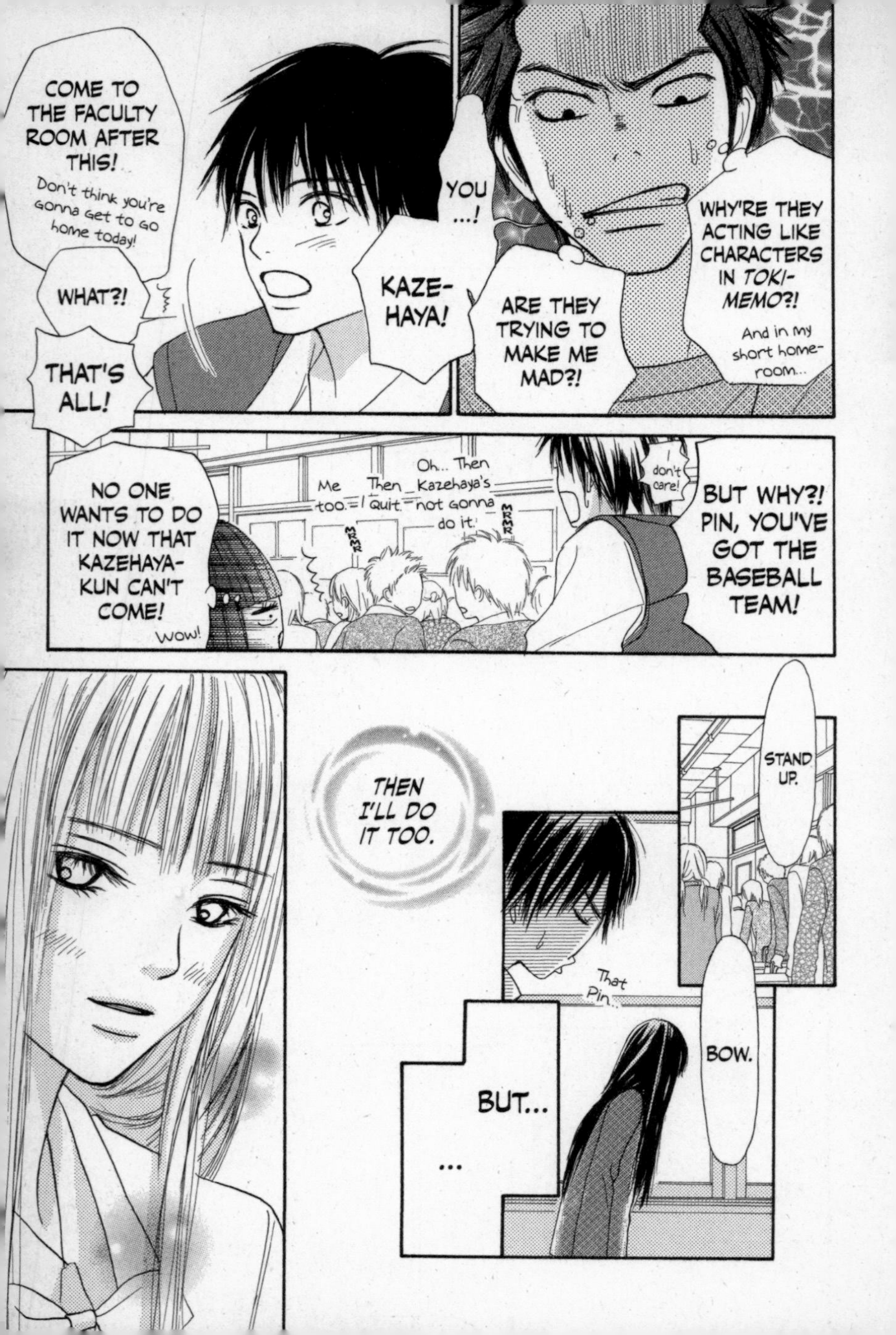
WHY'RE THEY ACTING LIKE CHARACTERS IN TOKI-MEMO?!
And in my short home-room...
ARE THEY TRYING TO MAKE ME MAD?!
YOU ...!
KAZE-HAYA!
COME TO THE FACULTY ROOM AFTER THIS!
Don't think you're gonna get to go home today!
WHAT?!
THAT'S ALL!
BUT WHY?! PIN, YOU'VE GOT THE BASEBALL TEAM!
I don't care!
MRMR
Oh... Then Kazehaya's not gonna do it.
Then I quit.
MRMR
Me too.
NO ONE WANTS TO DO IT NOW THAT KAZEHAYA-KUN CAN'T COME!
Wow!
STAND UP.
That Pin...
BOW.
BUT...
...
THEN I'LL DO IT TOO.

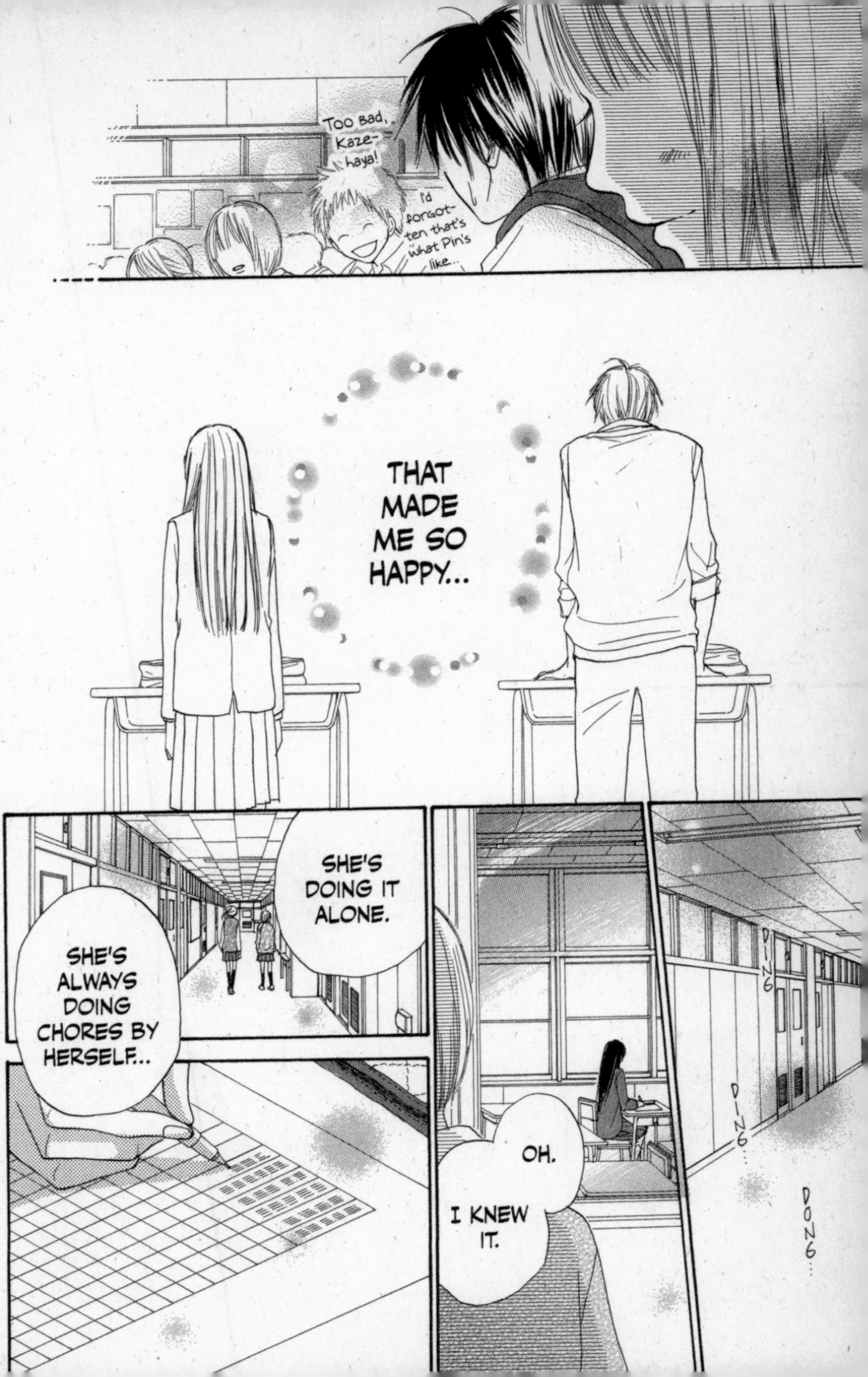
Too bad, Kaze-haya!
I'd forgot-ten that's what Pin's like...
THAT MADE ME SO HAPPY...
DING DING... DONG...
OH.
I KNEW IT.
SHE'S DOING IT ALONE.
SHE'S ALWAYS DOING CHORES BY HERSELF...

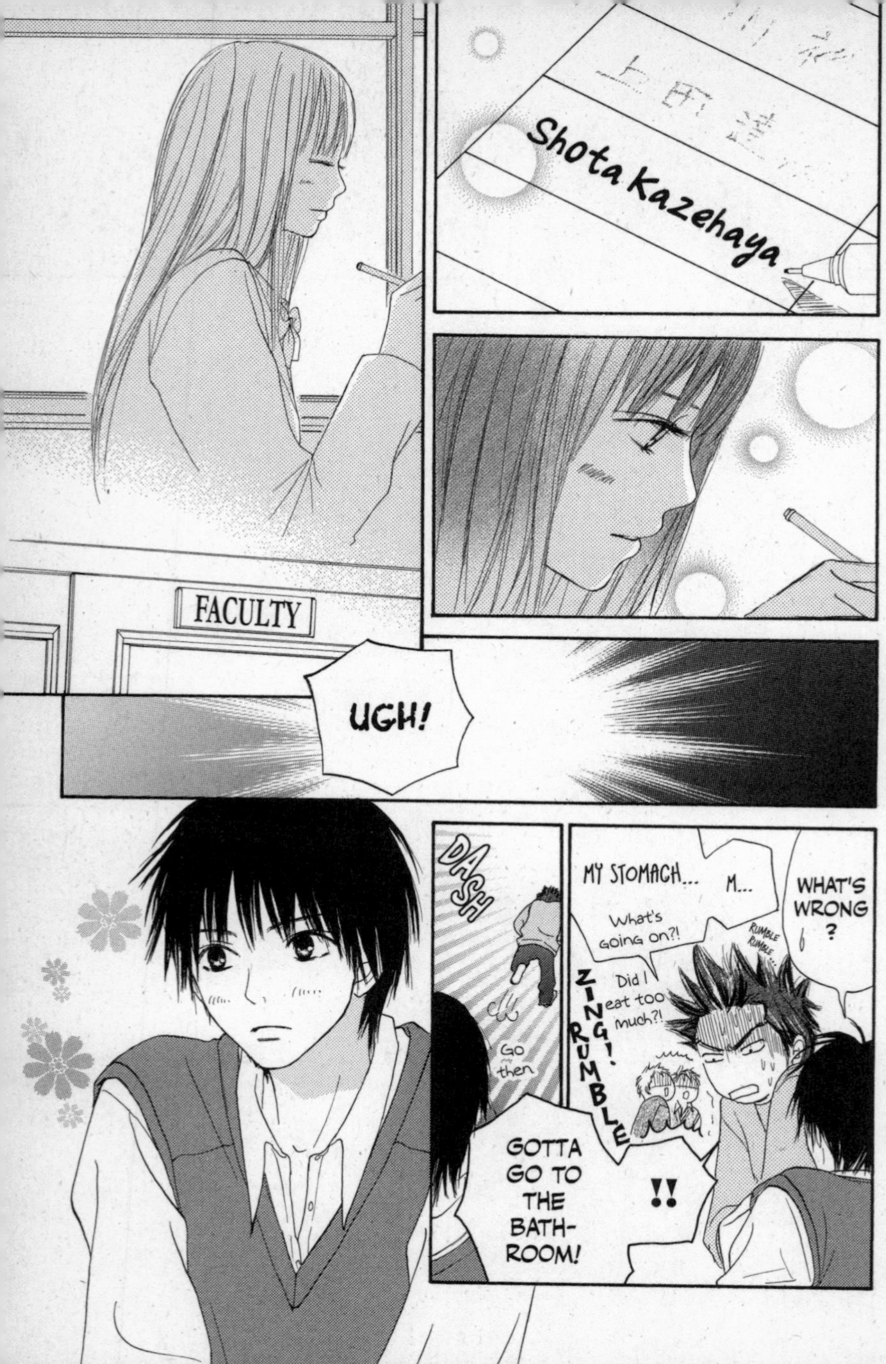
Shota Kazehaya
FACULTY
UGH!
WHAT'S WRONG?
M...
MY STOMACH...
RUMBLE RUMBLE
What's going on?!
Did I eat too much?!
ZING!
RUMBLE
GOTTA GO TO THE BATH-ROOM!
!!
DASH
Go then

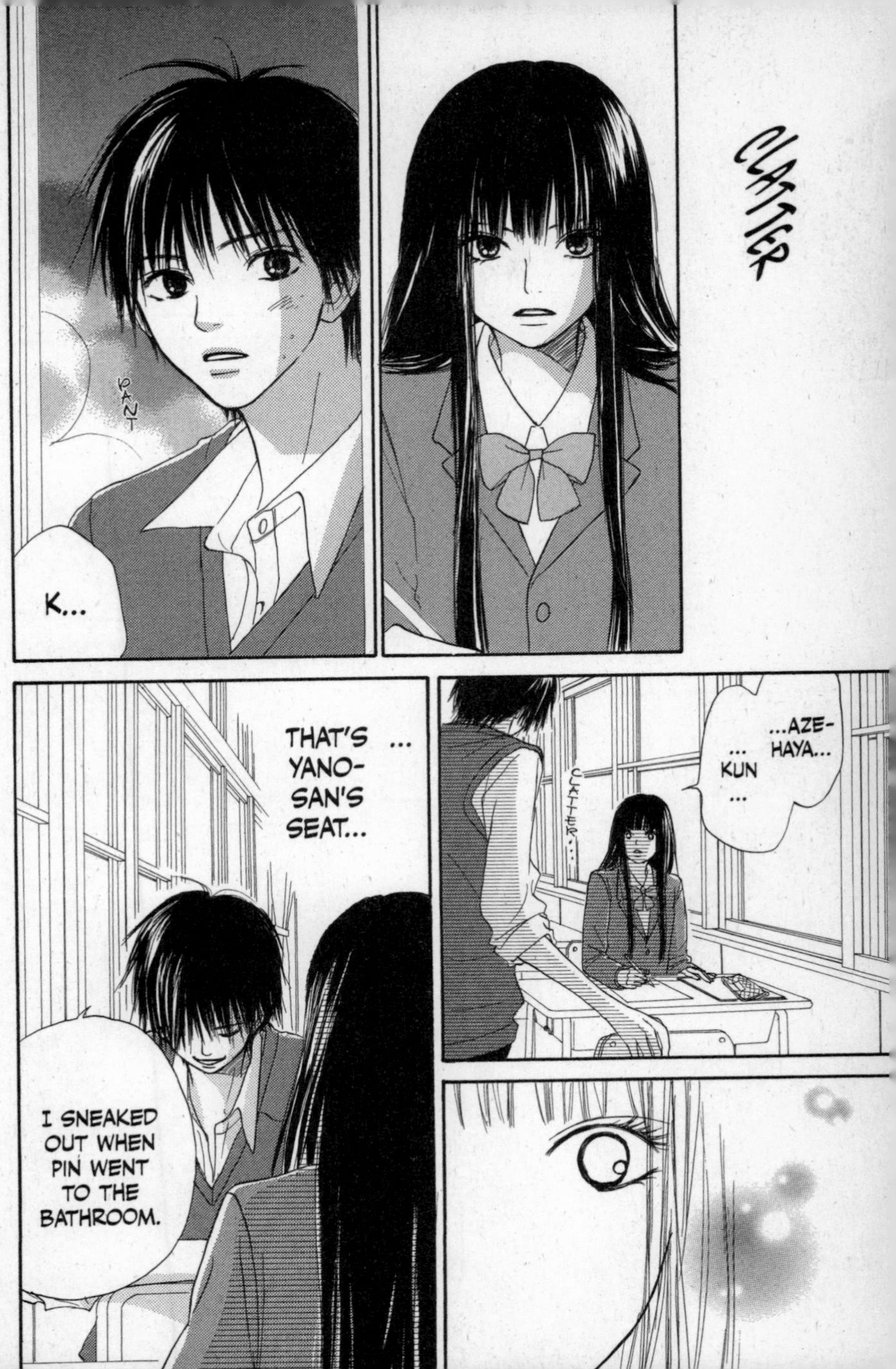
CLATTER
PANT
K...
...AZE-HAYA...
... KUN ...
CLATTER...
THAT'S YANO-SAN'S SEAT...
...
I SNEAKED OUT WHEN PIN WENT TO THE BATHROOM.

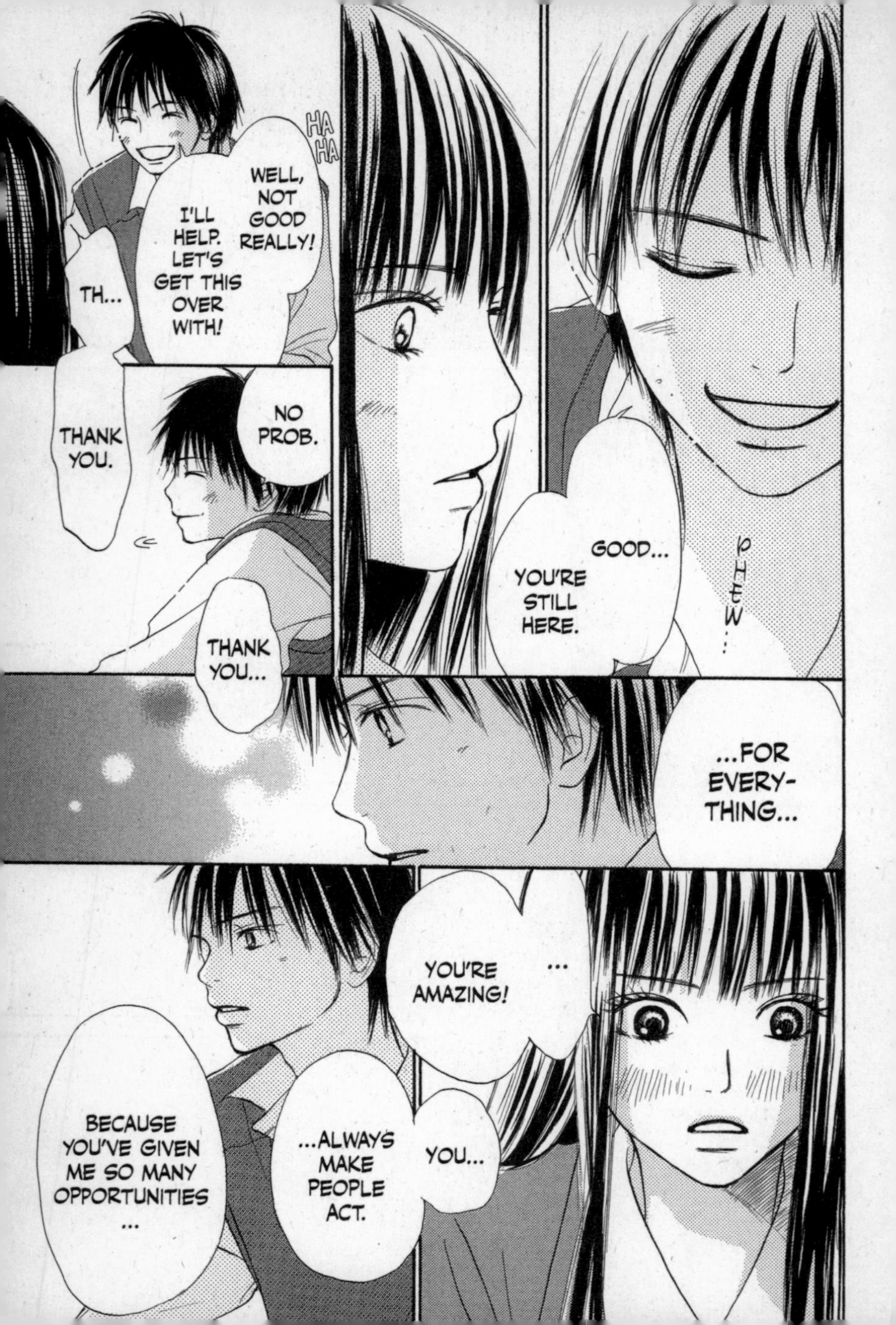
GOOD...
YOU'RE STILL HERE.
PHEW...
WELL, NOT GOOD REALLY!
HA HA
I'LL HELP. LET'S GET THIS OVER WITH!
TH...
NO PROB.
THANK YOU.
THANK YOU...
...FOR EVERY-THING...
...
YOU'RE AMAZING!
YOU...
...ALWAYS MAKE PEOPLE ACT.
BECAUSE YOU'VE GIVEN ME SO MANY OPPORTUNITIES...

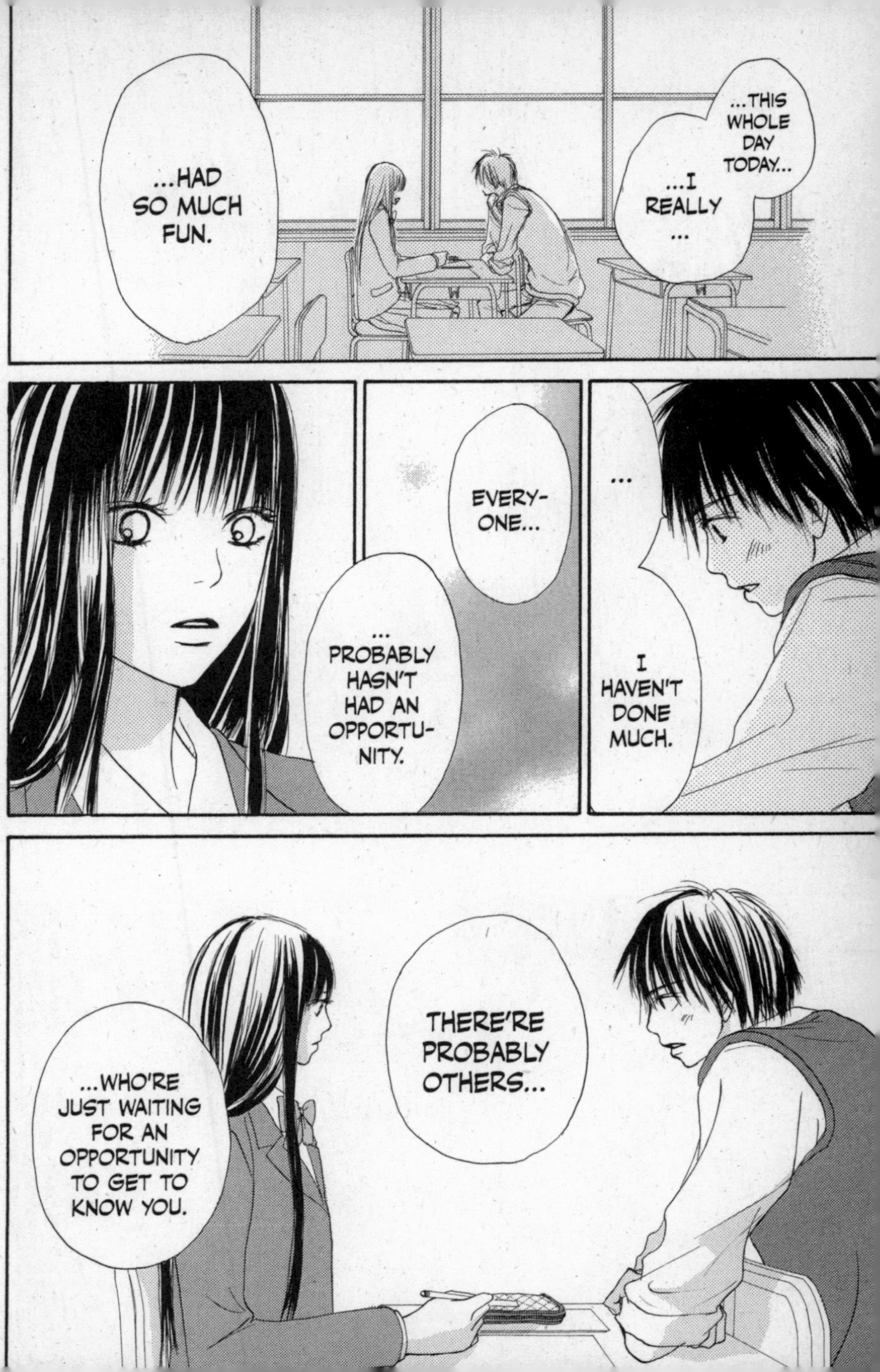
...THIS WHOLE DAY TODAY...
...I REALLY ...
...HAD SO MUCH FUN.
...
I HAVEN'T DONE MUCH.
EVERY-ONE...
... PROBABLY HASN'T HAD AN OPPORTU-NITY.
THERE'RE PROBABLY OTHERS...
...WHO'RE JUST WAITING FOR AN OPPORTUNITY TO GET TO KNOW YOU.

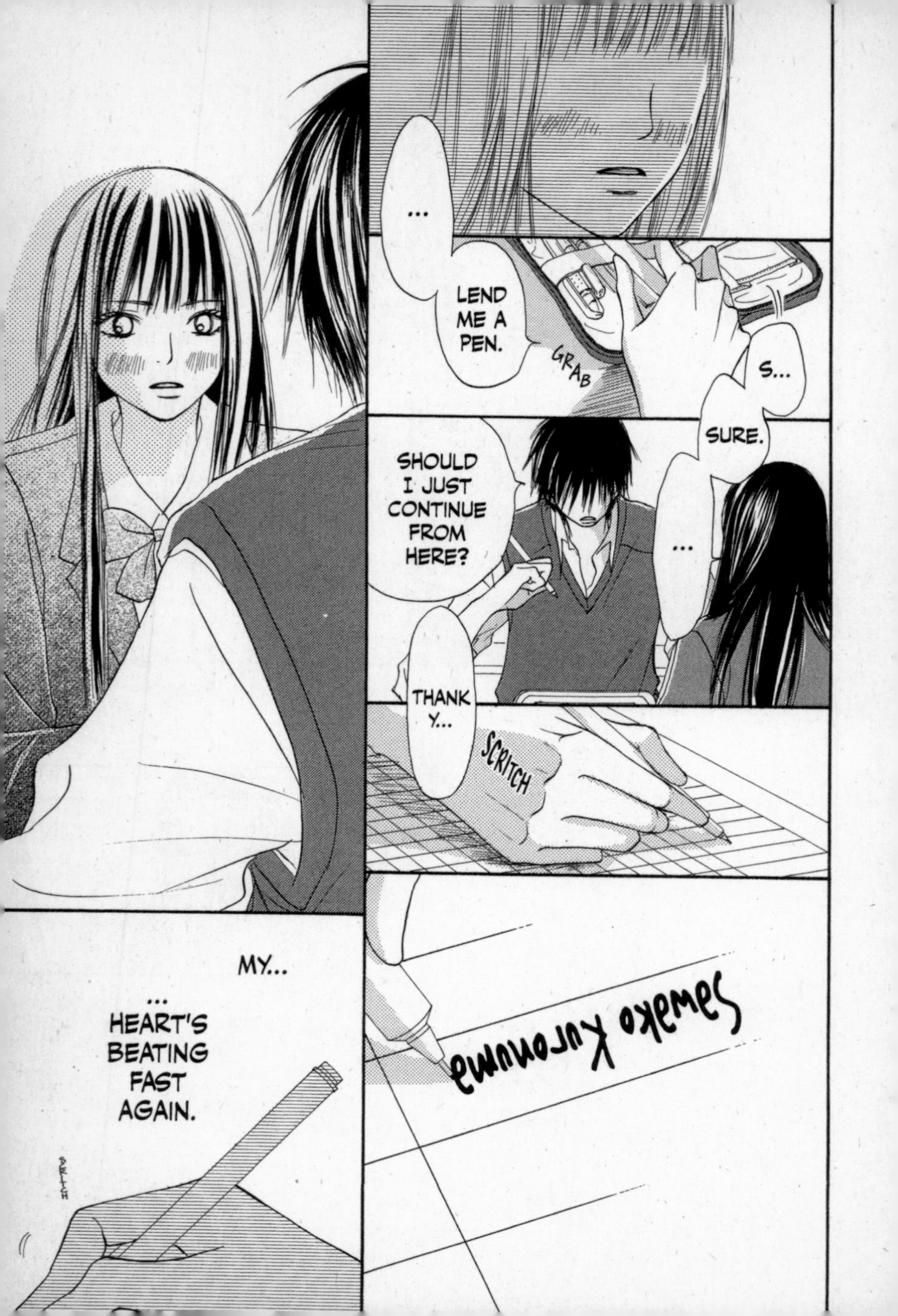
...
LEND ME A PEN.
GRAB
S...
SURE.
...
SHOULD I JUST CONTINUE FROM HERE?
THANK Y...
SCRITCH
Sawako Kuronuma
MY...
... HEART'S BEATING FAST AGAIN.
SCRITCH

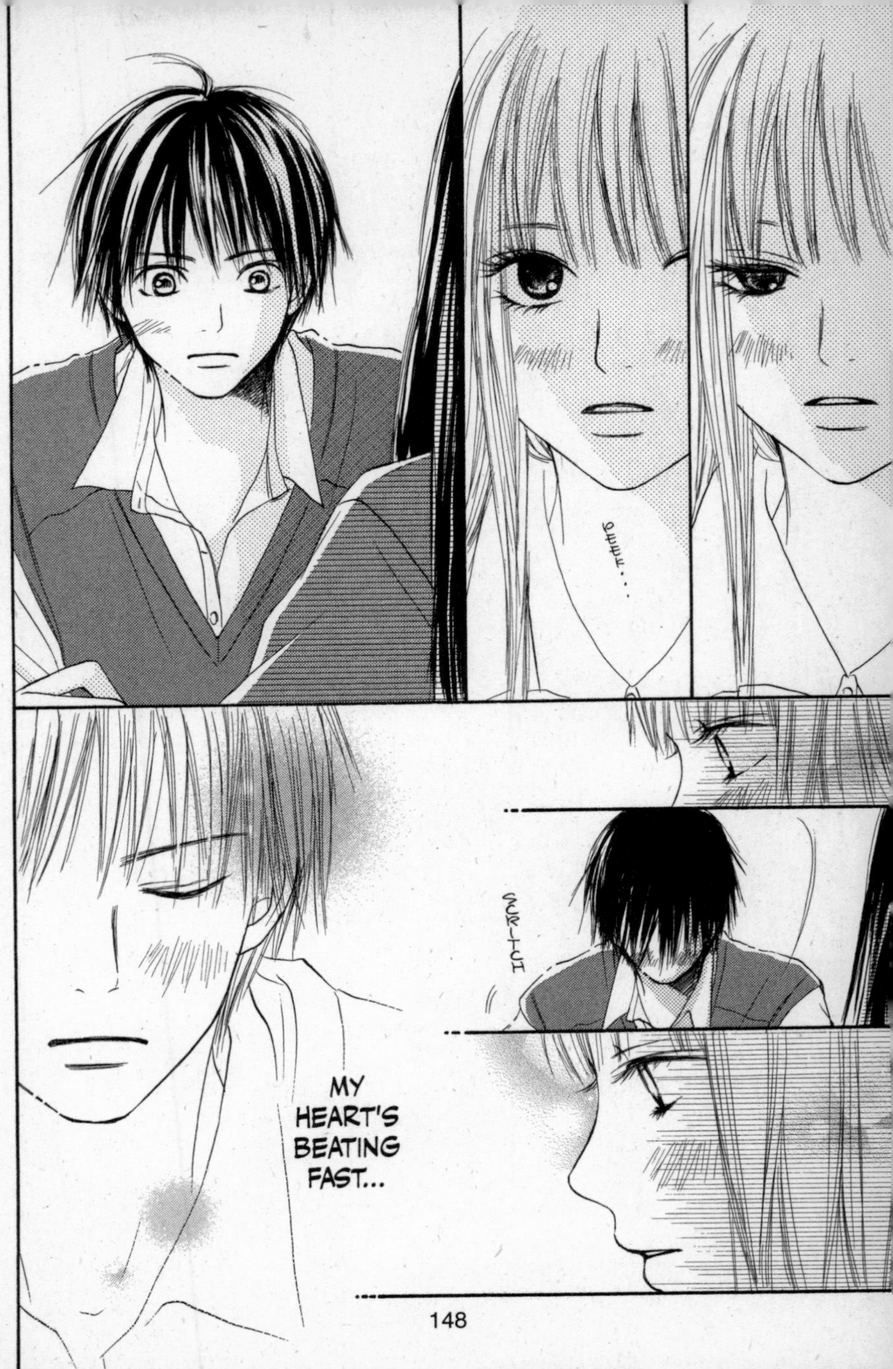
SEEE...
SCRITCH
MY HEART'S BEATING FAST...

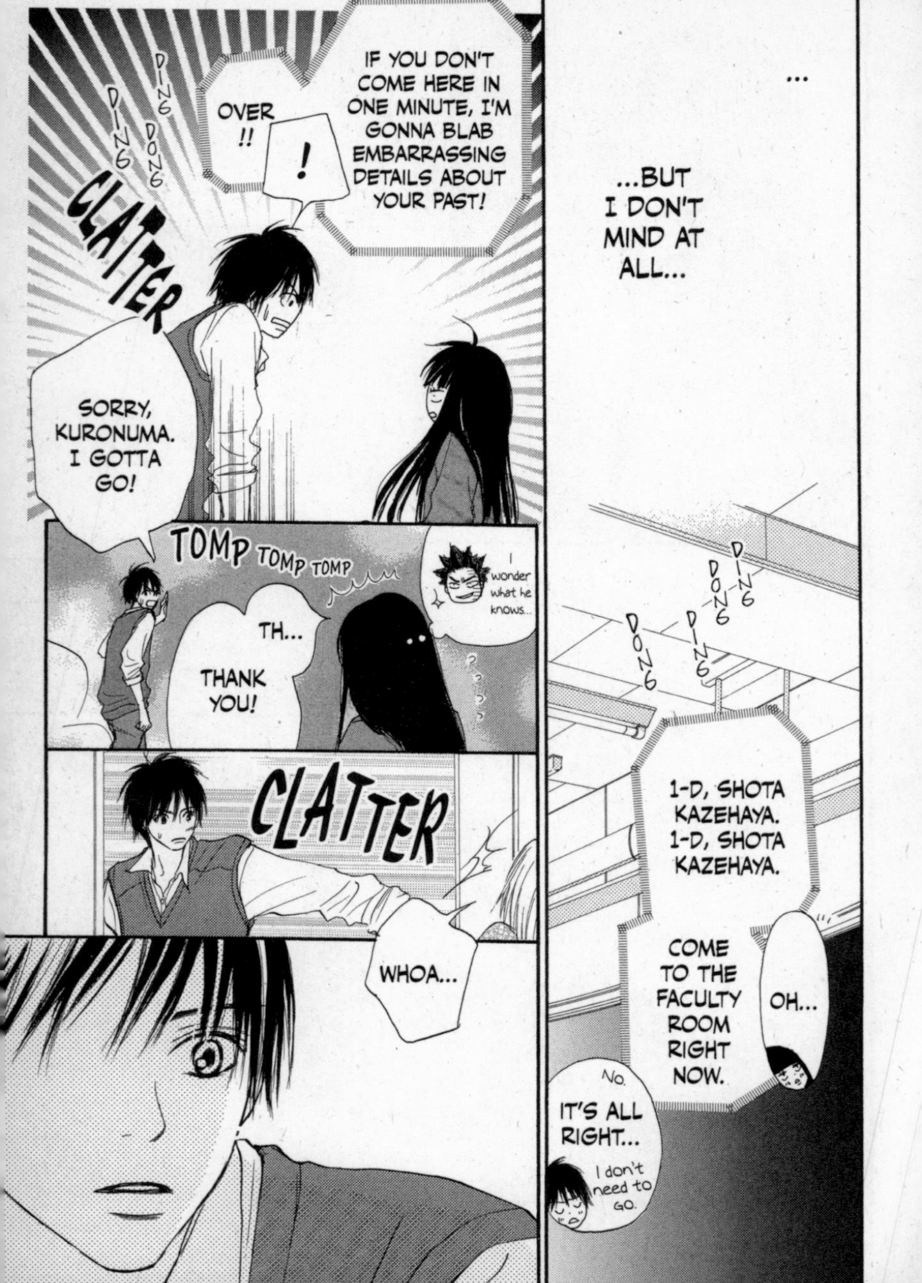
...
...BUT I DON'T MIND AT ALL...
DING DONG DING DONG
1-D, SHOTA KAZEHAYA. 1-D, SHOTA KAZEHAYA.
COME TO THE FACULTY ROOM RIGHT NOW.
OH...
No.
IT'S ALL RIGHT...
I don't need to GO.
IF YOU DON'T COME HERE IN ONE MINUTE, I'M GONNA BLAB EMBARRASSING DETAILS ABOUT YOUR PAST!
OVER !!
!
DING DONG DING DONG
CLATTER
SORRY, KURONUMA. I GOTTA GO!
I wonder what he knows...
TOMP TOMP TOMP
TH...
THANK YOU!
CLATTER
WHOA...

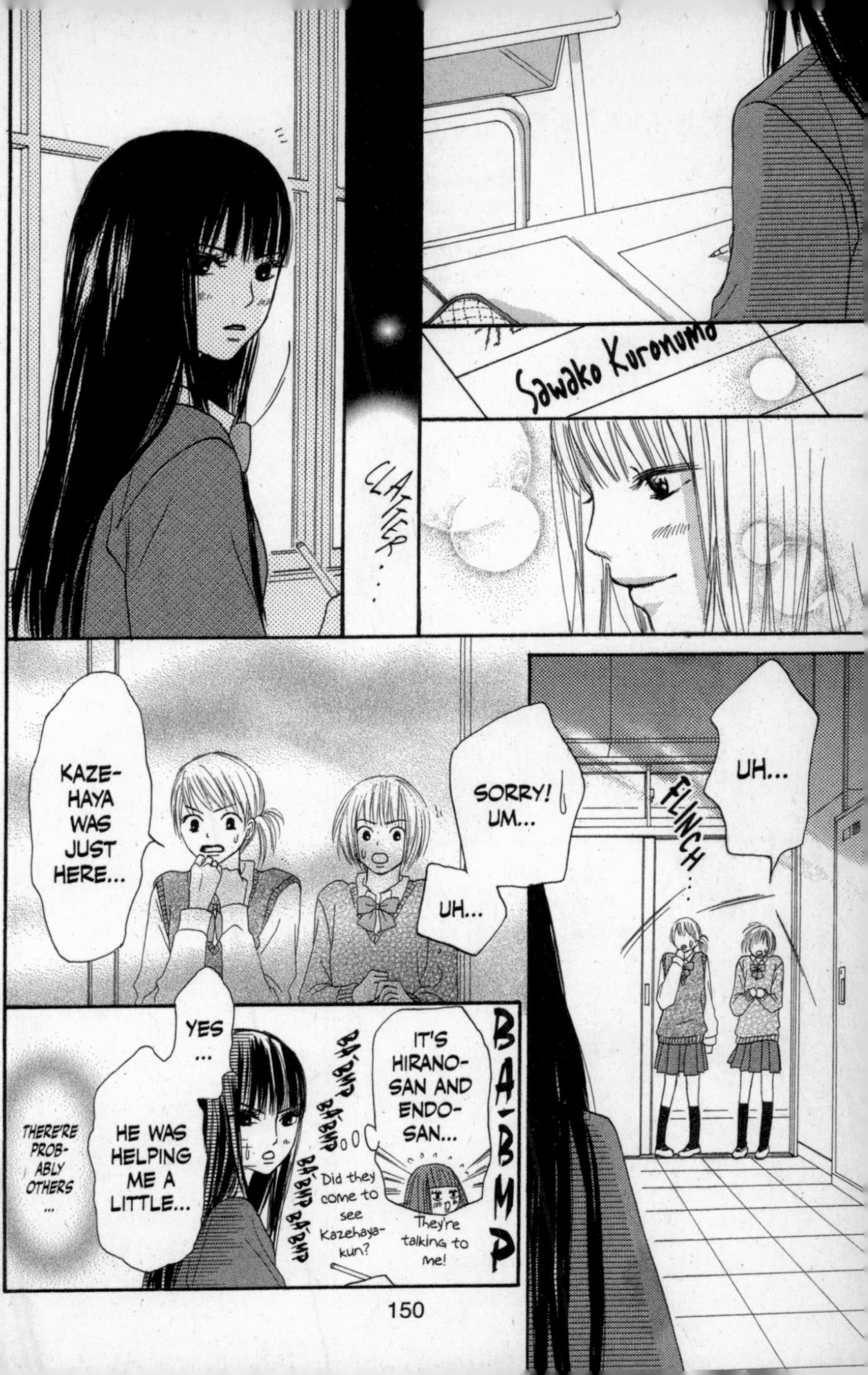
Sawako Kuronuma
CLATTER...
UH...
FLINCH...
SORRY! UM...
UH...
KAZE-HAYA WAS JUST HERE...
BA-BMP
IT'S HIRANO-SAN AND ENDO-SAN...
They're talking to me!
Did they come to see Kazehaya-kun?
BA-BMP BA-BMP BA-BMP BA-BMP
YES...
HE WAS HELPING ME A LITTLE...
THERE'RE PROB-ABLY OTHERS...

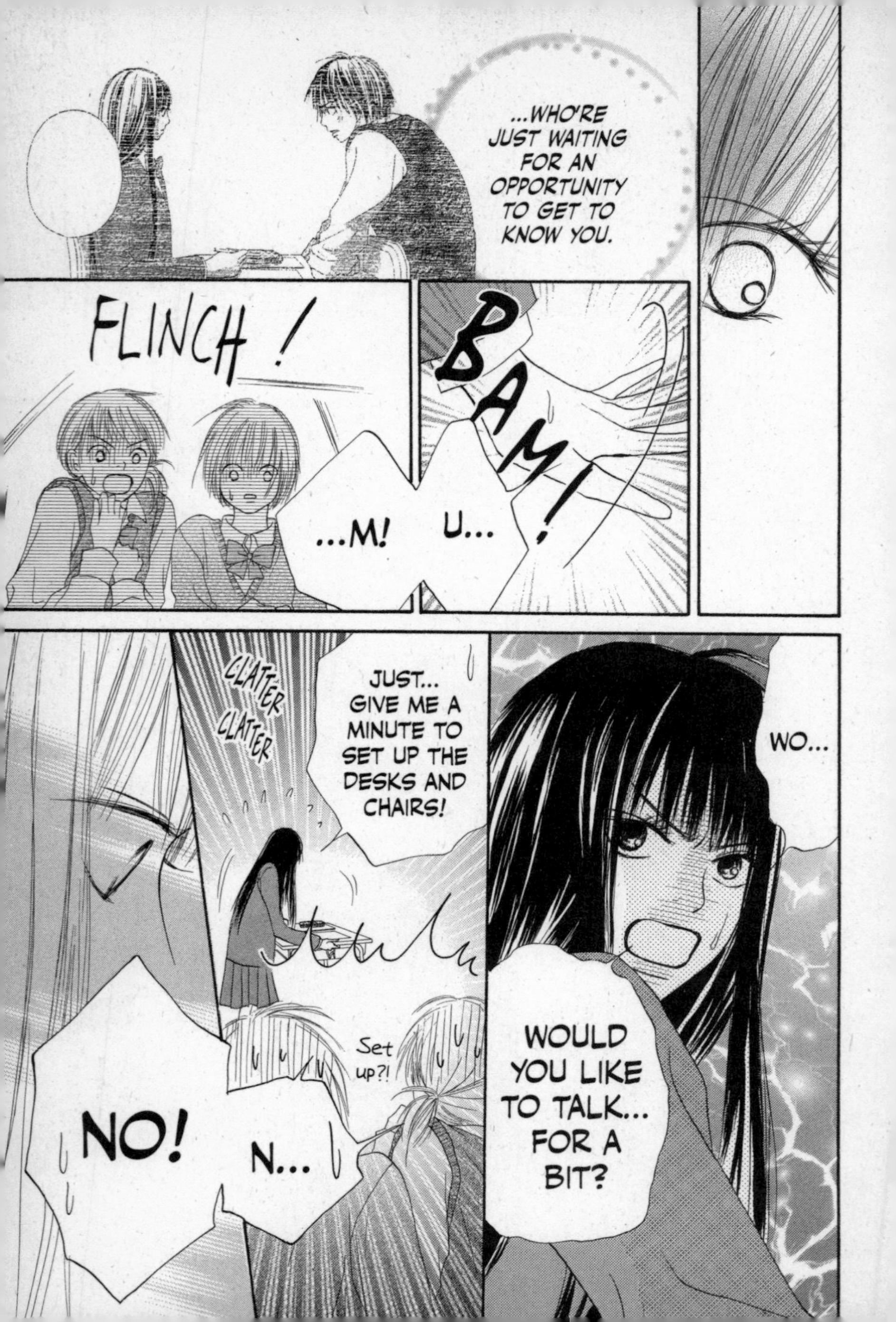
...WHO'RE JUST WAITING FOR AN OPPORTUNITY TO GET TO KNOW YOU.
BAM!
U...
...M!
FLINCH!
WO...
WOULD YOU LIKE TO TALK... FOR A BIT?
JUST... GIVE ME A MINUTE TO SET UP THE DESKS AND CHAIRS!
CLATTER CLATTER
Set up?!
N...
NO!

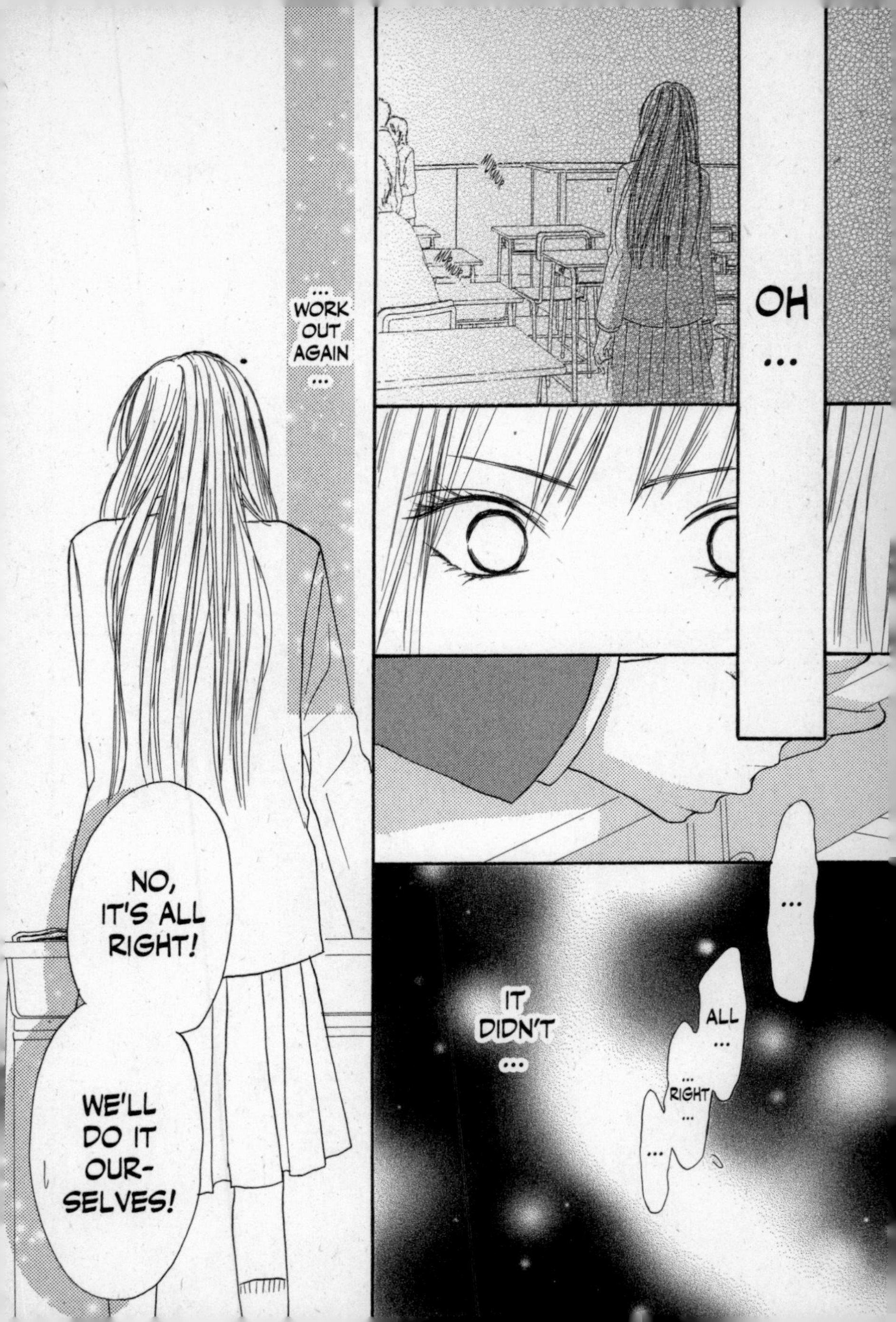
OH ...
MURMUR
MURMUR
...
ALL ... ... RIGHT ... ...
IT DIDN'T ...
... WORK OUT AGAIN ...
NO, IT'S ALL RIGHT!
WE'LL DO IT OUR-SELVES!

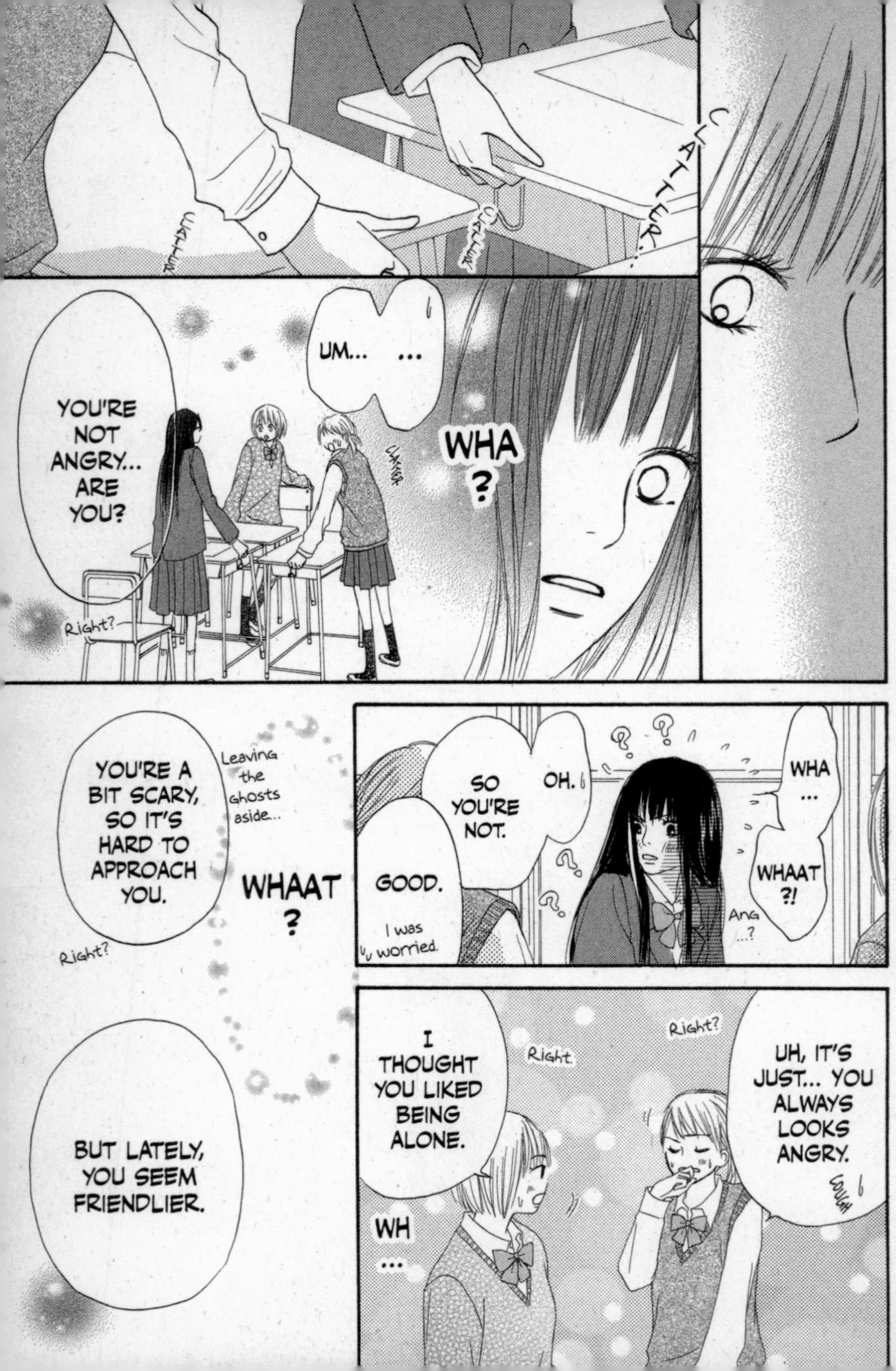
CLATTER...
CLATTER
CLATTER
UM... ...
WHA?
YOU'RE NOT ANGRY... ARE YOU?
Right?
CLATTER
WHA... WHAAT?!
Ang...?
OH.
SO YOU'RE NOT.
GOOD.
I was worried.
YOU'RE A BIT SCARY, SO IT'S HARD TO APPROACH YOU.
Leaving the ghosts aside...
WHAAT?
Right?
UH, IT'S JUST... YOU ALWAYS LOOKS ANGRY.
COUGH
Right?
Right.
I THOUGHT YOU LIKED BEING ALONE.
WH...
BUT LATELY, YOU SEEM FRIENDLIER.

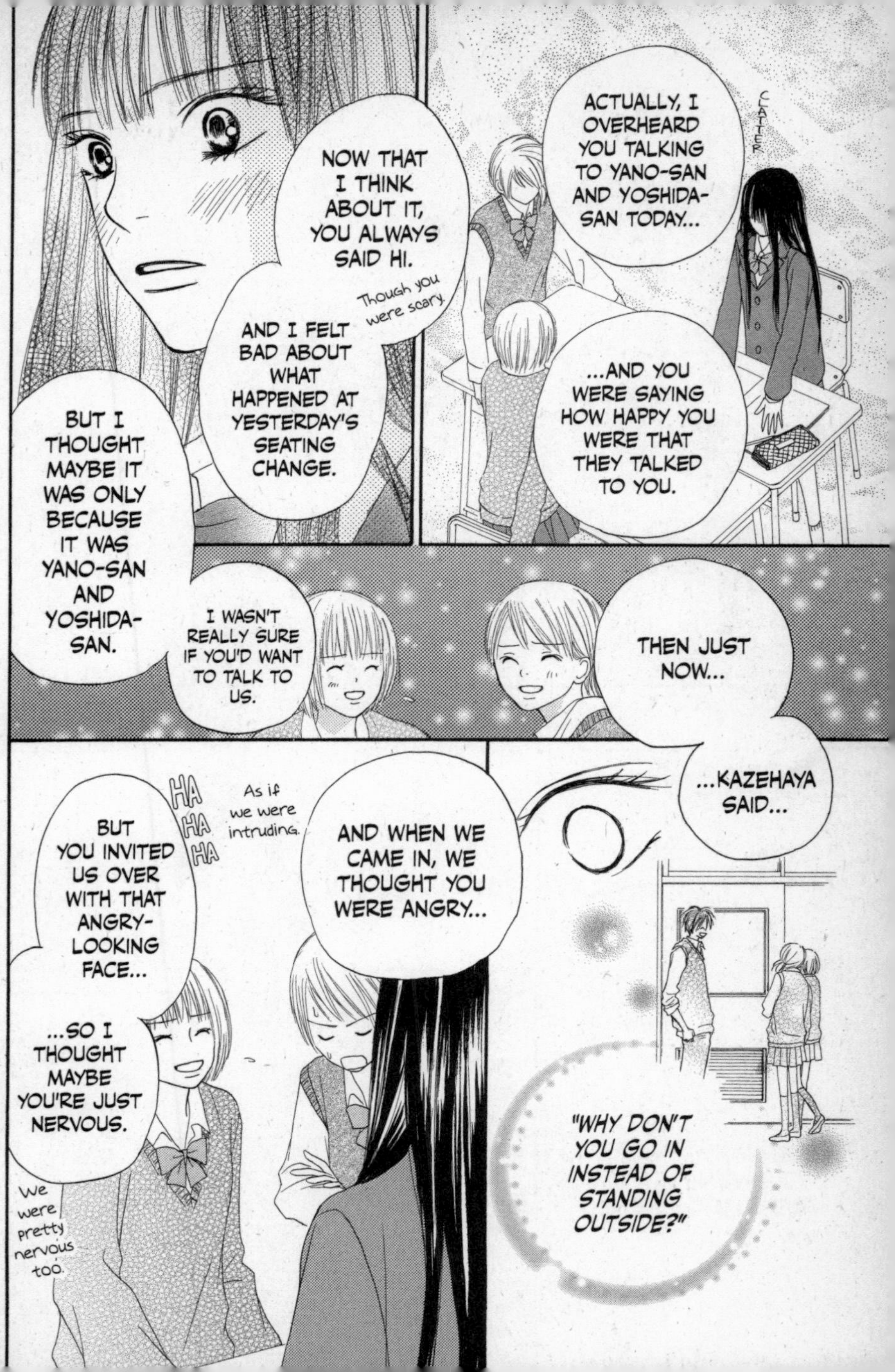
ACTUALLY, I OVERHEARD YOU TALKING TO YANO-SAN AND YOSHIDA-SAN TODAY...
CLATTER
...AND YOU WERE SAYING HOW HAPPY YOU WERE THAT THEY TALKED TO YOU.
NOW THAT I THINK ABOUT IT, YOU ALWAYS SAID HI.
Though you were scary.
AND I FELT BAD ABOUT WHAT HAPPENED AT YESTERDAY'S SEATING CHANGE.
BUT I THOUGHT MAYBE IT WAS ONLY BECAUSE IT WAS YANO-SAN AND YOSHIDA-SAN.
I WASN'T REALLY SURE IF YOU'D WANT TO TALK TO US.
THEN JUST NOW...
...KAZEHAYA SAID...
"WHY DON'T YOU GO IN INSTEAD OF STANDING OUTSIDE?"
AND WHEN WE CAME IN, WE THOUGHT YOU WERE ANGRY...
As if we were intruding.
BUT YOU INVITED US OVER WITH THAT ANGRY-LOOKING FACE...
HA HA HA
...SO I THOUGHT MAYBE YOU'RE JUST NERVOUS.
We were pretty nervous too.

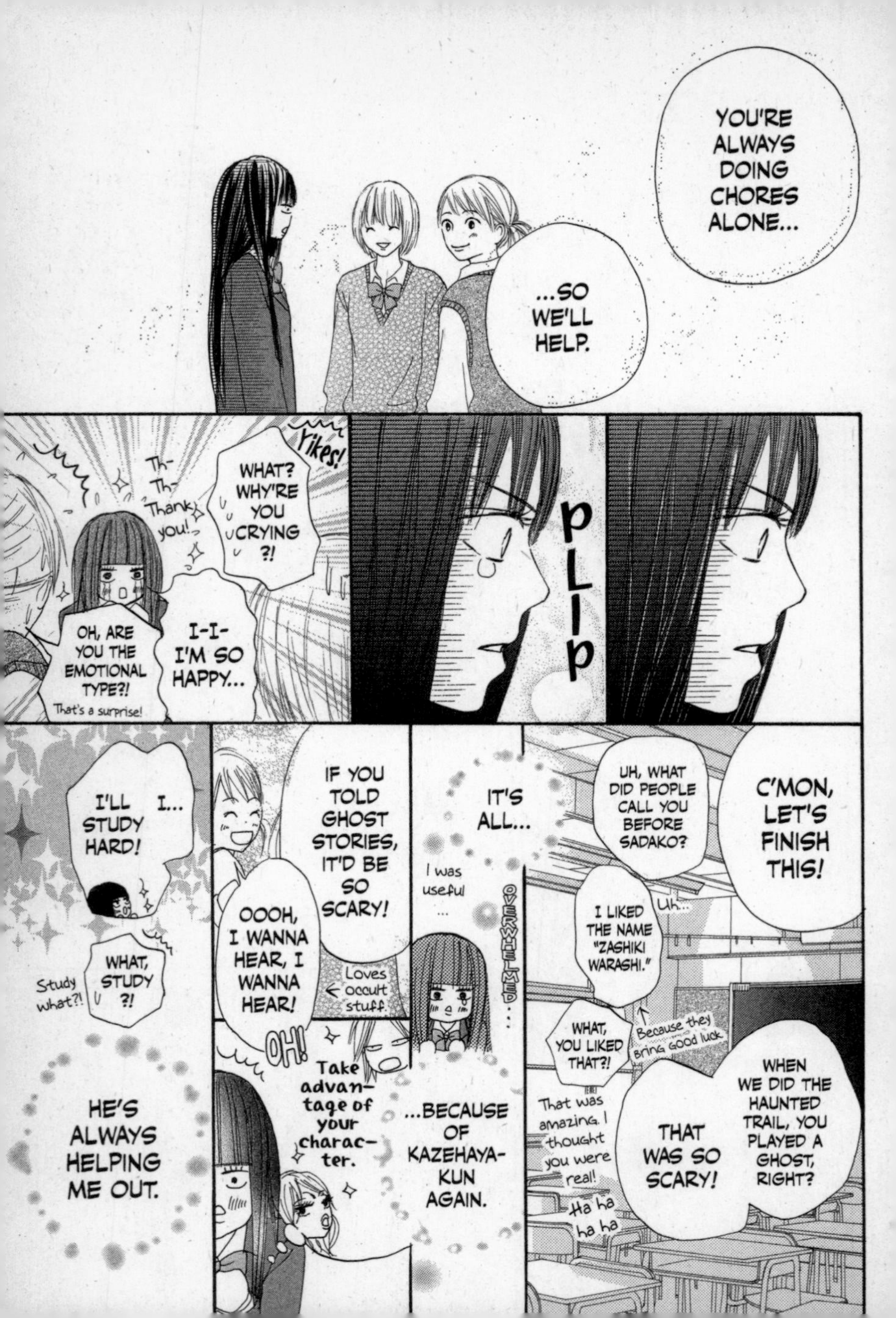
YOU'RE ALWAYS DOING CHORES ALONE...
...SO WE'LL HELP.
PLIP
Yikes!
WHAT? WHY'RE YOU CRYING?!
Th- Th- Thank you!
I-I-I'M SO HAPPY...
OH, ARE YOU THE EMOTIONAL TYPE?!
That's a surprise!
C'MON, LET'S FINISH THIS!
UH, WHAT DID PEOPLE CALL YOU BEFORE SADAKO?
Uh...
I LIKED THE NAME "ZASHIKI WARASHI."
Because they bring good luck
WHAT, YOU LIKED THAT?!
WHEN WE DID THE HAUNTED TRAIL, YOU PLAYED A GHOST, RIGHT?
THAT WAS SO SCARY!
That was amazing. I thought you were real!
Ha ha ha ha
IT'S ALL...
I was useful ...
OVERWHELMED...
IF YOU TOLD GHOST STORIES, IT'D BE SO SCARY!
OOOH, I WANNA HEAR, I WANNA HEAR!
Loves occult stuff.
...BECAUSE OF KAZEHAYA-KUN AGAIN.
OH!
Take advantage of your character.
I...
I'LL STUDY HARD!
WHAT, STUDY?!
Study what?!
HE'S ALWAYS HELPING ME OUT.

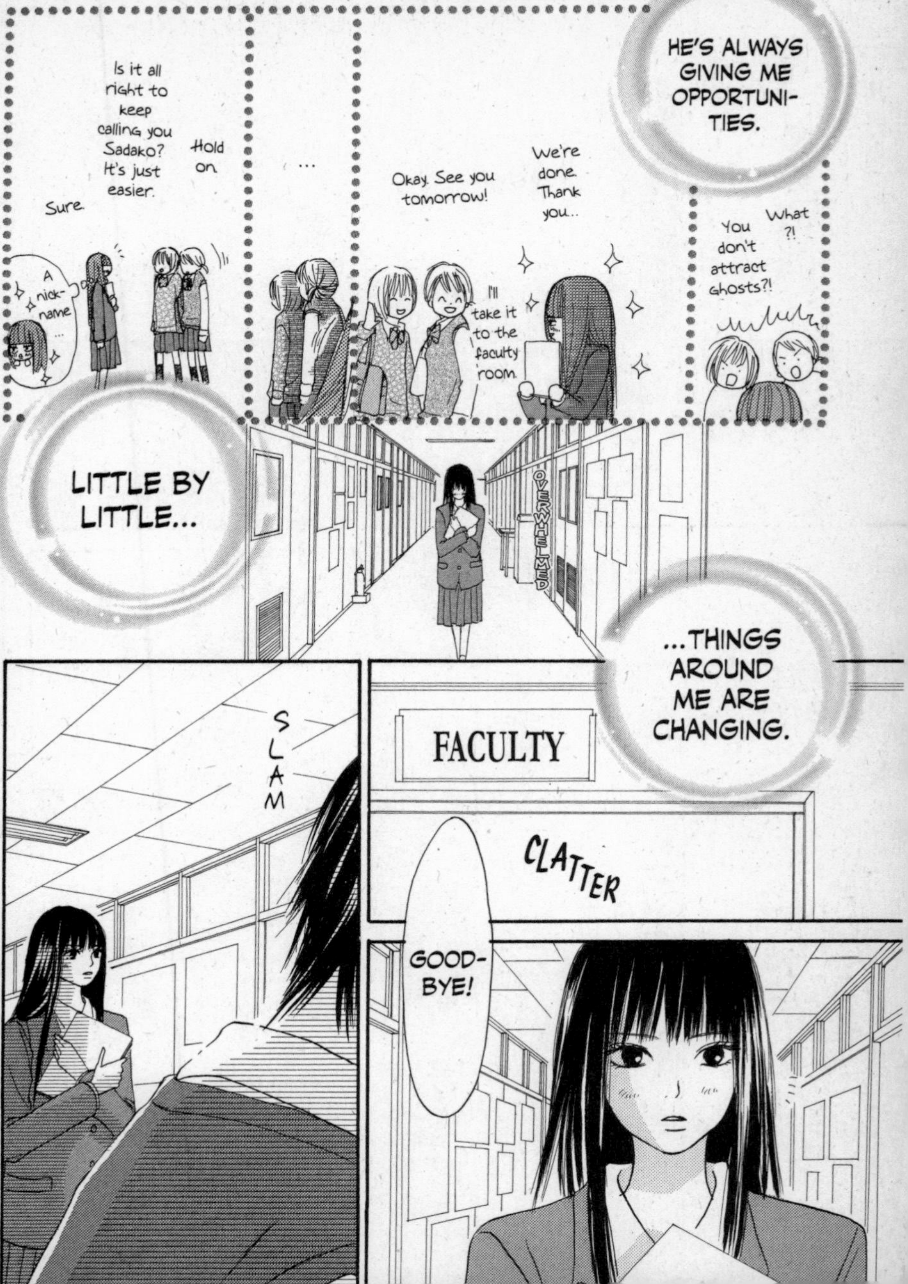
HE'S ALWAYS GIVING ME OPPORTUNI-TIES.
What?!
You don't attract ghosts?!
We're done. Thank you...
Okay. See you tomorrow!
I'll take it to the faculty room.
...
Hold on.
Is it all right to keep calling you Sadako? It's just easier.
Sure.
A nick-name...
LITTLE BY LITTLE...
OVERWHELMED
...THINGS AROUND ME ARE CHANGING.
FACULTY
CLATTER
GOOD-BYE!
SLAM

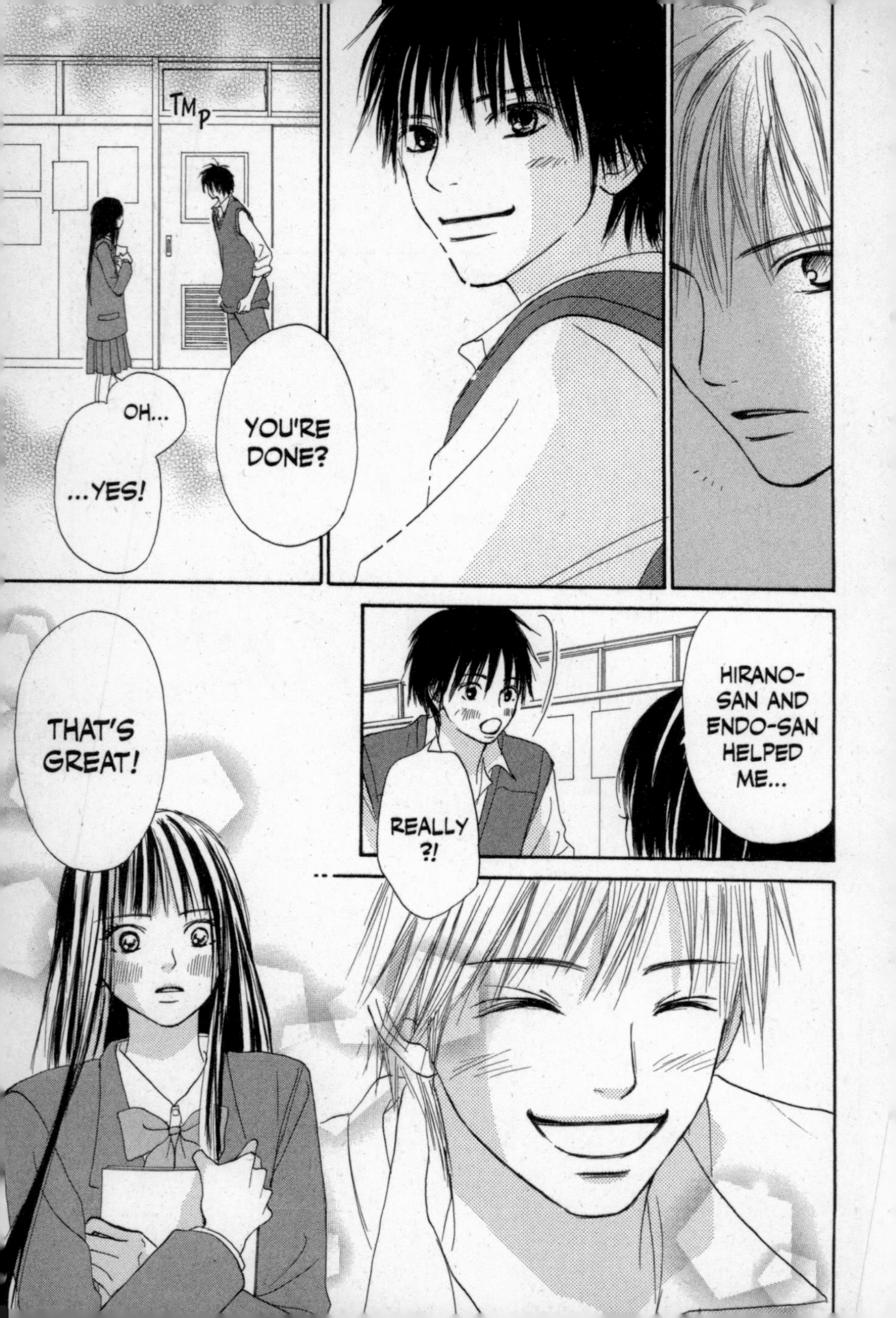
TMP
YOU'RE DONE?
OH... ...YES!
HIRANO-SAN AND ENDO-SAN HELPED ME...
REALLY?!
THAT'S GREAT!

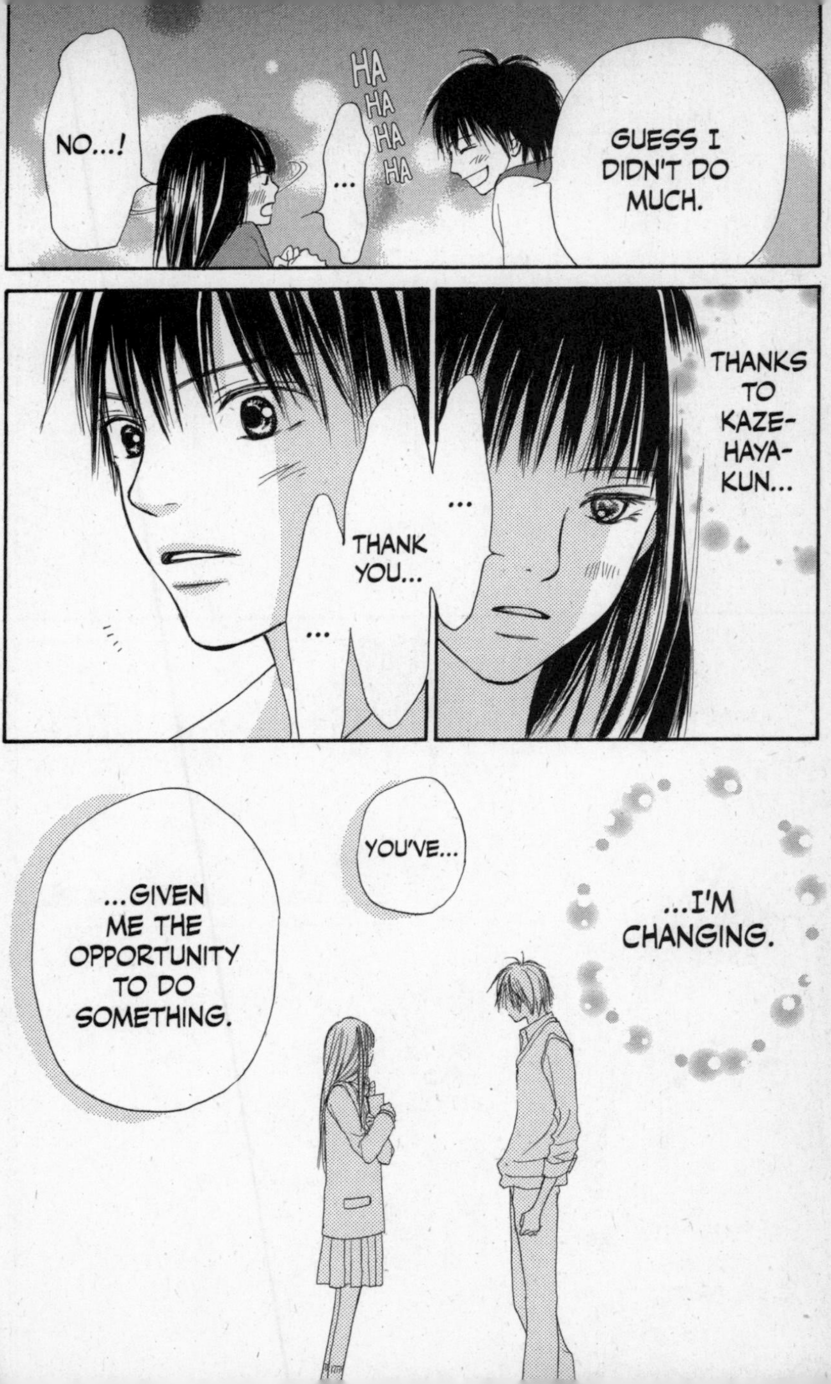
GUESS I DIDN'T DO MUCH.
HA HA HA HA
...
NO...!
THANKS TO KAZE-HAYA-KUN...
... THANK YOU... ...
...I'M CHANGING.
YOU'VE...
...GIVEN ME THE OPPORTUNITY TO DO SOMETHING.

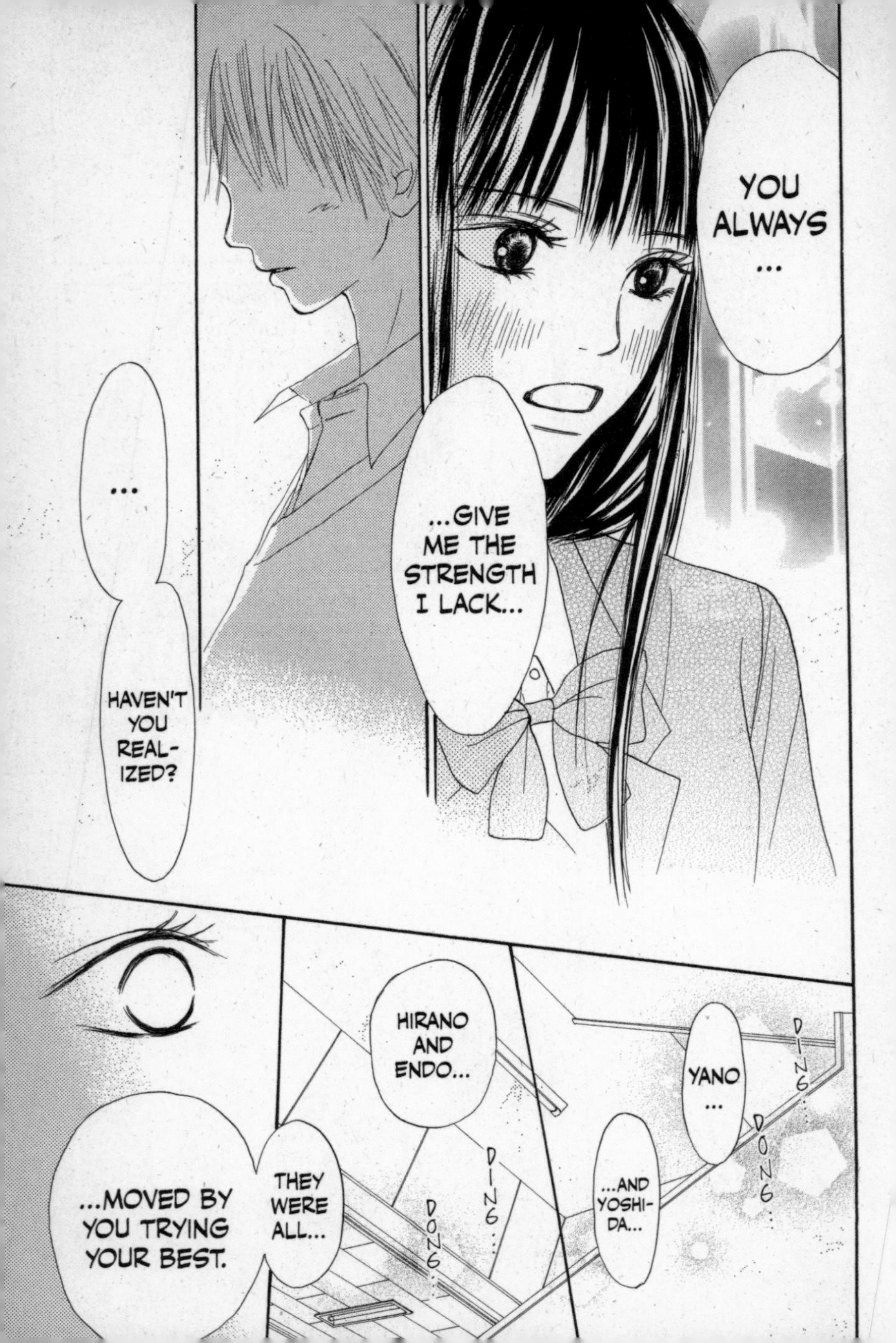
YOU ALWAYS ...
...GIVE ME THE STRENGTH I LACK...
...
HAVEN'T YOU REALIZED?
YANO ...
DING... DONG...
...AND YOSHIDA...
HIRANO AND ENDO...
DING... DONG...
THEY WERE ALL...
...MOVED BY YOU TRYING YOUR BEST.

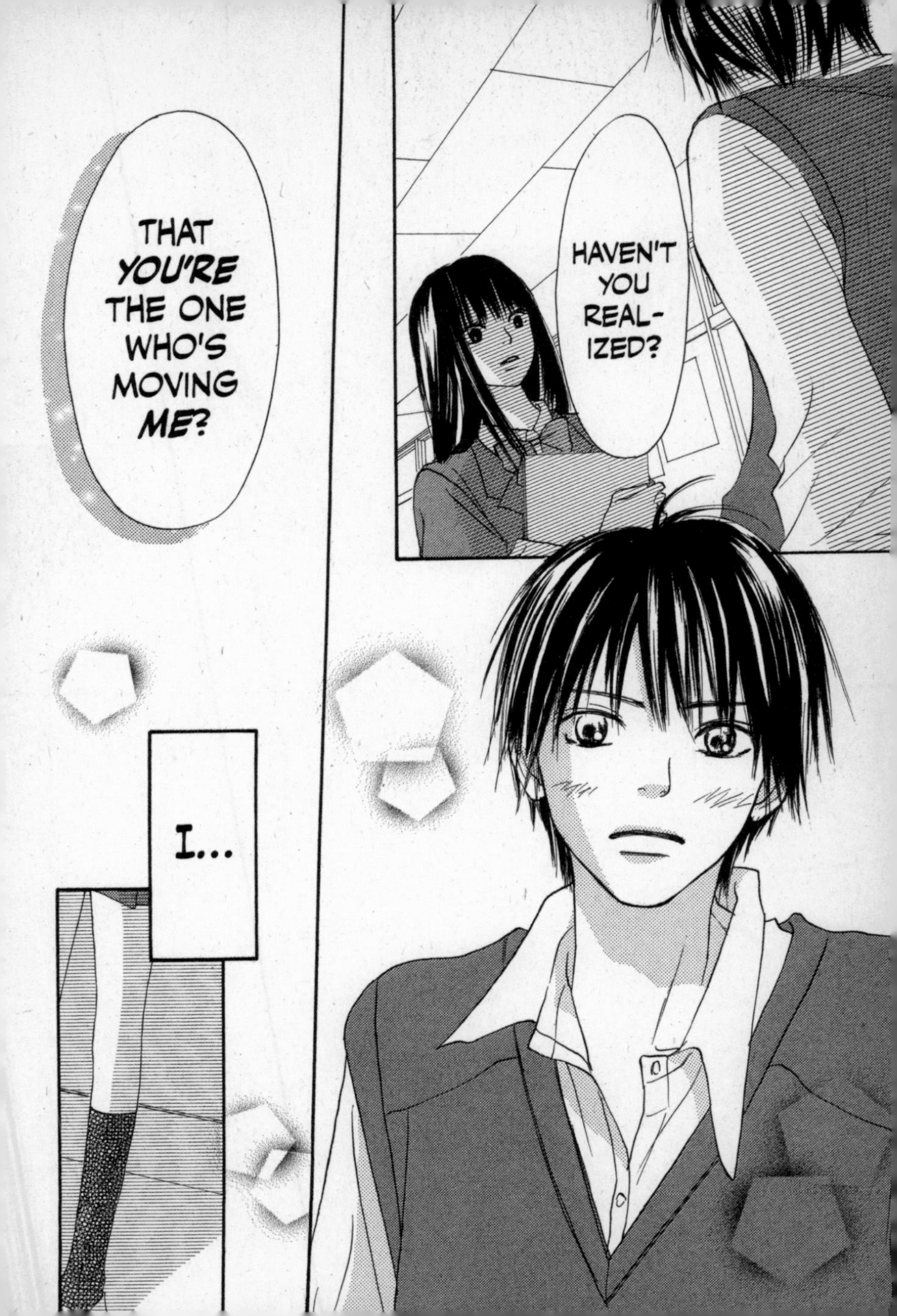
HAVEN'T YOU REALIZED?
THAT *YOU'RE* THE ONE WHO'S MOVING *ME*?
I...

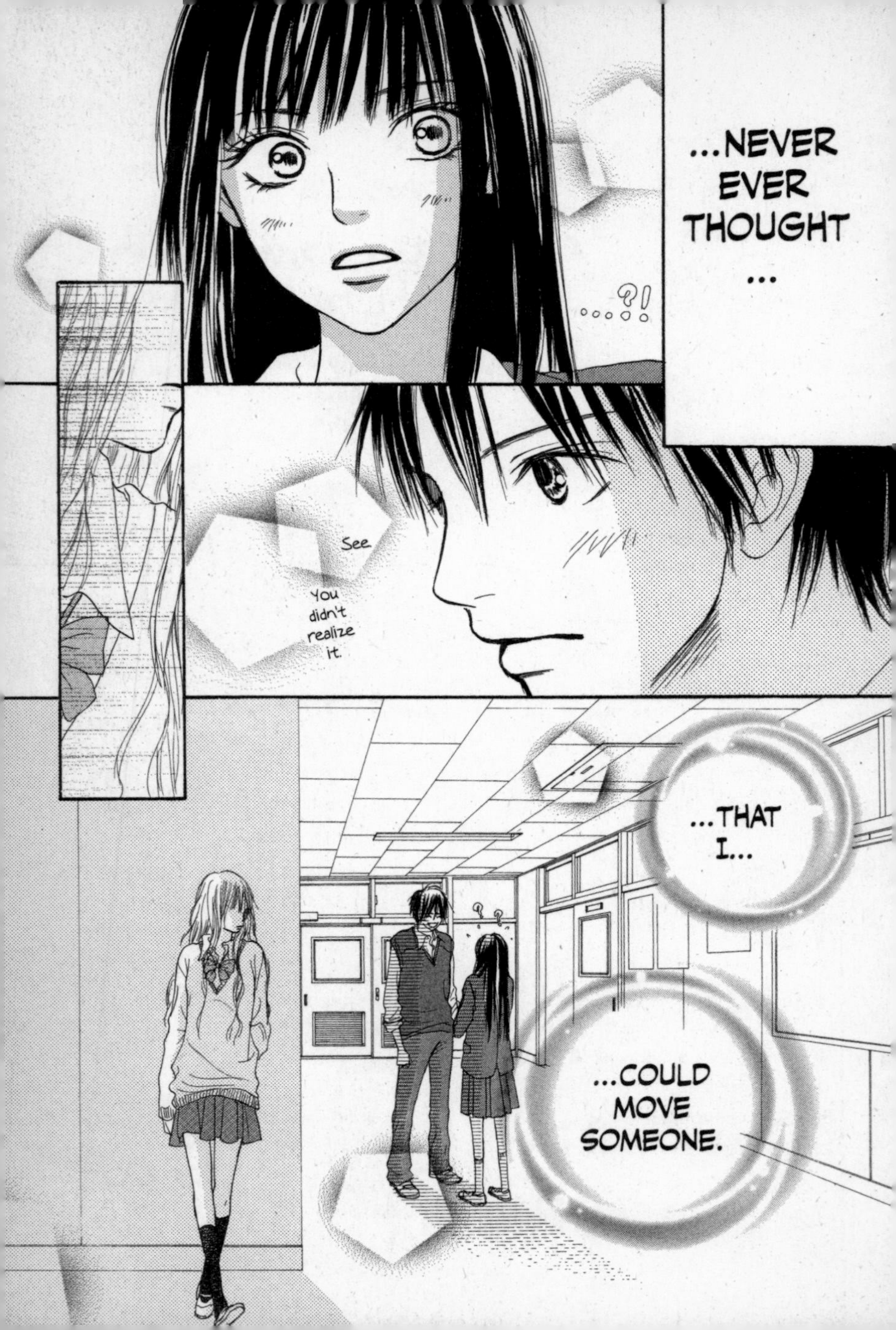
...NEVER EVER THOUGHT ...
...?!
See
You didn't realize it.
...THAT I...
...COULD MOVE SOMEONE.

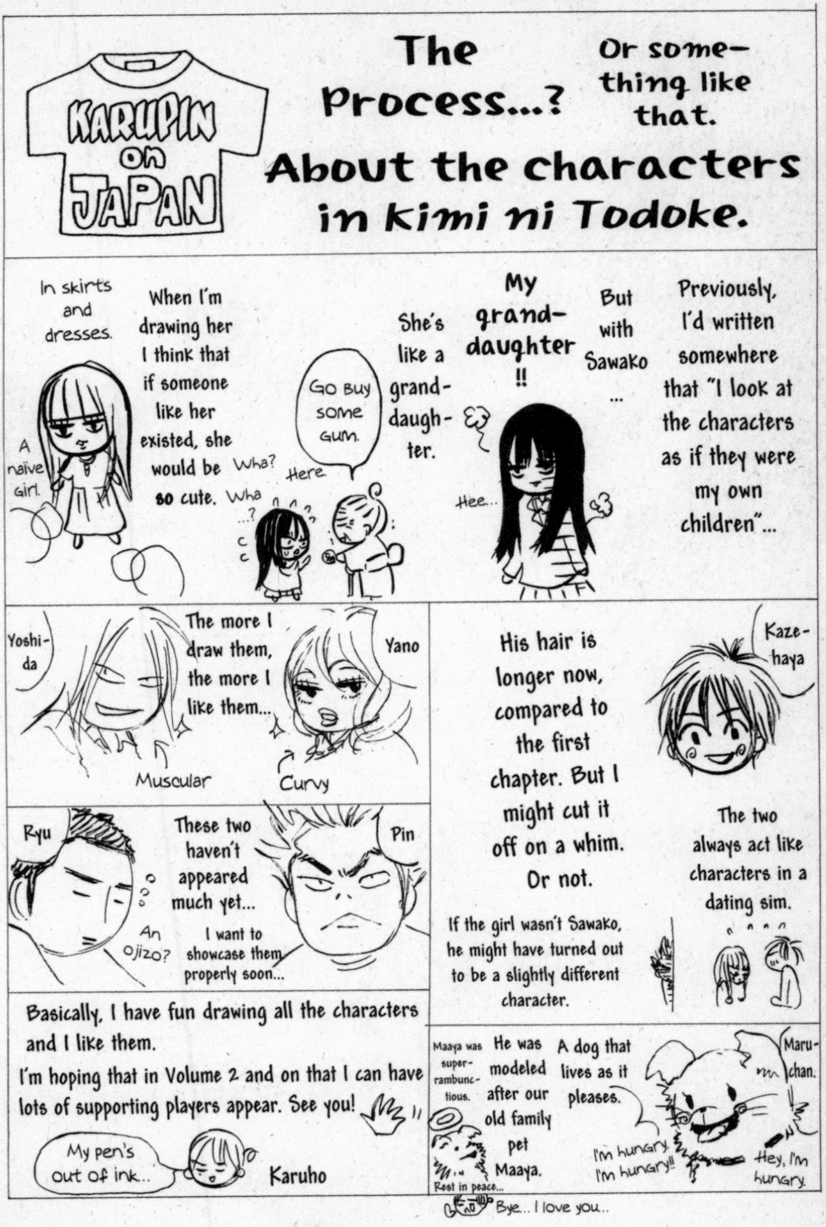
KARUPIN on JAPAN
The Process...?
Or some-thing like that.
About the characters in Kimi ni Todoke.
Previously, I'd written somewhere that "I look at the characters as if they were my own children"...
But with Sawako...
My grand-daughter!!
She's like a grand-daugh-ter.
Hee...
Go buy some gum.
Here.
Wha?
Wha...?
When I'm drawing her I think that if someone like her existed, she would be so cute.
In skirts and dresses.
A naïve girl.
Kaze-haya
His hair is longer now, compared to the first chapter. But I might cut it off on a whim. Or not.
The two always act like characters in a dating sim.
If the girl wasn't Sawako, he might have turned out to be a slightly different character.
Yano
The more I draw them, the more I like them...
Yoshi-da
Curvy
Muscular
Pin
These two haven't appeared much yet...
Ryu
I want to showcase them properly soon...
An ojizo?
Maru-chan.
A dog that lives as it pleases.
He was modeled after our old family pet Maaya.
Maaya was super-rambunc-tious.
I'm hungry. I'm hungry!!
Hey, I'm hungry.
Rest in peace...
Basically, I have fun drawing all the characters and I like them.
I'm hoping that in Volume 2 and on that I can have lots of supporting players appear. See you!
My pen's out of ink...
Karuho
Bye... I love you...

Episode 3: Smile

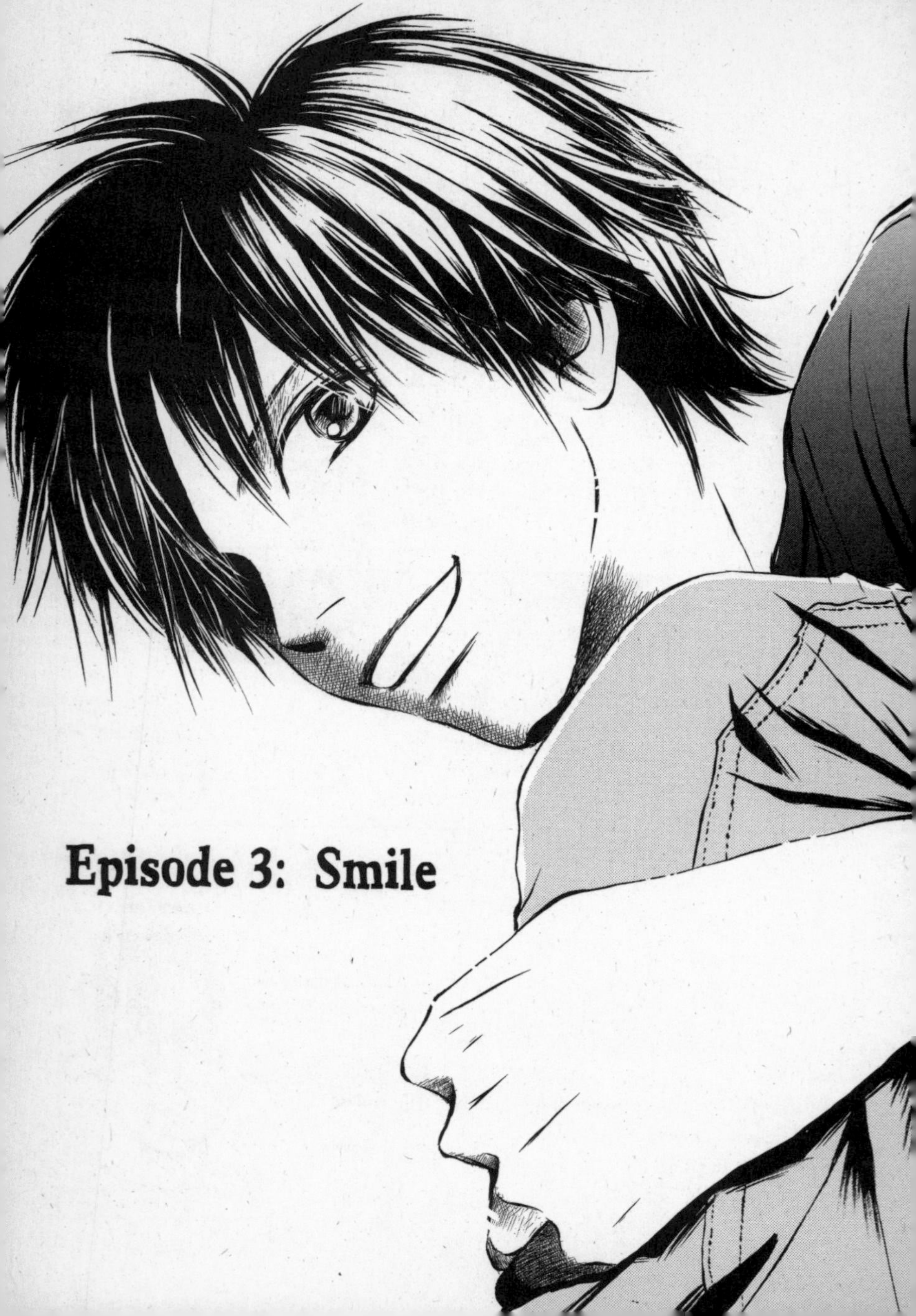

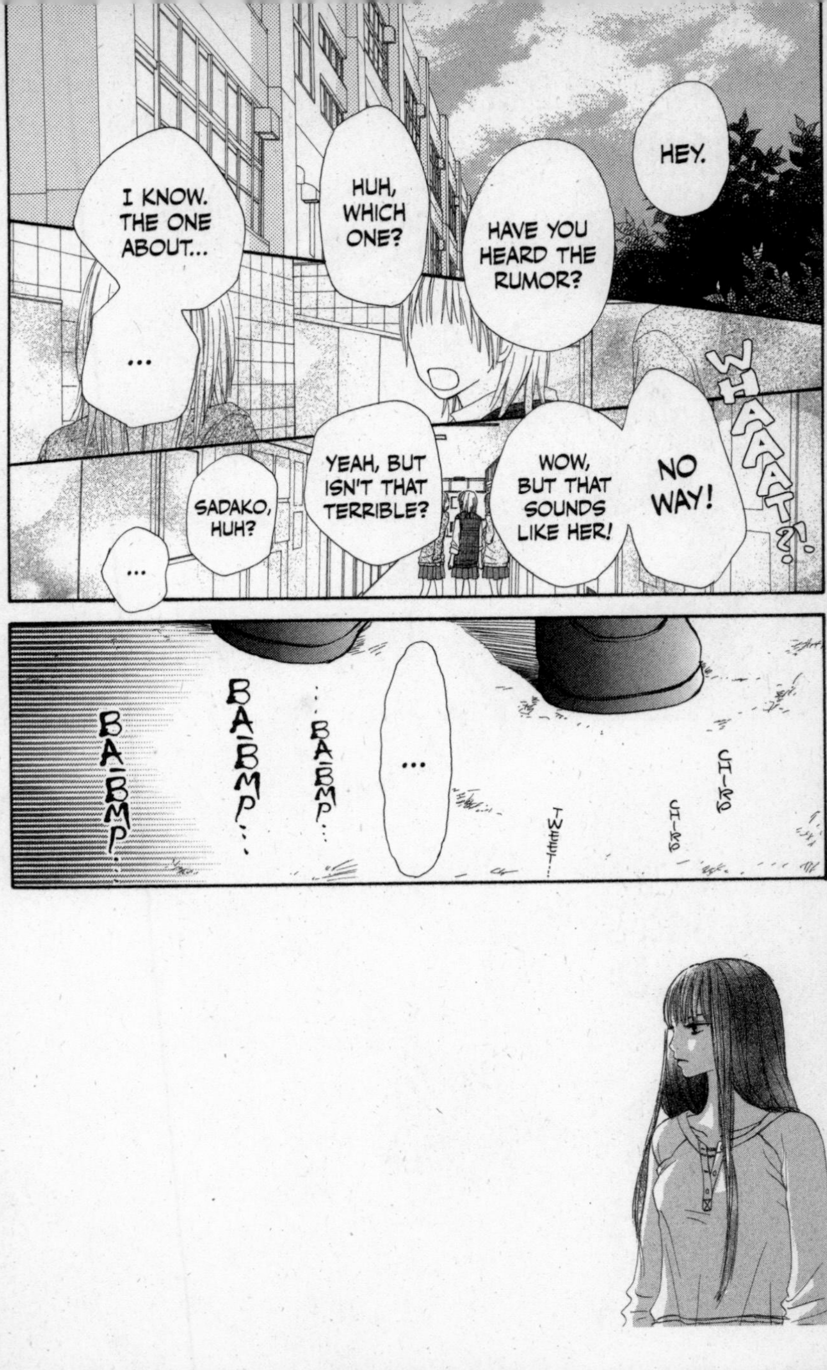
HEY.
HAVE YOU HEARD THE RUMOR?
HUH, WHICH ONE?
I KNOW. THE ONE ABOUT...
...
WHAAAT?!
NO WAY!
WOW, BUT THAT SOUNDS LIKE HER!
YEAH, BUT ISN'T THAT TERRIBLE?
SADAKO, HUH?
...
CHIRP
CHIRP
TWEET...
...
...BA-BMP...
BA-BMP...
BA-BMP...

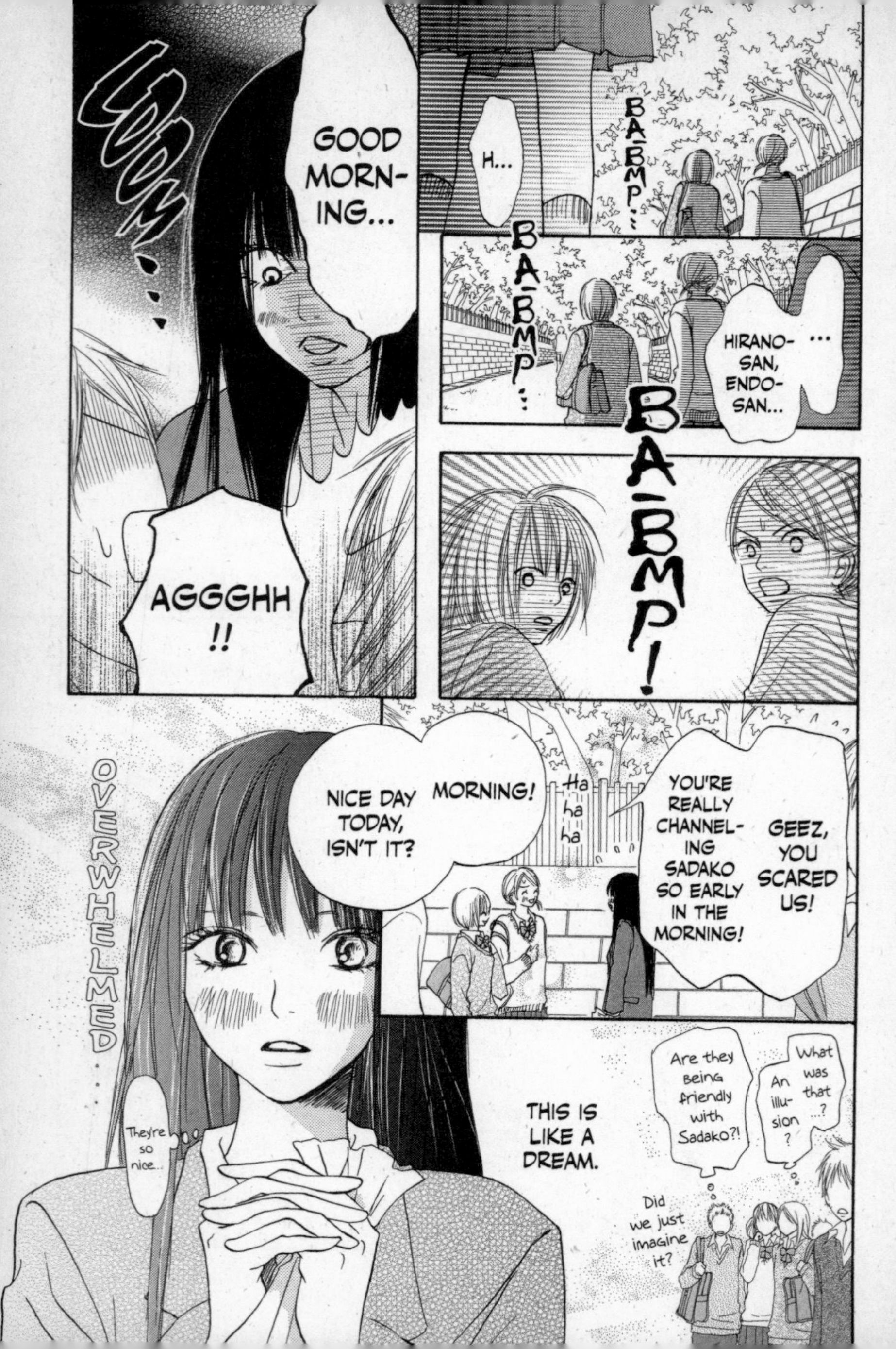
BA-BMP...
H...
...
HIRANO-SAN, ENDO-SAN...
BA-BMP...
BA-BMP!
GOOD MORNING...
LOOOM...
AGGGHH!!
GEEZ, YOU SCARED US!
YOU'RE REALLY CHANNELING SADAKO SO EARLY IN THE MORNING!
Ha ha ha
MORNING!
NICE DAY TODAY, ISN'T IT?
What was that ...?
An illusion?
Are they being friendly with Sadako?!
THIS IS LIKE A DREAM.
Did we just imagine it?
OVERWHELMED...
They're so nice...

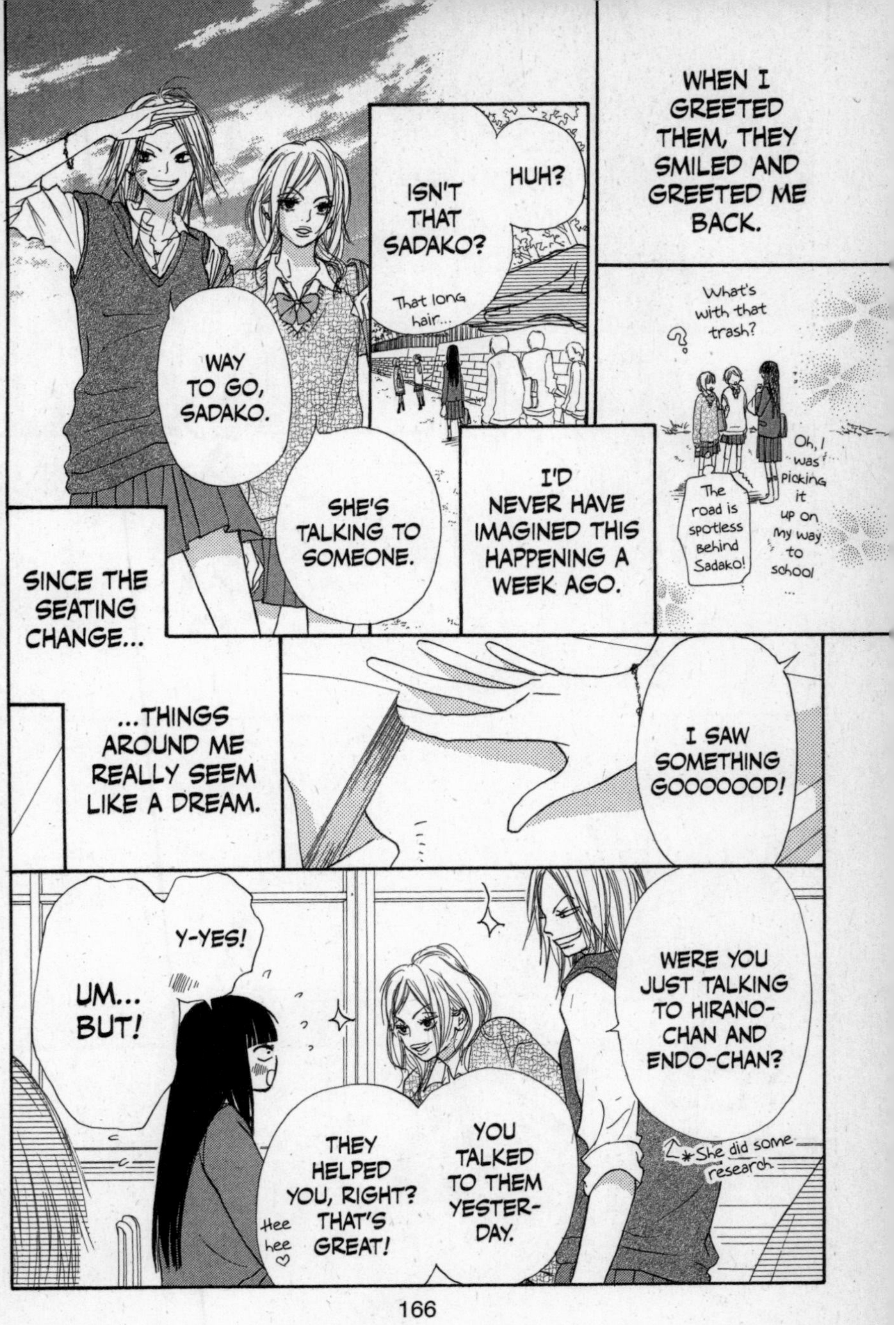
WHEN I GREETED THEM, THEY SMILED AND GREETED ME BACK.
HUH?
ISN'T THAT SADAKO?
That long hair...
WAY TO GO, SADAKO.
SHE'S TALKING TO SOMEONE.
What's with that trash?
Oh, I was picking it up on my way to school...
The road is spotless behind Sadako!
I'D NEVER HAVE IMAGINED THIS HAPPENING A WEEK AGO.
SINCE THE SEATING CHANGE...
I SAW SOMETHING GOOOOOOD!
...THINGS AROUND ME REALLY SEEM LIKE A DREAM.
WERE YOU JUST TALKING TO HIRANO-CHAN AND ENDO-CHAN?
*She did some research.
YOU TALKED TO THEM YESTERDAY.
THEY HELPED YOU, RIGHT? THAT'S GREAT!
Hee hee
Y-YES!
UM... BUT!

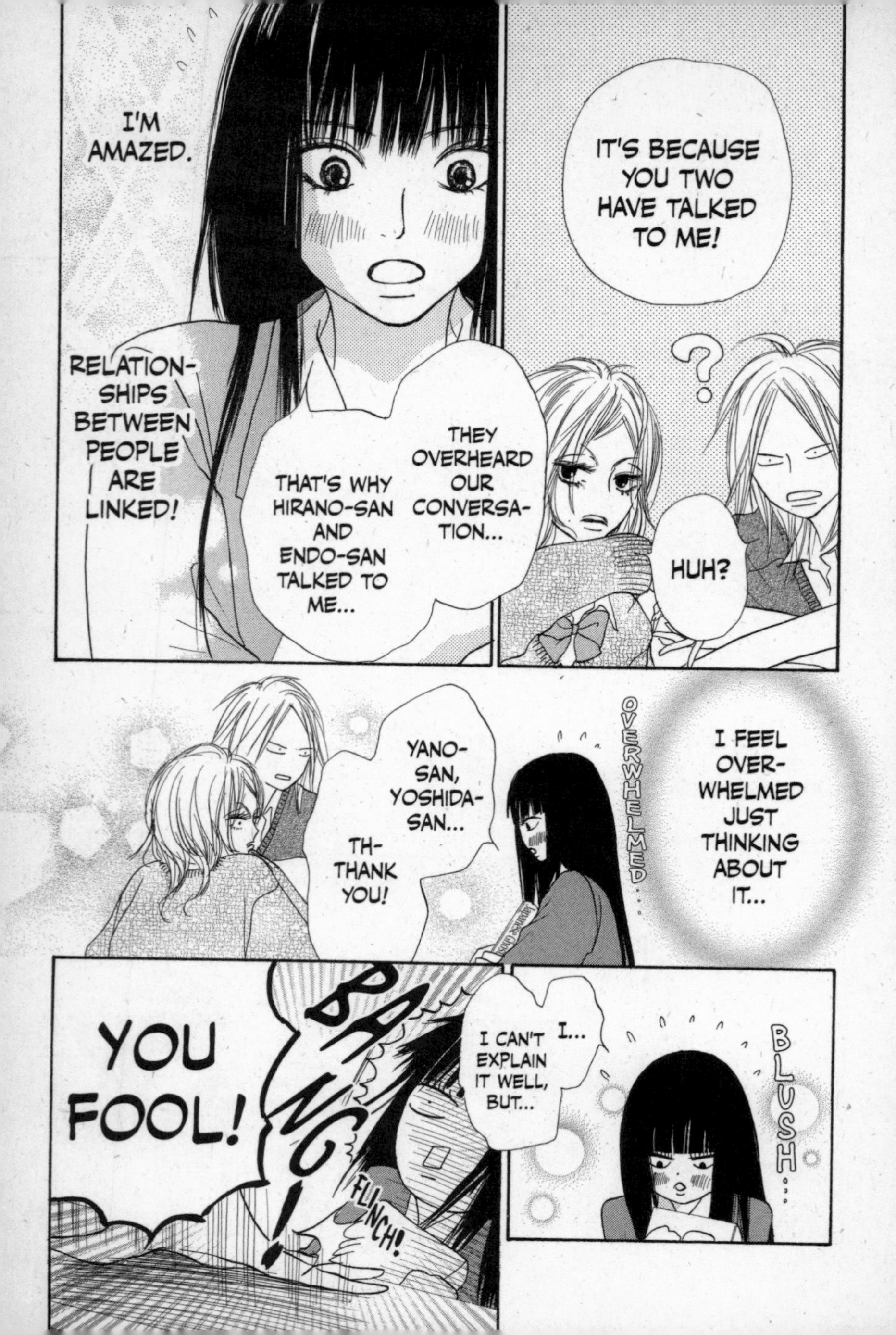
IT'S BECAUSE YOU TWO HAVE TALKED TO ME!
?
HUH?
I'M AMAZED.
THEY OVERHEARD OUR CONVERSATION...
THAT'S WHY HIRANO-SAN AND ENDO-SAN TALKED TO ME...
RELATIONSHIPS BETWEEN PEOPLE ARE LINKED!
I FEEL OVERWHELMED JUST THINKING ABOUT IT...
OVERWHELMED...
YANO-SAN, YOSHIDA-SAN...
TH-THANK YOU!
BLUSH...
I...
I CAN'T EXPLAIN IT WELL, BUT...
BANG!
YOU FOOL!
FLINCH!

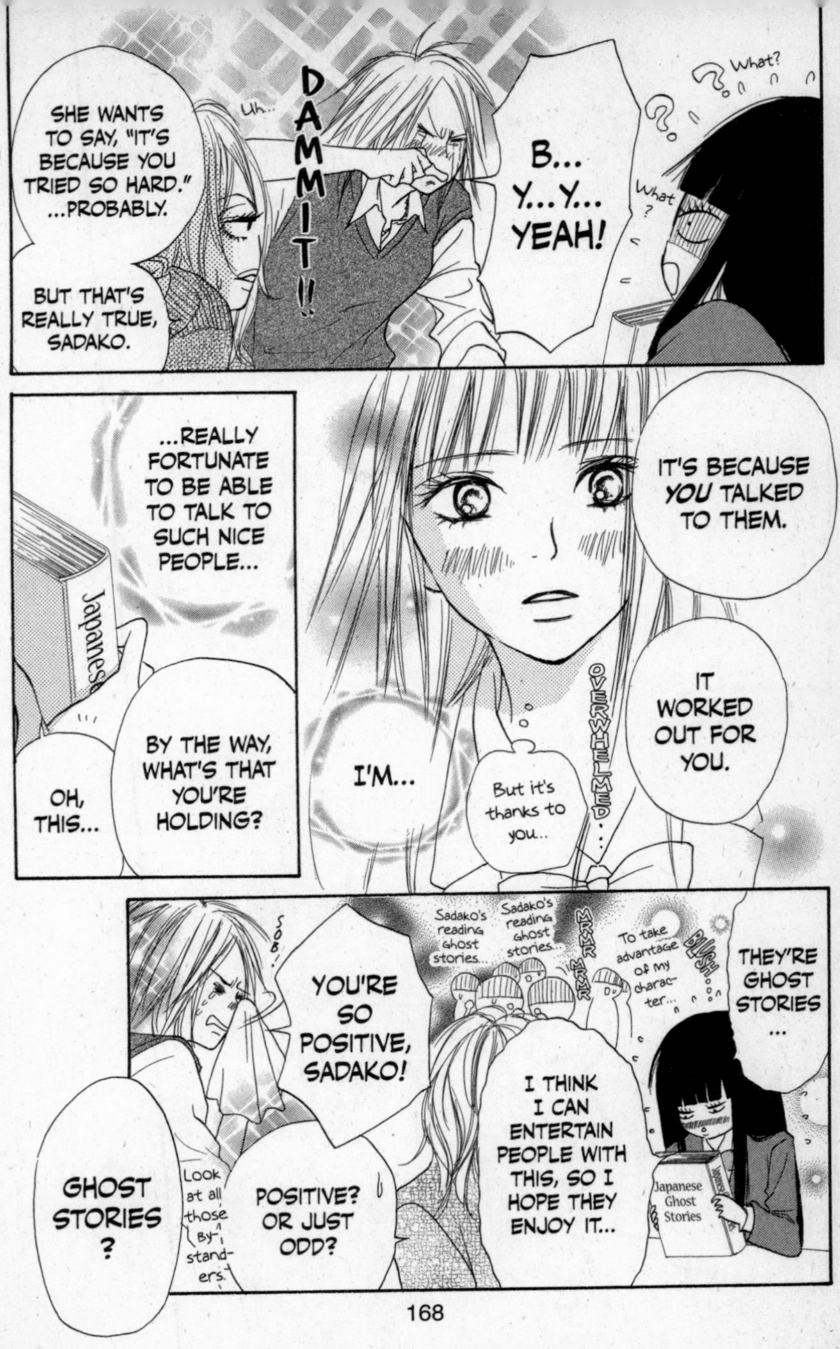
What?
What?
B... Y...Y... YEAH!
DAMMIT!!
Uh...
SHE WANTS TO SAY, "IT'S BECAUSE YOU TRIED SO HARD." ...PROBABLY.
BUT THAT'S REALLY TRUE, SADAKO.
IT'S BECAUSE *YOU* TALKED TO THEM.
IT WORKED OUT FOR YOU.
OVERWHELMED...
But it's thanks to you...
I'M...
...REALLY FORTUNATE TO BE ABLE TO TALK TO SUCH NICE PEOPLE...
Japanese
BY THE WAY, WHAT'S THAT YOU'RE HOLDING?
OH, THIS...
THEY'RE GHOST STORIES ...
BLUSH
To take advantage of my character...
MRMR MRMR
Sadako's reading ghost stories...
Sadako's reading ghost stories...
I THINK I CAN ENTERTAIN PEOPLE WITH THIS, SO I HOPE THEY ENJOY IT...
Japanese Ghost Stories
YOU'RE SO POSITIVE, SADAKO!
SOB
POSITIVE? OR JUST ODD?
Look at all those By-standers.
GHOST STORIES?

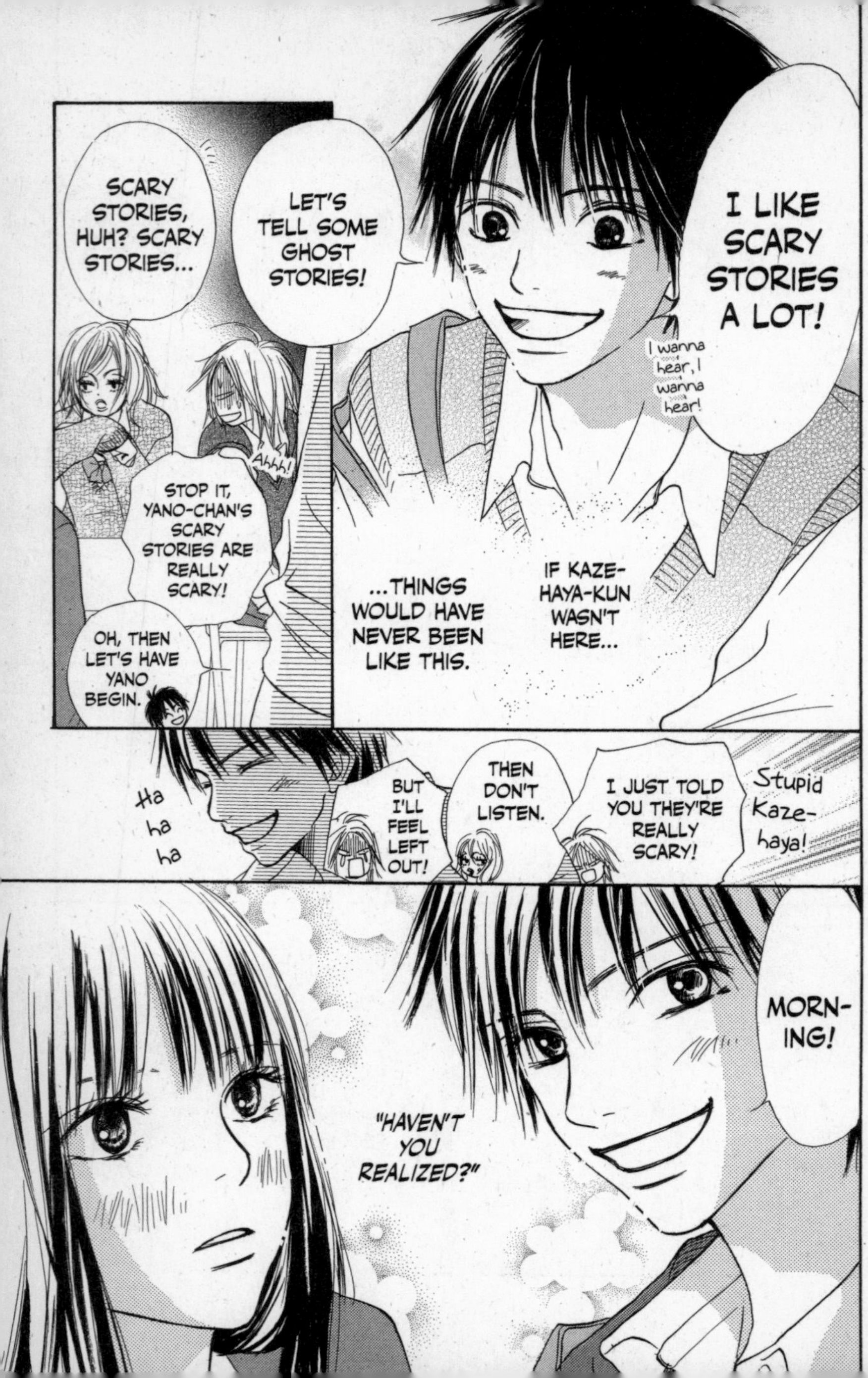
LET'S TELL SOME GHOST STORIES!
SCARY STORIES, HUH? SCARY STORIES...
Ahhh!
STOP IT, YANO-CHAN'S SCARY STORIES ARE REALLY SCARY!
OH, THEN LET'S HAVE YANO BEGIN.
I LIKE SCARY STORIES A LOT!
I wanna hear, I wanna hear!
IF KAZE-HAYA-KUN WASN'T HERE...
...THINGS WOULD HAVE NEVER BEEN LIKE THIS.
Stupid Kaze-haya!
I JUST TOLD YOU THEY'RE REALLY SCARY!
THEN DON'T LISTEN.
BUT I'LL FEEL LEFT OUT!
Ha ha ha
MORN-ING!
"HAVEN'T YOU REALIZED?"

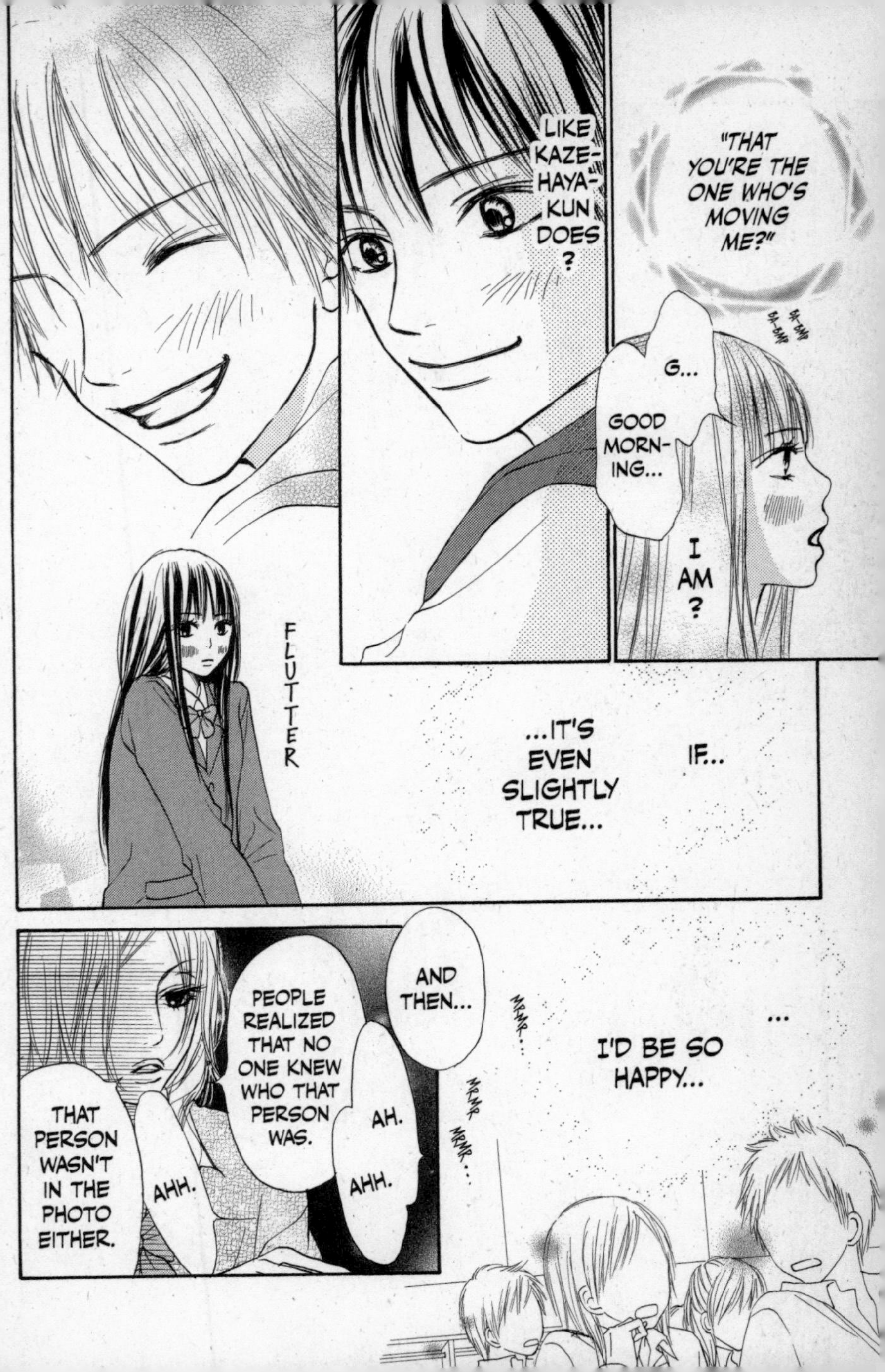
"THAT YOU'RE THE ONE WHO'S MOVING ME?"
BA-DMP BA-DMP
G...
GOOD MORN-ING...
I AM?
LIKE KAZE-HAYA-KUN DOES?
FLUTTER
IF...
...IT'S EVEN SLIGHTLY TRUE...
...
I'D BE SO HAPPY...
MRMR...
MRMR
MRMR...
AND THEN...
PEOPLE REALIZED THAT NO ONE KNEW WHO THAT PERSON WAS.
AH.
AHH.
THAT PERSON WASN'T IN THE PHOTO EITHER.
AHH.

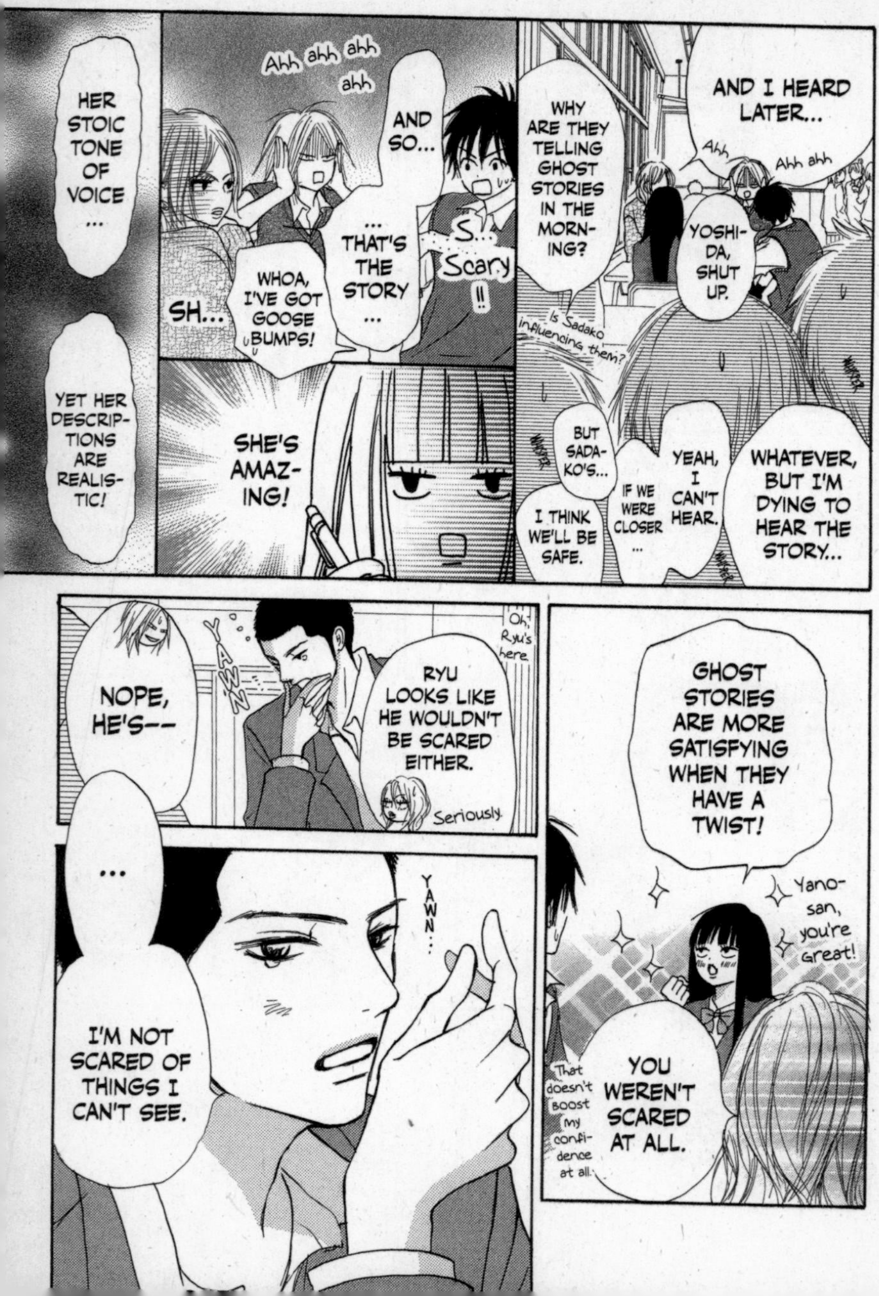
AND I HEARD LATER...
Ahh
Ahh ahh
WHY ARE THEY TELLING GHOST STORIES IN THE MORNING?
YOSHIDA, SHUT UP.
Is Sadako influencing them?
WHATEVER, BUT I'M DYING TO HEAR THE STORY...
YEAH, I CAN'T HEAR.
IF WE WERE CLOSER...
BUT SADAKO'S...
I THINK WE'LL BE SAFE.
Ahh ahh ahh ahh
AND SO...
... THAT'S THE STORY ...
S... Scary!!
WHOA, I'VE GOT GOOSE BUMPS!
SH...
SHE'S AMAZING!
HER STOIC TONE OF VOICE ...
YET HER DESCRIPTIONS ARE REALISTIC!
GHOST STORIES ARE MORE SATISFYING WHEN THEY HAVE A TWIST!
Yano-san, you're Great!
YOU WEREN'T SCARED AT ALL.
That doesn't boost my confidence at all.
Oh, Ryu's here
RYU LOOKS LIKE HE WOULDN'T BE SCARED EITHER.
YAWN
Seriously.
NOPE, HE'S--
YAWN...
...
I'M NOT SCARED OF THINGS I CAN'T SEE.

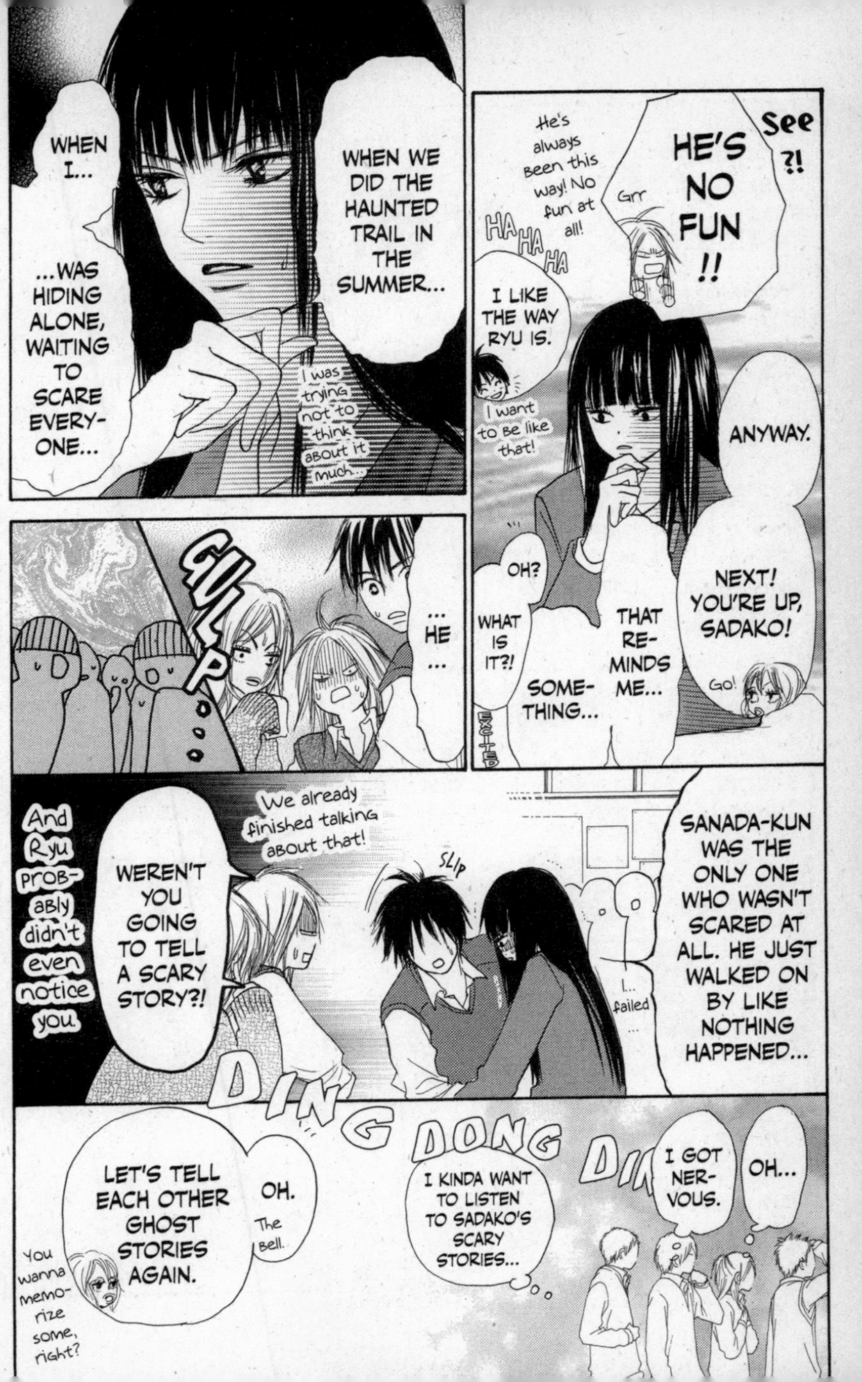
See ?!
HE'S NO FUN !!
He's always Been this way! No fun at all!
Grr
HA HA HA HA
I LIKE THE WAY RYU IS.
I want to be like that!
ANYWAY.
WHEN WE DID THE HAUNTED TRAIL IN THE SUMMER...
WHEN I...
...WAS HIDING ALONE, WAITING TO SCARE EVERY-ONE...
I was trying not to think about it much...
NEXT! YOU'RE UP, SADAKO!
Go!
THAT RE-MINDS ME...
SOME-THING...
OH?
WHAT IS IT?!
EXCITED
... HE ...
GULP...
SANADA-KUN WAS THE ONLY ONE WHO WASN'T SCARED AT ALL. HE JUST WALKED ON BY LIKE NOTHING HAPPENED...
I... failed ...
SLIP
We already finished talking about that!
WEREN'T YOU GOING TO TELL A SCARY STORY?!
And Ryu probably didn't even notice you
DING DONG DING DONG DI
OH...
I GOT NER-VOUS.
I KINDA WANT TO LISTEN TO SADAKO'S SCARY STORIES...
OH.
The Bell.
LET'S TELL EACH OTHER GHOST STORIES AGAIN.
You wanna memo-rize some, right?

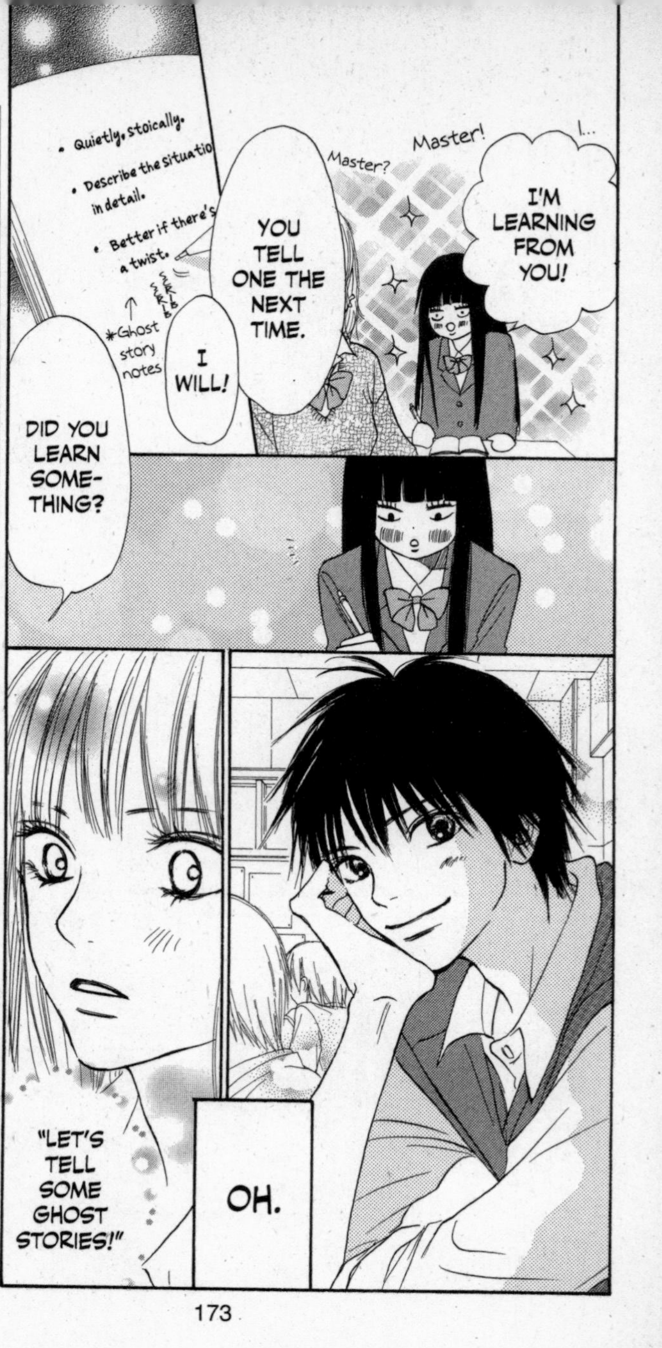
I...
Master!
I'M LEARNING FROM YOU!
Master?
YOU TELL ONE THE NEXT TIME.
• Quietly, stoically.
• Describe the situatio
in detail.
• Better if there's
a twist.
*Ghost story notes
I WILL!
DID YOU LEARN SOME-THING?
OH.
"LET'S TELL SOME GHOST STORIES!"

KARUPIN on JAPAN 4

And so, the only time I get to go out is to head to the neighborhood supermarket. So I don't get much exercise.

My lower back... My lower back hurts... It's probably because my muscles have weakened...

When it's spring, I like to go out for a bit and walk around.

My tummy is getting fat.
No, actually, my whole body is getting fat!

This year, I'm going to exercise properly!!
It's decided!!
Though it's already April...

Oh, there's no more space!

Goodbye for now.

Hope to see you in vol. 2 as well!!

Karuho Shiina ✧
April 2006

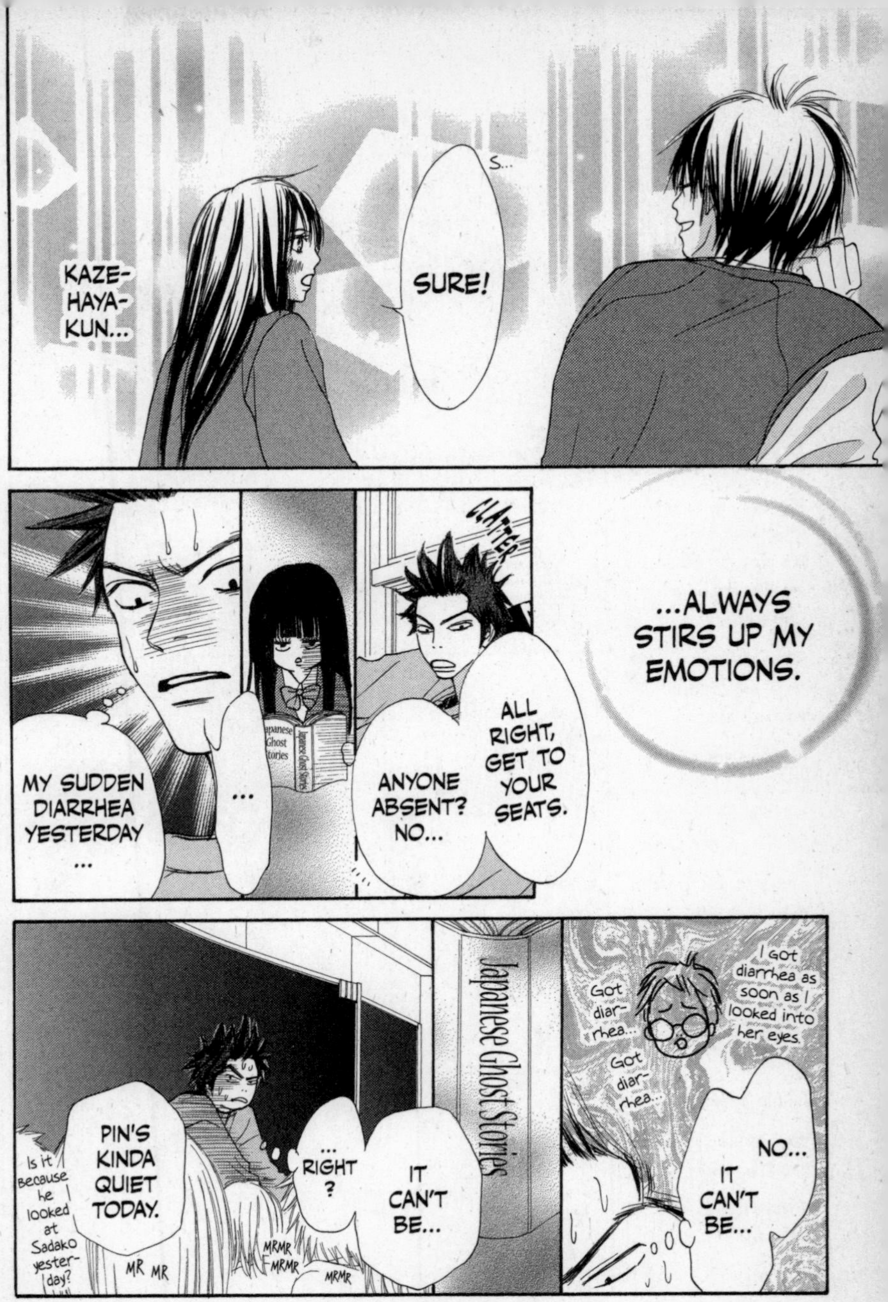
S...
SURE!
KAZE-HAYA-KUN...
...ALWAYS STIRS UP MY EMOTIONS.
CLATTER
ALL RIGHT, GET TO YOUR SEATS.
ANYONE ABSENT? NO...
Japanese Ghost Stories
...
MY SUDDEN DIARRHEA YESTERDAY ...
I got diarrhea as soon as I looked into her eyes.
Got diar-rhea...
Got diar-rhea...
NO...
IT CAN'T BE...
Japanese Ghost Stories
IT CAN'T BE...
... RIGHT?
MRMR MRMR
MRMR
PIN'S KINDA QUIET TODAY.
Is it because he looked at Sadako yester-day?
MR MR

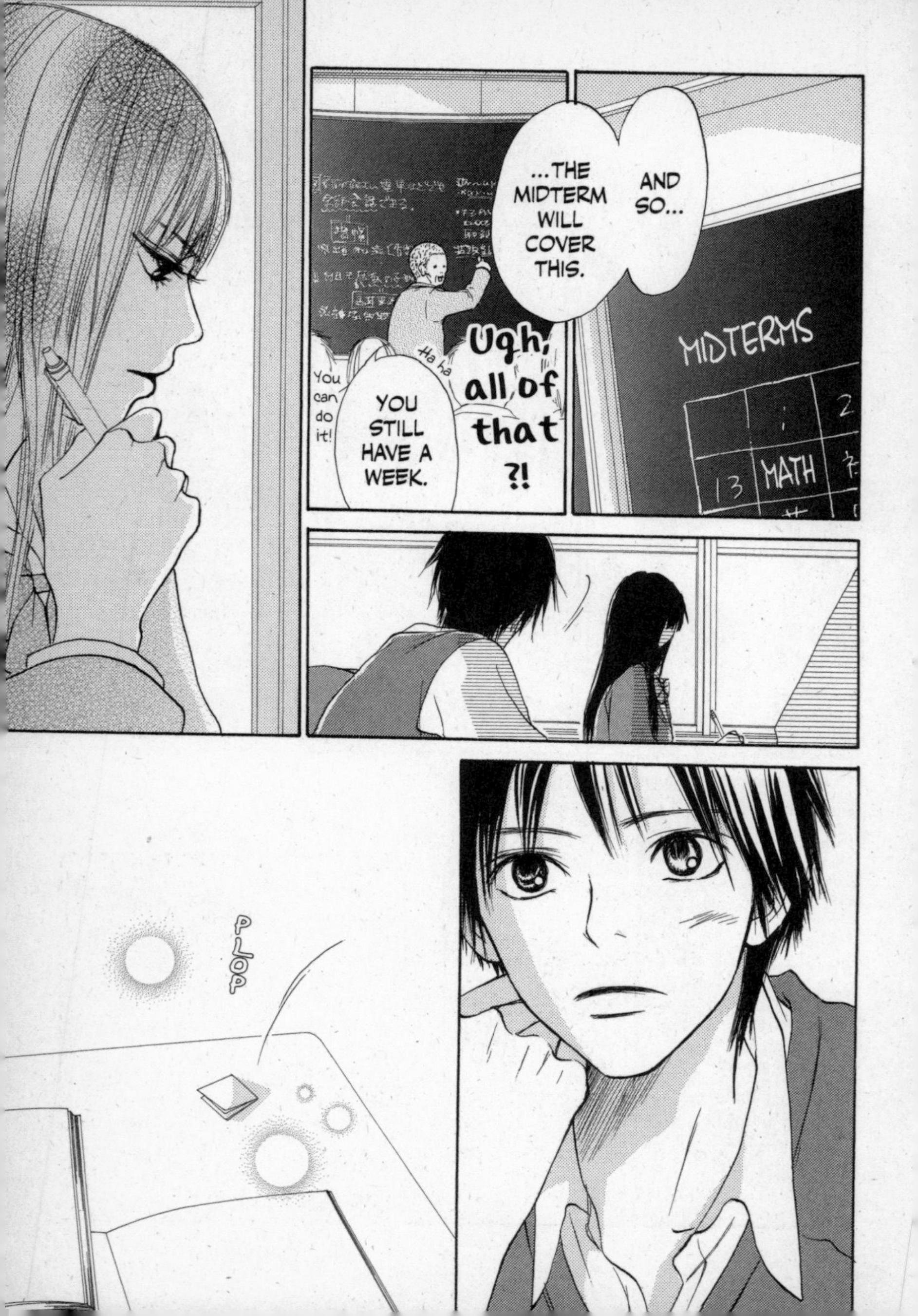
AND SO...
...THE MIDTERM WILL COVER THIS.
MIDTERMS
13 MATH
Ugh, all of that?!
Ha ha
YOU STILL HAVE A WEEK.
You can do it!
PLOP

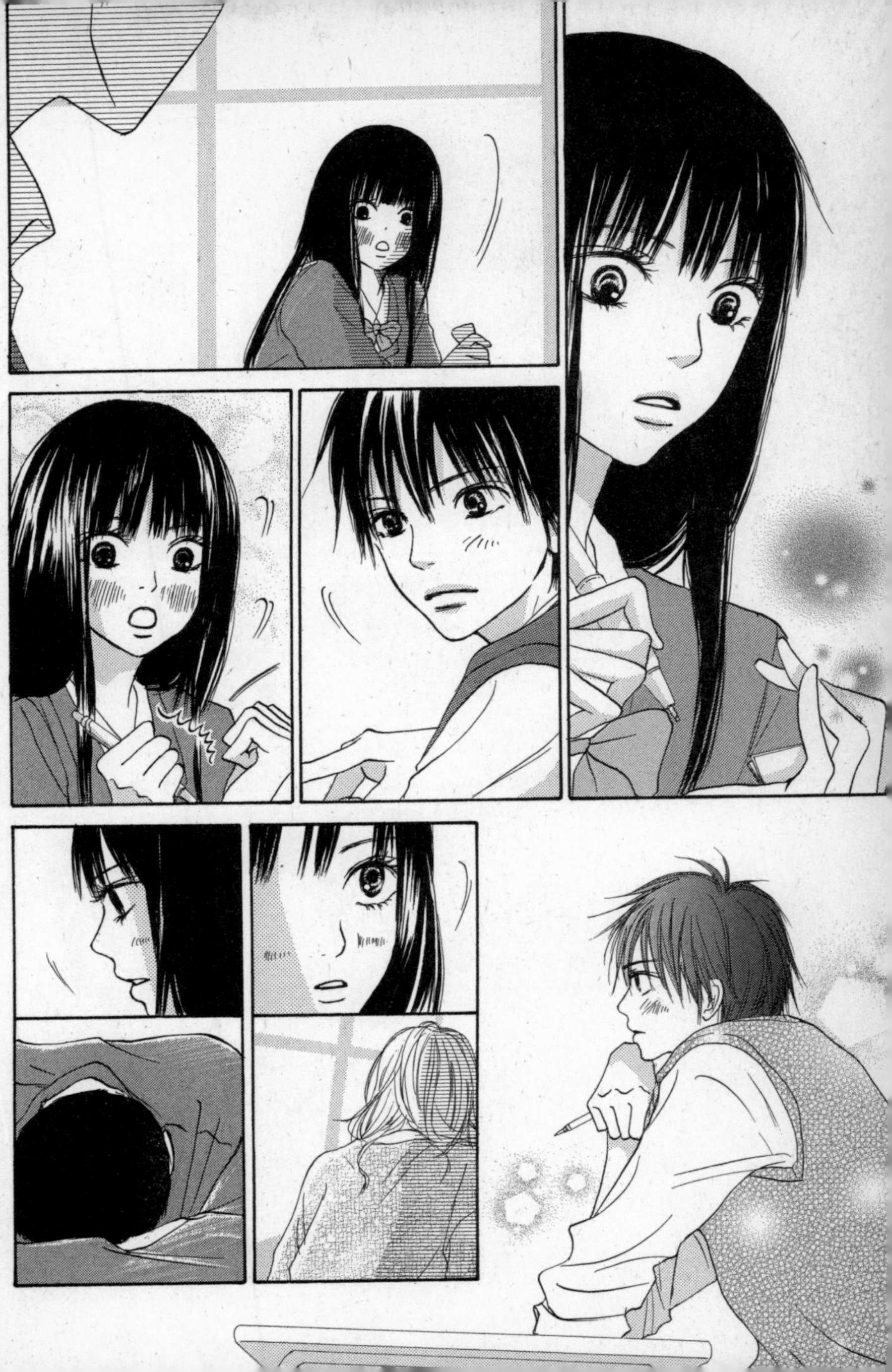

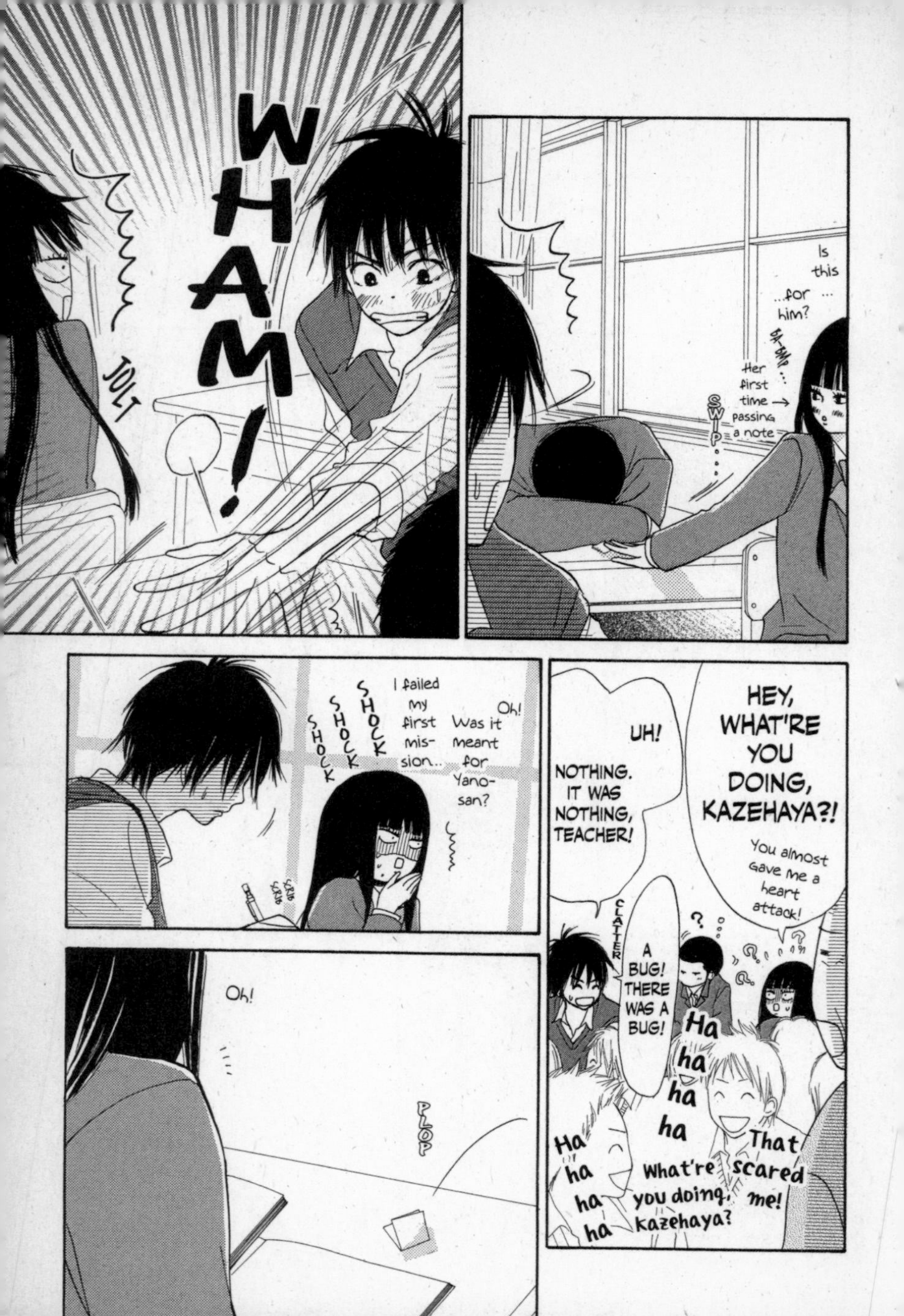
Is this ...for ... him?
BA-BMP...
Her first time passing a note
SWIP...
WHAM!
JOLT
HEY, WHAT'RE YOU DOING, KAZEHAYA?!
You almost gave me a heart attack!
UH!
NOTHING. IT WAS NOTHING, TEACHER!
CLATTER
A BUG! THERE WAS A BUG!
Ha ha ha ha ha
That scared me!
What're you doing, Kazehaya?
Ha ha ha ha
Oh! Was it meant for Yano-san?
I failed my first mission..
SHOCK SHOCK SHOCK
SCRIB SCRIB
Oh!
PLOP

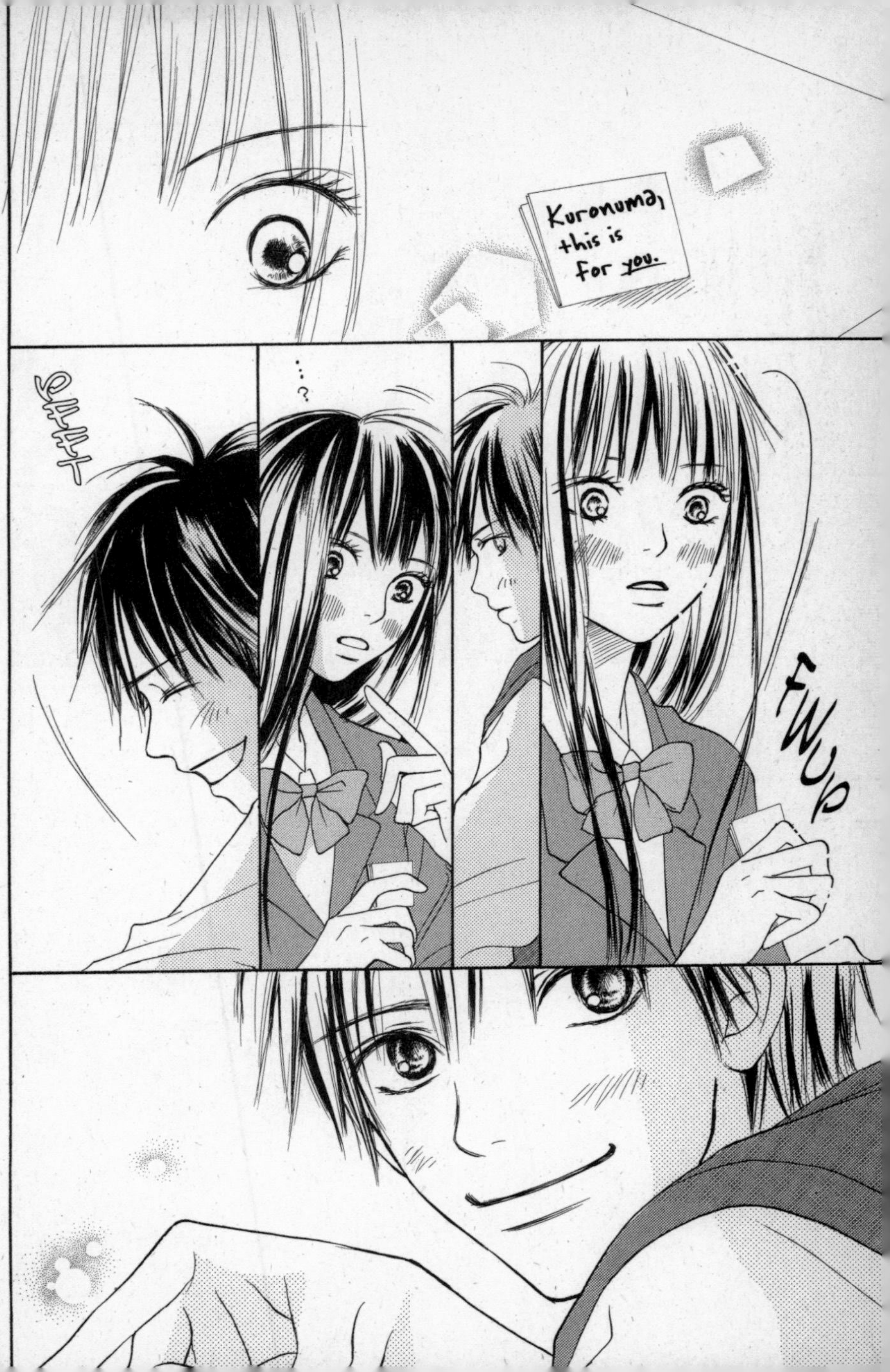
Kuronuma, this is for you.
FWUP
...?
SEET

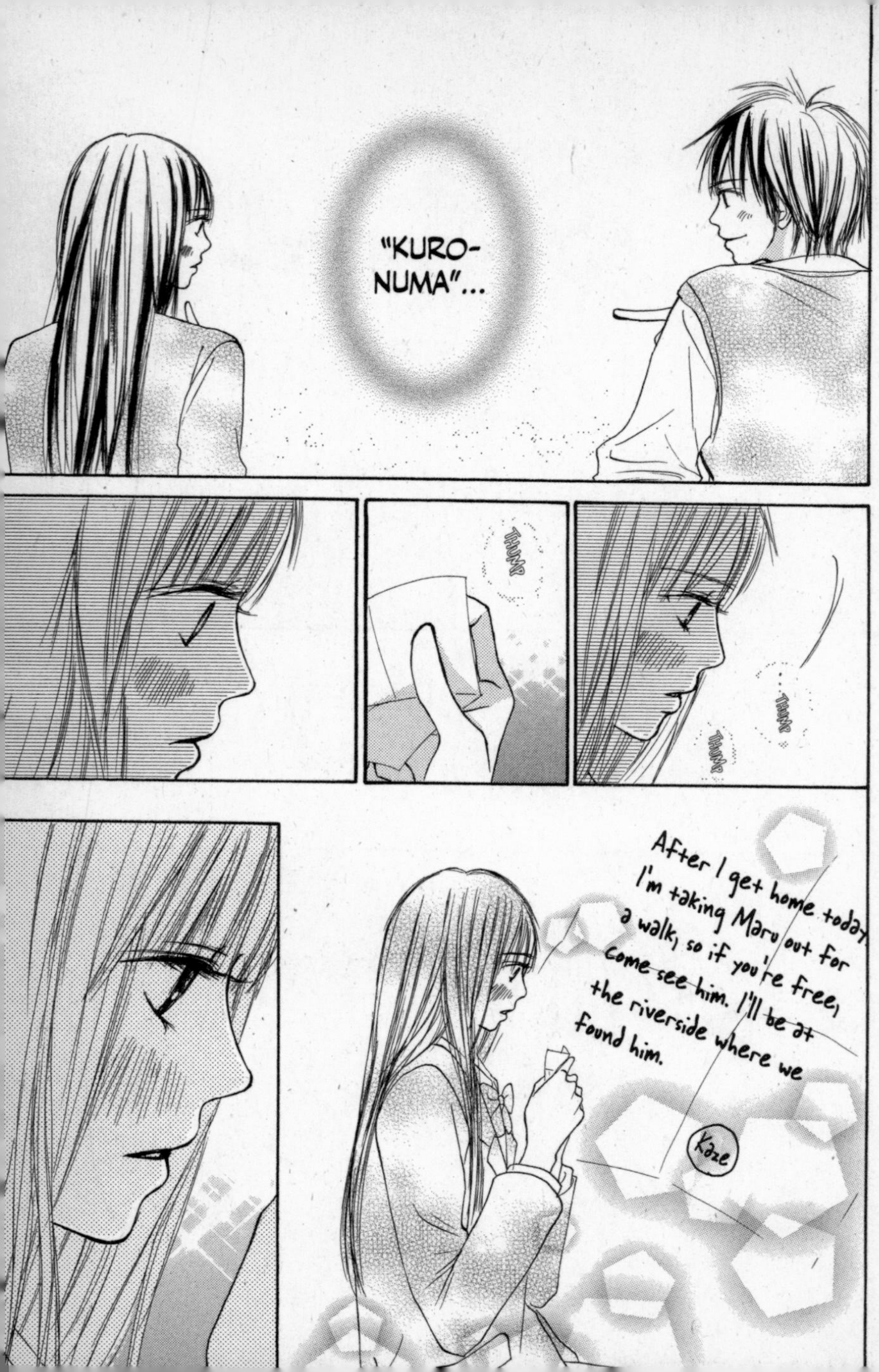
"KURO-
NUMA"...
THUMP
THUMP
THUMP
After I get home today I'm taking Maru out for a walk, so if you're free, come see him. I'll be at the riverside where we found him.
Kaze

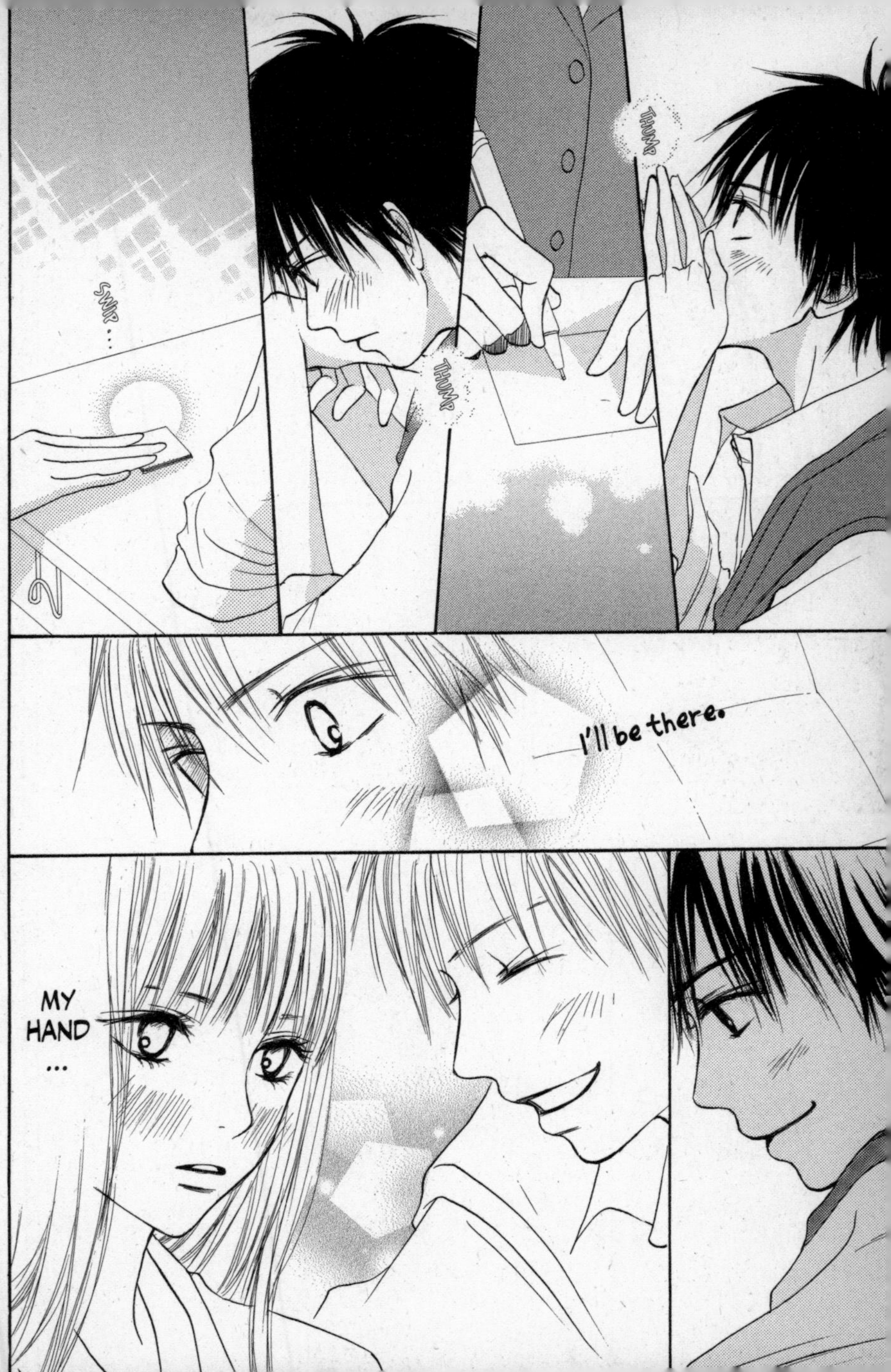
THUMP
THUMP
SWIP...
I'll be there.
MY HAND ...

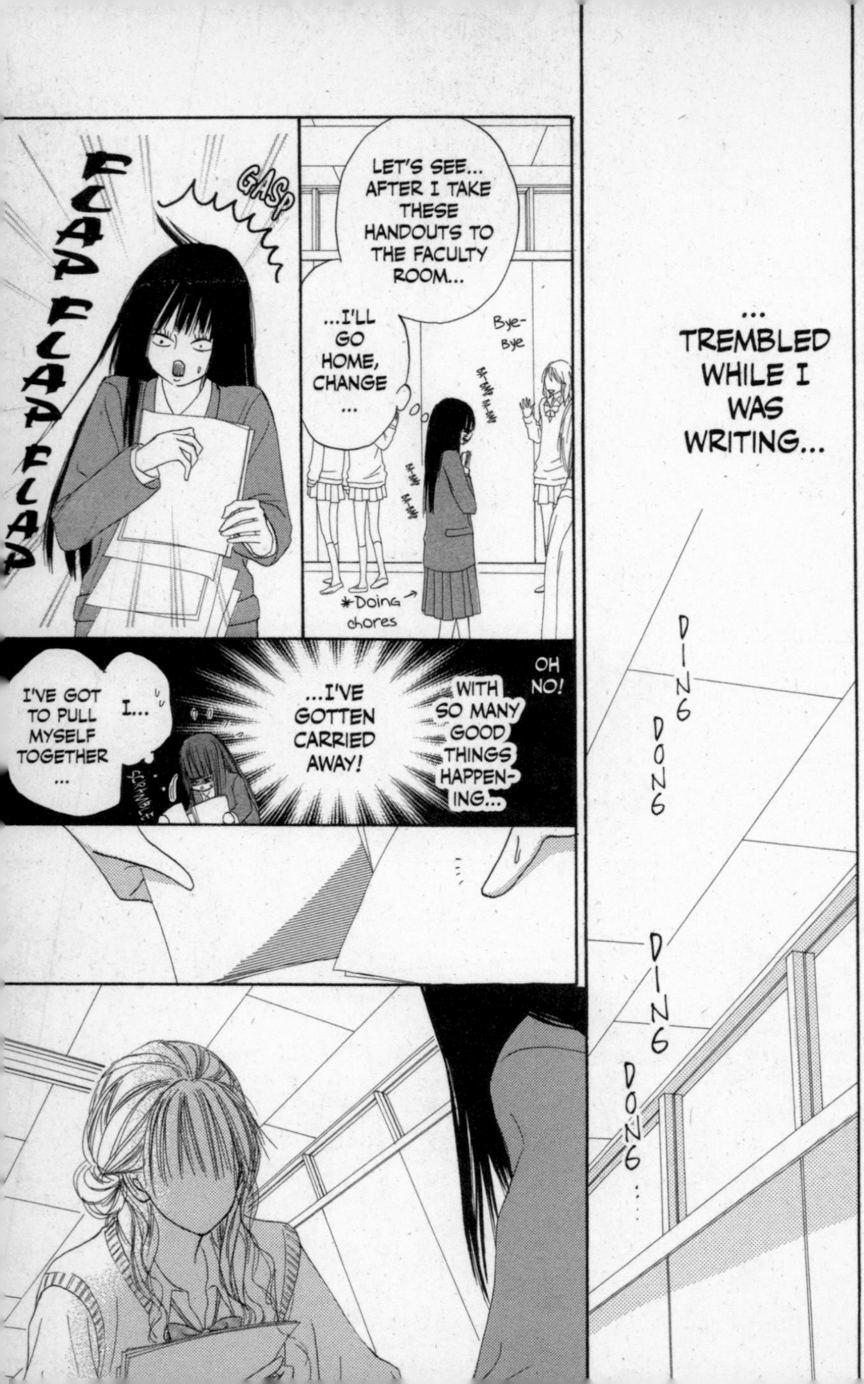
... TREMBLED WHILE I WAS WRITING...
DING DONG
DING DONG...
LET'S SEE... AFTER I TAKE THESE HANDOUTS TO THE FACULTY ROOM...
...I'LL GO HOME, CHANGE ...
Bye-Bye
*Doing chores
GASP
FLAP FLAP FLAP
OH NO!
WITH SO MANY GOOD THINGS HAPPENING...
...I'VE GOTTEN CARRIED AWAY!
I...
I'VE GOT TO PULL MYSELF TOGETHER ...
SCRAMBLE

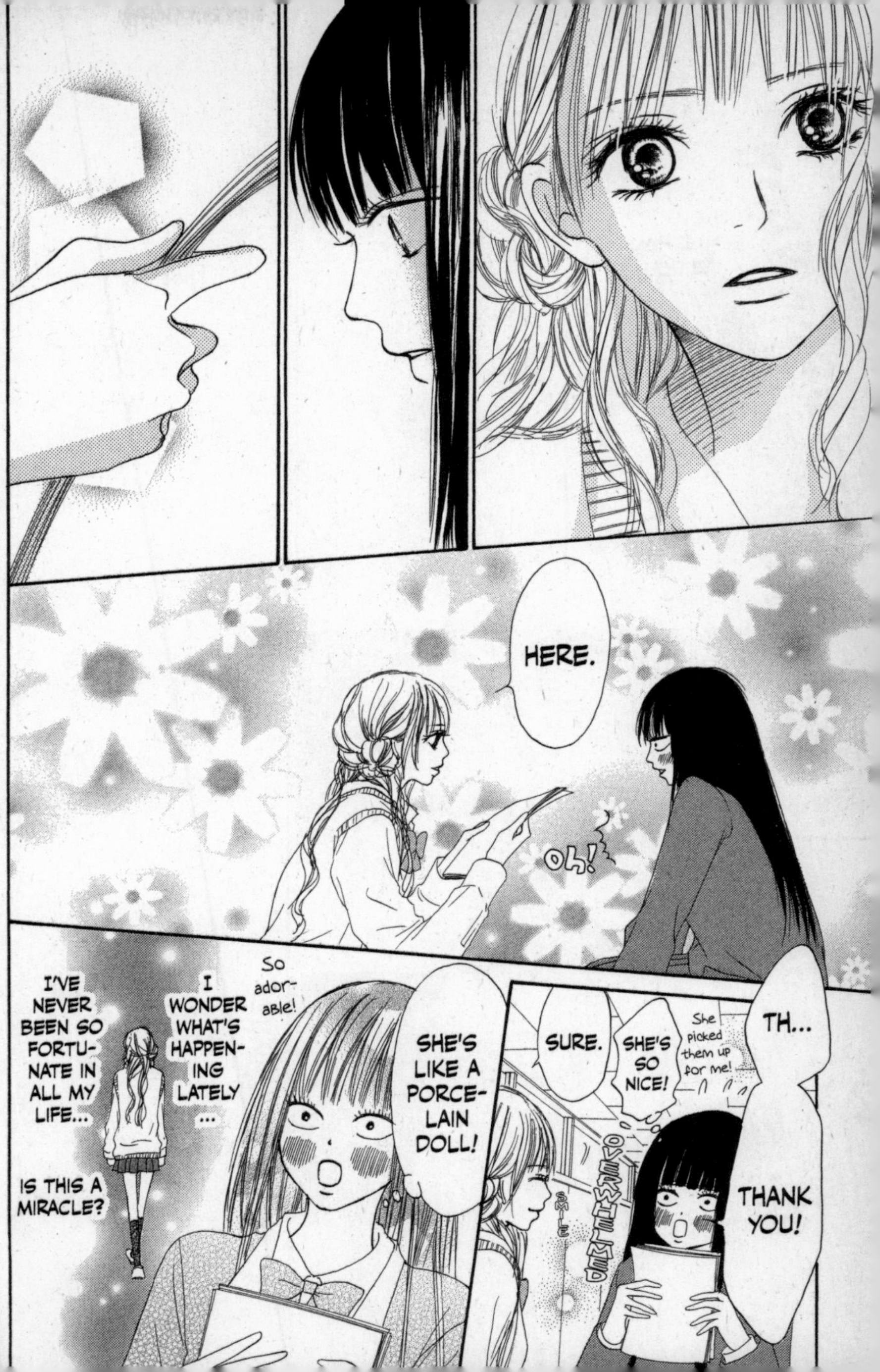
HERE.
Oh!
TH...
She picked them up for me!
SHE'S SO NICE!
SURE.
THANK YOU!
OVERWHELMED
SMILE
SHE'S LIKE A PORCE-LAIN DOLL!
So ador-able!
I WONDER WHAT'S HAPPEN-ING LATELY ...
I'VE NEVER BEEN SO FORTU-NATE IN ALL MY LIFE...
IS THIS A MIRACLE?

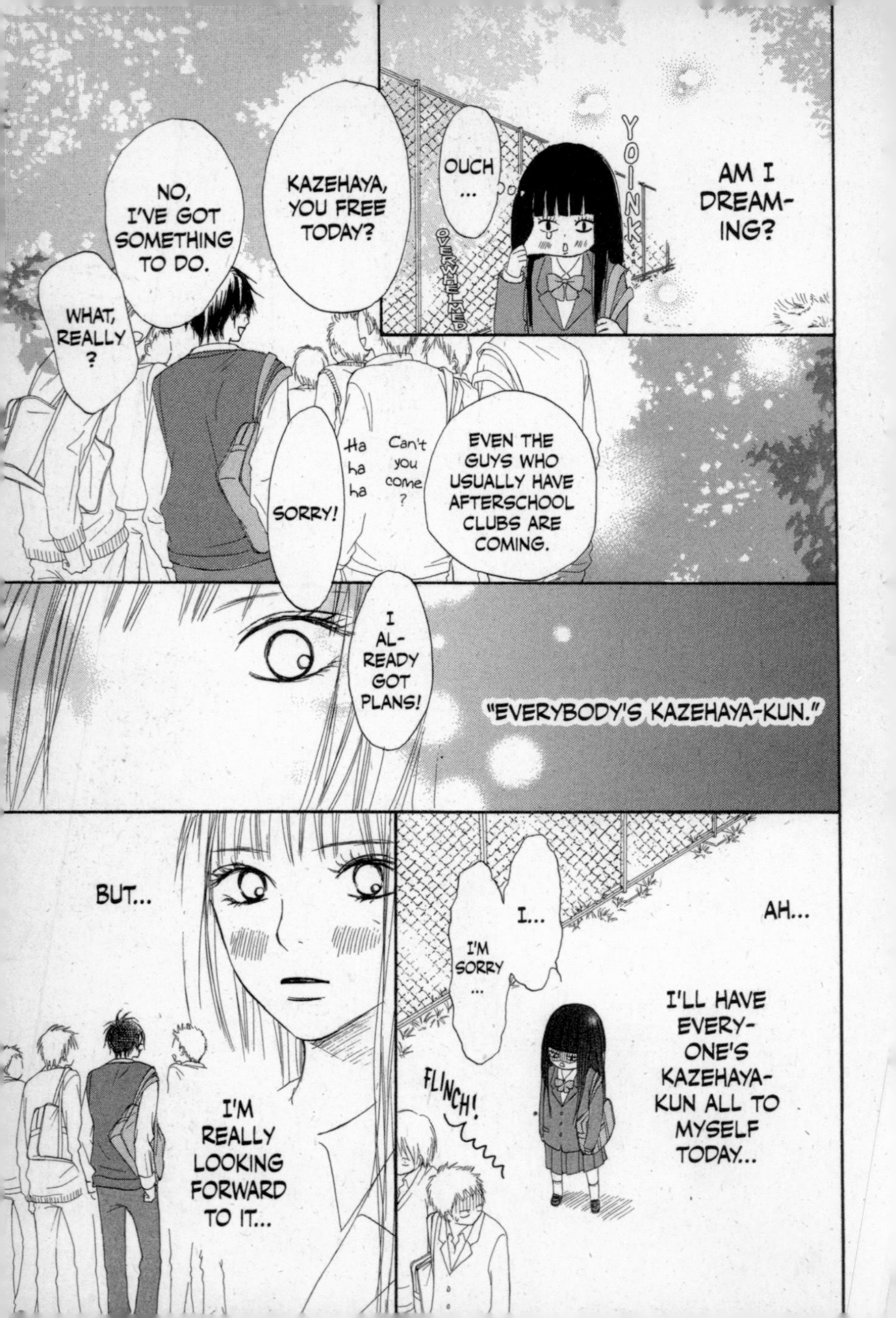
AM I DREAMING?
YOINK
OUCH ...
OVERWHELMED
KAZEHAYA, YOU FREE TODAY?
NO, I'VE GOT SOMETHING TO DO.
WHAT, REALLY ?
EVEN THE GUYS WHO USUALLY HAVE AFTERSCHOOL CLUBS ARE COMING.
Can't you come ?
Ha ha ha
SORRY!
I AL-READY GOT PLANS!
"EVERYBODY'S KAZEHAYA-KUN."
AH...
I'LL HAVE EVERY-ONE'S KAZEHAYA-KUN ALL TO MYSELF TODAY...
I...
I'M SORRY ...
FLINCH!
BUT...
I'M REALLY LOOKING FORWARD TO IT...

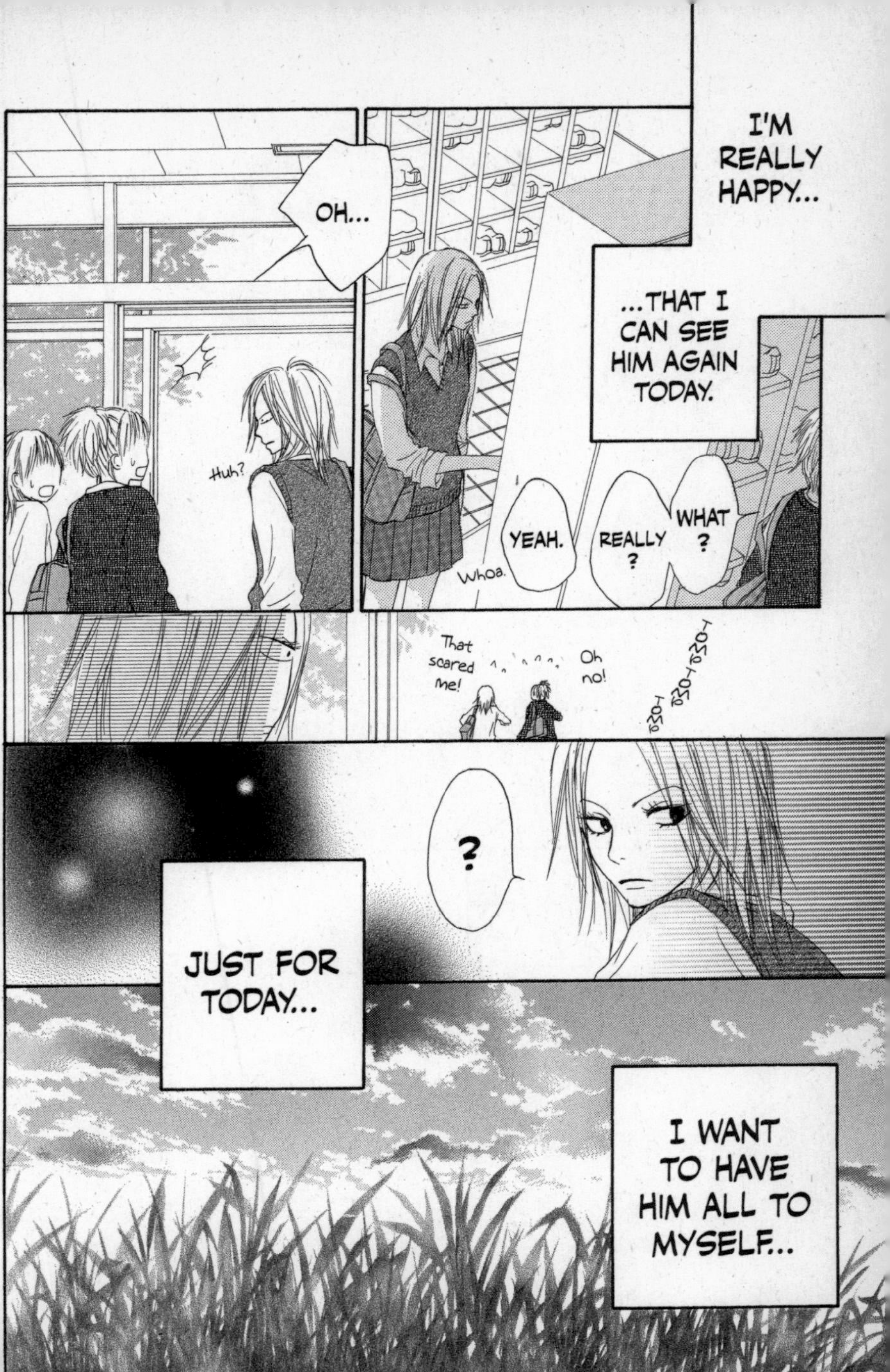
I'M REALLY HAPPY...
...THAT I CAN SEE HIM AGAIN TODAY.
WHAT?
REALLY?
YEAH.
Whoa.
OH...
Huh?
TOMO TOMO TOMO
Oh no!
That scared me!
?
JUST FOR TODAY...
I WANT TO HAVE HIM ALL TO MYSELF...

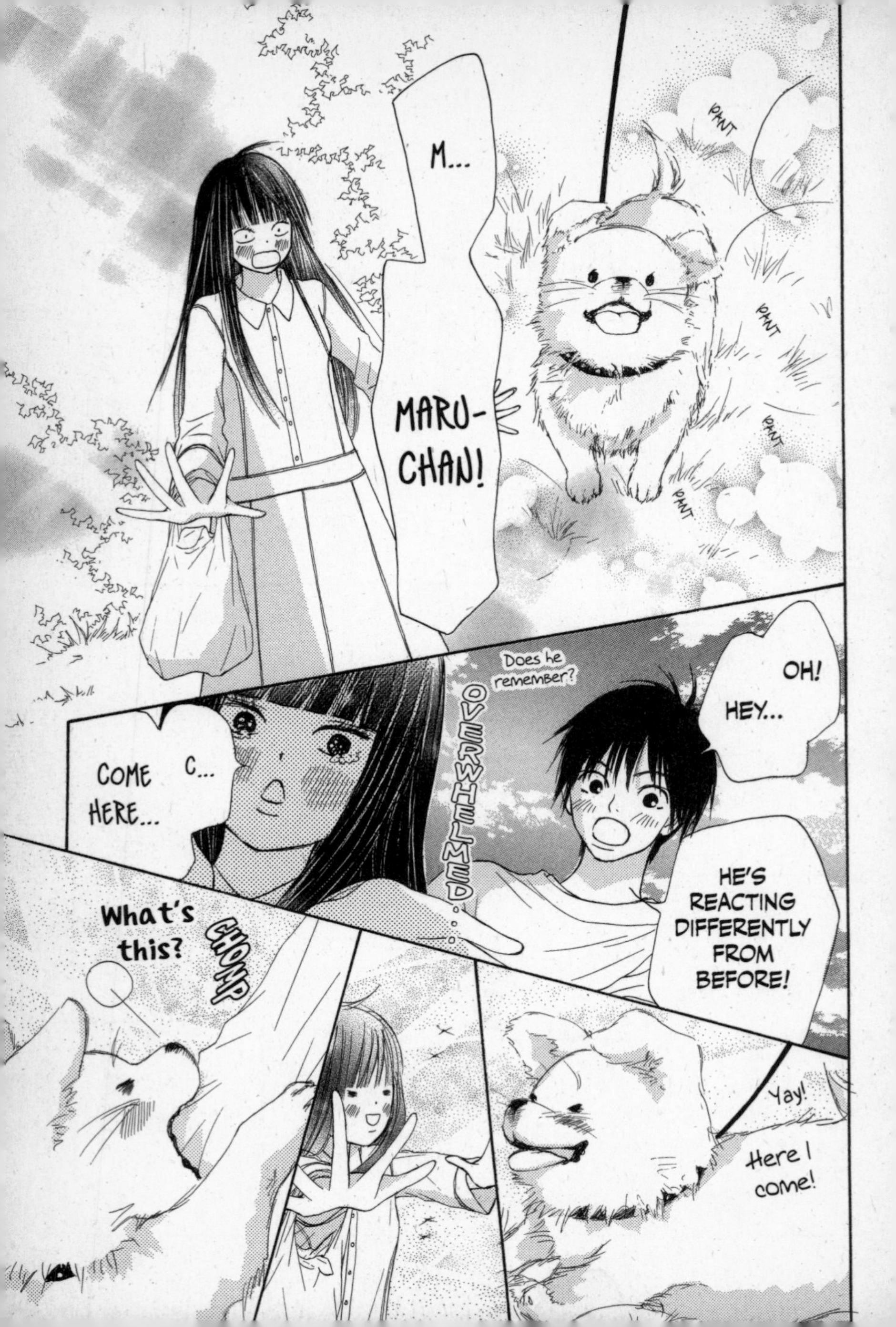
PANT
PANT
PANT
PANT
M...
MARU-CHAN!
OH! HEY...
HE'S REACTING DIFFERENTLY FROM BEFORE!
Does he remember?
OVERWHELMED...
C...
COME HERE...
Yay!
Here I come!
What's this?
CHOMP

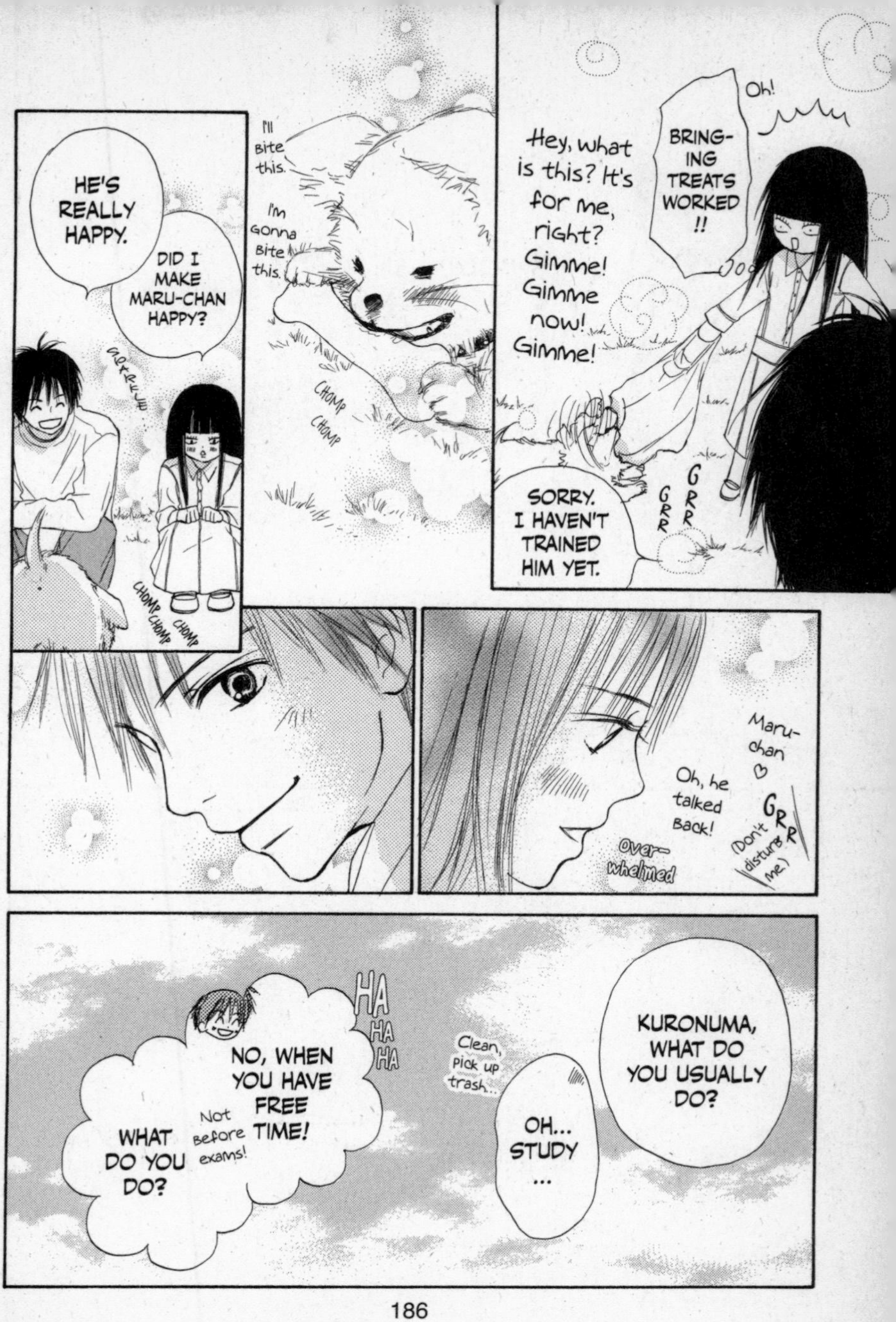

Oh!
BRING-ING TREATS WORKED !!
Hey, what is this? It's for me, right? Gimme! Gimme now! Gimme!
SORRY. I HAVEN'T TRAINED HIM YET.
GRR GRR
I'll bite this.
I'm gonna bite this.
CHOMP CHOMP
HE'S REALLY HAPPY.
DID I MAKE MARU-CHAN HAPPY?
CHOMP CHOMP CHOMP
Maru-chan ♡
Oh, he talked back!
GRR
(Don't disturb me)
over-whelmed
KURONUMA, WHAT DO YOU USUALLY DO?
Clean, pick up trash...
OH... STUDY ...
HA HA HA
NO, WHEN YOU HAVE FREE TIME!
Not before exams!
WHAT DO YOU DO?

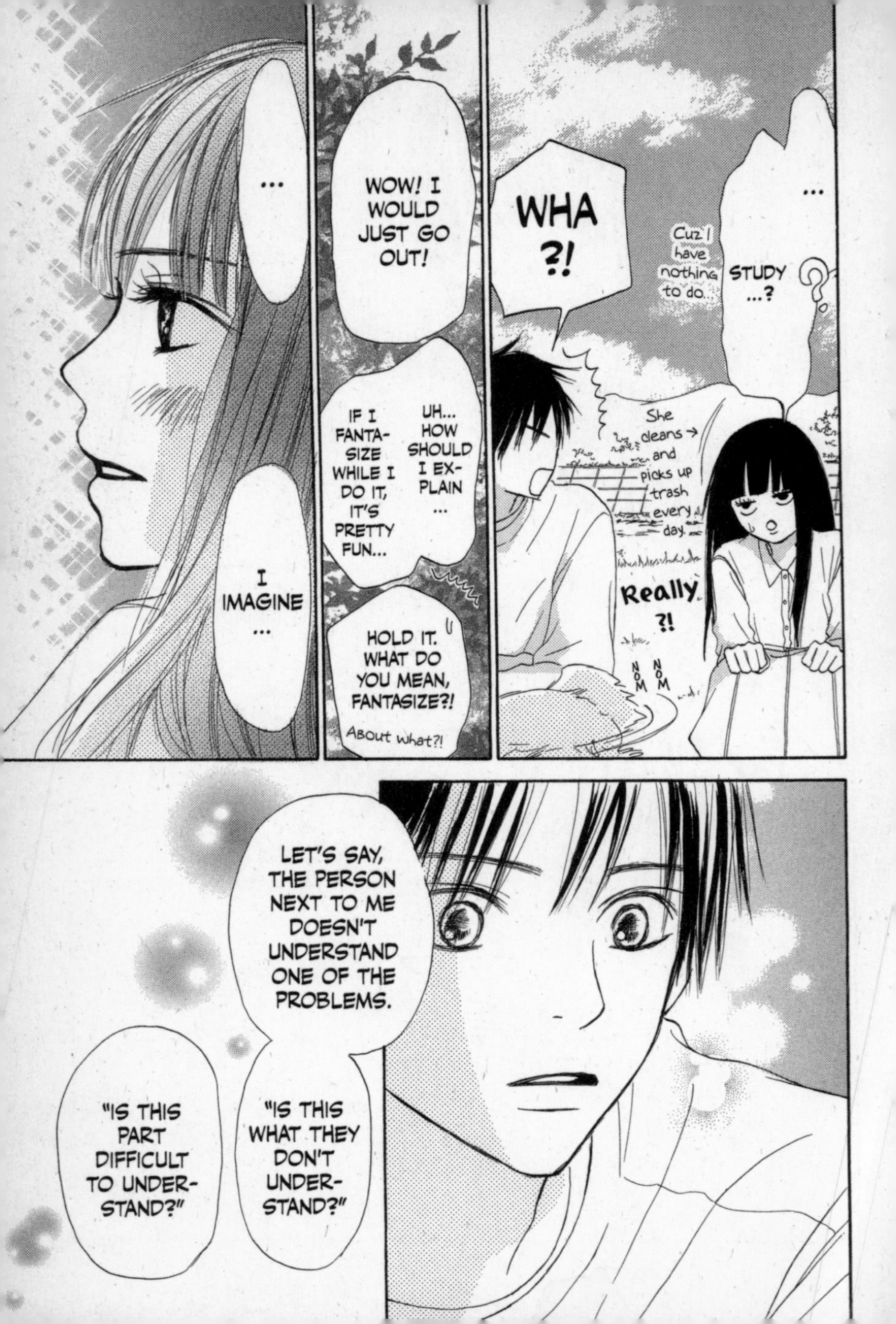
...
STUDY ...?
Cuz I have nothing to do...
WHA ?!
She cleans → and picks up trash every day.
Really ?!
NOM NOM
WOW! I WOULD JUST GO OUT!
UH... HOW SHOULD I EX-PLAIN ...
IF I FANTA-SIZE WHILE I DO IT, IT'S PRETTY FUN...
HOLD IT. WHAT DO YOU MEAN, FANTASIZE?!
About what?!
...
I IMAGINE ...
LET'S SAY, THE PERSON NEXT TO ME DOESN'T UNDERSTAND ONE OF THE PROBLEMS.
"IS THIS WHAT THEY DON'T UNDER-STAND?"
"IS THIS PART DIFFICULT TO UNDER-STAND?"

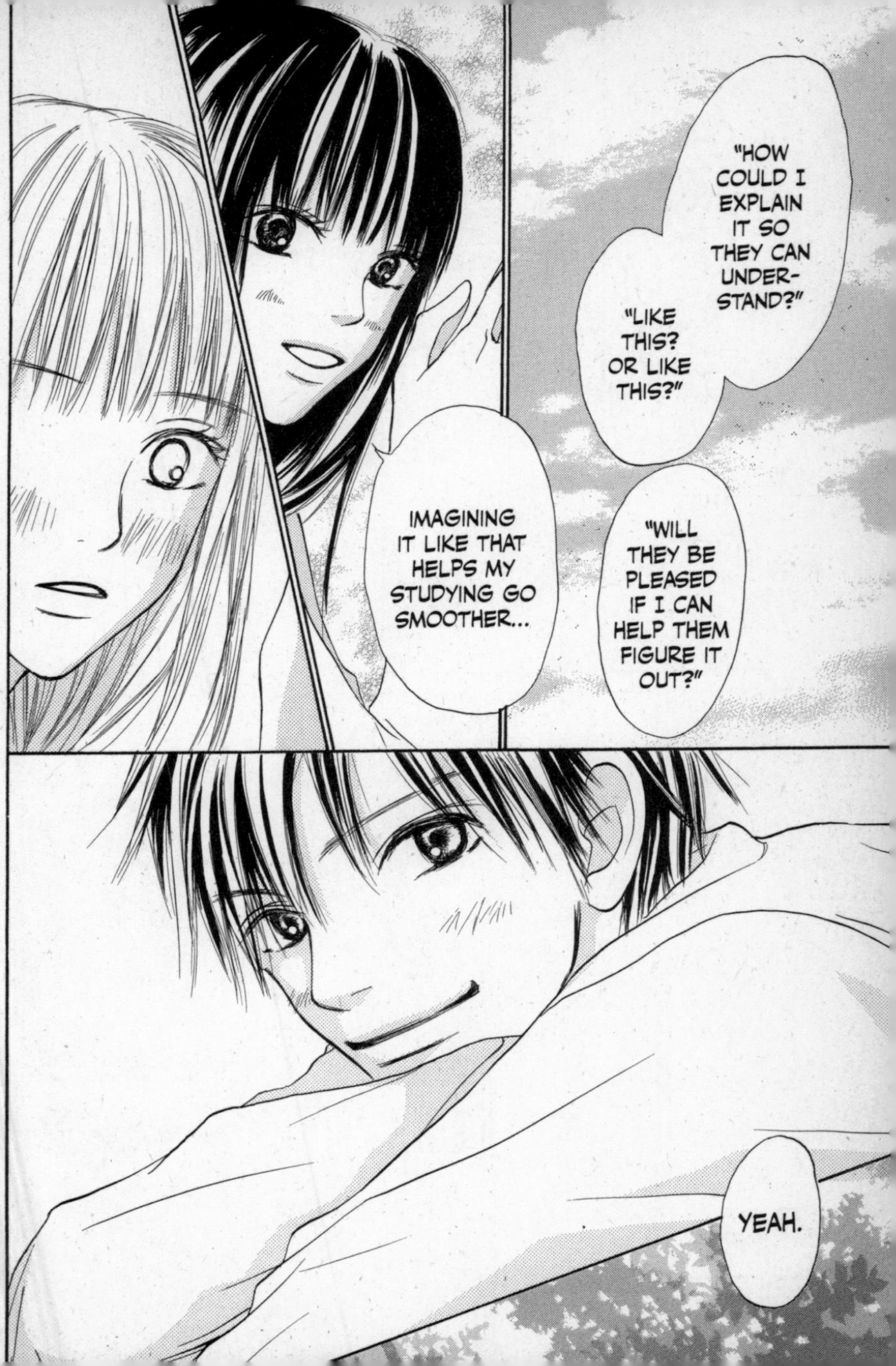
"HOW COULD I EXPLAIN IT SO THEY CAN UNDER-STAND?"
"LIKE THIS? OR LIKE THIS?"
"WILL THEY BE PLEASED IF I CAN HELP THEM FIGURE IT OUT?"
IMAGINING IT LIKE THAT HELPS MY STUDYING GO SMOOTHER...
YEAH.

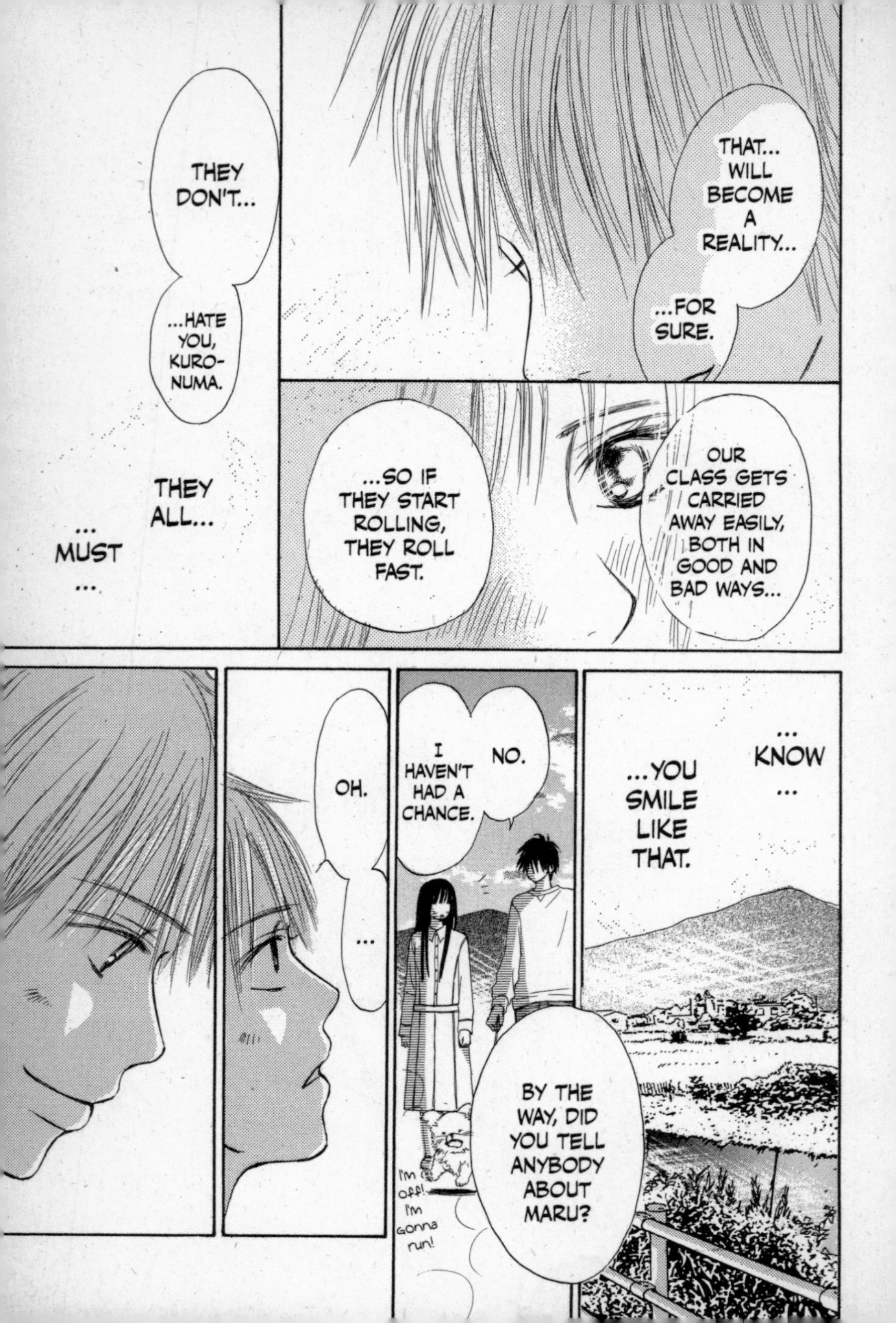
THAT... WILL BECOME A REALITY...
...FOR SURE.
OUR CLASS GETS CARRIED AWAY EASILY, BOTH IN GOOD AND BAD WAYS...
...SO IF THEY START ROLLING, THEY ROLL FAST.
THEY DON'T...
...HATE YOU, KURO-NUMA.
THEY ALL...
... MUST ...
... KNOW ...
...YOU SMILE LIKE THAT.
BY THE WAY, DID YOU TELL ANYBODY ABOUT MARU?
NO.
I HAVEN'T HAD A CHANCE.
I'm off! I'm gonna run!
OH.
...

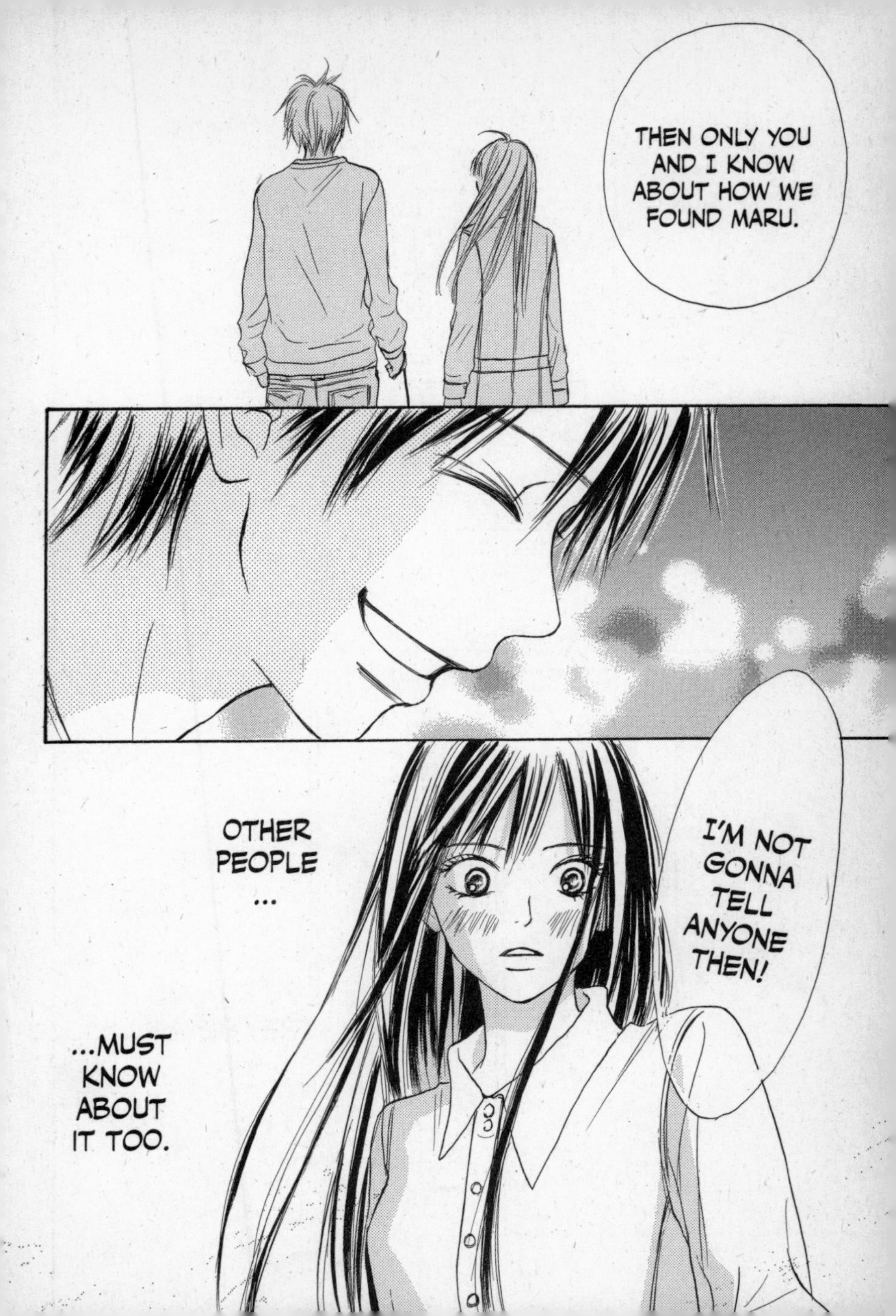
THEN ONLY YOU AND I KNOW ABOUT HOW WE FOUND MARU.
I'M NOT GONNA TELL ANYONE THEN!
OTHER PEOPLE ...
...MUST KNOW ABOUT IT TOO.

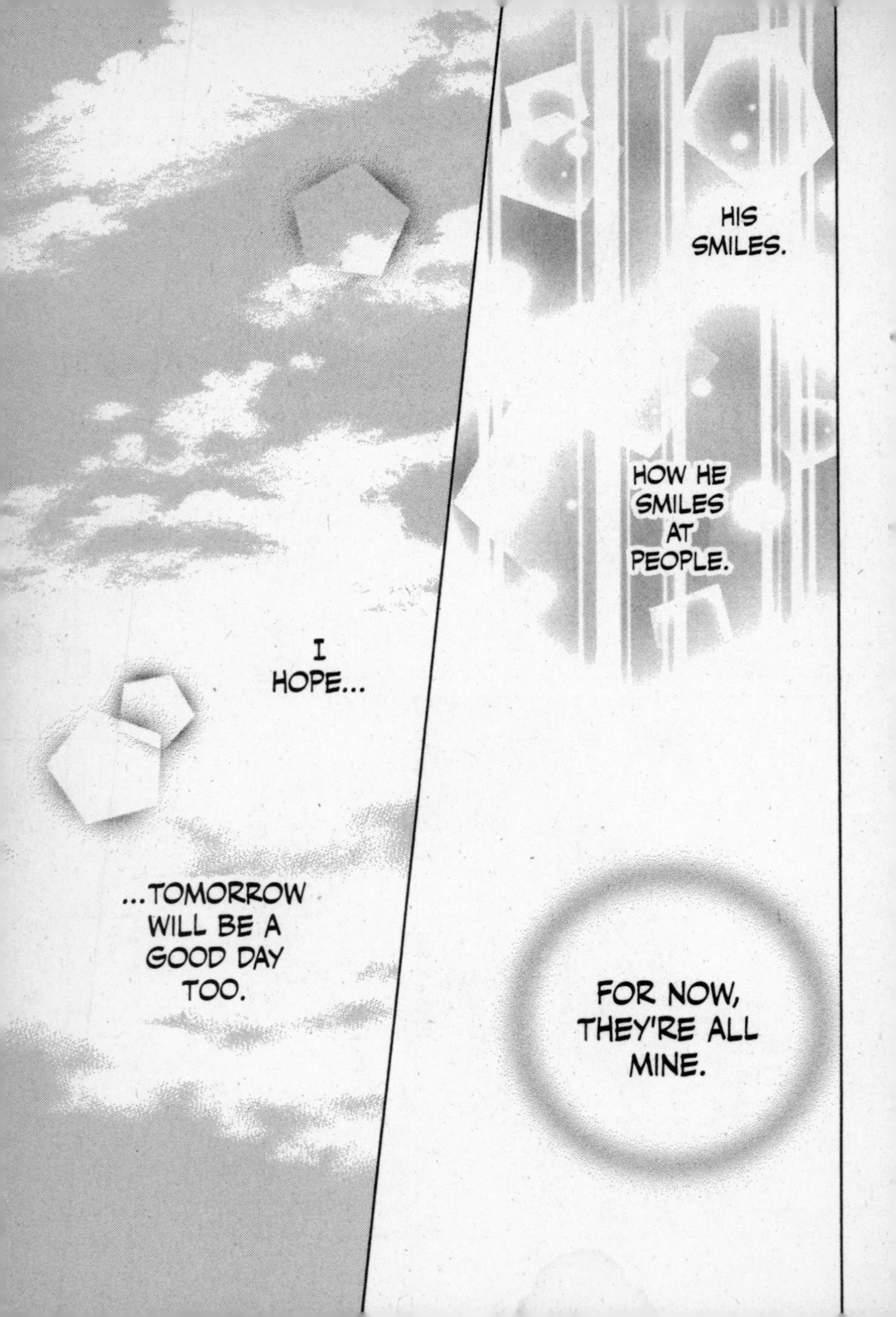
HIS SMILES.
HOW HE SMILES AT PEOPLE.
FOR NOW, THEY'RE ALL MINE.
I HOPE...
...TOMORROW WILL BE A GOOD DAY TOO.

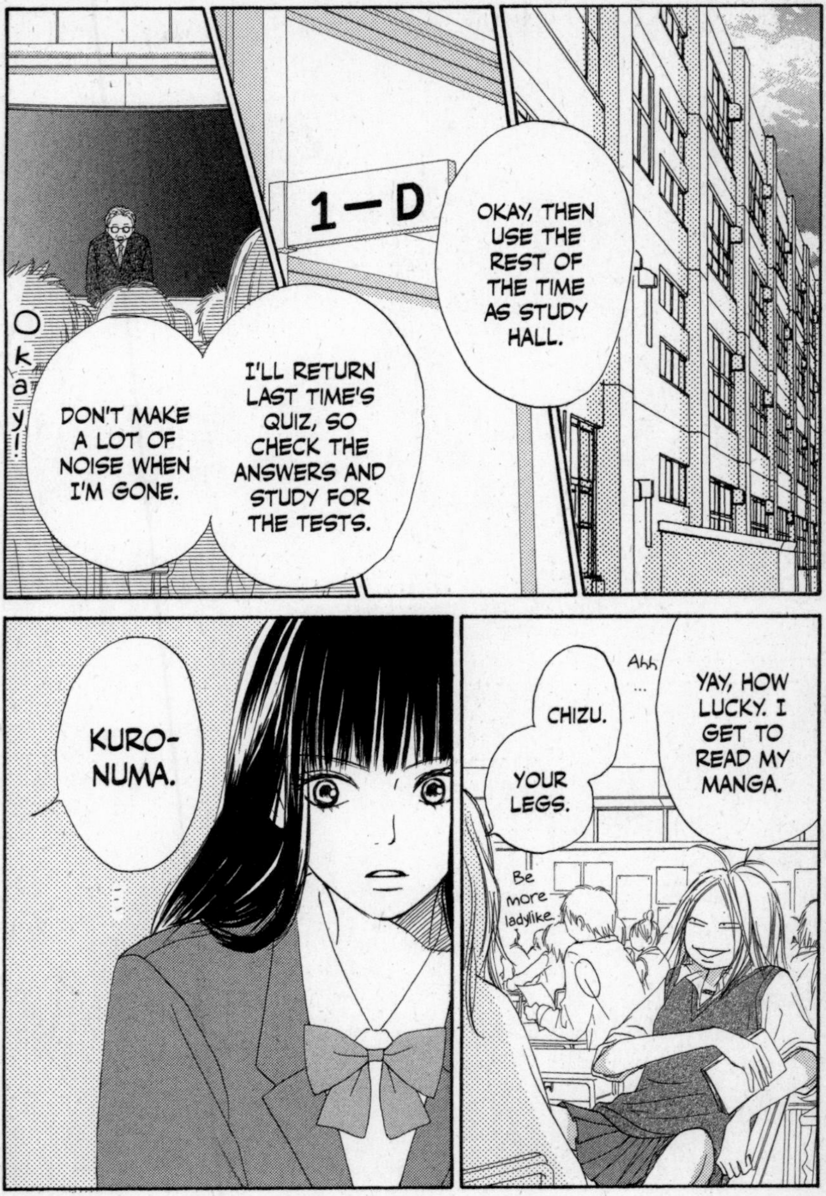
OKAY, THEN USE THE REST OF THE TIME AS STUDY HALL.
1—D
I'LL RETURN LAST TIME'S QUIZ, SO CHECK THE ANSWERS AND STUDY FOR THE TESTS.
DON'T MAKE A LOT OF NOISE WHEN I'M GONE.
Okay!
YAY, HOW LUCKY. I GET TO READ MY MANGA.
Ahh...
CHIZU.
YOUR LEGS.
Be more ladylike.
KURO-NUMA.
...

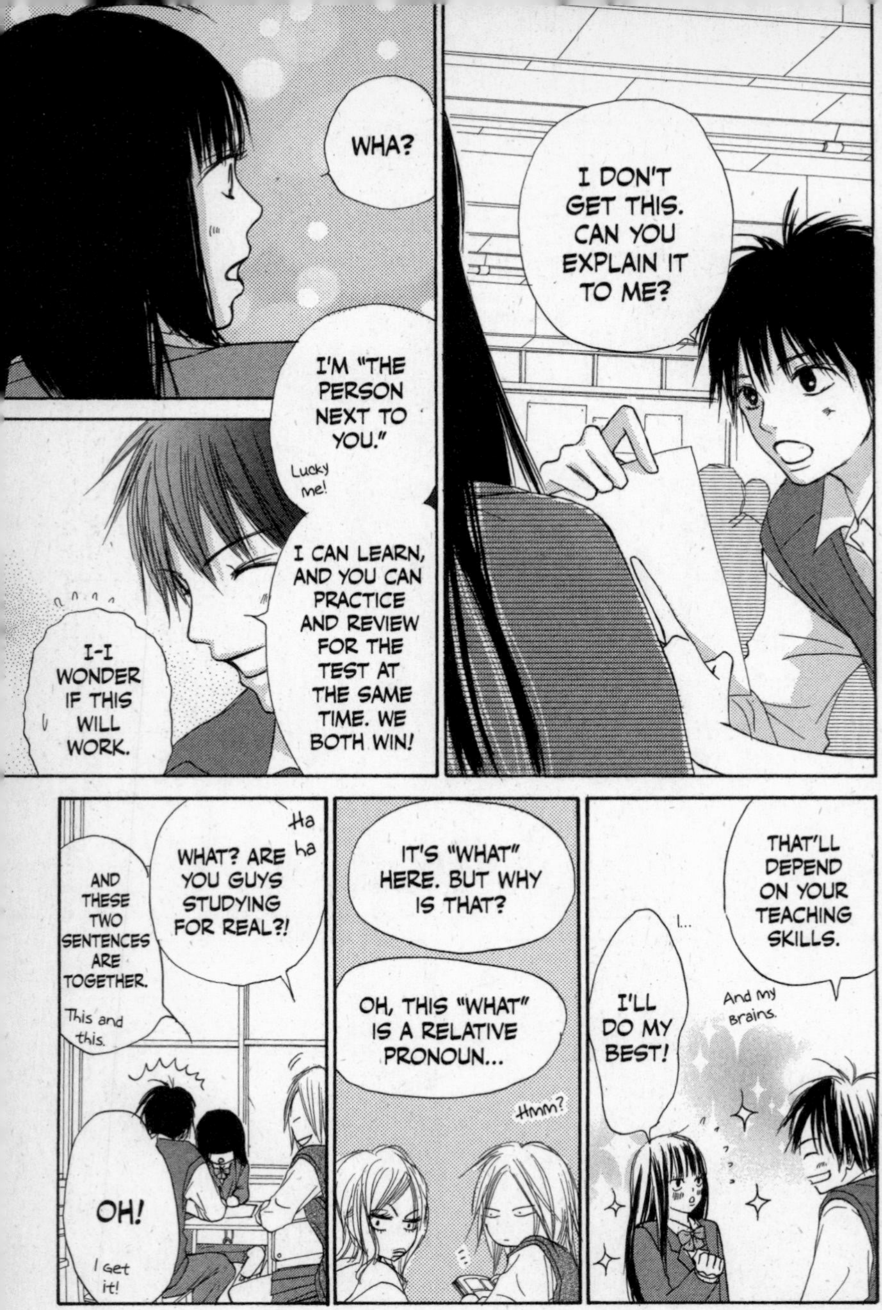
I DON'T GET THIS. CAN YOU EXPLAIN IT TO ME?
WHA?
I'M "THE PERSON NEXT TO YOU."
Lucky me!
I CAN LEARN, AND YOU CAN PRACTICE AND REVIEW FOR THE TEST AT THE SAME TIME. WE BOTH WIN!
I-I WONDER IF THIS WILL WORK.
THAT'LL DEPEND ON YOUR TEACHING SKILLS.
And my brains.
I...
I'LL DO MY BEST!
IT'S "WHAT" HERE. BUT WHY IS THAT?
OH, THIS "WHAT" IS A RELATIVE PRONOUN...
Hmm?
WHAT? ARE YOU GUYS STUDYING FOR REAL?!
Ha ha
AND THESE TWO SENTENCES ARE TOGETHER.
This and this.
OH!
I get it!

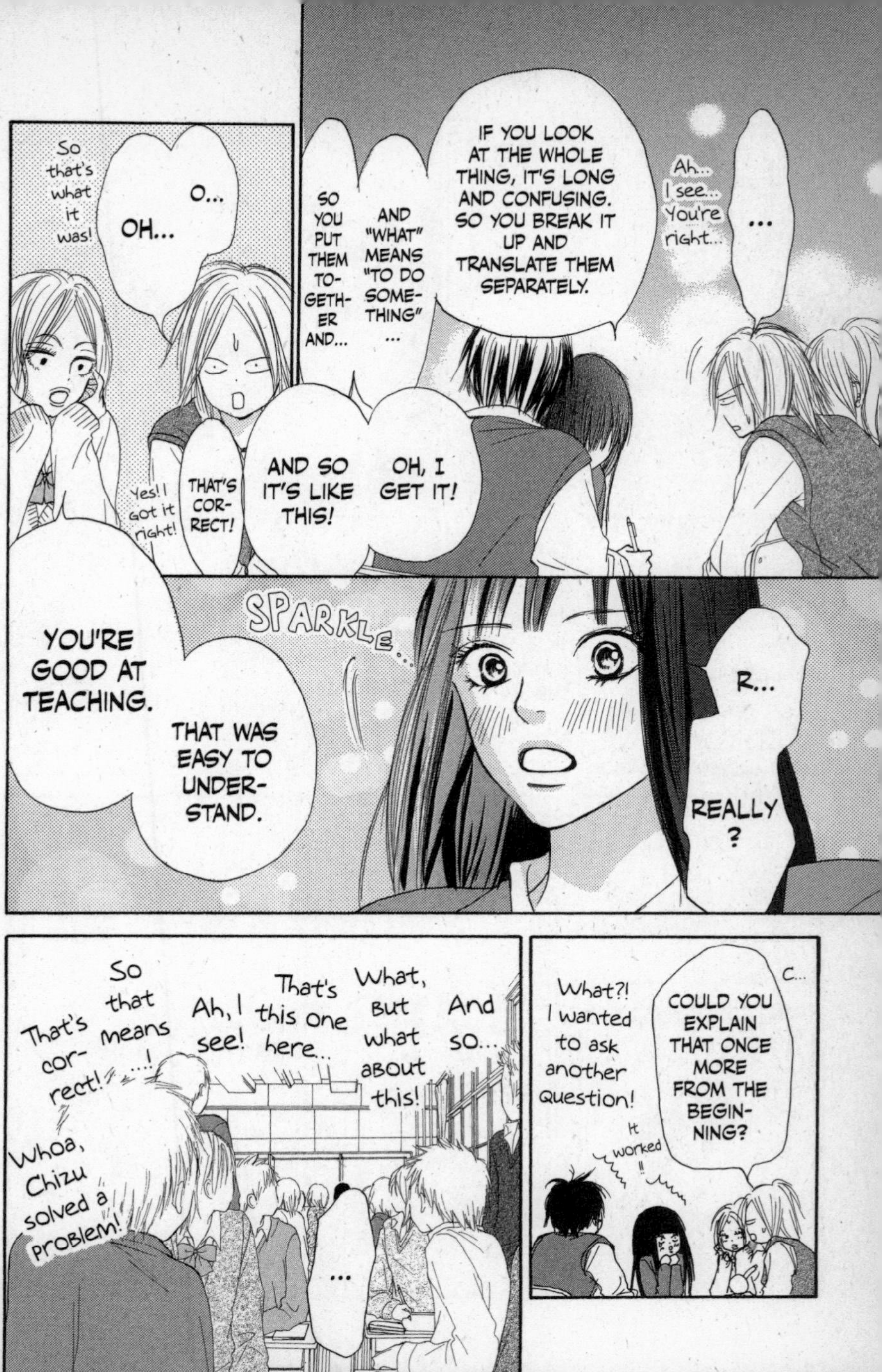
...
Ah... I see... You're right...
IF YOU LOOK AT THE WHOLE THING, IT'S LONG AND CONFUSING. SO YOU BREAK IT UP AND TRANSLATE THEM SEPARATELY.
AND "WHAT" MEANS "TO DO SOMETHING"...
SO YOU PUT THEM TOGETHER AND...
OH, I GET IT!
AND SO IT'S LIKE THIS!
O... OH...
So that's what it was!
THAT'S CORRECT!
Yes!! Got it right!
R... REALLY?
SPARKLE...
YOU'RE GOOD AT TEACHING. THAT WAS EASY TO UNDERSTAND.
C... COULD YOU EXPLAIN THAT ONCE MORE FROM THE BEGINNING?
What?! I wanted to ask another question!
It worked!!
And so...
What, but what about this!
That's this one here...
Ah, I see!
So that means...!
That's correct!
Whoa, Chizu solved a problem!
...

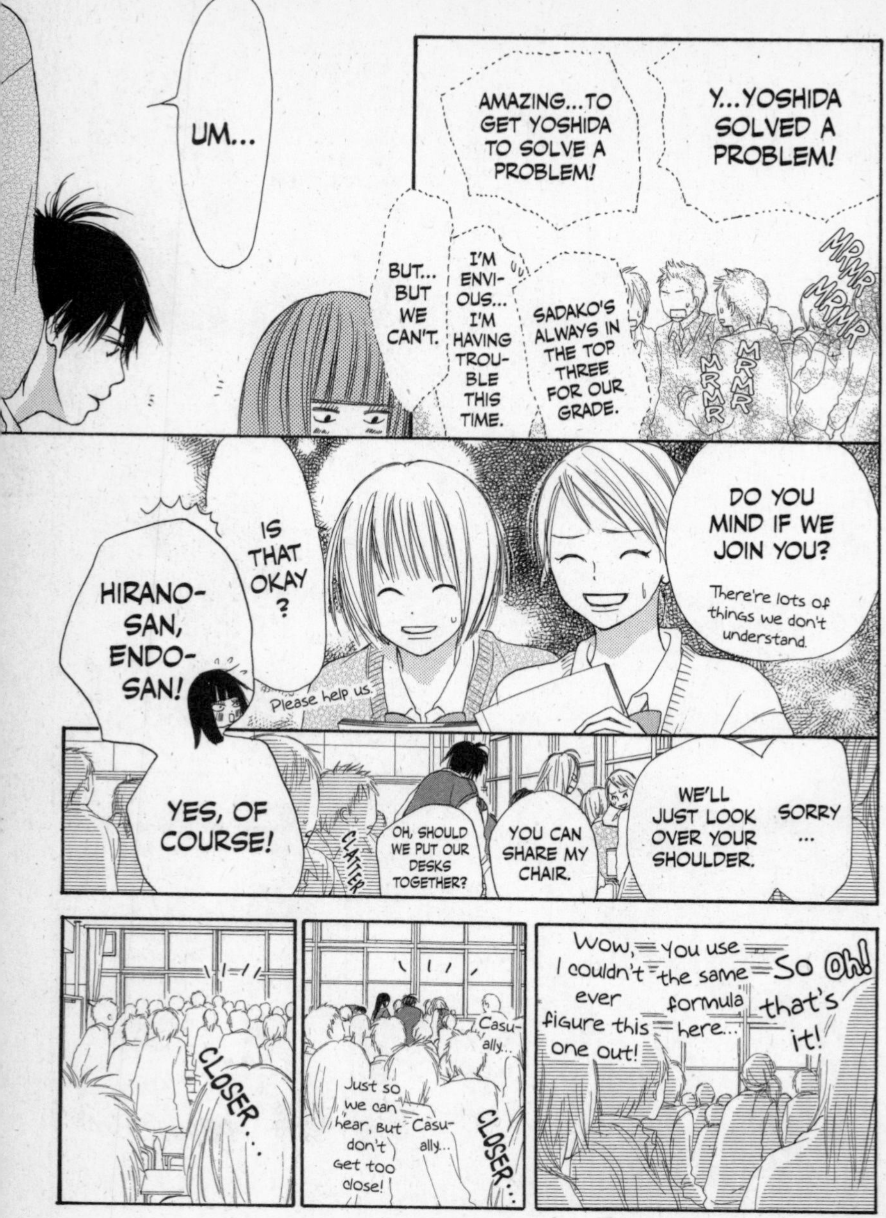
Y...YOSHIDA SOLVED A PROBLEM!
AMAZING...TO GET YOSHIDA TO SOLVE A PROBLEM!
MRMR MRMR
MRMR
MRMR
SADAKO'S ALWAYS IN THE TOP THREE FOR OUR GRADE.
I'M ENVIOUS... I'M HAVING TROUBLE THIS TIME.
BUT... BUT WE CAN'T.
UM...
DO YOU MIND IF WE JOIN YOU?
There're lots of things we don't understand.
IS THAT OKAY?
Please help us.
HIRANO-SAN, ENDO-SAN!
SORRY...
WE'LL JUST LOOK OVER YOUR SHOULDER.
YOU CAN SHARE MY CHAIR.
OH, SHOULD WE PUT OUR DESKS TOGETHER?
CLATTER
YES, OF COURSE!
Oh!
So that's it!
You use the same formula here...
Wow, I couldn't ever figure this one out!
Casu-ally...
CLOSER...
Casu-ally...
Just so we can hear, but don't get too close!
CLOSER...

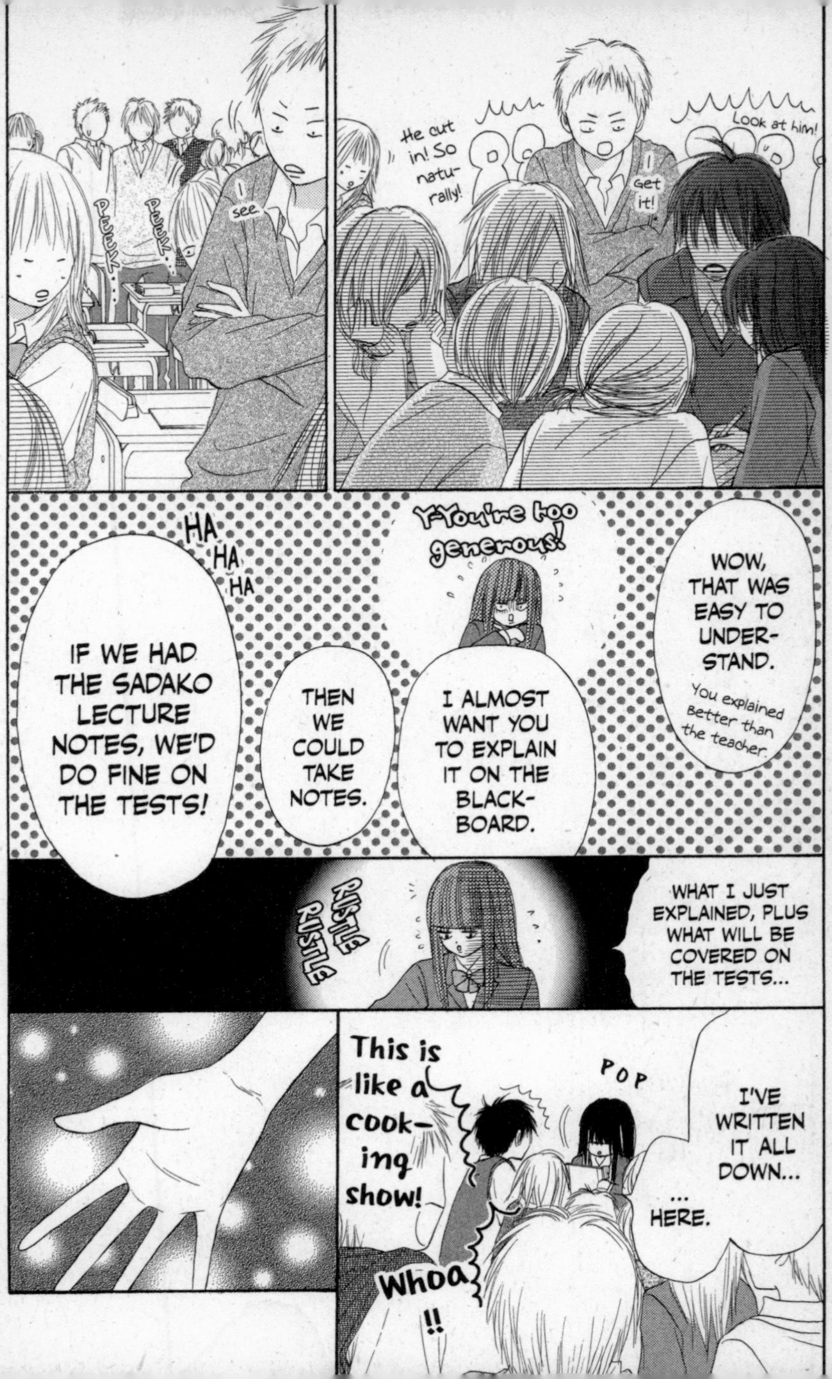
Look at him!
I Get it!
He cut in! So naturally!
I see.
PEEK
PEEK
WOW, THAT WAS EASY TO UNDERSTAND.
You explained better than the teacher.
Y-You're too generous!
I ALMOST WANT YOU TO EXPLAIN IT ON THE BLACKBOARD.
THEN WE COULD TAKE NOTES.
HA HA HA
IF WE HAD THE SADAKO LECTURE NOTES, WE'D DO FINE ON THE TESTS!
WHAT I JUST EXPLAINED, PLUS WHAT WILL BE COVERED ON THE TESTS...
RUSTLE RUSTLE
I'VE WRITTEN IT ALL DOWN...
POP
... HERE.
This is like a cooking show!
Whoa!!

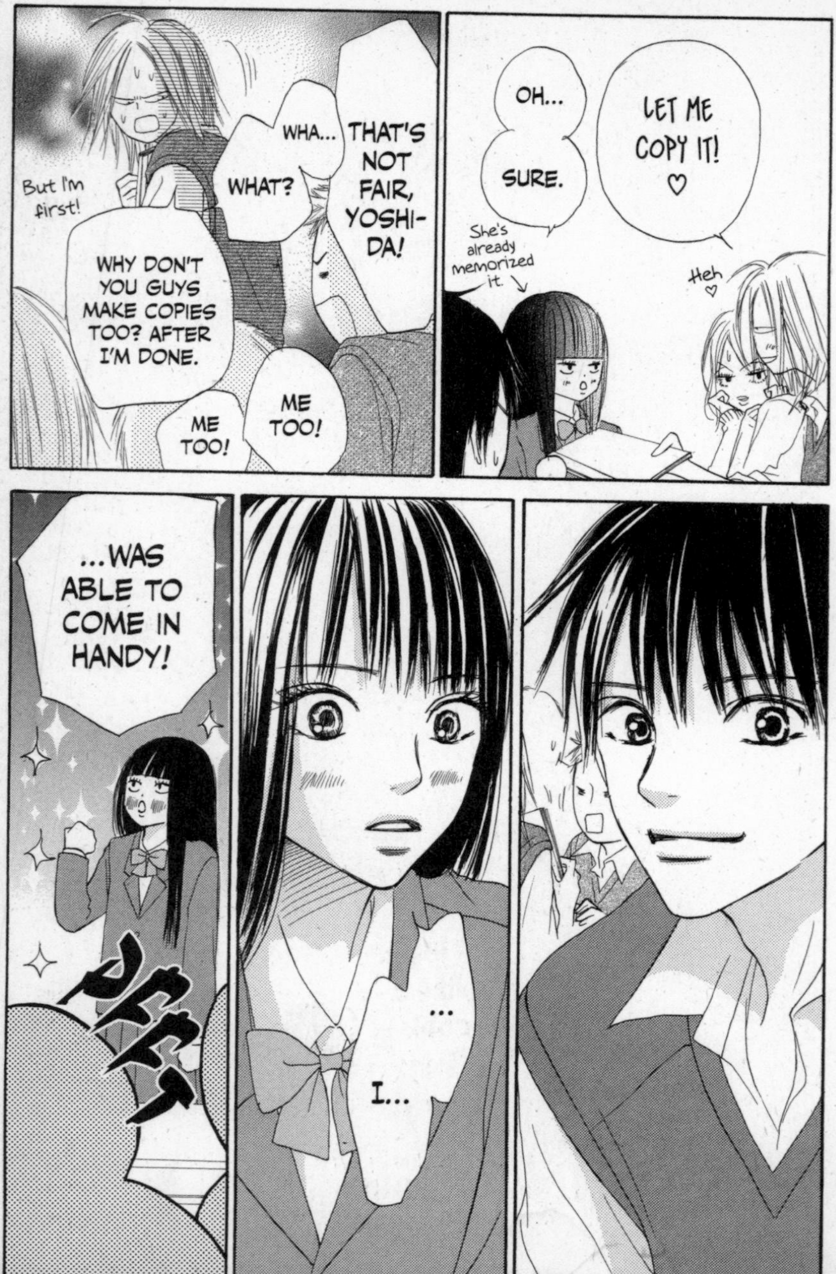
LET ME COPY IT! ♡
OH... SURE.
She's already memorized it.
Heh ♡
THAT'S NOT FAIR, YOSHIDA!
WHA...
WHAT?
But I'm first!
WHY DON'T YOU GUYS MAKE COPIES TOO? AFTER I'M DONE.
ME TOO!
ME TOO!
...
I...
...WAS ABLE TO COME IN HANDY!

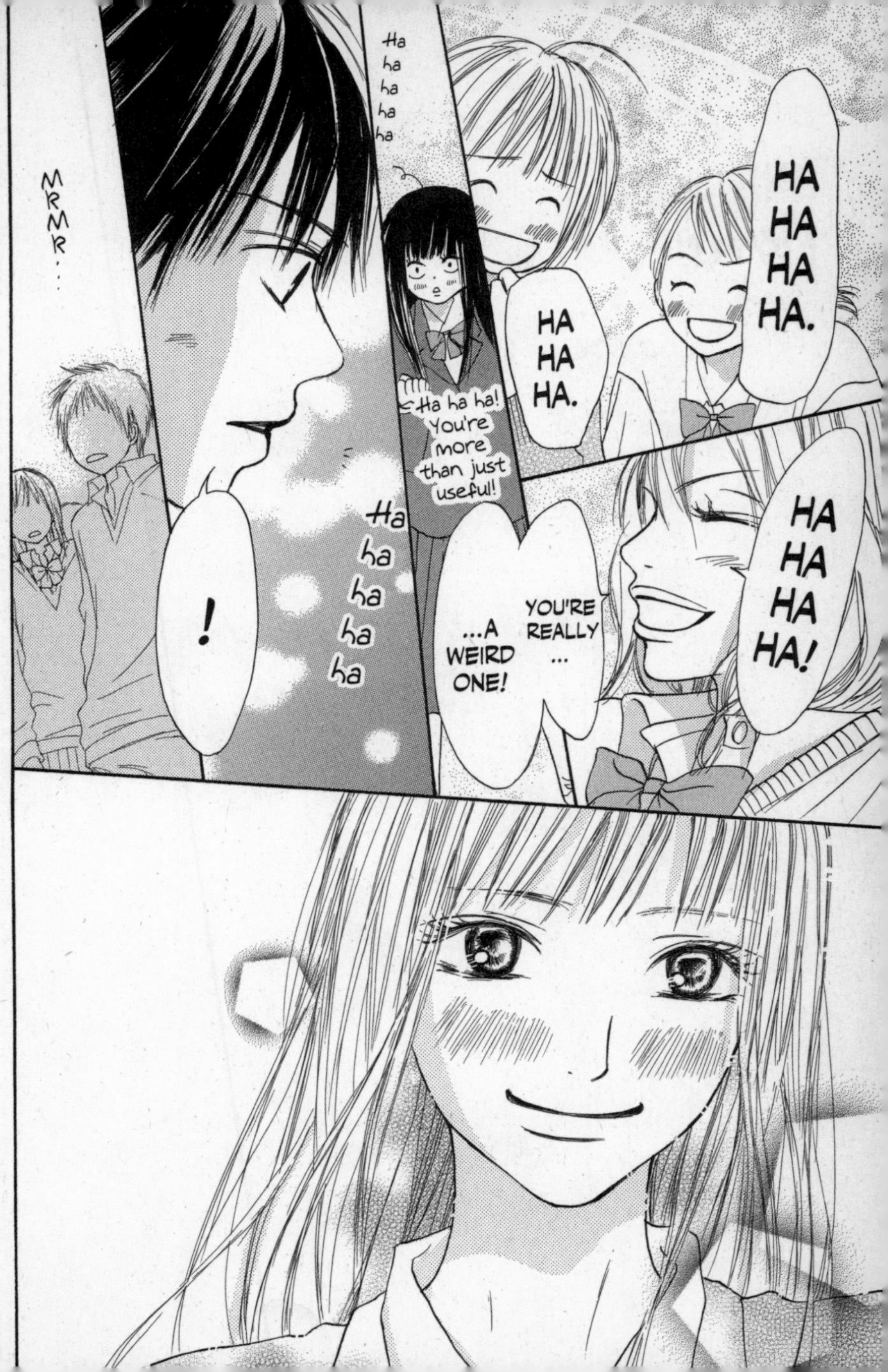
HA HA HA HA.
HA HA HA.
HA HA HA HA!
YOU'RE REALLY ...
...A WEIRD ONE!
Ha ha ha ha ha
Ha ha ha! You're more than just useful!
Ha ha ha ha ha
!
MRMR...

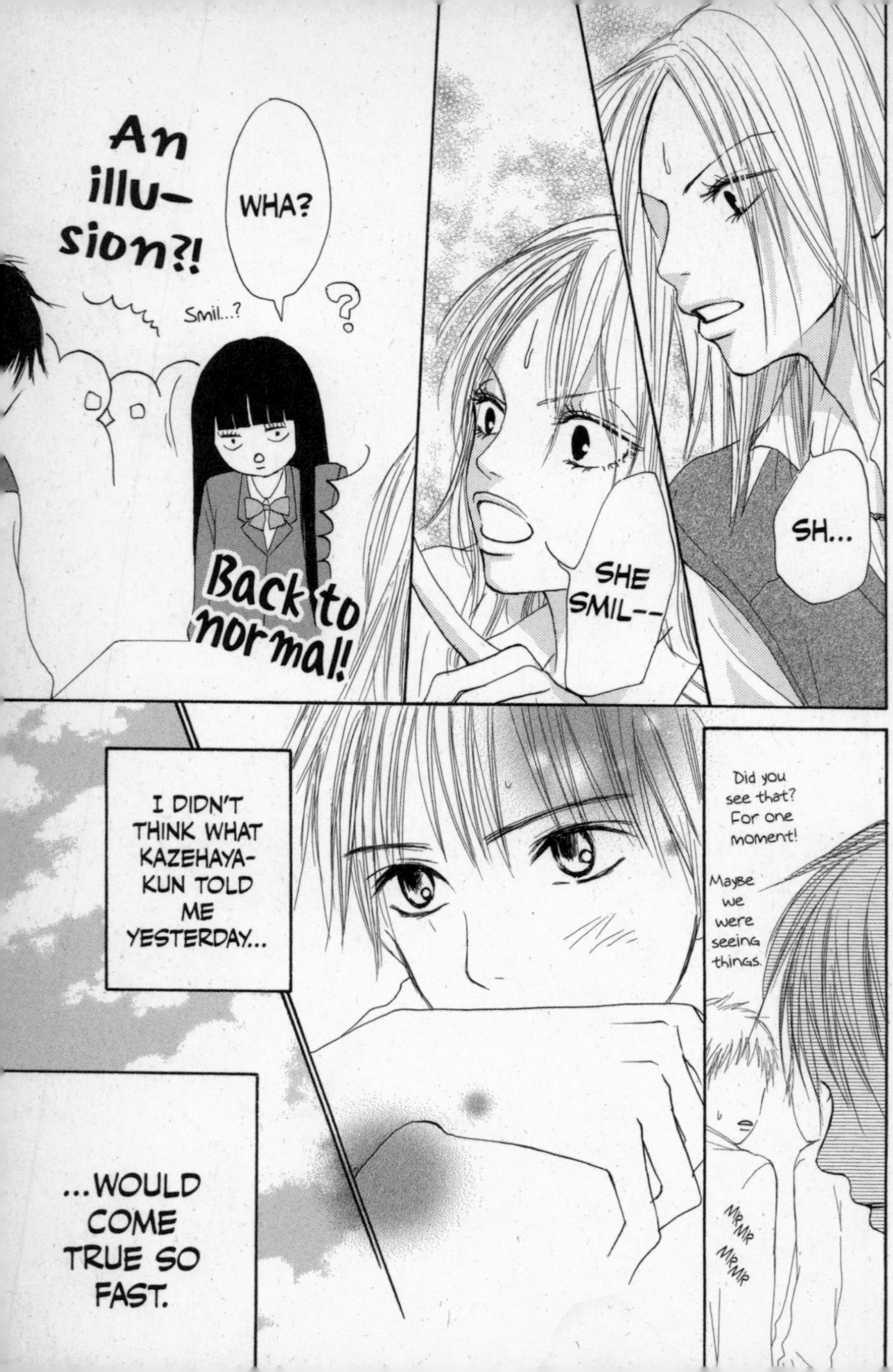
SH...
SHE SMIL--
WHA?
An illu-sion?!
Smil...?
Back to normal!
Did you see that? For one moment!
Maybe we were seeing things.
MRMR
MRMR
I DIDN'T THINK WHAT KAZEHAYA-KUN TOLD ME YESTERDAY...
...WOULD COME TRUE SO FAST.

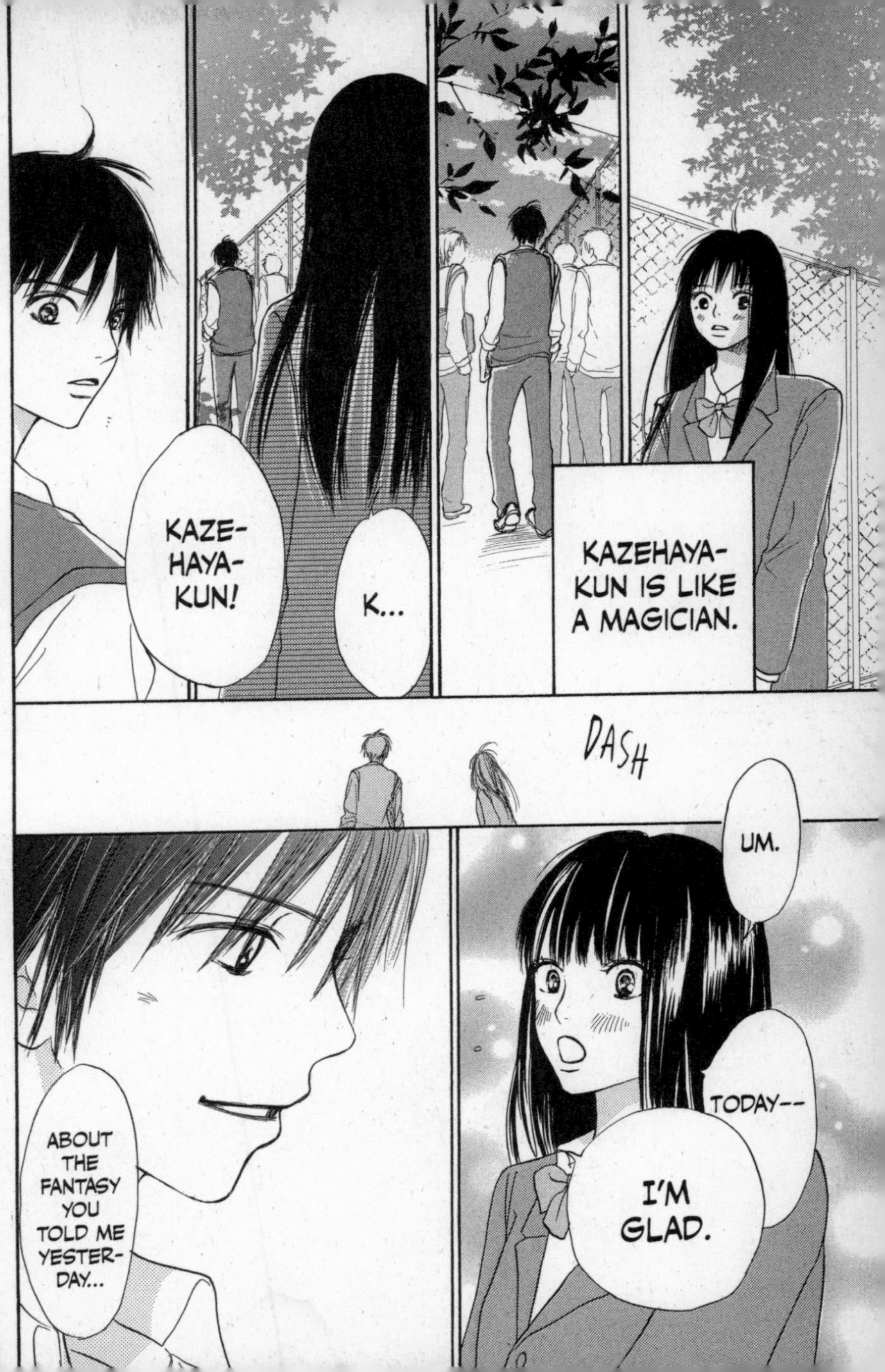
KAZEHAYA-KUN IS LIKE A MAGICIAN.
K...
KAZE-HAYA-KUN!
DASH
UM.
TODAY--
I'M GLAD.
ABOUT THE FANTASY YOU TOLD ME YESTER-DAY...

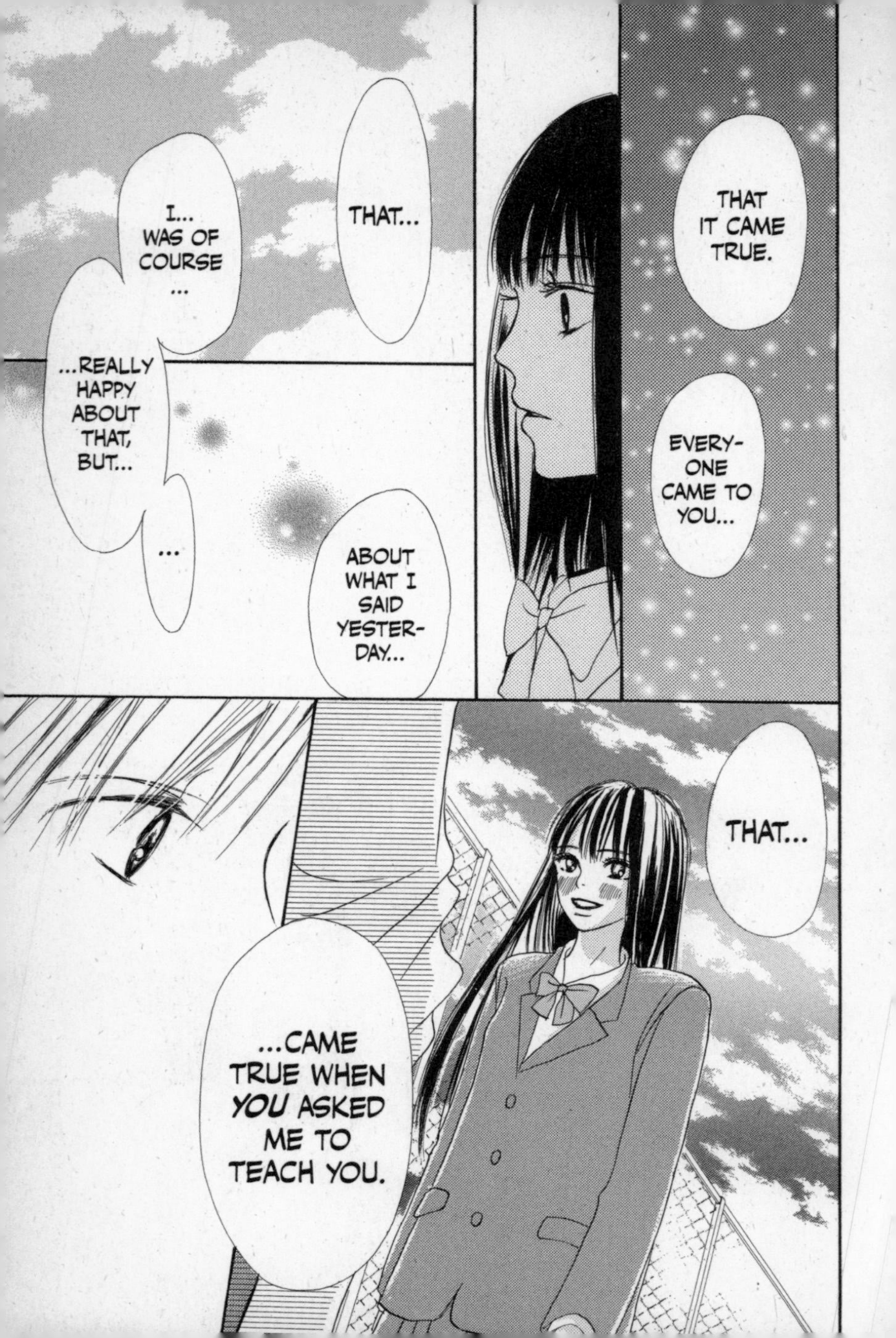
THAT IT CAME TRUE.
EVERYONE CAME TO YOU...
THAT...
I... WAS OF COURSE ...
...REALLY HAPPY ABOUT THAT, BUT...
...
ABOUT WHAT I SAID YESTERDAY...
THAT...
...CAME TRUE WHEN *YOU* ASKED ME TO TEACH YOU.

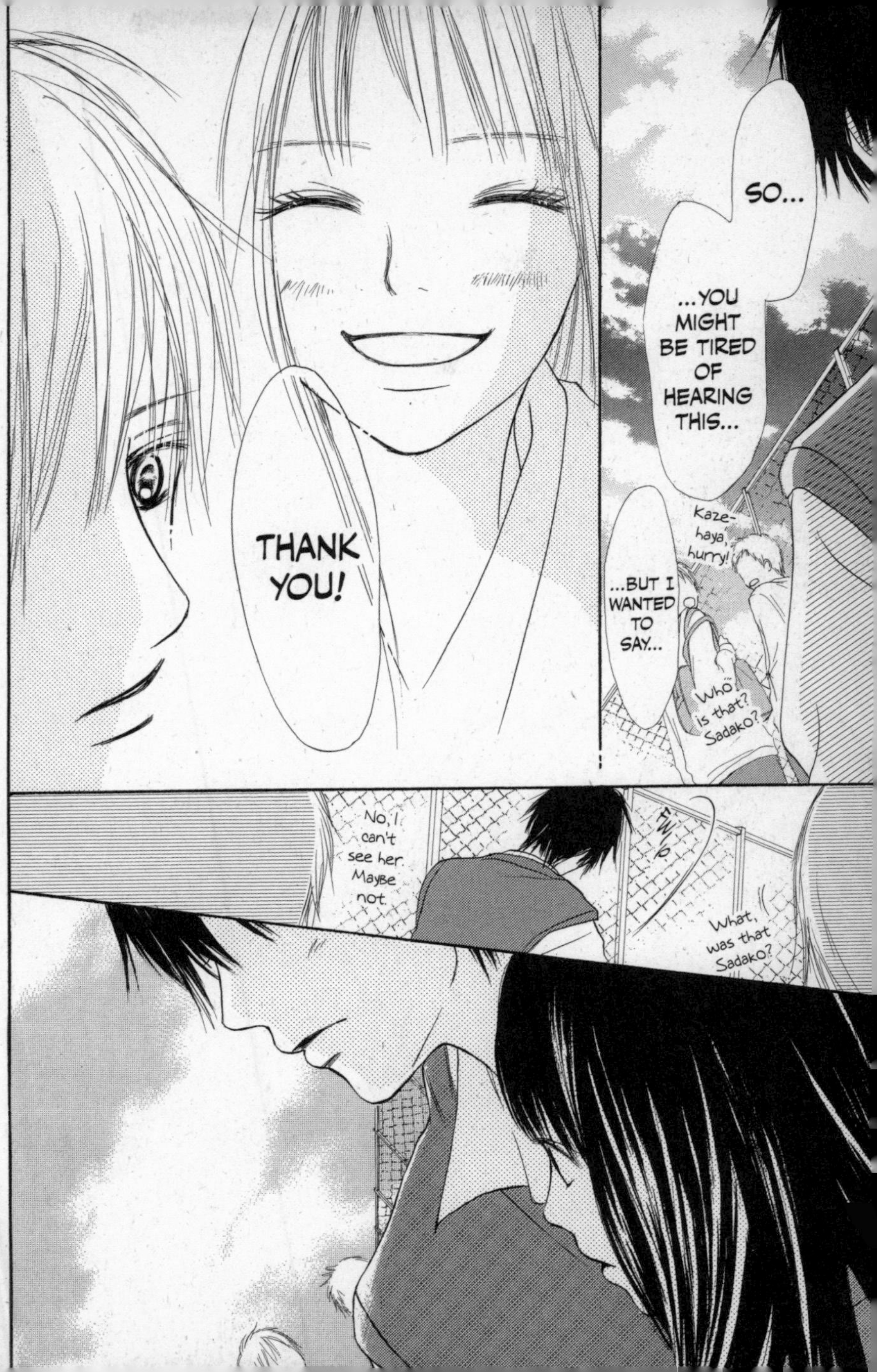
SO...
...YOU MIGHT BE TIRED OF HEARING THIS...
Kaze-haya, hurry!
...BUT I WANTED TO SAY...
Who is that? Sadako?
THANK YOU!
FWIP
What, was that Sadako?
No, I can't see her. Maybe not.

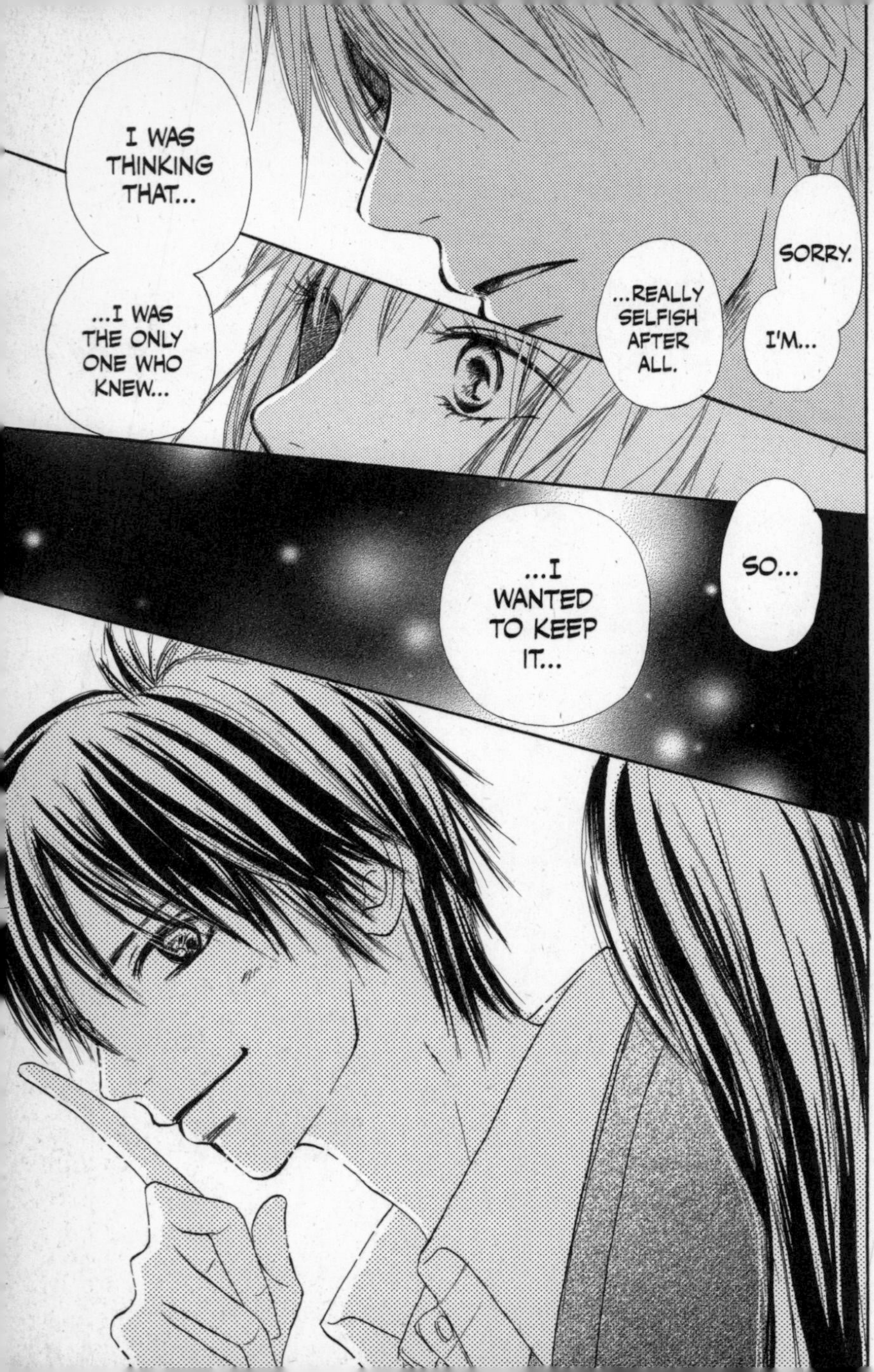
SORRY.
I'M...
...REALLY SELFISH AFTER ALL.
I WAS THINKING THAT...
...I WAS THE ONLY ONE WHO KNEW...
SO...
...I WANTED TO KEEP IT...

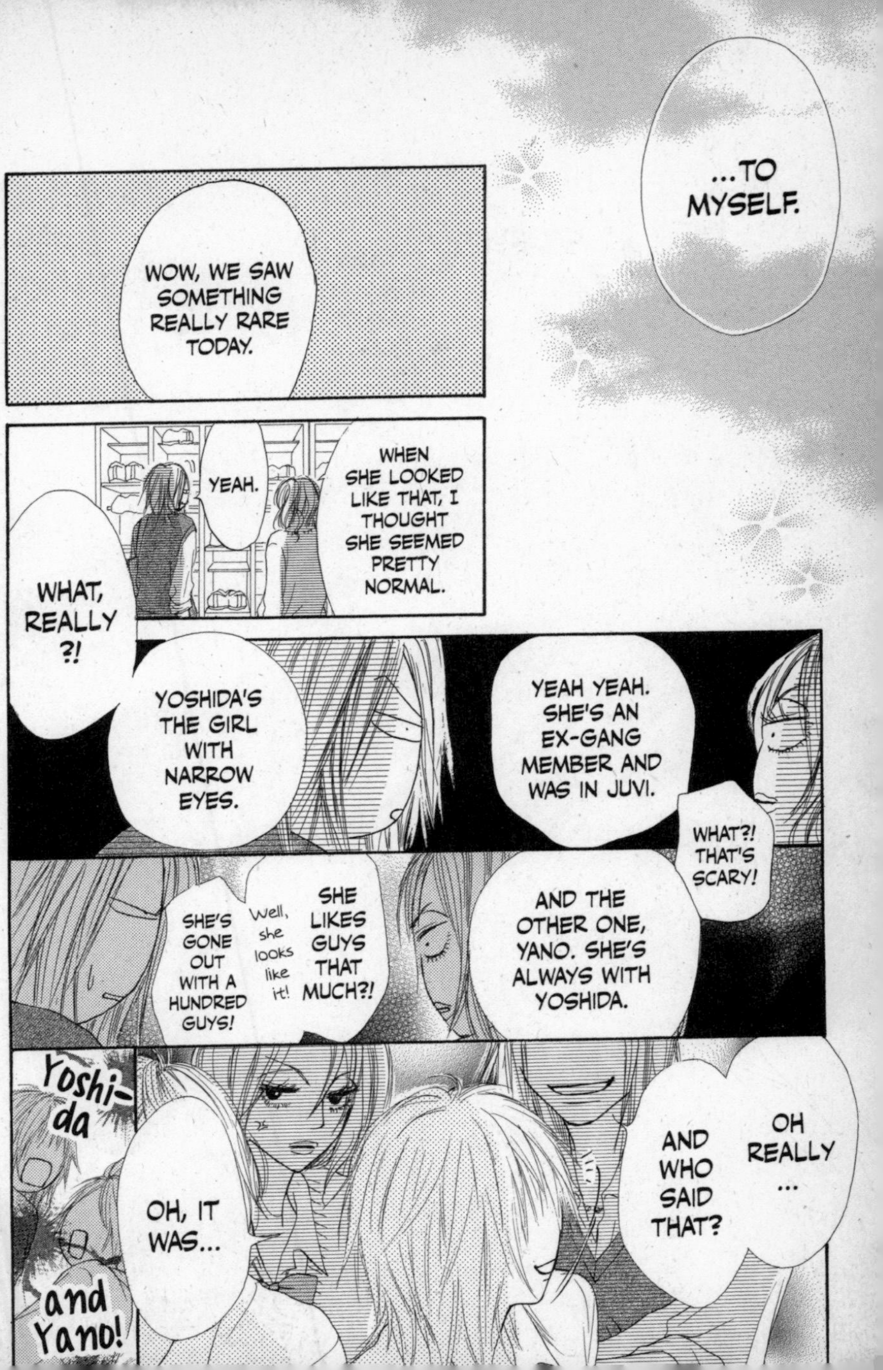
...TO MYSELF.
WOW, WE SAW SOMETHING REALLY RARE TODAY.
WHEN SHE LOOKED LIKE THAT, I THOUGHT SHE SEEMED PRETTY NORMAL.
YEAH.
WHAT, REALLY?!
YEAH YEAH. SHE'S AN EX-GANG MEMBER AND WAS IN JUVI.
YOSHIDA'S THE GIRL WITH NARROW EYES.
WHAT?! THAT'S SCARY!
AND THE OTHER ONE, YANO. SHE'S ALWAYS WITH YOSHIDA.
SHE'S GONE OUT WITH A HUNDRED GUYS!
SHE LIKES GUYS THAT MUCH?!
Well, she looks like it!
OH REALLY...
AND WHO SAID THAT?
OH, IT WAS...
Yoshi-da
and Yano!

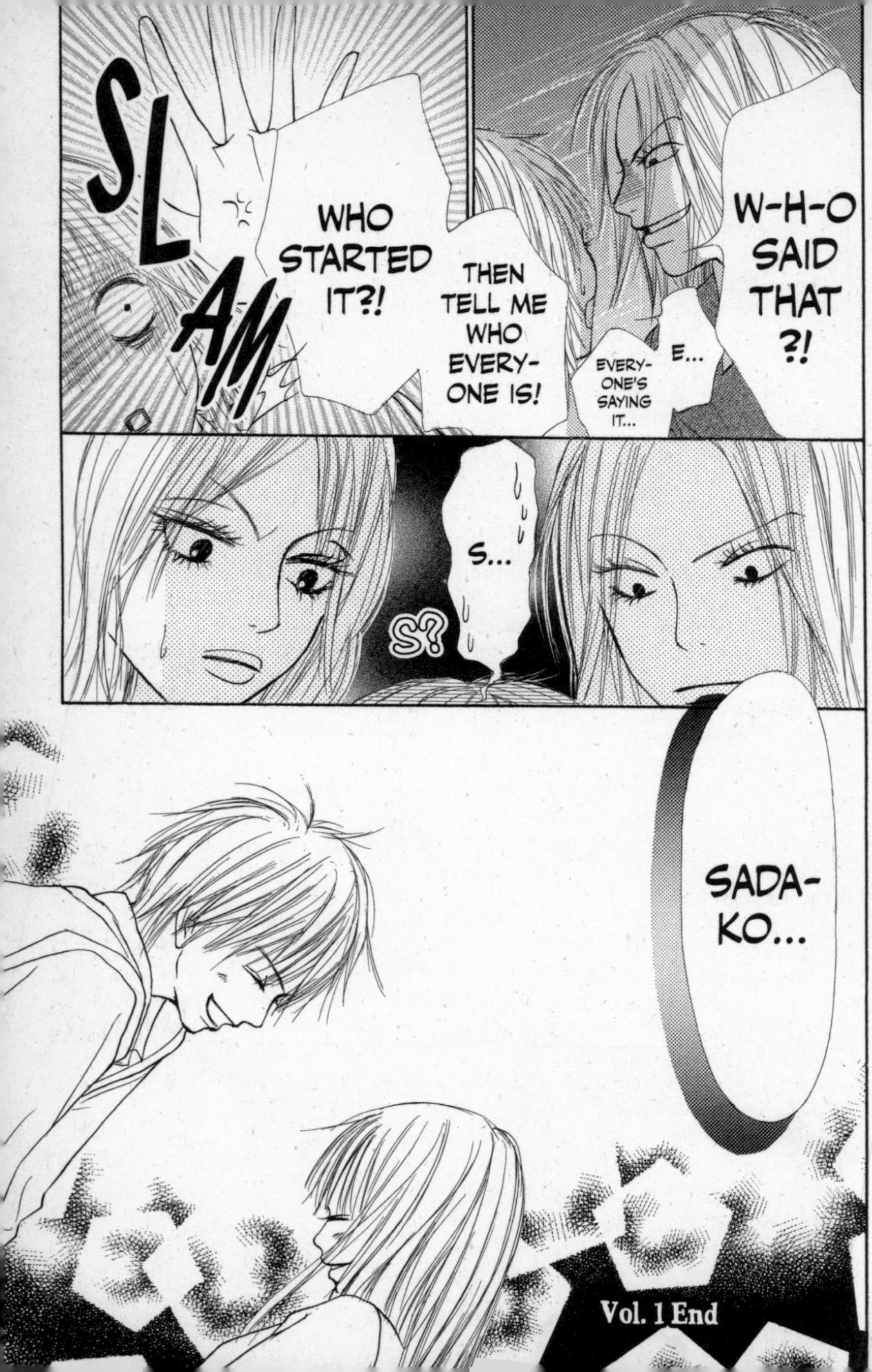
W-H-O SAID THAT ?!
E...
EVERY-ONE'S SAYING IT...
THEN TELL ME WHO EVERY-ONE IS!
WHO STARTED IT?!
SLAM
S...
S?!
SADA-KO...
Vol. 1 End

From me (the editor) to you (the reader).

Here are some Japanese culture explanations that will help you better understand the references in the *Kimi ni Todoke* world.

Honorifics:
When saying someone's name in Japanese, a suffix is often attached to indicate how familiar the speaker is with the person. Some are more polite and respectful, while others are endearing. Calling someone by just their first name is the most informal.
-kun is used for young men or boys, usually someone you are familiar with.
-chan is used for young women, girls or young children and can be used as a term of endearment.
-san is used for someone you respect or are not close to, or to be polite.

Page 6, Sadako:
Taken from a horror movie whose main character was named "Sadako," the name is now synonymous with the image of a girl with straight, long black hair that covers her face. Though it has a negative ring to it now, it was an ordinary girl's name a generation back.

Page 9, Haunted Trail:
Called *kimodameshi* in Japan, it's literally a "test of one's guts (courage)" and is usually done in unlit areas, such as graveyards or in the wilderness. Participants may pretend to be ghosts to frighten the ones walking by for an added spooky factor. It can also be a prime opportunity for girls and boys to get close to each other while pretending to be scared.

Page 15, summer vacation:
Summer vacation in Japan runs from mid-July to the end of August. Though technically it's a vacation, there are still days that students have to come to school for lectures and club activities.

Page 15, "Today's the 14th, so...":
To keep it fair and simple, some teachers call on students depending on what day of the month it is, since every student is assigned a number. On the plus side, students can predict that they'll be called on that particular day and at least have their homework done.

Page 23, Kazehaya:
Kaze means "wind" and *haya* means "fast."

Page 23, Kuronuma:
Kuro means "black" and *numa* means "swamp."

Page 23, Sawako:
The kanji character for *Sawa* means "pleasant" or "refreshing."

Page 28, "...get her to wear white":
Ghosts in Japan typically wear white and don't have legs that reach the ground. The white clothing would also help her stand out in the dark.

Page 45, penalty game:
Not only do you suffer the indignity of losing a game, but in Japan many people must also suffer the dreaded penalty game (or *batsu game*) on top of that. The penalty game can be anything (but the more embarrassing the better).

Page 77, Ojizo-san:
A deity sometimes represented on the side of the road as a stone statue with a scarf covering its head and a red bib. You can see one on page 32, in the 5th panel.

Page 99, changing seats:
In Japan, students stay in the same class for most of the day with the teachers coming to them. To break up the monotony, students will switch around their seating positions every few months, but they usually take their desks with them.

Page 121, Horror Newspaper:
In Jiro Tsunoda's manga, *Kyofu Shinbun* (Horror Newspaper), whoever reads the cursed newspaper shortens their life by a hundred days.

Page 127, Zen & Pin:
The kanji character for *Yoshi* in "Yoshiyuki" can also be read as *Zen* (meaning "good" or "righteous"). The kanji character for *Kazu* in "Kazuichi" can also be read as *Ichi* (meaning "one"). *Pin* is a play on this word since it means "one." Also, *pin* comedians are those who have a solo act since many comedians in Japan work in pairs.

Page 133, Kazune Kawahara:
The popular manga artist of *High School Debut*.

Page 141, Toki Memo:
Short for *Tokimeki Memorial*, a popular dating simulation game.

Page 155, Zashikiwarashi:
A deity who protects old traditional manor homes in Tohoku (the northern part of Honshu, the main island of Japan). Usually portrayed as a young girl with a straight black haircut and a kimono.

It feels as if I just started this series, but the book is now coming out. Time is passing by awfully fast. This is the first volume for this series, so I want to start fresh and do my best. Even though I am far from it, I always want to have the spirit and enthusiasm of a newbie. Heh heh. Too bad every time I see myself in the mirror I look older!

--Karuho Shiina

Karuho Shiina was born and raised in Hokkaido, Japan. Though *Kimi ni Todoke* is only her second series following many one-shot stories, it has already racked up accolades from various "Best Manga of the Year" lists. Winner of the 2008 Kodansha Manga Award for the shojo category, *Kimi ni Todoke* also placed fifth in the first-ever Manga Taisho (Cartoon Grand Prize) contest in 2008.

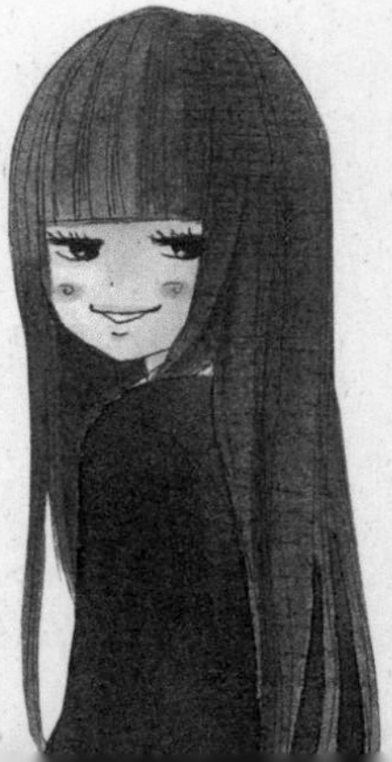

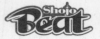

Kimi ni Todoke
VOL. 1

Shojo Beat Manga Edition

STORY AND ART BY
KARUHO SHIINA

Translation/Tomo Kimura
Touch-up Art & Lettering/Vanessa Satone
Design/Yukiko Whitley
Editor/Yuki Murashige

VP, Production/Alvin Lu
VP, Sales & Product Marketing/Gonzalo Ferreyra
VP, Creative/Linda Espinosa
Publisher/Hyoe Narita

KIMI NI TODOKE © 2005 by Karuho Shiina
All rights reserved. First published in Japan in 2005 by
SHUEISHA Inc., Tokyo. English translation rights arranged
by SHUEISHA Inc.

Printed in the U.S.A.

Published by VIZ Media, LLC
P.O. Box 77010
San Francisco, CA 94107

10 9 8 7 6 5 4 3 2
First printing, August 2009
Second printing, September 2009

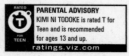
 www.viz.com

 www.shojobeat.com

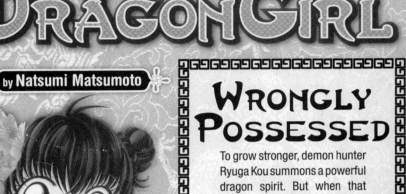
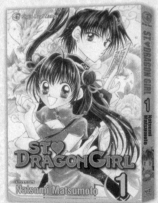
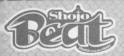

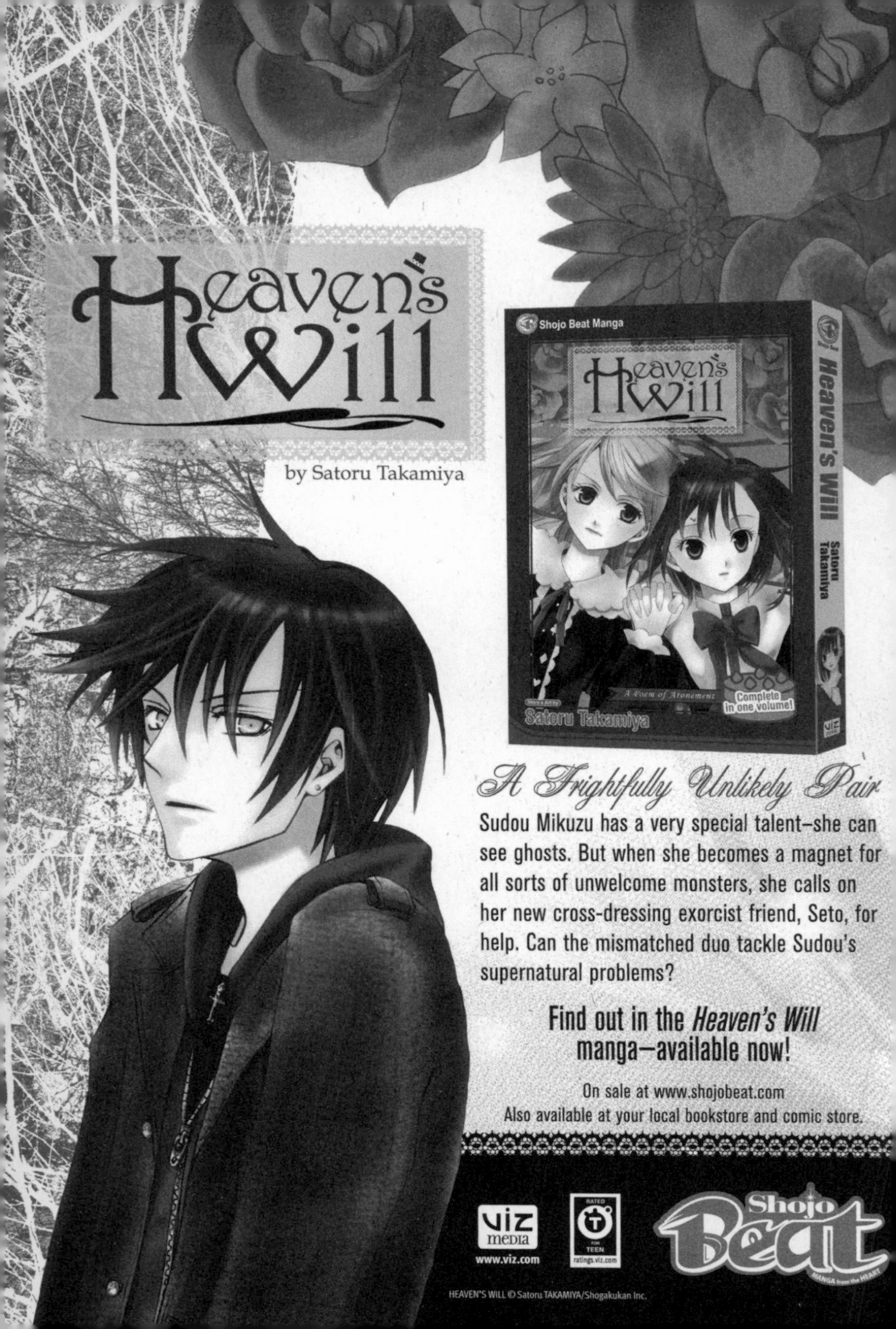
Heaven's Will
by Satoru Takamiya
Shojo Beat Manga
Heaven's Will
Satoru Takamiya
A Poem of Atonement
Complete in one volume!
Satoru Takamiya
A Frightfully Unlikely Pair
Sudou Mikuzu has a very special talent—she can see ghosts. But when she becomes a magnet for all sorts of unwelcome monsters, she calls on her new cross-dressing exorcist friend, Seto, for help. Can the mismatched duo tackle Sudou's supernatural problems?
Find out in the Heaven's Will manga—available now!
On sale at www.shojobeat.com
Also available at your local bookstore and comic store.
VIZ media
www.viz.com
RATED T FOR TEEN
ratings.viz.com
Shojo Beat
MANGA from the HEART
HEAVEN'S WILL © Satoru TAKAMIYA/Shogakukan Inc.

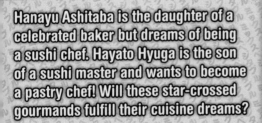
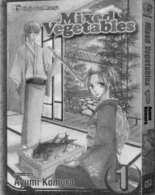
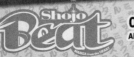
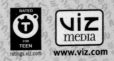

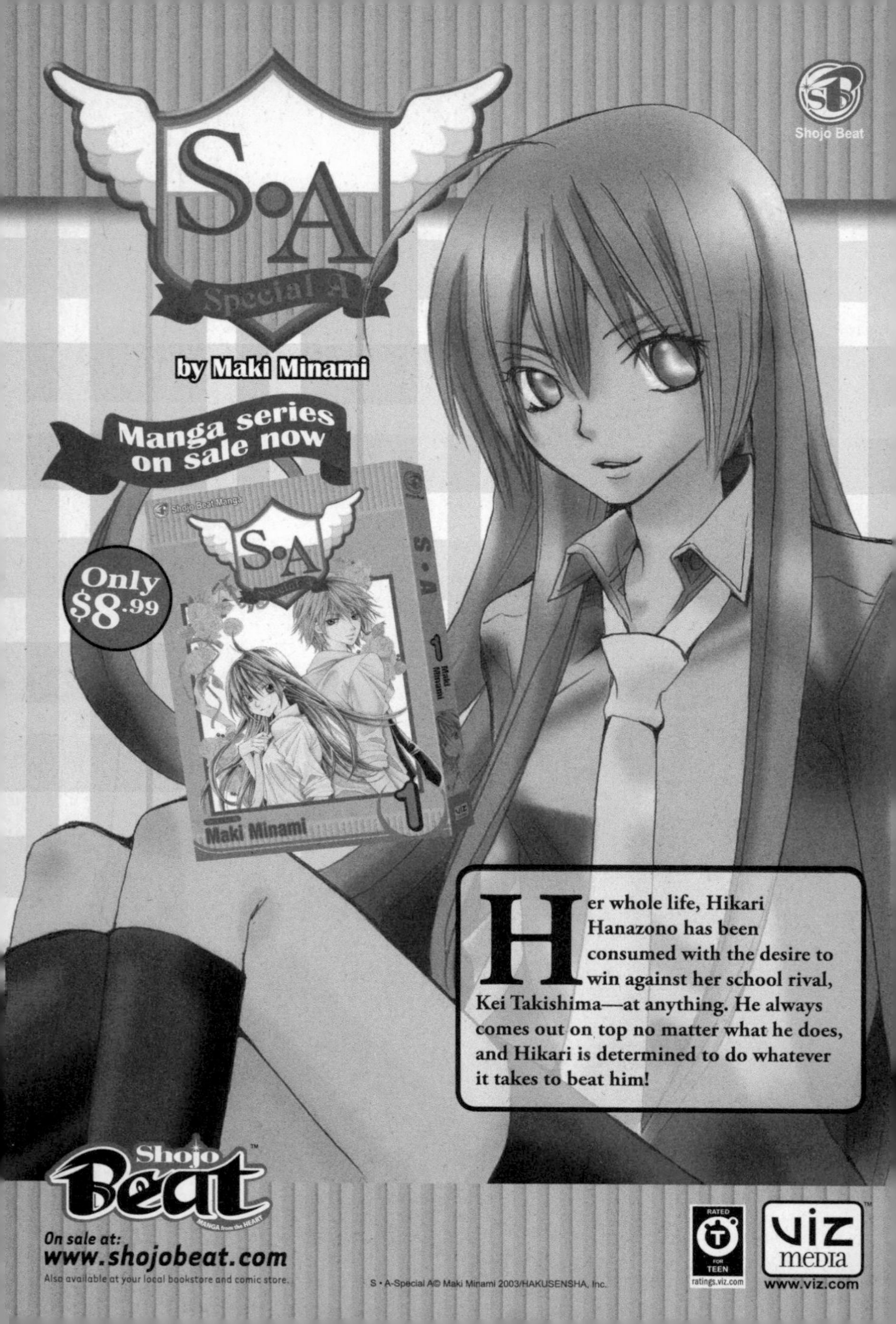
Shojo Beat
S•A
Special A
by Maki Minami
Manga series on sale now
Only $8.99
Shojo Beat Manga
S•A
1
Maki Minami
Her whole life, Hikari Hanazono has been consumed with the desire to win against her school rival, Kei Takishima—at anything. He always comes out on top no matter what he does, and Hikari is determined to do whatever it takes to beat him!
Shojo Beat
MANGA from the HEART
On sale at:
www.shojobeat.com
Also available at your local bookstore and comic store.
S • A-Special A© Maki Minami 2003/HAKUSENSHA, Inc.
RATED T FOR TEEN
ratings.viz.com
VIZ media
www.viz.com

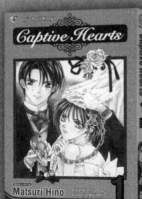

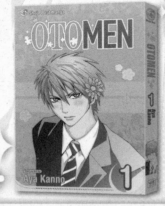
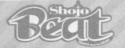
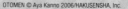

Tell us what you think about Shojo Beat Manga!

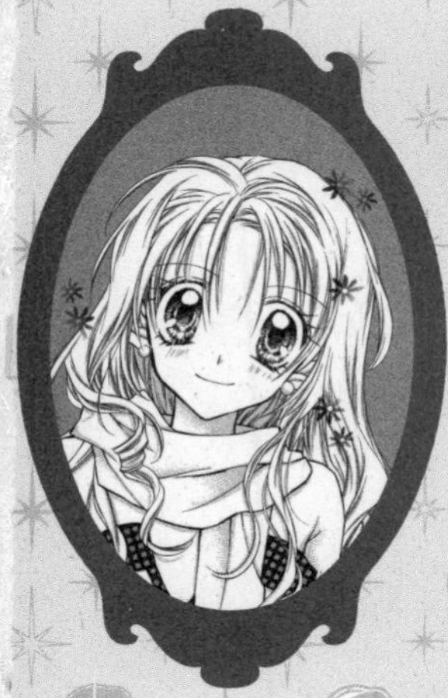

Our survey is now available online. Go to:

shojobeat.com/mangasurvey

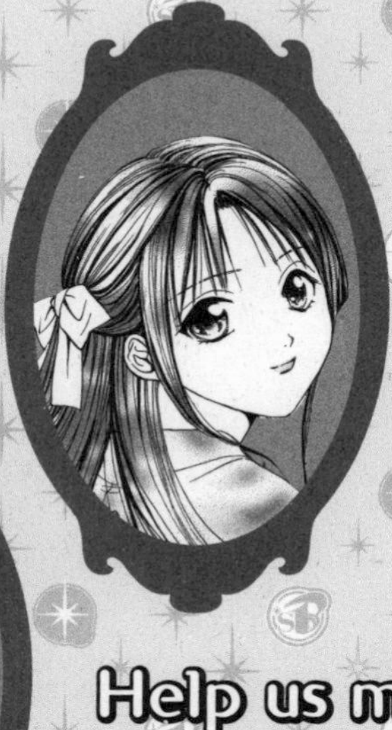

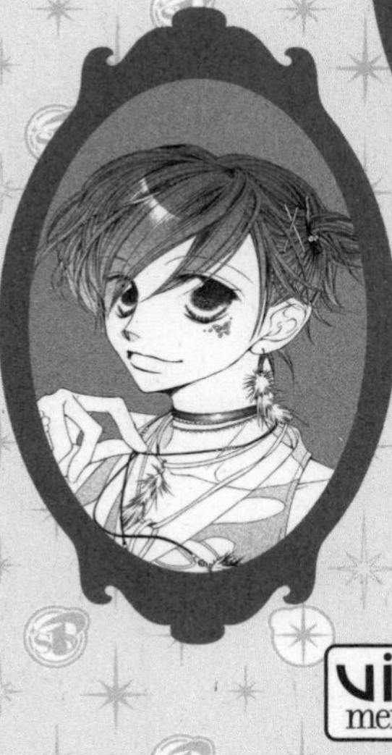

Help us make our product offerings better!

VIZ media

Shojo Beat
THE REAL DRAMA BEGINS IN...
MANGA from the HEART